JESUS
NAME ABOVE ALL NAMES

JESUS
NAME ABOVE ALL NAMES

ELLEN G. WHITE

Pacific Press®
Publishing Association
Nampa, Idaho | www.pacificpress.com

Cover design by Siloe Olivera
Cover design illustration has been adapted from Elfred Lee's *Christ of the Narrow Way* ©
The White Estate, Inc.

Printed by Pacific Press® Publishing Association
Printed in the United States of America

The Ellen G. White Estate, Inc., assumes full responsibility for the accuracy of all facts and quotations as cited in this book.

Bible texts used by Ellen G. White are from either the King James Version, the Revised Version (identified R. V.), or the American Revised Version (identified A.R.V.).

Purchase additional copies of this book by calling toll-free 1-800-765-6955
or by visiting http://www.adventistbookcenter.com.

ISBN 978-0-8280-2865-3

June 2020

FOREWORD

One cannot read the inspired writings of Ellen G. White without experiencing numerous encounters with Jesus. In the wide expanse of her literary output He is there. Around every corner and in every hidden place, glimpses of Jesus remind readers of Ellen White's deep love for the Savior and her constant desire to make Him known.

In this devotional you will meet the Jesus whom Ellen White knew intimately. Her voluminous descriptions of Christ represent an anthology unlike that of any other Christian writer—past or present. Reading Ellen White's counsels gives one the abiding sense that she lived a Christ-centered life and did so in the presence of Jesus.

That Jesus would become so central to Ellen White's life and work was by no means a foregone conclusion. As a young teenager she feared having to "endure the flames of hell forever" (LS 30, 31), but at the urging of her mother, she counseled briefly with Levi Stockman, a Methodist minister who had accepted Millerism. The teenager Stockman met was a struggling, forlorn believer, completely unsure of her salvation. Ellen White later wrote of that visit, "He knew there was hope for me through the love of Jesus," (LS 36). "I had obtained more knowledge on the subject of God's love and pitying tenderness, than from all the sermons and exhortations to which I had ever listened" (LS 37). From that moment, the darkness smothering Ellen White's growing faith lifted. Her spiritual life became transformed as she beheld Christ.

Ellen White's deepening love for her Redeemer can be seen through the amazing variety of names by which she referred to Jesus in her published writings—more than 840 in total. Space does not permit the inclusion of readings in which all the names are mentioned, so 365 of the best are captured here. The careful student of Ellen White's writings can come to but one conclusion as to the Source of such a powerful collection of appellations: Ellen White was inspired.

As you read *Names of Jesus*, you will also meet the Jesus on whom Ellen White depended to fulfill her unique calling. In 1892 she called Him "my Tried Stone," perhaps owing to the challenges she faced at the beginning of her sojourn in Australia. In other writings Jesus is the Alpha and Omega, Creator of Heaven and Earth, Giver of Every Good and Perfect Gift, and our Great Burden Bearer. To the distracted among us she wrote of One who is the Great Center of Attraction. To those broken by sin she offers the Complete Saviour, Great Intercessor, All-Powerful Mediator, and Captain of Our Salvation. For every need Ellen White has a Jesus!

In this devotional, each reading features a reflection thought or question to help the reader apply to his or her life that day's message. In addition, when words such as *man, men, brethren, he, him,* and *his* have been used as generic representations for the whole of humanity, we have changed these pronouns to be more inclusive, while preserving Ellen White's meaning and message.

It is our hope that this devotional will introduce you to Jesus if you have yet to meet the One who gave His life for you. If you have already felt the loving touch of the Savior, we are certain that each day's reading will enrich your walk with Him. Sharing Jesus was the great heartbeat of Ellen White's life and ministry. Our prayer is that this legacy will continue through you, until all call on Jesus—the name above all names.

THE TRUSTEES OF THE
ELLEN G. WHITE ESTATE®

JANUARY

ALPHA AND OMEGA

"I am the Alpha and the Omega, the Beginning and the End, the First and the Last."

—Revelation 22:13

He [Paul] approached the Gentiles, not by exalting the law at first, but by exalting Christ, and then showing the binding claims of the law. He showed them plainly how the light from the cross of Calvary gave significance and glory to the whole Jewish economy. Thus he varied his manner of labor, always shaping his message to the circumstances under which he was placed; and though after patient labor he was successful to a large degree, many would not be convinced. There are some who will not be convinced by any presentation of the truth. The laborer for God should, nevertheless, study carefully the best method, in order that he may not arouse prejudice or stir up combativeness in his hearers.

Christ said to His disciples, "I have yet many things to say unto you, but ye cannot bear them now." As the result of their early education, their ideas upon many points were incorrect, and they were not then prepared to understand and receive some things which He would otherwise have taught them. His instructions would have confused their minds, and raised questioning and unbelief that would have been difficult to remove.

Christ drew the hearts of His hearers to Him by the manifestation of His love, and then, little by little, as they were able to bear it, He unfolded to them the great truths of the kingdom. We also must learn to adapt our labors to the condition of the people—to meet humans where they are. While the claims of the law of God are to be presented to the world, we should never forget that love, the love of Christ, is the only power that can soften the heart, and lead to obedience. All the great truths of the Scriptures center in Christ; and rightly understood, all lead to Him. Let Christ be presented as the **Alpha and Omega**, the beginning and the end of the great plan of redemption. Present to the people such subjects as will strengthen their confidence in God and in His word, and lead them to investigate its teachings for themselves. And as they go forward, step by step, in the study of the Bible, they will be better prepared to appreciate the beauty and harmony of its precious truths.—*Review and Herald*, November 25, 1890.

Further Reflection: *In what ways has Jesus drawn my heart to Him by clear demonstrations of His love for me?*

BURDEN BEARER

"For I, the LORD your God, will hold your right hand, saying to you, 'Fear not, I will help you.' "

—Isaiah 41:13

In these words Christ is speaking to every human being. Whether they know it or not, all are weary and heavy-laden. All are weighed down with burdens that only Christ can remove. The heaviest burden that we bear is the burden of sin. If we were left to bear this burden, it would crush us. But the Sinless One has taken our place. "The Lord hath laid on Him the iniquity of us all." (Isaiah 53:6) He has borne the burden of our guilt. He will take the load from our weary shoulders. He will give us rest. The burden of care and sorrow also He will bear. He invites us to cast all our care upon Him; for He carries us upon His heart.

The Elder Brother of our race is by the eternal throne. He looks upon every soul who is turning his face toward Him as the Saviour. He knows by experience what are the weaknesses of humanity, what are our wants, and where lies the strength of our temptations; for He was in all points tempted like as we are, yet without sin. He is watching over you, trembling child of God. Are you tempted? He will deliver. Are you weak? He will strengthen. Are you ignorant? He will enlighten. Are you wounded? He will heal. The Lord "telleth the number of the stars;" and yet "He healeth the broken in heart, and bindeth up their wounds." (Psalm 147:4, 3) "Come unto Me," is His invitation. Whatever your anxieties and trials, spread out your case before the Lord. Your spirit will be braced for endurance. The way will be opened for you to disentangle yourself from embarrassment and difficulty. The weaker and more helpless you know yourself to be, the stronger will you become in His strength. The heavier your burdens, the more blessed the rest in casting them upon the **Burden Bearer**. The rest that Christ offers depends upon conditions, but these conditions are plainly specified. They are those with which all can comply. He tells us just how His rest is to be found.

"Take My yoke upon you," Jesus says. The yoke is an instrument of service. Cattle are yoked for labor, and the yoke is essential that they may labor effectually. By this illustration Christ teaches us that we are called to service as long as life shall last.—*The Desire of Ages*, pp. 328, 329.

Further Reflection: *What burden am I carrying that Jesus is waiting to take from me?*

JANUARY 3

LIVING VINE

"I am the vine, you are the branches. He who abides in Me, and I in him, bears much fruit; for without Me you can do nothing."

—John 15:5

I have frequently seen that the children of the Lord neglect prayer, especially secret prayer, altogether too much; that many do not exercise that faith which it is their privilege and duty to exercise, often waiting for that feeling which faith alone can bring. Feeling is not faith; the two are distinct. Faith is ours to exercise, but joyful feeling and the blessing are God's to give. The grace of God comes to the soul through the channel of living faith, and that faith it is in our power to exercise.

True faith lays hold of and claims the promised blessing before it is realized and felt. We must send up our petitions in faith within the second veil, and let our faith take hold of the promised blessing, and claim it as ours. We are then to believe that we receive the blessing, because our faith has hold of it, and according to the word it is ours. "What things soever ye desire, when ye pray, believe that ye receive them, and ye shall have them." (Mark 11:24) Here is faith, naked faith, to believe that we receive the blessing, even before we realize it. When the promised blessing is realized and enjoyed, faith is swallowed up. But many suppose they have much faith when sharing largely of the Holy Spirit, and that they cannot have faith unless they feel the power of the Spirit. Such confound faith with the blessing that comes through faith.

The very time to exercise faith is when we feel destitute of the Spirit. When thick clouds of darkness seem to hover over the mind, then is the time to let living faith pierce the darkness and scatter the clouds.

True faith rests on the promises contained in the word of God, and those only who obey that word can claim its glorious promises. . . .

We should be much in secret prayer. Christ is the vine, we are the branches. And if we would grow and flourish, we must continually draw sap and nourishment from the **Living Vine**; for separated from the Vine, we have no strength.—*Christian Experience and Teachings of Ellen G. White*, pp. 126, 127.

Further Reflection: *If faith is the channel through which feelings of assurance come, how can I reorient my life to make decisions based not on feeling but on faith in God's promises?*

TRIED STONE

"Behold, I lay in Zion a stone for a foundation, a tried stone, a precious cornerstone, a sure foundation; whoever believes will not act hastily."
—Isaiah 28:16

Our Redeemer is a "Tried Stone." The experiment has been made, the great test has been applied, and with perfect success. In Him is fulfilled all the purpose of God for the saving of a lost world. Never was a foundation subject to so severe a trial and test as this "Tried Stone." The Lord Jehovah knew what this foundation stone could sustain. The sins of the whole world could be piled upon it. The Lord's chosen were to be revealed, heaven's gates to be thrown open to all who would believe; its untold glories were to be given to the overcomers.

"A Tried Stone" is Christ, tried by the perversity of human beings. Thou, O our Saviour, hast taken the burden; Thou hast given peace and rest; Thou hast been tried, proved by believers who have taken their trials to Thy sympathy, their sorrows to Thy love, their wounds to Thy healing, their weakness to Thy strength, their emptiness to Thy fullness; and never, never has one soul been disappointed. Jesus, my **Tried Stone**, to Thee will I come, moment by moment. In Thy presence I am lifted above pain. "When my heart is overwhelmed, lead me to the Rock that is higher than I." (Psalm 61:2)

It is our privilege to enjoy sweet communion with God. Precious to the believer is His atoning blood, precious is His justifying righteousness. "Unto you therefore which believe He is precious." (1 Peter 2:7)

When I meditate upon this fountain of living power from which we may draw, I mourn that so many are losing the delight they might have had in considering His goodness. We are to be sons and daughters of God, growing into a holy temple in the Lord. "No more strangers and foreigners, but fellow-citizens with the saints, and of the household of God. . . . Built upon the foundation of the apostles and prophets, Jesus Christ Himself being the chief corner stone." (Ephesians 2:19, 20) This is our privilege. How is Heaven amazed at the present condition of the church that could be so much to the world were every stone, in its proper place, a living stone to emit light.—*Review and Herald*, March 19, 1895.

Further Reflection: *Is Jesus a proven Tried Stone to you, One on whom I can depend? Do I trust Jesus with my most painful trials?*

JUDGE OF ALL

"For many are called, but few are chosen."

—Matthew 22:14

When the householder went to the market and found men unhired, he said, "Why stand ye here all the day idle?" And the reply was, "Because no man hath hired us." None of those called later in the day were there in the morning. They had not refused the call. Those who refuse and afterward repent, do well to repent; but it is not safe to trifle with the first call of mercy. . . .

The Lord requires that sacred fire be used in His service. We are to bear the message of the divine householder to our fellow human beings. This will impress hearts. In whatever part of the Lord's vineyard men and women are working, they need closely to examine their own hearts.

If they are inclined to exalt themselves and disparage others, their hearts need to be changed, till they shall no longer place their own estimate upon their own work and the work of others.

We need a spirit of love and of true dependence upon God. When we have implicit faith in Him who is Truth, we shall realize that worry and anxiety are unnecessary.

Whatever work we do, we are to do it for Christ. There are many kinds of temporal work to be done for God. An unbeliever would do this work mechanically, for the wages they receive. They do not know the joy of co-operation with the Master Worker. There is no spirituality in the work of them who serve themselves. Common motives, common aspirations, common inspirations, a desire to be thought clever by people, rule in their life. Such a one may receive praise from people, but not from God. Those who are truly united with Christ do not work for the wages they receive. Laborers together with God, they do not strive to exalt self.

In the last great day decisions will be made that will be a surprise to many. Human judgment will have no place in the decisions then made. Christ can and will judge every case; for all judgment has been committed to Him by the Father. He will estimate service by that which is invisible to humans. The most secret things lie open to His all-seeing eye. When the **Judge of all** human beings shall make His investigation, many of those whom human estimation has placed first will be placed last, and those who have been put in the lowest place by men and women will be taken out of the ranks and made first.—*Review and Herald*, July 31, 1900.

Further Reflection: *When was the last time that I heard the applause of heaven for some selfless act of service?*

GREAT MASTER ARTIST

"Even Solomon in all his glory was not arrayed like one of these."
—Matthew 6:29

Christ taught His disciples that the measure of divine attention bestowed on any of God's work is proportionate to the rank which that object occupies in the scale of creation. The little brown sparrow, apparently the most inferior of birds, is watched over by Providence. Not one falls to the ground without the notice of our heavenly Father. The flowers of the field, the grass which clothes the earth with verdure—all share the notice and care of our heavenly Father.

"Behold the fowls of the air," Christ said, "for they sow not, neither do they reap, nor gather into barns; yet your heavenly Father feedeth them. Are ye not much better than they? Which of you by taking thought can add one cubit unto his stature? And why take ye thought for raiment? Consider the lilies of the field, how they grow; they toil not, neither do they spin: and yet I say unto you, That even Solomon in all his glory was not arrayed like one of these." (Matthew 6:26–29) If the lilies of the field are objects upon which the **great Master Artist** has bestowed care, making them so beautiful that they out-rival the glory of Solomon, the greatest king that ever wielded a scepter; if the grass of the field is made into a beautiful carpet for the earth, can we form any idea of the regard which God bestows upon humanity, who was formed in His image?

God has given human beings intellect in order that they may comprehend greater things than these beautiful objects in nature. He carries the human agent into a higher department of truth, leading the mind higher and still higher, and opening to them the divine mind. And in the book of God's providence, the volume of life, each one is given a page. That page contains every particular of his history. Even the hairs of his head are numbered. God's children are never absent from His mind.

And though sin existed for ages, seeking to counteract the merciful tide of love flowing from God to the human race, yet the love and care that God bestows upon the beings He has created in His own image has not ceased to increase in richness and abundance. . . . He crowned His benevolence by the inestimable gift of Jesus.—*Manuscript Releases*, vol. 17, pp. 182, 183.

Further Reflection: *If God cares so much for me, why do I allow the cares of the world to worry me?*

AUTHOR OF OUR BEING

"For in Him we live and move and have our being."
—Acts 17:28

In tilling the soil, in disciplining and subduing the land, lessons may constantly be learned. No one would think of settling upon a raw piece of land, expecting it at once to yield a harvest. Earnestness, diligence, and persevering labor are to be put forth in treating the soil preparatory to sowing the seed. So it is in the spiritual work in the human heart. Those who would be benefited by the tilling of the soil must go forth with the word of God in their hearts. They will then find the fallow ground of the heart broken by the softening, subduing influence of the Holy Spirit. Unless hard work is bestowed on the soil, it will not yield a harvest. So with the soil of the heart: the Spirit of God must work upon it to refine and discipline it before it can bring forth fruit to the glory of God.

The soil will not produce its riches when worked by impulse. It needs thoughtful, daily attention. It must be plowed often and deep, with a view to keeping out the weeds that take nourishment from the good seed planted. Thus those who plow and sow prepare for the harvest. None need stand in the field amid the sad wreck of their hopes.

The blessing of the Lord will rest upon those who thus work the land, learning spiritual lessons from nature. In cultivating the soil the worker knows little what treasures will open up before him. While he is not to despise the instruction he may gather from minds that have had an experience, and from the information that intelligent persons may impart, he should gather lessons for himself. . . . The cultivation of the soil will prove an education to the soul.

He who causes the seed to spring up, who tends it day and night, who gives it power to develop, is the **Author of our being**, the King of heaven, and He exercises still greater care and interest in behalf of His children. While the human sower is planting the seed to sustain our earthly life, the Divine Sower will plant in the soul the seed that will bring forth fruit unto life everlasting.—*Christ's Object Lessons*, pp. 88, 89.

Further Reflection: *Is the soil of my heart ready for the seed that the Divine Sower wishes to plant in me today?*

DELIVERER

Finally, my brethren, be strong in the Lord and in the power of His might.

—Ephesians 6:10

The Christian must be upright while dwelling with the corrupt and with traitors. With a heart true to God, and imbued with His Spirit, he will see much to grieve over while surrounded by commandment-breakers—those who are on the side of the great rebel, having thrown off their allegiance to the God of Heaven. The fact that iniquity abounds is a strong reason why he should be watchful, and diligent, and faithful in his Master's service, that he may rightly represent the religion of Jesus Christ.

On all sides the Christian soldier will hear treasonable plottings and rebellious utterances from those who make void the law of God. This should increase his zeal to act as a faithful sentinel for God, and to use every effort to bring souls to enlist beneath the blood-stained banner of Prince Immanuel. The more dense the moral darkness, the more earnest should be the endeavor to walk with God, that light and power from Him may be reflected upon those in darkness. The love of genuine Christians will not grow cold because iniquity abounds. As society grows more and more corrupt, as in the days of Noah and of Lot, there will be yearning of soul over deceived, deluded, perishing sinners, who are preparing themselves for a fate similar to that of the transgressors who perished in the waters of the flood and in the fires of Sodom. . . .

We have only a little while to urge the warfare; then Christ will come, and this scene of rebellion will close. . . . As never before, resistance must be made against sin—against the powers of darkness. The time demands energetic and determined activity on the part of those who believe present truth. They should teach the truth by both precept and example. If the time seems long to wait for our **Deliverer** to come, if, bowed by affliction and worn with toil, we feel impatient for our commission to close, and to receive an honorable release from the warfare, let us remember—and let the remembrance check every murmur—that God leaves us on earth to encounter storms and conflicts, to perfect Christian character, to become better acquainted with God our Father and Christ our elder Brother, and to do work for the Master in winning many souls to Christ.—*Review and Herald*, October 25, 1881.

Further Reflection: *Does the antagonism of those who hate Christianity increase my zeal to share the gospel, that even the scoffer might have an opportunity to be saved?*

JANUARY 9

AUTHOR OF THE RESURRECTION

Jesus said to her, "I am the resurrection and the life.
He who believes in Me, though he may die, he shall live."
—John 11:25

Jesus encouraged her faith, saying, "Thy brother shall rise again." His answer was not intended to inspire hope of an immediate change. He carried Martha's thoughts beyond the present restoration of her brother, and fixed them upon the resurrection of the just. This He did that she might see in the resurrection of Lazarus a pledge of the resurrection of all the righteous dead, and an assurance that it would be accomplished by the Saviour's power.

Martha answered, "I know that he shall rise again in the resurrection at the last day."

Still seeking to give a true direction to her faith, Jesus declared, "I am the resurrection, and the life." In Christ is life, original, unborrowed, underived. "He that hath the Son hath life." (1 John 5:12) The divinity of Christ is the believer's assurance of eternal life. "He that believeth in Me," said Jesus, "though he were dead, yet shall he live: and whosoever liveth and believeth in Me shall never die. Believest thou this?" Christ here looks forward to the time of His Second Coming. Then the righteous dead shall be raised incorruptible, and the living righteous shall be translated to heaven without seeing death. The miracle which Christ was about to perform, in raising Lazarus from the dead, would represent the resurrection of all the righteous dead. By His word and His works He declared Himself the **Author of the resurrection**. He who Himself was soon to die upon the cross stood with the keys of death, a conqueror of the grave, and asserted His right and power to give eternal life.

To the Saviour's words, "Believest thou?" Martha responded, "Yea, Lord: I believe that Thou art the Christ, the Son of God, which should come into the world." She did not comprehend in all their significance the words spoken by Christ, but she confessed her faith in His divinity, and her confidence that He was able to perform whatever it pleased Him to do.—*The Desire of Ages*, p. 530.

Further Reflection: *Martha's heart was breaking when Jesus spoke words she had never heard before, let alone fully understood. How much of my belief in Jesus is dependent on that which I can understand? Does what I don't know about Jesus affect what I do know about Him?*

BELOVED

But God forbid that I should boast except in the cross of our Lord Jesus Christ, by whom the world has been crucified to me, and I to the world.

—Galatians 6:14

The consecrated messengers who in the early days of Christianity carried to a perishing world the glad tidings of salvation, allowed no thought of self-exaltation to mar their presentation of Christ and Him crucified. They coveted neither authority nor pre-eminence. Hiding self in the Saviour, they exalted the great plan of salvation, and the life of Christ, the Author and Finisher of this plan. Christ, the same yesterday, today, and forever, was the burden of their teaching.

If those who today are teaching the word of God, would uplift the cross of Christ higher and still higher, their ministry would be far more successful. If sinners can be led to give one earnest look at the cross, if they can obtain a full view of the crucified Saviour, they will realize the depth of God's compassion and the sinfulness of sin.

Christ's death proves God's great love for human beings. It is our pledge of salvation. To remove the cross from the Christian would be like blotting the sun from the sky. The cross brings us near to God, reconciling us to Him. With the relenting compassion of a father's love, Jehovah looks upon the suffering that His Son endured in order to save the race from eternal death, and accepts us in the **Beloved**.

Without the cross, humanity could have no union with the Father. On it depends our every hope. From it shines the light of the Saviour's love, and when at the foot of the cross the sinner looks up to the One who died to save him, he may rejoice with fullness of joy, for his sins are pardoned. Kneeling in faith at the cross, he has reached the highest place to which human beings can attain.

Through the cross we learn that the heavenly Father loves us with a love that is infinite. Can we wonder that Paul exclaimed, "God forbid that I should glory, save in the cross of our Lord Jesus Christ"? (Galatians 6:14)—*The Acts of the Apostles*, pp. 209, 210.

Further Reflection: *If my every hope depends on what Jesus accomplished at the cross, how often should I thank God for the amazing sacrifice of His Beloved? How often do I kneel at the pinnacle of my existence—the foot of Jesus' cross?*

JANUARY 11

CONQUEROR CLAIMING HIS VICTORY

He gives power to the weak, and to those who have no might He increases strength.

—Isaiah 40:29

It is Satan's special device to lead human beings into sin, and then leave them, helpless and trembling, fearing to seek for pardon. But why should we fear, when God has said, "Let him take hold of My strength, that he may make peace with Me; and he shall make peace with Me"? (Isaiah 27:5) Every provision has been made for our infirmities, every encouragement offered us to come to Christ.

Christ offered up His broken body to purchase back God's heritage, to give human beings another trial. "Wherefore He is able also to save them to the uttermost that come unto God by Him, seeing He ever liveth to make intercession for them." (Hebrews 7:25) By His spotless life, His obedience, His death on the cross of Calvary, Christ interceded for the lost race. And now, not as a mere petitioner does the Captain of our salvation intercede for us, but as a **Conqueror claiming His victory**. His offering is complete, and as our Intercessor He executes His self-appointed work, holding before God the censer containing His own spotless merits and the prayers, confessions, and thanksgiving of His people. . . . The offering is wholly acceptable, and pardon covers all transgression.

Christ has pledged Himself to be our substitute and surety, and He neglects no one. He who could not see human beings exposed to eternal ruin without pouring out His soul unto death in their behalf, will look with pity and compassion upon every soul who realizes that he cannot save himself.

He will look upon no trembling suppliant without raising him up. He who through His own atonement provided for man an infinite fund of moral power, will not fail to employ this power in our behalf. We may take our sins and sorrows to His feet; for He loves us. His every look and word invites our confidence. He will shape and mold our characters according to His own will.

In the whole Satanic force there is not power to overcome one soul who in simple trust casts himself on Christ. "He giveth power to the faint; and to them that have no might He increaseth strength." (Isaiah 40:29)—*Christ's Object Lessons*, pp. 156,157.

Further Reflection: *How can I access Christ's "infinite fund of moral power"?*

INFINITE LOVE

"But if you do not forgive men their trespasses, neither will your Father forgive your trespasses."

—Matthew 6:15

When one turns away from human imperfections to behold Jesus, a divine transformation takes place in the character. The Spirit of Christ working upon the heart conforms it to His image. Then let it be your effort to lift up Jesus. Let the mind's eye be directed to "the Lamb of God, which taketh away the sin of the world." (John 1:29) And as you engage in this work, remember that "he which converteth the sinner from the error of his way, shall save a soul from death, and shall hide a multitude of sins." (James 5:20)

"But if ye forgive not men their trespasses, neither will your Father forgive your trespasses." (Matthew 6:15) Nothing can justify an unforgiving spirit. He who is unmerciful toward others shows that he himself is not a partaker of God's pardoning grace. In God's forgiveness the heart of the erring one is drawn close to the great heart of **infinite Love**. The tide of divine compassion flows into the sinner's soul, and from him to the souls of others. The tenderness and mercy that Christ has revealed in His own precious life will be seen in those who become sharers of His grace. . . . But "if any man have not the Spirit of Christ, he is none of His." (Romans 8:9) He is alienated from God, fitted only for eternal separation from Him.

It is true that he may once have received forgiveness; but his unmerciful spirit shows that he now rejects God's pardoning love. He has separated himself from God, and is in the same condition as before he was forgiven. He has denied his repentance, and his sins are upon him as if he had not repented.

But the great lesson of the parable lies in the contrast between God's compassion and man's hardheartedness; in the fact that God's forgiving mercy is to be the measure of our own. . . .

We are not forgiven *because* we forgive, but *as* we forgive. The ground of all forgiveness is found in the unmerited love of God, but by our attitude toward others we show whether we have made that love our own.—*Christ's Object Lessons*, pp. 250, 251.

Further Reflection: *Do I tend to grade sins, seeing some as worse than others? How does this tendency affect my ability to forgive sins of which I may not be guilty?*

FOUNDATION

For no other foundation can anyone lay than that which is laid, which is Jesus Christ.

—1 Corinthians 3:11

Every act of life, however unimportant, has its influence in forming the character. A good character is more precious than worldly possessions, and the work of forming it is the noblest in which men and women can engage.

Characters formed by circumstance are changeable and discordant—a mass of contraries. Their possessors have no high aim or purpose in life. They have no ennobling influence upon the characters of others. They are purposeless and powerless.

God expects us to build characters in accordance with the pattern set before us. We are to lay brick by brick, adding grace to grace, finding our weak points and correcting them in accordance with the directions given. When a crack is seen in the walls of a mansion, we know that something about the building is wrong. In our character building, cracks are often seen. Unless these defects are remedied, the house will fall when the tempest of trial beats upon it.

God gives us strength, reasoning power, time, in order that we may build characters on which He can place His stamp of approval. He desires each child of His to build a noble character, by the doing of pure, noble deeds, that in the end he may present a symmetrical structure, a fair temple, honored by humanity and God.

In our character building we must build on Christ. He is the sure **Foundation**—a foundation which can never be moved. The tempest of temptation and trial cannot move the building which is riveted to the Eternal Rock.

He who would grow into a beautiful building for the Lord must cultivate every power of the being. It is only by the right use of the talents that the character can develop harmoniously. Thus we bring to the foundation that which is represented in the Word as gold, silver, precious stones—material that will stand the test of God's purifying fires. In our character building Christ is our example.—*Child Guidance*, pp. 165, 166.

Further Reflection: *Am I using my talents in a way that will contribute to the development of a Godly character?*

BEST FRIEND

"No longer do I call you servants, for a servant does not know what his master is doing; but I have called you friends, for all things that I heard from My Father I have made known to you."

—John 15:15

I saw it was the privilege of every Christian to enjoy the deep movings of the Spirit of God. A sweet, heavenly peace will pervade the mind, and you will love to meditate upon God and heaven. You will feast upon the glorious promises of His word.

But know first that you have begun the Christian course. Know that the first steps are taken in the road to everlasting life. Be not deceived. I fear, yea, I know that many of you know not what religion is. You have felt some excitement, some emotions, but you have never seen sin in its enormity. You have never felt your undone condition, and turned from your evil ways with bitter sorrow. You never have died to the world. You still love its pleasures; you love to engage in conversation on worldly matters. But when the truth of God is introduced, you have nothing to say. Why so silent? Why so talkative upon worldly things, and so silent upon the subject that should most concern you? A subject that should engage your whole soul. The truth of God does not dwell in you.

I saw that many were fair in their profession, but within is corruption. Deceive not yourselves, false-hearted professors. God looks at the heart. "Out of the abundance of the heart the mouth speaketh." The world, I saw, was in the heart of such, but the religion of Jesus is not there. If the professed Christian loves Jesus better than the world, he will love to speak of Him, his **best friend** in whom his highest affections are centered.

He came to their aid when they felt their lost and perishing condition. When weary and heavy laden with sin, they turned unto Him. He removed their burden of guilt and sin, took away their sorrow and mourning, and turned the whole current of their affections. The things they once loved, they now hate; and the things they hated, they now love.—*Spiritual Gifts*, vol. 2, pp. 258, 259.

Further Reflection: *Is Jesus my Best Friend? If someone were observing me, would they hear me speak about Him more than I speak about my earthly friends?*

HIGH PRIEST

For such a High Priest was fitting for us, who is holy, harmless, undefiled, separate from sinners, and has become higher than the heavens.
—Hebrews 7:26

The command was communicated to Moses while in the mount with God, "Let them make Me a sanctuary; that I may dwell among them;" and full directions were given for the construction of the tabernacle. By their apostasy the Israelites forfeited the blessing of the divine Presence, and for the time rendered impossible the erection of a sanctuary for God among them. But after they were again taken into favor with Heaven, the great leader proceeded to execute the divine command.

Chosen men were especially endowed by God with skill and wisdom for the construction of the sacred building. God Himself gave to Moses the plan of that structure, with particular directions as to its size and form, the materials to be employed, and every article of furniture which it was to contain. The holy places made with hands were to be "figures of the true," "patterns of things in the heavens" (Hebrews 9:24, 23)—a miniature representation of the heavenly temple where Christ, our great **High Priest**, after offering His life as a sacrifice, was to minister in the sinner's behalf. God presented before Moses in the mount a view of the heavenly sanctuary, and commanded him to make all things according to the pattern shown him. All these directions were carefully recorded by Moses, who communicated them to the leaders . . .

For the building of the sanctuary great and expensive preparations were necessary; a large amount of the most precious and costly material was required; yet the Lord accepted only freewill offerings. "Of every man that giveth it willingly with his heart ye shall take My offering" was the divine command repeated by Moses to the congregation. Devotion to God and a spirit of sacrifice were the first requisites in preparing a dwelling place for the Most High.

All the people responded with one accord. "They came, every one whose heart stirred him up, and every one whom His spirit made willing, and they brought the Lord's offering to the work of the tabernacle of the congregation, and for all His service, and for the holy garments." —*Christ in His Sanctuary*, pp. 34, 35.

Further Reflection: *Does anything happening at your church stir your heart to give?*

SELF-EXISTENT ONE

Jesus said to them, "Most assuredly, I say to you, before Abraham was, I am."

—John 8:58

Abraham learned of God the greatest lesson ever given to mortal. His prayer that he might see Christ before he should die was answered. He saw Christ; he saw all that mortal can see, and live. By making an entire surrender, he was able to understand the vision of Christ, which had been given him. He was shown that in giving His only-begotten Son to save sinners from eternal ruin, God was making a greater and more wonderful sacrifice than ever humans could make.

Abraham's experience answered the question: "Wherewith shall I come before the Lord, and bow myself before the high God? Shall I come before Him with burnt offerings, with calves of a year old? Will the Lord be pleased with thousands of rams, or with ten thousands of rivers of oil? shall I give my first-born for my transgression, the fruit of my body for the sin of my soul?" (Micah 6:6, 7) In the words of Abraham, "My son, God will provide Himself a lamb for a burnt offering," (Genesis 22:8), and in God's provision of a sacrifice instead of Isaac, it was declared that no person could make expiation for himself. The pagan system of sacrifice was wholly unacceptable to God. . . . The Son of God alone can bear the guilt of the world.

Through his own suffering, Abraham was enabled to behold the Saviour's mission of sacrifice. But Israel would not understand that which was so unwelcome to their proud hearts. Christ's words concerning Abraham conveyed to His hearers no deep significance. The Pharisees saw in them only fresh ground for caviling. They retorted with a sneer, as if they would prove Jesus to be a madman, "Thou art not yet fifty years old, and hast Thou seen Abraham?"

With solemn dignity Jesus answered, "Verily, verily, I say unto you, Before Abraham was, I AM."

Silence fell upon the vast assembly. The name of God, given to Moses to express the idea of the eternal presence, had been claimed as His own by this Galilean Rabbi. He had announced Himself to be the **self-existent One**, He who had been promised to Israel, "whose goings forth have been from of old, from the days of eternity." (Micah 5:2, margin)—*The Desire of Ages*, pp. 469, 470.

Further Reflection: *Jesus beheld my every need before the foundation of the world. How can I thank Him today for loving me before the foundation of the world?*

HEAVEN'S KING

But with the precious blood of Christ, as of a lamb without blemish and without spot.

—1 Peter 1:19

Jesus looked upon the innocent victims of sacrifice, and saw how the Jews had made these great convocations scenes of bloodshed and cruelty. In place of humble repentance of sin, they had multiplied the sacrifice of beasts, as if God could be honored by a heartless service. The priests and rulers had hardened their hearts through selfishness and avarice. The very symbols pointing to the Lamb of God they had made a means of getting gain. Thus in the eyes of the people the sacredness of the sacrificial service had been in a great measure destroyed. The indignation of Jesus was stirred; He knew that His blood, so soon to be shed for the sins of the world, would be as little appreciated by the priests and elders as was the blood of beasts which they kept incessantly flowing.

Against these practices Christ had spoken through the prophets. Samuel had said, "Hath the Lord as great delight in burnt offerings and sacrifices, as in obeying the voice of the Lord? Behold, to obey is better than sacrifice, and to hearken than the fat of rams." (1 Samuel 15:22) . . .

He who had Himself given these prophecies now for the last time repeated the warning. In fulfillment of prophecy the people had proclaimed Jesus king of Israel. He had received their homage, and accepted the office of king. In this character He must act. He knew that His efforts to reform a corrupt priesthood would be in vain; nevertheless His work must be done; to an unbelieving people the evidence of His divine mission must be given.

Again the piercing look of Jesus swept over the desecrated court of the temple. All eyes were turned toward Him. Priest and ruler, Pharisee and Gentile, looked with astonishment and awe upon Him who stood before them with the majesty of **heaven's King**. Divinity flashed through humanity, investing Christ with a dignity and glory He had never manifested before. . . . Christ spoke with a power that swayed the people like a mighty tempest: "It is written, My house shall be called the house of prayer; but ye have made it a den of thieves." His voice sounded like a trumpet through the temple.—*The Desire of Ages*, pp. 590, 591.

Further Reflection: *When have I felt the righteous indignation that Jesus did at the temple?*

ONE THAT IS MIGHTY TO SAVE

"The LORD your God in your midst,
The Mighty One, will save;
He will rejoice over you with gladness,
He will quiet you with His love,
He will rejoice over you with singing."

—Zephaniah 3:17

Now you may cling to your righteousness, and you may think that you have tried to do about right, and that, after all, you will be saved in doing this. You cannot see that Christ does it all. "I must repent first," some say. "I must go so far on my own without Christ, and then Christ meets me and accepts me."

You cannot have a thought without Christ. You cannot have an inclination to come to Him unless He sets in motion influences and impresses His Spirit upon the human mind. And if there is a person on the face of the earth who has any inclination toward God, it is because of the many influences that are set to work to bear upon his mind and heart. Those influences call for the allegiance to God and an appreciation of the great work that God has done for him.

Then don't let us ever say that we can repent of ourselves, and then Christ will pardon. No, indeed. It is the favor of God that pardons. It is the favor of God that leads us by His power to repentance. Therefore, it is all of Jesus Christ, everything of Him, and you want to just give back glory to God. Why don't you respond more when you meet together in your meetings? Why don't you have the quickening influence of the Spirit of God when the love of Jesus and His salvation are presented to you? It is because you do not see that Christ is first and last and best, and the Alpha and the Omega, the beginning and the end, the very Author and Finisher of our faith. You don't realize this, and therefore you remain in your sins. Why is this? It is because Satan is here wrestling and battling for the souls of human beings. He casts his hellish shadow right athwart our pathway, and all that you can see is the enemy and his power.

Look away from his power to the **One that is mighty to save** to the utmost. Why doesn't your faith plow through the shadow to where Christ is? He has led captivity captive and given gifts unto men and women. He will teach you that Satan claims every soul that does not join with Him as His property.—*Faith and Works*, pp. 72, 73.

Further Reflection: *What in my life is preventing me from taking a sustained, consistent look at Jesus? What is the Devil using to distract me from God?*

BRIDEGROOM

Arise, shine; For your light has come!
And the glory of the LORD is risen upon you.

—Isaiah 60:1

To those who go out to meet the **Bridegroom** is this message given. Christ is coming with power and great glory. He is coming with His own glory and with the glory of the Father. He is coming with all the holy angels with Him. While all the world is plunged in darkness, there will be light in every dwelling of the saints. They will catch the first light of His second appearing. The unsullied light will shine from His splendor, and Christ the Redeemer will be admired by all who have served Him.

While the wicked flee from His presence, Christ's followers will rejoice. The patriarch Job, looking down to the time of Christ's second advent, said, "Whom I shall see for myself, and mine eyes shall behold, and not a stranger." (Job 19:27) To His faithful followers Christ has been a daily companion and familiar Friend. They have lived in close contact, in constant communion with God. Upon them the glory of the Lord has risen. In them the light of the knowledge of the glory of God in the face of Jesus Christ has been reflected. Now they rejoice in the undimmed rays of the brightness and glory of the King in His majesty. They are prepared for the communion of heaven; for they have heaven in their hearts.

With uplifted heads, with the bright beams of the Sun of Righteousness shining upon them, with rejoicing that their redemption draweth nigh, they go forth to meet the Bridegroom, saying, "Lo, this is our God; we have waited for Him, and He will save us." (Isaiah 25:9)

"And I heard as it were the voice of a great multitude, and as the voice of many waters, and as the voice of mighty thunderings, saying, Alleluia; for the Lord God omnipotent reigneth. Let us be glad and rejoice, and give honour to Him; for the marriage of the Lamb is come, and His wife hath made herself ready." (Revelation 19:6–9)—*Christ's Object Lessons*, p. 421.

Further Reflection: *Before Jesus returns in His full glorified state, His glory will be reflected in those who live in close, constant contact with Him. Am I reflecting Christ's glory to the world?*

DIVINE VOICE

He came to His own, and His own did not receive Him.
—John 1:11

Jesus came by the authority of God, bearing His image, fulfilling His word, and seeking His glory; yet He was not accepted by the leaders in Israel; but when others should come, assuming the character of Christ, but actuated by their own will and seeking their own glory, they would be received. And why? Because he who is seeking his own glory appeals to the desire for self-exaltation in others. To such appeals the Jews could respond. They would receive the false teacher because he flattered their pride by sanctioning their cherished opinions and traditions. But the teaching of Christ did not coincide with their ideas. It was spiritual, and demanded the sacrifice of self; therefore they would not receive it. They were not acquainted with God, and to them His voice through Christ was the voice of a stranger.

Is not the same thing repeated in our day? Are there not many, even religious leaders, who are hardening their hearts against the Holy Spirit, making it impossible for them to recognize the voice of God? Are they not rejecting the word of God, that they may keep their own traditions?

"Had ye believed Moses," said Jesus, "ye would have believed Me: for he wrote of Me. But if ye believe not his writings, how shall ye believe My words?" It was Christ who had spoken to Israel through Moses. If they had listened to the **divine voice** that spoke through their great leader, they would have recognized it in the teachings of Christ. Had they believed Moses, they would have believed Him of whom Moses wrote.

Jesus knew that the priests and rabbis were determined to take His life; yet He clearly explained to them His unity with the Father, and His relation to the world. They saw that their opposition to Him was without excuse, yet their murderous hatred was not quenched. Fear seized them as they witnessed the convincing power that attended His ministry; but they resisted His appeals, and locked themselves in darkness.

They had signally failed to subvert the authority of Jesus or to alienate the respect and attention of the people, many of whom were convicted by His words.—*The Desire of Ages*, pp. 212, 213.

Further Reflection: *How can I hear Jesus clearly and follow His leading when He speaks to me?*

ALL-POWERFUL HELPER

Therefore, in all things He had to be made like His brethren, that He might be a merciful and faithful High Priest in things pertaining to God, to make propitiation for the sins of the people.

—Hebrews 2:17

Wonderful—almost too wonderful for human beings to comprehend—is the Saviour's sacrifice in our behalf, shadowed forth in all the sacrifices of the past, in all the services of the typical sanctuary. And this sacrifice was called for. When we realize that His suffering was necessary in order to secure our eternal well-being, our hearts are touched and melted. He pledged Himself to accomplish our full salvation in a way satisfactory to the demands of God's justice, and consistent with the exalted holiness of His law.

No one less holy than the Only Begotten of the Father, could have offered a sacrifice that would be efficacious to cleanse all—even the most sinful and degraded—who accept the Saviour as their atonement and become obedient to Heaven's law. Nothing less could have reinstated human beings in God's favor.

What right had Christ to take the captives out of the enemy's hands?—The right of having made a sacrifice that satisfies the principles of justice by which the kingdom of heaven is governed. He came to this earth as the Redeemer of the lost race, to conquer the wily foe, and, by His steadfast allegiance to right, to save all who accept Him as their Saviour. On the cross of Calvary He paid the redemption price of the race. And thus He gained the right to take the captives from the grasp of the great deceiver, who, by a lie, framed against the government of God, caused the fall of humanity, and thus forfeited all claim to be called a loyal subject of God's glorious everlasting kingdom.

Our ransom has been paid by our Saviour. No one need be enslaved by Satan. Christ stands before us as our **all-powerful helper**. "In all things it behooved Him to be made like unto His brethren, that He might be a merciful and faithful high priest in things pertaining to God, to make reconciliation for the sins of the people." (Hebrews 2:17, 18)—*Selected Messages*, book 1, pp. 309, 310.

Further Reflection: *When was the last time Jesus delivered me from the enemy?*

CAPTAIN OF THE LORD'S HOST

"The Lord will fight for you, and you shall hold your peace."
—Exodus 14:14

I think of the meditation of Christ and the promise, "I will not leave you comfortless: I will come to you." (John 14:18) The agency of the Holy Spirit is to combine with human effort and all heaven is engaged in the work of preparing a people for to stand in these last days. The end is near, and we want to keep the future world in view. The burden of my prayer is that the churches may be aroused from their moral torpor and awaken to earnest, interested endeavor. Oh, that they could see and understand that in this last conflict the **Captain of the Lord's host** is leading on the armies of heaven and mingling in the ranks and fighting our battles for us. We shall have apostasies; we expect them. "They will go out from us because they were not of us." (1 John 2:19) "Every plant, which My heavenly Father hath not planted, shall be rooted up." (Matthew 15:13)

The angel, the mighty angel from heaven, is to "lighten the earth with His glory" while He cries mightily with a loud voice, "Babylon the great is fallen, is fallen." (Revelation 18:1, 2) Oh, how I wish the church to arise and shine because the glory of the Lord has risen upon her. What can we not do in God if every human agency is doing its very utmost. "Without Me ye can do nothing." (John 15:5)

We would lose faith and courage in the conflict if we were not sustained by the power of God. Every form of evil is to spring into intense activity. Evil angels unite their powers with evil people and, as they have been in constant conflict and attained an experience in the best modes of deception and battle, and have been strengthening for centuries, they will not yield the last great final contest without a desperate struggle. All the world will be on one side or the other of the question. The battle of Armageddon will be fought. And that day must find none of us sleeping. Wide awake we must be, as wise virgins having oil in our vessels with our lamps. What is this? Grace, grace! The power of the Holy Ghost must be upon us and the Captain of the Lord's Host will stand at the head of the angels of heaven to direct the battle.—Letter 112, 1890.

Further Reflection: *Satan and his evil army will do everything within their power to fight the armies of God. Am I ready to take my place in the great battle to come? What can I do today to prepare?*

GREAT REMEDY FOR SIN

"For God did not send His Son into the world to condemn the world, but that the world through Him might be saved."

—John 3:17

Christ said to His disciples, "Ye are the light of the world." As the sun goes forth in the heavens to fill the world with brightness, so must the followers of Jesus shed the light of truth upon those who are groping in the darkness of error and superstition. But Christ's followers have no light of themselves. It is the light of Heaven that falls upon them, which is to be reflected by them to the world. . . .

The light of life is freely proffered to all. Everyone who will may be guided by the bright beams of the Sun of Righteousness. Christ is the **great remedy for sin**. None can plead their circumstances, their education, or their temperament as an excuse for living in rebellion against God. Sinners are such by their own deliberate choice. Said our Savior, "This is the condemnation, that light is come into the world, and men loved darkness rather than light, because their deeds were evil. For everyone that doeth evil hateth the light, neither cometh to the light, lest his deeds should be reproved." . . .

When the claims of God are presented, those who love sin evince their true character by the satisfaction with which they point to the faults and errors of professed Christians. They are actuated by the same spirit as their master, Satan, whom the Bible declares to be the "accuser of the brethren." Let an evil report be started, and how rapidly it will be exaggerated and passed from lip to lip! How many will feast upon it, like vultures upon a heap of garbage. . . .

The true Christian, "he that doeth truth, cometh to the light, that his deeds may be made manifest, that they are wrought in God." His godly life and holy conversation are a daily testimony against sin and sinners. He is a living representative of the truth which he professes. Of these true-hearted followers, Jesus declares that He is not ashamed to call them brethren. Everyone who at last secures eternal life will here manifest zeal and devotion in the service of God. . . . To know their duty is to do it heartily and fearlessly. They follow the light as it shines upon their path, regardless of consequences. The God of truth is on their side and will never forsake them.—*The Signs of the Times*, March 9, 1882.

Further Reflection: *Is my life a testimony for or against sin? How can I know the answer?*

BRIGHT AND MORNING STAR

Here is the patience of the saints; here are those who keep the commandments of God and the faith of Jesus.

—Revelation 14:12

Mysteries into which angels desire to look, which prophets and kings and righteous men and women desired to understand, the remnant church will carry in messages from God to the world. The prophets prophesied of these things, and they longed to understand that which they foretold; but to them this privilege was not given. . . .

The truths of the third angel's message have been presented by some as a dry theory; but in this message is to be presented Christ the Living One. He is to be revealed as the first and the last, as the I AM, the Root and the Offspring of David, and the **bright and morning Star**. Through this message the character of God in Christ is to be manifested to the world. The call is to be sounded: "O Jerusalem, that bringest good tidings, lift up thy voice with strength; lift it up, be not afraid; say unto the cities of Judah, Behold your God! Behold, the Lord God will come with strong hand, and His arm shall rule for Him: behold, His reward is with Him, and His work before Him. He shall feed His flock like a shepherd: He shall gather the lambs with His arm, and carry them in His bosom." (Isaiah 40:9–11)

Now, with John the Baptist, we are to point to Jesus, saying: "Behold the Lamb of God, which taketh away the sin of the world." (John 1:29) Now as never before is to be sounded the invitation: "If any man thirst, let him come unto Me, and drink." "The Spirit and the bride say, Come. And let him that heareth say, Come. And let him that is athirst come. And whosoever will, let him take the water of life freely." (John 7:37; Revelation 22:17)

There is a great work to be done, and every effort possible must be made to reveal Christ as the sin-pardoning Saviour, Christ as the Sin Bearer, Christ as the bright and morning Star; and the Lord will give us favor before the world until our work is done.—*Testimonies for the Church*, vol. 6, p. 20.

Further Reflection: *When was the last time that God granted me favor as I tried to reveal Christ to someone? How did it feel to know that God used me to share the Bright and Morning Star with others?*

DIVINE PHYSICIAN

" 'For I will restore health to you and heal you of your wounds,' says the LORD."

—Jeremiah 30:17

Christ has all power in heaven and in earth. He is the Great Physician, upon whom we are to call when suffering from physical or spiritual disease. Over the winds and the waves and over men possessed with demons, He showed that He possessed absolute control. To Him have been given the keys of death and of hell. Principalities and powers were made subject to Him, even while in His humiliation. . . .

Why do we not exercise greater faith in the **Divine Physician**? As He worked for the man with the palsy, so He will work today for those who come to Him for healing. We have great need of more faith. I am alarmed as I see the lack of faith among our people. We need to come right into the presence of Christ, believing that He will heal our physical and spiritual infirmities.

We are too faithless. Oh, how I wish that I could lead our people to have faith in God! They need not feel that in order to exercise faith they must be wrought up into a high state of excitement. All they have to do is to believe God's Word, just as they believe one another's word. He hath said it, and He will perform His Word. Calmly rely on His promise, because He means all that He says. Say, He has spoken to me in His Word, and He will fulfill every promise that He has made. Do not become restless. Be trustful. God's Word is true. Act as if your heavenly Father could be trusted. . . .

No one lives to himself. In God's work each one is assigned a post of duty. The union of all strengthens the work of each. As the faith and love and unity of the church grow stronger their circle of influence enlarges, and ever they are to reach to the farthest limit of this influence, constantly extending the triumphs of the cross.—*Selected Messages*, book 1, pp. 83, 84.

Further Reflection: *How can I practice complete faith and trust in heaven's Divine Physician? What situations most cause me to distrust Jesus?*

CENTER OF ALL GOODNESS

You are good, and do good; teach me Your statutes.
—Psalm 119:68

In the humanity of Christ there are golden threads that bind the believing, trusting poor person to His own soul of infinite love. He is the great Physician. In our world He bore our infirmities and carried our burdens. He is the mighty Healer of all diseases. He was poor, and yet He was the **center of all goodness**, all blessings. He is a reservoir of power to all to consecrate their powers to the work of becoming sons God.

Christ has ever been the poor person's friend. He chose poverty and honored it by making it His lot. He has stripped from it forever the reproach of scorn by blessing the poor, the inheritors of God's kingdom. Such was His work. By consecrating Himself to a life of poverty, He redeemed poverty from its humiliation. He took His position with the poor that He might lift from poverty the stigma that the world had attached to it. He knew the danger of the love of riches. He knew that this love is ruinous to many souls. It places those who are rich where they indulge every wish for grandeur. It teaches them to look down on those who are suffering the pressure of poverty. It develops the weakness of human minds and shows that, notwithstanding the abundance of wealth, the rich are not rich toward God.

The characters of many have been molded by the false estimate placed on worldly rich people. The person possessed of houses and lands, lauded and deceived by the respect given him or her, may look down upon the poor person, who possesses virtues that the rich person does not. When weighed in the golden scales of the sanctuary, the selfish, covetous rich person will be found wanting, while the poor person, who has depended in faith upon God alone for his virtue and goodness, will be pronounced heir to eternal riches in the kingdom of God.—Manuscript 22, 1898.

Further Reflection: *Why did Jesus choose to become poor, to make His lot with the powerless and the marginalized? How do I emulate Jesus' love for the suffering and the oppressed?*

HOLY ONE OF ISRAEL

"They will respect my son."

—Matthew 21:37

With a father's heart, God bore with His people. He pleaded with them by mercies given and mercies withdrawn. Patiently He set their sins before them, and in forbearance waited for their acknowledgment. Prophets and messengers were sent to urge God's claim upon the husbandmen; but instead of being welcomed, they were treated as enemies. The husbandmen persecuted and killed them. God sent still other messengers, but they received the same treatment as the first, only that the husbandmen showed still more determined hatred.

As a last resource, God sent His Son, saying, "They will reverence My Son." But their resistance had made them vindictive, and they said among themselves, "This is the heir; come, let us kill Him, and let us seize on His inheritance." . . .

The Jewish rulers did not love God; therefore they cut themselves away from Him, and rejected all His overtures for a just settlement. Christ, the Beloved of God, came to assert the claims of the Owner of the vineyard; but the husbandmen treated Him with marked contempt, saying, We will not have this man to rule over us. They envied Christ's beauty of character. His manner of teaching was far superior to theirs, and they dreaded His success. He remonstrated with them, unveiling their hypocrisy, and showing them the sure results of their course of action. This stirred them to madness. They smarted under the rebukes they could not silence. They hated the high standard of righteousness which Christ continually presented. They saw that His teaching was placing them where their selfishness would be uncloaked, and they determined to kill Him. They hated His example of truthfulness and piety and the elevated spirituality revealed in all He did. His whole life was a reproof to their selfishness, and when the final test came, the test which meant obedience unto eternal life or disobedience unto eternal death, they rejected the **Holy One of Israel**. When they were asked to choose between Christ and Barabbas, they cried out, "Release unto us Barabbas!" (Luke 23:18) And when Pilate asked, "What shall I do then with Jesus?" they cried fiercely, "Let Him be crucified." (Matthew 27:22)—*Christ's Object Lessons*, pp. 293, 294.

Further Reflection: *When have I sought to silence the voice of Jesus because He rebuked some cherished sin in my life? Am I any different from the mob that yelled "Crucify Him!"?*

DIVINE HEAD

"Therefore by their fruits you will know them."
—Matthew 7:20

The work for this time is to appeal to the Christian's mind as the most important work that can be done. It is the question of cultivating the Lord's vineyard. In this vineyard every person has a lot and a place, which the Lord has assigned him. And the success of each depends on his individual relationship to the one **Divine Head**.

The grace and love of our Lord Jesus Christ and His tender relationship to His church on earth are to be revealed by the growth of His work and the evangelization of people in many places. The heavenly principles of truth and righteousness are to be seen more and still more plainly in the lives of Christ's followers. More unselfishness and uncovetousness is to be seen in business transactions than has been seen in the churches since the pouring out of the Holy Spirit on the day of Pentecost. Not a vestige of the influence of selfish, worldly monopolies is to make the slightest impression on the people who are watching and working and praying for the second coming of our Lord and Saviour Jesus Christ in the clouds of heaven with power and great glory.

As a people we are not ready for the Lord's appearing. If we would close the windows of the soul earthward and open them heavenward, every institution established would be a bright and shining light in the world. Each member of the church, if he lived the great, elevated, ennobling truths for this time, would be a bright, shining light. God's people cannot please Him unless they are surcharged with the Holy Spirit's efficiency. So pure and true is to be their relationship to one another that by their words, their affections, their attributes, they will show that they are one with Christ. They are to be as signs and wonders in our world, carrying forward intelligently every line of the work. And the different parts of the work are to be so harmoniously related to one another that all will move like well-regulated machinery. Then will the joy of Christ's salvation be understood. There will then be none of the representation now made by those who have been given the light of truth to communicate, but who have not revealed the principles of truth in their association with one another, who have not done the Lord's work in a way that glorifies Him.—*Selected Messages,* book 1, pp. 113, 114.

Further Reflection: *What good is knowing truth if I lack the love shown by Christ?*

PERFECT MODEL

For to this you were called, because Christ also suffered for us, leaving us an example, that you should follow His steps.
—1 Peter 2:21

Those who talk unbelief will have a little enthusiasm when the sky is bright, and everything encouraging; but when the battle goes hard, when we have to hope against hope, and urge our petitions to the throne of grace through deep darkness, then the unbelieving ones will talk of the good land of Canaan, but will make prominent the dangers to be encountered. They will dwell on the strong walls, and the giants that we shall meet, when the language of faithful Caleb should be heard: "The land is an exceeding good land. If the Lord delight in us, then He will bring us into this land, and give it us."

People of courage are wanted now; people who will venture something for the truth's sake; individuals who will be sober, but not gloomy and desponding; persons who will watch unto prayer, and whose prayers will be mingled with living, active faith. We may be cheerful and even joyful. Even under temptation, our language may be that of faith and hope and courage. But no lightness, no trifling, should be indulged in; no low witticism should escape our lips, for these things give Satan great advantage. And we are living in the solemn hour of the judgment, when we should afflict our souls, confess our errors, repent of our sins, and pray one for another that we may be healed.

If we are converted, we shall no longer represent Satan by warped, one-sided characters; but in character, in words, and in actions, we shall conform to the **perfect model** given us in the life of Christ. Unless we follow this example, evil practices will confirm us in Satan's snare. We cannot afford to dally with the tempter—to persist in one wrong habit, to cherish one darling sin. If we confess and forsake our sins; if we come to Jesus in penitence and humility of soul, acknowledging our inability to remove one spot or stain of sin, and relying wholly on the merits of a crucified Saviour, we may expect forgiveness; for His word is pledged. He has said that He will pardon our transgressions, and blot out our sins. We must dwell upon the matchless love and compassion of Jesus, and not upon our own unworthiness and sinfulness.—*Review and Herald*, May 13, 1884.

Further Reflection: *Is there anything in my life preventing me from following Christ fully?*

CHIEF AMONG TEN THOUSAND

And suddenly, a woman who had a flow of blood for twelve years came from behind and touched the hem of His garment.
—Matthew 9:20

When you respond to the drawing of Christ, and join yourself to Him, you manifest saving faith. To talk of religious things in a casual way, to pray for spiritual blessings without real soul hunger and living faith, avails little. The wondering crowd that pressed close about Jesus realized no accession of vital power from the contact. But when the poor, suffering woman, who for twelve years had been an invalid, in her great need put forth her hand and touched the hem of His garment, she felt the healing virtue. Hers was the touch of faith, and Christ recognized that touch. . . . The faith which avails to bring us in vital contact with Christ expresses on our part supreme preference, perfect reliance, entire consecration. This faith works by love and purifies the soul. It works in the life of the follower of Christ true obedience to God's commandments; for love to God and love to men and women will be the result of vital connection with Christ. . . .

Jesus says, "I am the vine, ye are the branches." (John 15:5) Can we conceive of a more intimate relation than this implies? The fibers of the branch are identical with those of the vine. The communication of life, strength, and nourishment from the trunk to the branches is unobstructed and constant. The root sends its nourishment through the branches. Such is the believer's relation to Christ, if he abides in Christ and draws his nourishment from Him. But this spiritual relation between Christ and the soul can be established only through the exercise of personal faith. "Without faith it is impossible to please Him" (Hebrews 11:6); for it is faith that connects us with the power of heaven, and brings us strength for coping with the powers of darkness. "This is the victory that overcometh the world, even our faith." (1 John 5:4) . . . Our souls become strong in spiritual power; for we are breathing the atmosphere of heaven, and realizing that God is at our right hand, that we shall not be moved. We are rising above the world, beholding Him who is the **Chief among ten thousand**, the one altogether lovely, and by beholding we are to become changed into His image. —*Selected Messages*, book 1, pp. 334, 335.

Further Reflection: *Is my faith in Jesus the result of a life totally consecrated to God?*

JANUARY 31

MIGHTIER THAN THE MIGHTIEST

And His name will be called Wonderful, Counselor, Mighty God, Everlasting Father, Prince of Peace.

—Isaiah 9:6

The wisdom of God, His power and His love are without a parallel. It is the divine guarantee that not one of even the straying sheep and lambs is overlooked, and not one left unsuccored. A golden chain—the mercy and compassion of divine power—is passed around every one of these imperiled souls. Then shall not the human agent cooperate with God? Shall he be sinful, failing, defective in character himself, regardless of the soul ready to perish? Christ has linked him to His eternal throne by His offering His own life.

Zechariah's description of Joshua, the high priest, is a striking representation of the sinner for whom Christ is mediating that he shall be brought to repentance. Satan is standing at the right hand of the Advocate, resisting the work of Christ, and pleading against Him that humanity is his property, through choosing him as their ruler. But the Defender of humanity, the Restorer, **mightier than the mightiest,** hears the demands and claims of Satan, and answers him: "The Lord rebuke thee, O Satan; even the Lord that hath chosen Jerusalem rebuke thee: is not this a brand plucked out of the fire? . . .

"And he answered and spake unto those that stood before Him, saying, Take away the filthy garments from him. And unto him he said, Behold I have caused thine iniquity to pass from thee, and I will clothe thee with change of raiment. And I said, Let them set a fair mitre upon his head. So they set a fair mitre upon his head, and clothed him with garments. And the angel of the Lord stood by." (Zechariah 3:2–5) . . .

Bear in mind that every teacher that takes the responsibility of dealing with human minds, that every soul who is inclined to err and is easily tempted, is the special object for whom Christ is solicitor. They that are whole need not a physician, but those that are sick. The compassionate Intercessor is pleading, and will sinful, finite men and women repulse a single soul?—Manuscript 34, 1893.

Further Reflection: *Do I believe that Jesus is willing to defend, forgive, and renew me?*

FEBRUARY

CHIEF MISSIONARY

And a vision appeared to Paul in the night. A man of Macedonia stood and pleaded with him, saying, "Come over to Macedonia and help us."

—Acts 16:9

God calls for personal effort from those that know the truth. He calls for Christian families to go into communities that are in darkness and error, to go into foreign fields, to become acquainted with a new class of society, and to work wisely and perseveringly for the cause of the Master. To answer this call, self-sacrifice must be experienced.

While many are waiting to have every obstacle removed, souls are dying without hope and without God in the world. Many, very many, for the sake of worldly advantage, for the sake of acquiring knowledge of the sciences, will venture into pestilential regions, and will go into countries where they think they can obtain commercial advantage; but where are the men and women who will change their location, and move their families into regions that are in need of the light of the truth, in order that their example may tell upon those who shall see in them the representatives of Christ?

The Macedonian cry is coming from every quarter of the world, and people are saying, "Come over . . . and help us," and why is there not a decided response? Thousands ought to be constrained by the Spirit of Christ to follow the example of Him who has given His life for the life of the world. Why decline to make decided, self-denying efforts, in order to instruct those who know not the truth for this time? The **Chief Missionary** came to our world, and He has gone before us to show us the way in which we should work. No one can mark out a precise line for those who would be witnesses for Christ.

Those who have means are doubly responsible; for this means has been entrusted to them of God, and they are to feel their accountability to forward the work of God in its various branches. The fact that the truth binds souls by its golden links to the throne of God, should inspire men and women to work with all their God-given energy, to trade upon their Lord's goods in regions beyond, disseminating the knowledge of Christ far hence among the Gentiles.—*Counsels on Stewardship*, pp. 55, 56.

Further Reflection: *Is there anything preventing me from being a missionary in my community if I am unable to travel abroad for the cause of God?*

BABE OF BETHLEHEM

"But you, Bethlehem Ephrathah,
though you are little among the thousands of Judah,
yet out of you shall come forth to Me
The One to be Ruler in Israel."

—Micah 5:2

Parents, in the training of your children, study the lessons that God has given in nature. . . . Ask the gardener by what process he makes every branch and leaf to flourish so beautifully, and to develop in symmetry and loveliness. He will tell you that it was by no rude touch, no violent effort; for this would only break the delicate stems. It was by little attentions, often repeated. He moistened the soil, and protected the growing plants from the fierce blasts and from the scorching sun, and God caused them to flourish and to blossom into loveliness. . . .

Encourage the expression of love toward God and toward one another. The reason why there are so many hardhearted men and women in the world is that true affection has been regarded as weakness, and has been discouraged and repressed. The better nature of these persons was stifled in childhood; and unless the light of divine love shall melt away their cold selfishness, their happiness will be forever ruined. If we wish our children to possess the tender spirit of Jesus, and the sympathy that angels manifest for us, we must encourage the generous, loving impulses of childhood.

Teach the children to see Christ in nature. Take them out into the open air, under the noble trees, into the garden; and in all the wonderful works of creation teach them to see an expression of His love. Teach them that He made the laws which govern all living things, that He has made laws for us, and that these laws are for our happiness and joy. Do not weary them with long prayers and tedious exhortations, but through nature's object lessons teach them obedience to the law of God.

As you win their confidence in you as followers of Christ, it will be easy to teach them of the great love wherewith He has loved us. As you try to make plain the truths of salvation, and point the children to Christ as a personal Saviour, angels will be by your side. The Lord will give to fathers and mothers grace to interest their little ones in the precious story of the **Babe of Bethlehem**, who is indeed the hope of the world. —*The Desire of Ages*, pp. 516, 517.

Further Reflection: *In a sometimes-cold-hearted world, how can I help the children in my life to develop tender hearts of love toward God and others?*

HEAVENLY VINE

"Every branch in Me that does not bear fruit He takes away; and every branch that bears fruit He prunes, that it may bear more fruit."

—John 15:2

Christ's followers are required to come out from the world, and be separate, and touch not the unclean, and they have the promise of being the sons and daughters of the Most High, members of the royal family. But if the conditions are not complied with on their part, they will not, cannot, realize the fulfillment of the promise. A profession of Christianity is nothing in the sight of God; but true, humble, willing obedience to His requirements designates the children of His adoption, the recipients of His grace, the partakers of His great salvation. Such will be peculiar, a spectacle unto the world, to angels, and to human beings. Their peculiar, holy character will be discernible, and will distinctly separate them from the world, from its affections and lust.

I saw that but few among us answer to this description. Their love to God is in word, not in deed and in truth. Their course of action, their works, testify of them that they are not children of the light but of darkness. Their works have not been wrought in God, but in selfishness, in unrighteousness. Their hearts are strangers to His renewing grace. They have not experienced the transforming power which leads them to walk even as Christ walked. Those who are living branches of the **heavenly Vine** will partake of the sap and nourishment of the Vine. They will not be withered and fruitless branches, but will show life and vigor, and will flourish and bear fruit to the glory of God. They will be careful to depart from all iniquity and to perfect holiness in the fear of God.

Like ancient Israel the church has dishonored her God by departing from the light, neglecting her duties, and abusing her high and exalted privilege of being peculiar and holy in character. Her members have violated their covenant to live for God and Him only. They have joined with the selfish and world-loving. Pride, the love of pleasure, and sin have been cherished, and Christ has departed. His Spirit has been quenched in the church. Satan works side by side with professed Christians; yet they are so destitute of spiritual discernment that they do not detect him. . . . By their fruits ye shall know them.—*Testimonies for the Church*, vol. 2, pp. 441, 442.

Further Reflection: *How can I avoid the hypocrisy of living as a Christian in name only?*

PRECIOUS SAVIOUR

" 'I was naked and you clothed Me; I was sick and you visited Me; I was in prison and you came to Me.' "

—Matthew 25:36

Every impulse of the Holy Spirit leading individuals to goodness and to God, is noted in the books of heaven, and in the day of God everyone who has given himself as an instrument for the Holy Spirit's working, will be permitted to behold what his life has wrought. . . .

Wonderful will be the revealing as the lines of holy influence, with their precious results, are brought to view. What will be the gratitude of souls that will meet us in the heavenly courts, as they understand the sympathetic, loving interest which has been taken in their salvation! All praise, honor, and glory will be given to God and to the Lamb for our redemption; but it will not detract from the glory of God to express gratitude to the instrumentality He has employed in the salvation of souls ready to perish.

The redeemed will meet and recognize those whose attention they have directed to the uplifted Saviour. What blessed converse they will have with these souls! "I was a sinner," it will be said, "without God and without hope in the world; and you came to me, and drew my attention to the **precious Saviour** as my only hope. And I believed in Him. I repented of my sins, and was made to sit together with His saints in heavenly places in Christ Jesus." Others will say: "I was a heathen in heathen lands. You left your friends and comfortable home, and came to teach me how to find Jesus, and believe in Him as the only true God. I demolished my idols, and worshiped God, and now I see Him face to face. I am saved, eternally saved, ever to behold Him whom I love. I then saw Him only with the eye of faith, but now I see Him as He is. I can now express my gratitude for His redeeming mercy to Him who loved me, and washed me from my sins in His own blood."

Others will express their gratitude to those who fed the hungry and clothed the naked. "When despair bound my soul in unbelief, the Lord sent you to me," they say, "to speak words of hope and comfort. You brought me food for my physical necessities, and you opened to me the word of God, awakening me to my spiritual needs. You treated me as a brother."—*Gospel Workers*, pp. 517–519.

Further Reflection: *Who most helped your decision to follow Jesus Christ? Do they know it?*

HOLY WATCHER

The eyes of the LORD are on the righteous,
And His ears are open to their cry.

—Psalm 34:15

It was while Peter was still at Joppa that he was called by God to take the gospel to Cornelius, in Caesarea.

Cornelius was a Roman centurion. He was a man of wealth and noble birth, and his position was one of trust and honor. A heathen by birth, training, and education, through contact with the Jews he had gained a knowledge of God, and he worshiped Him with a true heart, showing the sincerity of his faith by compassion to the poor. He was known far and near for his beneficence, and his righteous life made him of good repute among both Jews and Gentiles. His influence was a blessing to all with whom he came in contact. The inspired record describes him as "a devout man, and one that feared God with all his house, which gave much alms to the people, and prayed to God alway."

Believing in God as the Creator of heaven and earth, Cornelius revered Him, acknowledged His authority, and sought His counsel in all the affairs of life. He was faithful to Jehovah in his home life and in his official duties. He had erected the altar of God in his home, for he dared not attempt to carry out his plans or to bear his responsibilities without the help of God.

Though Cornelius believed the prophecies and was looking for the Messiah to come, he had not a knowledge of the gospel as revealed in the life and death of Christ. He was not a member of the Jewish church and would have been looked upon by the rabbis as a heathen and unclean. But the same **Holy Watcher** who said of Abraham, "I know him," knew Cornelius also, and sent a message direct from heaven to him.

The angel appeared to Cornelius while he was at prayer. As the centurion heard himself addressed by name, he was afraid, yet he knew that the messenger had come from God. . . .

The explicitness of these directions, in which was named even the occupation of the man with whom Peter was staying, shows that Heaven is acquainted with the history and business of human beings in every station of life. God is familiar with the experience and work of the humble laborer, as well as with that of the king upon his throne.—*The Acts of the Apostles*, pp. 132–134.

Further Reflection: *Who in my neighborhood has been seeking God, faithfully waiting for a special message from God, which He might want to deliver through me?*

FAULTLESS EXAMPLE

He who says he abides in Him ought himself also to walk just as He walked.

—1 John 2:6

There must be a revival of the strait testimony. The path to heaven is no smoother now than in the days of our Saviour. All our sins must be put away. Every darling indulgence that hinders our religious life must be cut off. The right eye or the right hand must be sacrificed if it cause us to offend. Are we willing to renounce our own wisdom and to receive the kingdom of heaven as a little child? Are we willing to part with self-righteousness? . . .

Every association we form, however limited, exerts some influence upon us. The extent to which we yield to that influence will be determined by the degree of intimacy, the constancy of the association, and our love and veneration for the one with whom we associate. Thus by acquaintance and association with Christ we may become like Him, the one **faultless Example.**

Communion with Christ—how unspeakably precious! Such communion it is our privilege to enjoy if we will seek it, if we will make any sacrifice to secure it. When the early disciples heard the words of Christ, they felt their need of Him. They sought, they found, they followed Him. They were with Him in the house, at the table, in the closet, in the field. They were with Him as pupils with a teacher, daily receiving from His lips lessons of holy truth. They looked to Him as servants to their master, to learn their duty. They served Him cheerfully, gladly. They followed Him, as soldiers follow their commander, fighting the good fight of faith. . . .

"He that saith he abideth in Him ought himself also so to walk, even as He walked." "Now if any man have not the spirit of Christ, he is none of His." This conformity to Jesus will not be unobserved by the world. It is a subject of notice and comment. The Christian may not be conscious of the great change; for the more closely he resembles Christ in character the more humble will be his opinion of himself; but it will be seen and felt by all around him. Those who have had the deepest experience in the things of God are the farthest removed from pride or self-exaltation. They have the humblest thoughts of self, and the most exalted conceptions of the glory and excellence of Christ. They feel that the lowest place in His service is too honorable for them.—*Testimonies for the Church,* vol. 5, pp. 222, 223.

Further Reflection: *What do I find most precious about communing with Christ?*

COMING KING

"Then they will see the Son of Man coming in a cloud with power and great glory."

—Luke 21:27

Christ had bidden His people watch for the signs of His advent and rejoice as they should behold the tokens of their **coming King**. "When these things begin to come to pass," He said, "then look up, and lift up your heads; for your redemption draweth nigh." He pointed His followers to the budding trees of spring, and said: "When they now shoot forth, ye see and know of your own selves that summer is now nigh at hand. So likewise ye, when ye see these things come to pass, know ye that the kingdom of God is nigh at hand." (Luke 21:28, 30, 31)

But as the spirit of humility and devotion in the church had given place to pride and formalism, love for Christ and faith in His coming had grown cold. Absorbed in worldliness and pleasure seeking, the professed people of God were blinded to the Saviour's instructions concerning the signs of His appearing. The doctrine of the Second Advent had been neglected; the Scriptures relating to it were obscured by misinterpretation, until it was, to a great extent, ignored and forgotten. Especially was this the case in the churches of America. The freedom and comfort enjoyed by all classes of society, the ambitious desire for wealth and luxury, begetting an absorbing devotion to money-making, the eager rush for popularity and power, which seemed to be within the reach of all, led people to center their interests and hopes on the things of this life, and to put far in the future that solemn day when the present order of things should pass away.

When the Saviour pointed out to His followers the signs of His return, He foretold the state of backsliding that would exist just prior to His second advent. There would be, as in the days of Noah, the activity and stir of worldly business and pleasure seeking—buying, selling, planting, building, marrying, and giving in marriage—with forgetfulness of God and the future life. For those living at this time, Christ's admonition is: "Take heed to yourselves, lest at any time your hearts be overcharged with surfeiting, and drunkenness, and cares of this life, and so that day come upon you unawares."—*The Great Controversy*, pp. 308, 309.

Further Reflection: *How much of my day today is planned with an eye on the second coming of Jesus?*

NEW-FOUND MASTER

And Jesus said to him, "Today salvation has come to this house, because he also is a son of Abraham."

—Luke 19:9

The streets were crowded, and Zacchaeus, who was small of stature, could see nothing over the heads of the people. None would give way for him; so, running a little in advance of the multitude, to where a wide-branching fig tree hung over the way, the rich tax collector climbed to a seat among the boughs, whence he could survey the procession as it passed below. The crowd comes near, it is going by, and Zacchaeus scans with eager eyes to discern the one figure he longs to see.

Above the clamor of priests and rabbis and the shouts of welcome from the multitude, that unuttered desire of the chief publican spoke to the heart of Jesus. Suddenly, just beneath the fig tree, a group halts, the company before and behind come to a standstill, and One looks upward whose glance seems to read the soul. Almost doubting his senses, the man in the tree hears the words, "Zacchaeus, make haste, and come down; for today I must abide at thy house."

The multitude give way, and Zacchaeus, walking as in a dream, leads the way toward his own home. But the rabbis look on with scowling faces, and murmur in discontent and scorn, "that He was gone to be guest with a man that is a sinner."

Zacchaeus had been overwhelmed, amazed, and silenced at the love and condescension of Christ in stooping to him, so unworthy. Now love and loyalty to his **new-found Master** unseal his lips. He will make public his confession and his repentance.

In the presence of the multitude, "Zacchaeus stood, and said unto the Lord; Behold, Lord, the half of my goods I give to the poor; and if I have taken anything from any man by false accusation, I restore him fourfold.

"And Jesus said unto him, this day is salvation come to this house, forsomuch as he also is a son of Abraham."—*The Desire of Ages*, pp. 553–555.

Further Reflection: *Throughout His earthly ministry, Jesus demonstrated an ability to hear the cry of human hearts above the din of everyday life. Do my needs move the heart of Jesus? Do I seek Him with the assurance that He will hear me?*

BREAD SENT DOWN FROM HEAVEN

"This is the bread which comes down from heaven, that one may eat of it and not die."

—John 6:50

The Bible is the only book giving a positive description of Christ Jesus; and if every human being would study it as their lesson book, and obey it, not a soul would be lost.

All the rays of light shining in the Scriptures point to Jesus Christ, and testify of Him, linking together the Old and New Testament Scriptures. Christ is presented as the author and finisher of their faith, Himself the one in whom their hopes of eternal life are centered. "For God so loved the world, that He gave His only-begotten Son, that whosoever believeth in Him should not perish, but have everlasting life."

What book can begin to compare with the Bible? It is essential for every child, for youth, and for those of mature age to understand; for it is the word of God, the word to guide all the human family to heaven. Then why does not the word from God contain the chief elements which constitute education? Uninspired authors are placed in the hands of children and youth in our schools as lesson books—books from which they are to be educated. They are kept before the youth, taking up their precious time in studying those things which they can never use. . . . These books do not in any sense voice the words of John, "Behold the Lamb of God, which taketh away the sin of the world." . . .

Jesus Christ is the knowledge of the Father, and Christ is our great teacher sent from God. Christ has declared in the sixth chapter of John that He is that **bread sent down from heaven**. "Verily, verily, I say unto you, He that believeth on Me hath everlasting life. I am that bread of life. Your fathers did eat manna in the wilderness, and are dead. This is the bread which cometh down from heaven, that a man may eat thereof, and not die. I am the living bread which came down from heaven: if any man eat of this bread, he shall live forever: and the bread that I will give is My flesh, which I will give for the life of the world." The disciples did not comprehend His words. Says Christ, "It is the Spirit that quickeneth; the flesh profiteth nothing: the words that I speak unto you, they are spirit, and they are life."—*Fundamentals of Christian Education*, pp. 383, 384.

Further Reflection: *How does one "eat" Jesus, the bread sent down from heaven? In what practical ways can I partake of His life today?*

MASTER WORKER

For I know that in me (that is, in my flesh) nothing good dwells.
—Romans 7:18

None of the apostles or prophets ever claimed to be without sin. Those who have lived nearest to God, those who would sacrifice life itself rather than knowingly commit a wrong act, those whom God had honored with divine light and power, have confessed the sinfulness of their own nature. They have put no confidence in the flesh, have claimed no righteousness of their own, but have trusted wholly in the righteousness of Christ. So will it be with all who behold Christ.

At every advance step in Christian experience our repentance will deepen. It is to those whom the Lord has forgiven, to those whom He acknowledges as His people, that He says, "Then shall ye remember your own evil ways, and your doings that were not good, and shall loathe yourselves in your own sight." (Ezekiel 36:31) Again He says, "I will establish My covenant with thee, and thou shalt know that I am the Lord; that thou mayest remember, and be confounded, and never open thy mouth any more because of thy shame, when I am pacified toward thee for all that thou hast done, saith the Lord God." (Ezekiel 16:62, 63) Then our lips will not be opened in self-glorification. We shall know that our sufficiency is in Christ alone. We shall make the apostle's confession our own. "I know that in me (that is, in my flesh) dwelleth no good thing." (Romans 7:18) . . .

In harmony with this experience is the command, "Work out your own salvation with fear and trembling. For it is God which worketh in you both to will and to do of His good pleasure." (Philippians 2:12, 13) God does not bid you fear that He will fail to fulfill His promises, that His patience will weary, or His compassion be found wanting. Fear lest your will shall not be held in subjection to Christ's will, lest your hereditary and cultivated traits of character shall control your life. "It is God which worketh in you both to will and to do of His good pleasure." Fear lest self shall interpose between your soul and the great **Master Worker**. . . . Fear to trust to your own strength, fear to withdraw your hand from the hand of Christ and attempt to walk life's pathway without His abiding presence.—*Christ's Object Lessons*, pp. 160, 161.

Further Reflection: *How can I avoid living in constant fear while soberly working out my personal salvation?*

COMMANDER OF THE HEAVENLY INTELLIGENCES

All things were made through Him, and without Him nothing was made that was made.

—John 1:3

If Christ made all things, He existed before all things. The words spoken in regard to this are so decisive that no one need be left in doubt. Christ was God essentially, and in the highest sense. He was with God from all eternity, God over all, blessed forevermore.

The Lord Jesus Christ, the divine Son of God, existed from eternity, a distinct person, yet one with the Father. He was the surpassing glory of heaven. He was the **commander of the heavenly intelligences,** and the adoring homage of the angels was received by Him as His right. This was no robbery of God. "The Lord possessed Me in the beginning of His way," He declares, "before His works of old. I was set up from everlasting, from the beginning, or ever the earth was. When there were no depths, I was brought forth; when there were no fountains abounding with water. Before the mountains were settled, before the hills was I brought forth: while as yet He had not made the earth, nor the fields, nor the highest part of the dust of the world. When He prepared the heavens, I was there: when He set a compass upon the face of the depth." (Proverbs 8:22–27)

There are light and glory in the truth that Christ was one with the Father before the foundation of the world was laid. This is the light shining in a dark place, making it resplendent with divine, original glory. This truth, infinitely mysterious in itself, explains other mysterious and otherwise unexplainable truths, while it is enshrined in light, unapproachable and incomprehensible.

"Before the mountains were brought forth, or ever Thou hadst formed the earth and the world, even from everlasting to everlasting, Thou art God." (Psalm 90:2) "The people which sat in darkness saw great light; and to them which sat in the region and shadow of death light is sprung up." (Matthew 4:16) Here the pre-existence of Christ and the purpose of His manifestation to our world are presented as living beams of light from the eternal throne. . . . "But thou, Bethlehem Ephratah, though thou be little among the thousands of Judah, yet out of thee shall He come forth unto Me that is to be ruler in Israel; whose goings forth have been from of old, from everlasting." (Micah 5:1, 2)—*Selected Messages*, book 1, pp. 247, 248.

Further Reflection: *How can I enjoy the truths of God which are shrouded in mystery?*

COMPANION

"Eye has not seen, nor ear heard, nor have entered into the heart of man the things which God has prepared for those who love Him."
—1 Corinthians 2:9

Fresh wonders will be revealed to the mind the more closely we apply it to divine things. We lose much by not talking more of Jesus and of heaven, the saints' inheritance. The more we contemplate heavenly things, the more new delights we shall see and the more will our hearts be brim full of thanks to our beneficent Creator.

Consider the wonderful love of God in giving His only begotten Son, that whosoever believeth in Him might not perish but have everlasting life. Oh, why do the professed followers of Christ become charmed and all absorbed with human frail beings and set their affections upon them and bow to them as to a deity, while Jesus is seeking to win our love and engage our thoughts, to bind us to His own heart by the disclosures of the tenderest sympathy and inexpressible love?

No earthly parent has pled more earnestly with an erring child than Christ pleads for us before His Father's throne, while we are transgressors of His law. No human lips have ever followed with more tender expostulations the erring ones. Have, then, a care how you treat this marvelous love. Read the rich promises of God and believe them. Ponder upon them. Listen to the voice of unspeakable love and pity. In Him we have redemption through His blood. As many as are led by the Spirit of God, they are the sons of God. . . .

Cut loose the tendrils; let them not entwine about earthly things, but let them entwine about God. You may never be lonesome, never feel that you are alone, if you will take Jesus as your **Companion** and your everlasting Friend. . . . Trust in Jesus fully as your Saviour, whose death has redeemed you; as your Intercessor, whose pleadings above avail with the Father and secure us peace, pardon. Our names are engraven on the palms of His hands, as our King to whom we must render a reverent and affectionate obedience. Jesus is the believer's life, his hope, his joy. Love is the growth of faith and trust, to have Christ formed in us, to look to Him as a Friend and Counselor.—Letter 4, 1885.

Further Reflection: *If no earthly parent has ever pled for a child as Christ pleads for me before the throne of God, what should be my response to such an expression of love?*

HONORED OF THE ANGELS

Then an angel appeared to Him from heaven, strengthening Him.
—Luke 22:43

The words of Christ teach that we should regard ourselves as inseparably bound to our Father in heaven. Whatever our position, we are dependent upon God, who holds all destinies in His hands. He has appointed us our work, and has endowed us with faculties and means for that work. So long as we surrender the will to God, and trust in His strength and wisdom, we shall be guided in safe paths, to fulfill our appointed part in His great plan. But the one who depends upon his own wisdom and power is separating himself from God. Instead of working in unison with Christ, he is fulfilling the purpose of the enemy of God and humanity.

The Saviour continued: "What things soever He [the Father] doeth, these also doeth the Son likewise. . . . As the Father raiseth up the dead, and quickeneth them; even so the Son quickeneth whom He will." The Sadducees held that there would be no resurrection of the body; but Jesus tells them that one of the greatest works of His Father is raising the dead, and that He Himself has power to do the same work. "The hour is coming, and now is, when the dead shall hear the voice of the Son of God: and they that hear shall live." The Pharisees believed in the resurrection of the dead. Christ declares that even now the power which gives life to the dead is among them, and they are to behold its manifestation. This same resurrection power is that which gives life to the soul "dead in trespasses and sins." (Ephesians 2:1) That spirit of life in Christ Jesus, "the power of His resurrection," sets humans "free from the law of sin and death." (Philippians 3:10; Romans 8:2) The dominion of evil is broken, and through faith the soul is kept from sin. He who opens his heart to the Spirit of Christ becomes a partaker of that mighty power which shall bring forth his body from the grave.

The humble Nazarene asserts His real nobility. He rises above humanity, throws off the guise of sin and shame, and stands revealed, the **Honored of the angels**, the Son of God, One with the Creator of the universe. His hearers are spellbound. No person has ever spoken words like His, or borne himself with such a kingly majesty. His utterances are clear and plain, fully declaring His mission, and the duty of the world.—*The Desire of Ages*, pp. 209, 210.

Further Reflection: *How can I be kept from sin through faith? What power does faith allow me to access?*

THE RESURRECTION AND THE LIFE

*Now Martha said to Jesus, "Lord, if You had been here,
my brother would not have died."*

—John 11:21

When Jesus therefore saw her weeping, and the Jews also weeping which came with her, He groaned in the spirit, and was troubled." He read the hearts of all assembled. He saw that with many, what passed as a demonstration of grief was only pretense. He knew that some in the company, now manifesting hypocritical sorrow, would erelong be planning the death, not only of the mighty miracle worker, but of the one to be raised from the dead. Christ could have stripped from them their robe of pretended sorrow. But He restrained His righteous indignation. The words He could in all truth have spoken, He did not speak, because of the loved one kneeling at His feet in sorrow, who truly believed in Him.

"Where have ye laid him?" He asked, "They said unto Him, Lord, come and see." Together they proceeded to the grave. It was a mournful scene. Lazarus had been much beloved, and his sisters wept for him with breaking hearts, while those who had been his friends mingled their tears with those of the bereaved sisters. In view of this human distress, and of the fact that the afflicted friends could mourn over the dead while the Saviour of the world stood by—"Jesus wept." Though He was the Son of God, yet He had taken human nature upon Him, and He was moved by human sorrow. His tender, pitying heart is ever awakened to sympathy by suffering. He weeps with those that weep, and rejoices with those that rejoice.

But it was not only because of His human sympathy with Mary and Martha that Jesus wept. In His tears there was a sorrow as high above human sorrow as the heavens are higher than the earth. Christ did not weep for Lazarus; for He was about to call him from the grave. He wept because many of those now mourning for Lazarus would soon plan the death of Him who was **the resurrection and the life**. But how unable were the unbelieving Jews rightly to interpret His tears! Some, who could see nothing more than the outward circumstances of the scene before Him as a cause for His grief, said softly, "Behold how He loved him!"—*The Desire of Ages*, pp. 533, 534.

Further Reflection: *How do I respond when someone whom I help betrays me?*

COMPASSIONATE REDEEMER

For it is the God who commanded light to shine out of darkness, who has shone in our hearts to give the light of the knowledge of the glory of God in the face of Jesus Christ.
—2 Corinthians 4:6

As disciples of Christ we shall not mingle with the world from a mere love of pleasure, to unite with them in folly. Such associations can result only in harm. We should never give sanction to sin by our words or our deeds, our silence or our presence. Wherever we go, we are to carry Jesus with us, and to reveal to others the preciousness of our Saviour. But those who try to preserve their religion by hiding it within stone walls lose precious opportunities of doing good. Through the social relations, Christianity comes in contact with the world. Everyone who has received the divine illumination is to brighten the pathway of those who know not the Light of life.

We should all become witnesses for Jesus. Social power, sanctified by the grace of Christ, must be improved in winning souls to the Saviour. Let the world see that we are not selfishly absorbed in our own interests, but that we desire others to share our blessings and privileges. Let them see that our religion does not make us unsympathetic or exacting. Let all who profess to have found Christ, minister as He did for the benefit of humanity.

We should never give to the world the false impression that Christians are a gloomy, unhappy people. If our eyes are fixed on Jesus, we shall see a **compassionate Redeemer,** and shall catch light from His countenance. Wherever His Spirit reigns, there peace abides. And there will be joy also, for there is a calm, holy trust in God.

Christ is pleased with His followers when they show that, though human, they are partakers of the divine nature. They are not statues, but living men and women. Their hearts, refreshed by the dews of divine grace, open and expand to the Sun of Righteousness. The light that shines upon them they reflect upon others in works that are luminous with the love of Christ.—*The Desire of Ages*, pp. 152, 153.

Further Reflection: *Am I a happy Christian? Do people enjoy being around me? How do I use my "social power" to build up the kingdom of God?*

ONLY MEDIATOR

And if anyone sins, we have an Advocate with the Father, Jesus Christ the righteous.

—1 John 2:1

All who endeavor to excuse or conceal their sins, and permit them to remain upon the books of heaven, unconfessed and unforgiven, will be overcome by Satan. The more exalted their profession and the more honorable the position which they hold, the more grievous is their course in the sight of God and the more sure the triumph of their great adversary. Those who delay a preparation for the day of God cannot obtain it in the time of trouble or at any subsequent time. The case of all such is hopeless.

It is not required of you to confess to those who know not your sin and errors. It is not your duty to publish a confession which will lead unbelievers to triumph; but to those to whom it is proper, who will take no advantage of your wrong, confess according to the word of God, and let them pray for you, and God will accept your work, and will heal you. For your soul's sake, be entreated to make thorough work for eternity. Lay aside your pride, your vanity, and make straight work. Come back again to the fold. The Shepherd is waiting to receive you. Repent, and do your first works, and again come into favor with God.

Christ is your Redeemer; He will take no advantage of your humiliating confessions. If you have sin of a private character, confess it to Christ, who is the **only Mediator** between God and humanity. "If any man sin, we have an advocate with the Father, Jesus Christ the righteous." (1 John 2:1) If you have sinned by withholding from God His own in tithes and offerings, confess your guilt to God and to the church, and heed the injunction that He has given you: "Bring ye all the tithes into the storehouse." (Malachi 3:10)

The people of God must move understandingly. They should not be satisfied until every known sin is confessed; then it is their privilege and duty to believe that Jesus accepts them. They must not wait for others to press through the darkness and obtain the victory for them to enjoy. Such enjoyment will last only till the meeting closes. But God must be served from principle instead of from feeling. . . . Let not your daily labor keep you from this. Take time to pray, and as you pray, believe that God hears you.—*Counsels for the Church*, pp. 258, 259.

Further Reflection: *Am I willing to accept the forgiveness that Jesus offers me today?*

GREAT HEAD OF THE CHURCH

"Son of man, I have made you a watchman for the house of Israel; therefore hear a word from My mouth, and give them warning from Me."

—Ezekiel 3:17

In His life and lessons Christ has given a perfect exemplification of the unselfish ministry which has its origin in God. God does not live for Himself. By creating the world, and by upholding all things, He is constantly ministering to others. "He maketh His sun to rise on the evil and on the good, and sendeth rain on the just and on the unjust." (Matthew 5:45) This ideal of ministry the Father committed to His Son. Jesus was given to stand at the head of humanity, by His example to teach what it means to minister. His whole life was under a law of service. He served all, ministered to all.

Again and again Jesus tried to establish His principle among His disciples. When James and John made their request for pre-eminence, He said, "Whosoever will be great among you, let him be your minister; and whosoever will be chief among you, let him be your servant: even as the Son of man came not to be ministered unto, but to minister, and to give His life a ransom for many." (Matthew 20:26–28)

Since His ascension Christ has carried forward His work on the earth by chosen ambassadors, through whom He speaks to the children of humanity and ministers to their needs. The **great Head of the church** superintends His work through the instrumentality of men and women ordained by God to act as His representatives.

The position of those who have been called of God to labor in word and doctrine for the upbuilding of His church, is one of grave responsibility. In Christ's stead they are to beseech men and women to be reconciled to God, and they can fulfill their mission only as they receive wisdom and power from above.

Christ's ministers are the spiritual guardians of the people entrusted to their care. Their work has been likened to that of watchmen. . . .

It is the privilege of the watchmen on the walls of Zion to live so near to God, and to be susceptible to the impressions of His Spirit, that He can work through them to tell men and women of their peril and point them to the place of safety.—*The Acts of the Apostles*, pp. 359–361.

Further Reflection: *How can I work more closely with Jesus to achieve His objectives?*

FRIEND THAT STICKETH CLOSER THAN A BROTHER

A man who has friends must himself be friendly,
But there is a friend who sticks closer than a brother.
—Proverbs 18:24

The Lord has not left you to yourself. He is looking upon you with tender compassion. His Spirit still strives for the mastery over the powers of darkness. If you will come to Christ, hungry and thirsty for the bread and water of life, the power of an abiding Christ will break down that harsh, cold, selfishness, which is the opposite of sympathy.

Christ is knocking at the door of your heart, asking for admittance. Shall He knock in vain? Will you refuse Him entrance, or will you welcome Him as an honored guest? Do not refuse to admit Him, for the love of Jesus is of more value to you than the whole world.

Its length, its depth, its height, its breadth cannot be estimated. It opens and expands the heart, giving it a new capacity for loving God. The calls and invitations made in the Bible mean all that the strongest language can express. The Lord is anxious for you to return to Him. He knows that you need Him, and He needs you, for He says, "Ye are My witnesses." (Isaiah 43:10) You do yourself a serious wrong when you turn your face from the living God. Fear not to make a full and decided consecration of yourself. Cast yourself without reserve on the grace of Jesus Christ; you will find that there is no compassion like that of infinite purity. Under His control, you will appreciate the goodness, longsuffering, and self-sacrificing love of God, and will reveal it to the world.

You may think that no one really understands your case, but there is One who is acquainted with every circumstance of it. He knows that you have no strength or wisdom of your own, that you do not even understand your own necessities; and He has promised to keep you from falling, and in this promise you may rely. At times you may feel like weeping because you have lost your joy and hope in the Lord; but Christ says to you, "Open the door of your heart and let Me in." He is a **friend that sticketh closer than a brother**, and to Him you may tell every trial, every sorrow, every need. He will teach you many things above price of gold or silver, and give you peace and joy.—Letter 109, 1896.

Further Reflection: *Have I shared what is on my heart with Jesus today?*

CONQUEROR

Jesus answered and said to them, "Destroy this temple, and in three days I will raise it up."

—John 2:19

Christ was the foundation and life of the temple. Its services were typical of the sacrifice of the Son of God. The priesthood was established to represent the mediatorial character and work of Christ. The entire plan of sacrificial worship was a foreshadowing of the Saviour's death to redeem the world. There would be no efficacy in these offerings when the great event toward which they had pointed for ages was consummated.

Since the whole ritual economy was symbolical of Christ, it had no value apart from Him. When the Jews sealed their rejection of Christ by delivering Him to death, they rejected all that gave significance to the temple and its services. Its sacredness had departed. It was doomed to destruction. From that day sacrificial offerings and the service connected with them were meaningless. Like the offering of Cain, they did not express faith in the Saviour. In putting Christ to death, the Jews virtually destroyed their temple. When Christ was crucified, the inner veil of the temple was rent in twain from top to bottom, signifying that the great final sacrifice had been made, and that the system of sacrificial offerings was forever at an end.

"In three days I will raise it up." In the Saviour's death the powers of darkness seemed to prevail, and they exulted in their victory. But from the rent sepulcher of Joseph, Jesus came forth a **conqueror**. "Having spoiled principalities and powers, He made a show of them openly, triumphing over them." (Colossians 2:15) By virtue of His death and resurrection He became the minister of the "true tabernacle, which the Lord pitched, and not man." (Hebrews 8:2) Human beings reared the Jewish tabernacle; humans builded the Jewish temple; but the sanctuary above, of which the earthly was a type, was built by no human architect. "Behold the Man whose name is The Branch. . . . He shall build the temple of the Lord; and He shall bear the glory, and shall sit and rule upon His throne; and He shall be a priest upon His throne." (Zechariah 6:12, 13)—*The Desire of Ages*, pp. 165, 166.

Further Reflection: *Satan believed that his plan to kill Jesus would end God's plan of salvation for humanity. It resulted in the opposite. How has God used moments of suffering to bring about even greater blessings in my life?*

CONSOLATION OF ISRAEL

"Lord, now You are letting Your servant depart in peace, according to Your word; for my eyes have seen Your salvation."

—Luke 2:29, 30

Spiritual things are spiritually discerned. In the temple the Son of God was dedicated to the work He had come to do. The priest looked upon Him as he would upon any other child. But though he neither saw nor felt anything unusual, God's act in giving His Son to the world was acknowledged. This occasion did not pass without some recognition of Christ. "There was a man in Jerusalem, whose name was Simeon; and the same man was just and devout, waiting for the Consolation of Israel: and the Holy Ghost was upon him. And it was revealed unto him by the Holy Ghost, that he should not see death, before he had seen the Lord's Christ."

As Simeon enters the temple, he sees a family presenting their first-born son before the priest. Their appearance bespeaks poverty; but Simeon understands the warnings of the Spirit, and he is deeply impressed that the infant being presented to the Lord is the **Consolation of Israel**, the One he has longed to see. To the astonished priest, Simeon appears like a man enraptured. The child has been returned to Mary, and he takes it in his arms and presents it to God, while a joy that he has never before felt enters his soul. As he lifts the infant Saviour toward heaven, he says, "Lord, now lettest Thou Thy servant depart in peace, according to Thy word: for mine eyes have seen Thy salvation, which Thou hast prepared before the face of all people; a light to lighten the Gentiles, and the glory of Thy people Israel."

The spirit of prophecy was upon this man of God, and while Joseph and Mary stood by, wondering at his words, he blessed them, and said unto Mary, "Behold, this child is set for the fall and rising again of many in Israel; and for a sign which shall be spoken against; (yea, a sword shall pierce through thy own soul also,) that the thoughts of many hearts may be revealed."—*The Desire of Ages*, p. 55.

Further Reflection: *Simeon yearned to see the Messiah who would take away the sins of the world. What am I yearning for God to show me at this moment in my life?*

CREATOR

"I will utter things kept secret from the foundation of the world."
—Matthew 13:35

The Scripture says, "All these things spake Jesus unto the multitude in parables; . . . that it might be fulfilled which was spoken by the prophet, saying, I will open My mouth in parables; I will utter things which have been kept secret from the foundation of the world." (Matthew 13:34, 35) Natural things were the medium for the spiritual; the things of nature and the life-experience of His hearers were connected with the truths of the written word. Leading thus from the natural to the spiritual kingdom, Christ's parables are links in the chain of truth that unites human beings with God, and earth with heaven.

In His teaching from nature, Christ was speaking of the things which His own hands had made, and which had qualities and powers that He Himself had imparted. In their original perfection all created things were an expression of the thought of God. To Adam and Eve in their Eden home nature was full of the knowledge of God, teeming with divine instruction. Wisdom spoke to the eye and was received into the heart; for they communed with God in His created works. As soon as the holy pair transgressed the law of the Most High, the brightness from the face of God departed from the face of nature. The earth is now marred and defiled by sin. Yet even in its blighted state much that is beautiful remains. God's object lessons are not obliterated; rightly understood, nature speaks of her **Creator**.

In the days of Christ these lessons had been lost sight of. Men and women had well-nigh ceased to discern God in His works. The sinfulness of humanity had cast a pall over the fair face of creation; and instead of manifesting God, His works became a barrier that concealed Him. Human beings "worshiped and served the creature more than the Creator." Thus the heathen "became vain in their imaginations, and their foolish heart was darkened." (Romans 1:25, 21) So in Israel, human teaching had been put in the place of God's. Not only the things of nature, but the sacrificial service and the Scriptures themselves—all given to reveal God—were so perverted that they became the means of concealing Him.—*Christ's Object Lessons*, pp. 17, 18.

Further Reflection: *The next time I have a chance to be in nature, what do I want God to say to me?*

DIVINE MEDIATOR

And when Moses had finished speaking with them,
he put a veil on his face.

—Exodus 34:33

Forty days and nights Moses remained in the mount; and during all this time, as at the first, he was miraculously sustained. No person had been permitted to go up with him, nor during the time of his absence were any to approach the mount. At God's command he had prepared two tables of stone, and had taken them with him to the summit; and again the Lord "wrote upon the tables the words of the covenant, the Ten Commandments."

During that long time spent in communion with God, the face of Moses had reflected the glory of the divine Presence; unknown to himself his face shone with a dazzling light when he descended from the mountain. Such a light illumined the countenance of Stephen when brought before his judges; "and all that sat in the council, looking steadfastly on him, saw his face as it had been the face of an angel." (Acts 6:15) Aaron as well as the people shrank away from Moses, and "they were afraid to come nigh him." Seeing their confusion and terror, but ignorant of the cause, he urged them to come near. . . .

By this brightness God designed to impress upon Israel the sacred, exalted character of His law, and the glory of the gospel revealed through Christ. While Moses was in the mount, God presented to him, not only the tables of the law, but also the plan of salvation. He saw that the sacrifice of Christ was pre-figured by all the types and symbols of the Jewish age; and it was the heavenly light streaming from Calvary, no less than the glory of the law of God, that shed such a radiance upon the face of Moses. That divine illumination symbolized the glory of the dispensation of which Moses was the visible mediator. . . .

Moses was a type of Christ. As Israel's intercessor veiled his countenance, because the people could not endure to look upon its glory, so Christ, the **divine Mediator**, veiled His divinity with humanity when He came to earth. Had He come clothed with the brightness of heaven, He could not have found access to men and women in their sinful state. They could not have endured the glory of His presence. Therefore He humbled Himself, and was made "in the likeness of sinful flesh" (Romans 8:3), that He might reach the fallen race, and lift them up.—*Patriarchs and Prophets*, pp. 329, 330.

Further Reflection: *Do I possess the glow that comes from obedience to God's sacred law?*

LORD AND MASTER

Peter said to Him, "You shall never wash my feet!"
Jesus answered him, "If I do not wash you, you have no part with Me."
—John 13:8

These words mean more than bodily cleanliness. Christ is still speaking of the higher cleansing as illustrated by the lower. He who came from the bath was clean, but the sandaled feet soon became dusty, and again needed to be washed. So Peter and his brethren had been washed in the great fountain opened for sin and uncleanness. Christ acknowledged them as His. But temptation had led them into evil, and they still needed His cleansing grace. When Jesus girded Himself with a towel to wash the dust from their feet, He desired by that very act to wash the alienation, jealousy, and pride from their hearts. This was of far more consequence than the washing of their dusty feet. With the spirit they then had, not one of them was prepared for communion with Christ. Until brought into a state of humility and love, they were not prepared to partake of the paschal supper, or to share in the memorial service which Christ was about to institute. Their hearts must be cleansed. Pride and self-seeking create dissension and hatred, but all this Jesus washed away in washing their feet. A change of feeling was brought about. Looking upon them, Jesus could say, "Ye are clean." Now there was union of heart, love for one another. They had become humble and teachable. Except Judas, each was ready to concede to another the highest place. Now with subdued and grateful hearts they could receive Christ's words.

Like Peter and his brethren, we too have been washed in the blood of Christ, yet often through contact with evil the heart's purity is soiled. We must come to Christ for His cleansing grace. Peter shrank from bringing his soiled feet in contact with the hands of his **Lord and Master**; but how often we bring our sinful, polluted hearts in contact with the heart of Christ! How grievous to Him is our evil temper, our vanity and pride! Yet all our infirmity and defilement we must bring to Him. He alone can wash us clean. We are not prepared for communion with Him unless cleansed by His efficacy.—*The Desire of Ages*, pp. 646–649.

Further Reflection: *Does the shame of my sins ever prevent me from bringing them to Jesus?*

LAMB

By that will we have been sanctified through the offering of the body of Jesus Christ once for all.
—Hebrews 10:10

Our Lord has said, "Except ye eat the flesh of the Son of man, and drink His blood, ye have no life in you. . . . For My flesh is meat indeed, and My blood is drink indeed." (John 6:53–55) This is true of our physical nature. To the death of Christ we owe even this earthly life. The bread we eat is the purchase of His broken body. The water we drink is bought by His spilled blood. Never one, saint or sinner, eats his daily food, but he is nourished by the body and the blood of Christ. The cross of Calvary is stamped on every loaf. . . .

And how much more are Christ's words true of our spiritual nature. He declares, "Whoso eateth My flesh, and drinketh My blood, hath eternal life." It is by receiving the life for us poured out on Calvary's cross, that we can live the life of holiness. And this life we receive by receiving His word, by doing those things which He has commanded. Thus we become one with Him. "He that eateth My flesh," He says, "and drinketh My blood, dwelleth in Me, and I in him. As the living Father hath sent Me, and I live by the Father: so he that eateth Me, even he shall live by Me." (John 6:54, 56, 57) To the holy Communion this scripture in a special sense applies. As faith contemplates our Lord's great sacrifice, the soul assimilates the spiritual life of Christ. That soul will receive spiritual strength from every Communion. The service forms a living connection by which the believer is bound up with Christ, and thus bound up with the Father. . . .

As we receive the bread and wine symbolizing Christ's broken body and spilled blood, we in imagination join in the scene of Communion in the upper chamber. . . . We witness the struggle by which our reconciliation with God was obtained. Christ is set forth crucified among us.

Looking upon the crucified Redeemer, we more fully comprehend the magnitude and meaning of the sacrifice made by the Majesty of heaven. The plan of salvation is glorified before us, and the thought of Calvary awakens living and sacred emotions in our hearts. Praise to God and the **Lamb** will be in our hearts and on our lips; for pride and self-worship cannot flourish in the soul that keeps fresh in memory the scenes of Calvary. —*The Desire of Ages*, pp. 660, 661.

Further Reflection: *I owe every earthly blessing to the sacrifice of Jesus Christ for me. What blessings has He sent me this week?*

DAYSMAN BETWEEN GOD AND HUMANITY

"God so loved the world that He gave His only begotten son, that whoever believes in Him should not perish but have everlasting life."
—John 3:16

Christ was treated as we deserve, that we might be treated as He deserves. He was condemned for our sins, in which He had no share, that we might be justified by His righteousness, in which we had no share. He suffered the death which was ours, that we might receive the life which was His. "With His stripes we are healed."

By His life and His death, Christ has achieved even more than recovery from the ruin wrought through sin. It was Satan's purpose to bring about an eternal separation between God and humanity; but in Christ we become more closely united to God than if we had never fallen. In taking our nature, the Saviour has bound Himself to humanity by a tie that is never to be broken. Through the eternal ages He is linked with us. "God so loved the world, that He gave His only-begotten Son." (John 3:16) He gave Him not only to bear our sins, and to die as our sacrifice; He gave Him to the fallen race. To assure us of His immutable counsel of peace, God gave His only-begotten Son to become one of the human family, forever to retain His human nature. This is the pledge that God will fulfill His word. "Unto us a child is born, unto us a son is given: and the government shall be upon His shoulder." God has adopted human nature in the person of His Son, and has carried the same into the highest heaven. It is the "Son of man" who shares the throne of the universe. It is the "Son of man" whose name shall be called, "Wonderful, Counselor, The mighty God, The everlasting Father, The Prince of Peace." (Isaiah 9:6) The I AM is the **Daysman between God and humanity**, laying His hand upon both. He who is "holy, harmless, undefiled, separate from sinners," is not ashamed to call us brethren. (Hebrews 7:26; 2:11) In Christ the family of earth and the family of heaven are bound together. Christ glorified is our Brother. Heaven is enshrined in humanity, and humanity is enfolded in the bosom of Infinite Love.—*The Desire of Ages*, pp. 25, 26.

Further Reflection: *Even though heaven seems far away, Jesus has bound me to the inhabitants of heaven with cords of love which cannot be broken. What is the first thing that I will do when I meet my heavenly family?*

MYSTERIOUS VICTIM

"Who shall not fear You, O Lord, and glorify Your name?
For You alone are holy."

—Revelation 15:4

At the cross of Calvary, love and selfishness stood face to face. Here was their crowning manifestation. Christ had lived only to comfort and bless, and in putting Him to death, Satan manifested the malignity of his hatred against God. He made it evident that the real purpose of his rebellion was to dethrone God, and to destroy Him through whom the love of God was shown.

By the life and the death of Christ, the thoughts of men and women also are brought to view. From the manger to the cross, the life of Jesus was a call to self-surrender, and to fellowship in suffering. It unveiled the purposes of men and women. Jesus came with the truth of heaven, and all who were listening to the voice of the Holy Spirit were drawn to Him. The worshipers of self belonged to Satan's kingdom. In their attitude toward Christ, all would show on which side they stood. And thus everyone passes judgment on himself.

In the day of final judgment, every lost soul will understand the nature of his own rejection of truth. The cross will be presented, and its real bearing will be seen by every mind that has been blinded by transgression. Before the vision of Calvary with its **mysterious Victim**, sinners will stand condemned. Every lying excuse will be swept away. Human apostasy will appear in its heinous character. People will see what their choice has been. Every question of truth and error in the long-standing controversy will then have been made plain. In the judgment of the universe, God will stand clear of blame for the existence or continuance of evil. It will be demonstrated that the divine decrees are not accessory to sin. There was no defect in God's government, no cause for disaffection. When the thoughts of all hearts shall be revealed, both the loyal and the rebellious will unite in declaring, "Just and true are Thy ways, Thou King of saints. Who shall not fear Thee, O Lord, and glorify Thy name? . . . for Thy judgments are made manifest." (Revelation 15:3, 4)—*The Desire of Ages*, pp. 57, 58.

Further Reflection: *How do I avoid the eternal implications of rejecting the Cross of Christ? Am I resisting the appeal of the Cross in some unsurrendered area of my life?*

ONE MIGHTIER THAN SATAN

And all who desire to live godly in Christ Jesus will suffer persecution.
—2 Timothy 3:12

Jesus does not present to His followers the hope of attaining earthly glory and riches, of living a life free from trial. Instead He calls upon them to follow Him in the path of self-denial and reproach. He who came to redeem the world was opposed by the united forces of evil. In an unpitying confederacy, evil human beings and evil angels arrayed themselves against the Prince of Peace. His every word and act revealed divine compassion, and His unlikeness to the world provoked the bitterest hostility.

So it will be with all who will live godly in Christ Jesus. Persecution and reproach await all who are imbued with the Spirit of Christ. The character of the persecution changes with the times, but the principle—the spirit that underlies it—is the same that has slain the chosen of the Lord ever since the days of Abel.

In all ages Satan has persecuted the people of God. He has tortured them and put them to death, but in dying they became conquerors. They bore witness to the power of **One mightier than Satan.** Wicked people may torture and kill the body, but they cannot touch the life that is hid with Christ in God. They can incarcerate men and women in prison walls, but they cannot bind the spirit.

Through trial and persecution the glory—the character—of God is revealed in His chosen ones. The believers in Christ, hated and persecuted by the world, are educated and disciplined in the school of Christ. On earth they walk in narrow paths; they are purified in the furnace of affliction. They follow Christ through sore conflicts; they endure self-denial and experience bitter disappointments; but thus they learn the guilt and woe of sin, and they look upon it with abhorrence. Being partakers of Christ's sufferings, they can look beyond the gloom to the glory, saying, "I reckon that the sufferings of this present time are not worthy to be compared with the glory which shall be revealed in us." (Romans 8:18) —*The Acts of the Apostles*, pp. 576, 577.

Further Reflection: *The problem of suffering remains one of the most troubling aspects of human life. How can I embrace the suffering that God allows in my life and avoid becoming bitter against Him or my fellow human beings?*

DEITY

And when we see Him, there is no beauty that we should desire Him.
—Isaiah 53:2

Nearly two thousand years ago, a voice of mysterious import was heard in heaven, from the throne of God, "Lo, I come." "Sacrifice and offering Thou wouldest not, but a body hast Thou prepared Me. . . . Lo, I come (in the volume of the Book it is written of Me,) to do Thy will, O God." (Hebrews 10:5–7) In these words is announced the fulfillment of the purpose that had been hidden from eternal ages. Christ was about to visit our world, and to become incarnate. He says, "A body hast Thou prepared Me." Had He appeared with the glory that was His with the Father before the world was, we could not have endured the light of His presence. That we might behold it and not be destroyed, the manifestation of His glory was shrouded. His divinity was veiled with humanity—the invisible glory in the visible human form.

This great purpose had been shadowed forth in types and symbols. The burning bush, in which Christ appeared to Moses, revealed God. The symbol chosen for the representation of the **Deity** was a lowly shrub, that seemingly had no attractions. This enshrined the Infinite. The all-merciful God shrouded His glory in a most humble type, that Moses could look upon it and live. So in the pillar of cloud by day and the pillar of fire by night, God communicated with Israel, revealing to humans His will, and imparting to them His grace. God's glory was subdued, and His majesty veiled, that the weak vision of finite men and women might behold it. So Christ was to come in "the body of our humiliation" (Philippians 3:21, R. V.), "in the likeness of men." In the eyes of the world He possessed no beauty that they should desire Him; yet He was the incarnate God, the light of heaven and earth. His glory was veiled, His greatness and majesty were hidden, that He might draw near to sorrowful, tempted men and women.

God commanded Moses for Israel, "Let them make Me a sanctuary; that I may dwell among them" (Exodus 25:8), and He abode in the sanctuary, in the midst of His people. Through all their weary wandering in the desert, the symbol of His presence was with them. So Christ set up His tabernacle in the midst of our human encampment. He pitched His tent by the side of the tents of human beings, that He might dwell among us, and make us familiar with His divine character and life.—*The Desire of Ages,* p. 23.

Further Reflection: *Jesus is willing to become whatever I need, whenever I need it. What do I need from Him today?*

MARCH

ADVOCATE AT THE THRONE OF GOD

*Who is he who condemns? It is Christ who died,
and furthermore is also risen, who is even at the right hand of God,
who also makes intercession for us.*

—Romans 8:34

As the disciples returned from Olivet to Jerusalem, the people looked on them, expecting to see on their faces expressions of sorrow, confusion, and defeat; but they saw there gladness and triumph. The disciples did not now mourn over disappointed hopes. They had seen the risen Saviour, and the words of His parting promise echoed constantly in their ears.

In obedience to Christ's command, they waited in Jerusalem for the promise of the Father—the outpouring of the Spirit. They did not wait in idleness. The record says that they were "continually in the temple, praising and blessing God." (Luke 24:53) They also met together to present their requests to the Father in the name of Jesus. They knew that they had a Representative in heaven, an **Advocate at the throne of God**. In solemn awe they bowed in prayer, repeating the assurance, "Whatsoever ye shall ask the Father in My name, He will give it you. Hitherto have ye asked nothing in My name: ask, and ye shall receive, that your joy may be full." (John 16:23, 24) Higher and still higher they extended the hand of faith, with the mighty argument, "It is Christ that died, yea rather, that is risen again, who is even at the right hand of God, who also maketh intercession for us." (Romans 8:34)

As the disciples waited for the fulfillment of the promise, they humbled their hearts in true repentance and confessed their unbelief. As they called to remembrance the words that Christ had spoken to them before His death they understood more fully their meaning. Truths which had passed from their memory were again brought to their minds, and these they repeated to one another. They reproached themselves for their misapprehension of the Saviour. Like a procession, scene after scene of His wonderful life passed before them. As they meditated upon His pure, holy life they felt that no toil would be too hard, no sacrifice too great, if only they could bear witness in their lives to the loveliness of Christ's character. Oh, if they could but have the past three years to live over, they thought, how differently they would act!—*The Acts of the Apostles*, pp. 35, 36.

Further Reflection: *Am I taking for granted what Jesus is currently doing in my life and in heaven on my behalf? How can I truly value every moment that I have with Jesus?*

DESPISED NAZARENE

"But first He must suffer many things and be rejected by this generation."

—Luke 17:25

Wealth is a power with which to do good or to do evil. If it is rightly used it becomes a source of continual gratitude, because the gifts of God are appreciated and the Giver acknowledged by using them as God intended they should be used. Those who rob God by withholding from His cause and from the suffering poor will meet His retributive justice. Our heavenly Father, who has given us in trust every good gift, pities our ignorance, our frailty, and our hopeless condition. In order to save us from death, He freely gave His beloved Son. He claims from us all that we claim as our own. A neglect of His suffering poor is a neglect of Christ, for He tells us that the poor are His representatives on earth. . . .

When the Lord's poor are neglected and forgotten or greeted with cold looks and cruel words, let the guilty one bear in mind that he is neglecting Christ in the person of His saints. Our Saviour identifies His interest with that of suffering humanity. As the heart of the parent yearns with pitying tenderness over the suffering one of her little flock, so the heart of our Redeemer sympathizes with the poorest and lowliest of His earthly children. He has placed them among us to awaken in our hearts that love which He feels toward the suffering and oppressed, and He will let His judgments fall upon anyone who wrongs, slights, or abuses them.

Let us consider that Jesus took all the woes and griefs, the poverty and suffering, of men and women into His own heart and made them a part of His own experience. Although He was the Prince of life, He did not take His position with the great and honorable, but with the lowly, the oppressed, and the suffering. He was the **despised Nazarene**. He had not where to lay His head. He became poor for our sakes, that we through His poverty might be made rich. He is now the King of glory, and should He come crowned with majesty, millions would do Him homage. All would vie with one another in bestowing honors upon Him; all would plead to be found in His presence. An opportunity is now granted us to receive Christ in the person of His saints.—*Testimonies for the Church*, vol. 4, pp. 620, 621.

Further Reflection: *What can I do today to relieve the suffering of the poor in my community? How can I motivate others to join me in this act of service?*

FIRST FRUITS OF THOSE THAT SLEPT

Blessed be the God and Father of our Lord Jesus Christ, who according to His abundant mercy has begotten us again to a living hope through the resurrection of Jesus Christ from the dead.

—1 Peter 1:3

When the voice of the mighty angel was heard at Christ's tomb, saying, Thy Father calls Thee, the Saviour came forth from the grave by the life that was in Himself. Now was proved the truth of His words, "I lay down My life, that I might take it again. . . . I have power to lay it down, and I have power to take it again." (John 10:17, 18; 2:19)

Over the rent sepulcher of Joseph, Christ had proclaimed in triumph, "I am the resurrection, and the life." These words could be spoken only by the Deity. All created beings live by the will and power of God. They are dependent recipients of the life of God. From the highest seraph to the humblest animate being, all are replenished from the Source of life. Only He who is one with God could say, I have power to lay down My life, and I have power to take it again. In His divinity, Christ possessed the power to break the bonds of death.

Christ arose from the dead as the **first fruits of those that slept**. He was the antitype of the wave sheaf, and His resurrection took place on the very day when the wave sheaf was to be presented before the Lord. For more than a thousand years this symbolic ceremony had been performed. From the harvest fields the first heads of ripened grain were gathered, and when the people went up to Jerusalem to the Passover, the sheaf of first fruits was waved as a thank offering before the Lord. Not until this was presented could the sickle be put to the grain, and it be gathered into sheaves. The sheaf dedicated to God represented the harvest. . . . His resurrection is the type and pledge of the resurrection of all the righteous dead. . . .

As Christ arose, He brought from the grave a multitude of captives. The earthquake at His death had rent open their graves, and when He arose, they came forth with Him. They were those who had been colaborers with God, and who at the cost of their lives had borne testimony to the truth. Now they were to be witnesses for Him who had raised them from the dead.—*The Desire of Ages*, pp. 785, 786.

Further Reflection: *Jesus offers physical resurrection to those who die in Christ, but have I experienced the spiritual resurrection He also came to give?*

HEAVENLY GIFT

"And this is the condemnation, that the light has come into the world, and men loved darkness rather than light, because their deeds were evil."

—John 3:19

In sending out the seventy, Jesus bade them, as He had bidden the twelve, not to urge their presence where they were unwelcome. "Into whatsoever city ye enter, and they receive you not," He said, "go your ways out into the streets of the same, and say, Even the very dust of your city, which cleaveth on us, we do wipe off against you: notwithstanding be ye sure of this, that the kingdom of God is come nigh unto you." They were not to do this from motives of resentment or through wounded dignity, but to show how grievous a thing it is to refuse the Lord's message or His messengers. To reject the Lord's servants is to reject Christ Himself. . . .

To those busy towns about the Sea of Galilee, heaven's richest blessings had been freely offered. Day after day the Prince of life had gone in and out among them. The glory of God, which prophets and kings had longed to see, had shone upon the multitudes that thronged the Saviour's steps. Yet they had refused the **heavenly Gift**.

With a great show of prudence the rabbis had warned the people against receiving the new doctrines taught by this new Teacher; for His theories and practices were contrary to the teachings of the fathers. The people gave credence to what the priests and Pharisees taught, in place of seeking to understand the word of God for themselves. They honored the priests and rulers instead of honoring God, and rejected the truth that they might keep their own traditions. Many had been impressed and almost persuaded; but they did not act upon their convictions, and were not reckoned on the side of Christ. Satan presented his temptations, until the light appeared as darkness. Thus many rejected the truth that would have proved the saving of the soul.

The True Witness says, "Behold, I stand at the door, and knock." (Revelation 3:20) Every warning, reproof, and entreaty in the word of God or through His messengers is a knock at the door of the heart. It is the voice of Jesus asking for entrance. . . . The impressions of the Holy Spirit if disregarded today, will not be as strong tomorrow.—*The Desire of Ages*, pp. 489, 490.

Further Reflection: *Exodus 34:7 reminds us that we have a merciful God, but He does not overlook sin. How does God reclaim one whose life has been marked by repeated transgression?*

DIVINE CONQUEROR

*And I looked, and behold, a white horse.
He who sat on it had a bow; and a crown was given to him,
and he went out conquering and to conquer.*
—Revelation 6:2

The time had come for Christ to ascend to His Father's throne. As a **divine conqueror** He was about to return with the trophies of victory to the heavenly courts. Before His death He had declared to His Father, "I have finished the work which Thou gavest Me to do." (John 17:4) After His resurrection He tarried on earth for a season, that His disciples might become familiar with Him in His risen and glorified body. Now He was ready for the leave-taking. . . .

As the place of His ascension, Jesus chose the spot so often hallowed by His presence while He dwelt among humanity. Not Mount Zion, the place of David's city, not Mount Moriah, the temple site, was to be thus honored. There Christ had been mocked and rejected. There the waves of mercy, still returning in a stronger tide of love, had been beaten back by hearts as hard as rock. Thence Jesus, weary and heart-burdened, had gone forth to find rest in the Mount of Olives. . . . From this mountain He was to ascend to heaven. Upon its summit His feet will rest when He shall come again. Not as a man of sorrows, but as a glorious and triumphant king He will stand upon Olivet, while Hebrew hallelujahs mingle with Gentile hosannas, and the voices of the redeemed as a mighty host shall swell the acclamation, Crown Him Lord of all! . . .

Upon reaching the Mount of Olives, Jesus led the way across the summit, to the vicinity of Bethany. Here He paused, and the disciples gathered about Him. Beams of light seemed to radiate from His countenance as He looked lovingly upon them. He upbraided them not for their faults and failures; words of the deepest tenderness were the last that fell upon their ears from the lips of their Lord. With hands outstretched in blessing, and as if in assurance of His protecting care, He slowly ascended from among them, drawn heavenward by a power stronger than any earthly attraction. . . .

While the disciples were still gazing upward, voices addressed them which sounded like richest music. . . . "Ye men of Galilee, why stand ye gazing up into heaven? this same Jesus, which is taken up from you into heaven, shall so come in like manner as ye have seen Him go into heaven."—*The Desire of Ages*, pp. 829–832.

Further Reflection: *Has Jesus ever returned me victorious to a place of previous suffering?*

GREAT MISSIONARY WORKER

"For I have come down from heaven, not to do My own will, but the will of Him who sent Me."

—John 6:38

The world's greatest need is consecrated effort for the salvation of souls. Christ desires by the fulness of His power so to strengthen His people that through them the whole world shall be encircled with an atmosphere of grace. When His people shall make a whole-hearted surrender of themselves to God, walking before Him in humility and faith, He will carry out through them His eternal purpose, enabling them to work harmoniously in giving to the world the truth as it is in Jesus. He will use all, men, women, and children, in making the light shine forth to the world, and calling out a people who will be true to His commandments.

"God so loved the world, that He gave His only begotten Son, that whosoever believeth in Him should not perish, but have everlasting life." The salvation of souls was the great object for which Christ sacrificed His royal robe and kingly crown, the glory of heaven, and the homage of angels, and laying aside His divinity, came to earth to labor and suffer with humanity upon Him. He who has been transformed into the likeness of Christ, he who cherishes the spirit of the **great Missionary Worker**, is filled with a desire to bear the tidings of salvation to the regions beyond, to those who know not the Saviour. To the work of soul-saving he consecrates time and strength, means and influence. He uses every jot of his ability in an effort to win souls to Christ. The sacrifice made on the cross of Calvary is the motive that inspires him to put forth untiring efforts and to show unflagging zeal. His determination is, "I will not fail nor be discouraged." By his consistent life he draws those around him to the Saviour.

Those who give their lives to Christian ministry know the meaning of true happiness. Their interests and their prayers reach far beyond self. They themselves are growing up as they try to reach others. They become familiar with the largest plans, the most stirring enterprises; and how can they but grow when they place themselves in the channel of light and blessing? They become more and more identified with Christ in all His plans. There is no opportunity for spiritual stagnation. Selfish ambition and self-seeking are rebuked by constant contact with the absorbing interests which belong to high and holy aspirations.—*Review and Herald*, November 21, 1907.

Further Reflection: *How will I use my gifts to help others be saved?*

DIVINE EXAMPLE

"The Holy Spirit will teach you in that very hour what you ought to say."
—Luke 12:12

The servants of Christ will be brought before the great men and women of the world, who, but for this, might never hear the gospel. The truth has been misrepresented to these persons. They have listened to false charges concerning the faith of Christ's disciples. Often their only means of learning its real character is the testimony of those who are brought to trial for their faith. Under examination these are required to answer, and their judges to listen to the testimony borne. God's grace will be dispensed to His servants to meet the emergency. "It shall be given you," says Jesus, "in that same hour what ye shall speak. For it is not ye that speak, but the Spirit of your Father which speaketh in you." As the Spirit of God illuminates the minds of His servants, the truth will be presented in its divine power and preciousness. Those who reject the truth will stand to accuse and oppress the disciples. But under loss and suffering, even unto death, the Lord's children are to reveal the meekness of their **divine Example**. Thus will be seen the contrast between Satan's agents and the representatives of Christ. The Saviour will be lifted up before the rulers and the people.

The disciples were not endowed with the courage and fortitude of the martyrs until such grace was needed. Then the Saviour's promise was fulfilled. When Peter and John testified before the Sanhedrin council, people "marveled; and they took knowledge of them, that they had been with Jesus." (Acts 4:13) Of Stephen it is written that "all that sat in the council, looking steadfastly on him, saw his face as it had been the face of an angel." People "were not able to resist the wisdom and the spirit by which he spake." (Acts 6:15, 10) . . .

The servants of Christ were to prepare no set speech to present when brought to trial. Their preparation was to be made day by day in treasuring up the precious truths of God's word, and through prayer strengthening their faith. When they were brought into trial, the Holy Spirit would bring to their remembrance the very truths that would be needed.—*The Desire of Ages*, pp. 354, 355.

Further Reflection: *The thought of going unprepared into trial fills most people with dread. How does trusting God in the small things in life prepare me to trust Him in the big moments of life?*

MARCH 8

CENTER OF THE SACRIFICIAL SYSTEM

God was in Christ reconciling the world to Himself, not imputing their trespasses to them, and has committed to us the word of reconciliation.

—2 Corinthians 5:19

While the Saviour's death brought to an end the law of types and shadows, it did not in the least detract from the obligation of the moral law. On the contrary, the very fact that it was necessary for Christ to die in order to atone for the transgression of that law, proves it to be immutable.

Those who claim that Christ came to abrogate the law of God and to do away with the Old Testament, speak of the Jewish age as one of darkness, and represent the religion of the Hebrews as consisting of mere forms and ceremonies. But this is an error. All through the pages of sacred history, where the dealings of God with His chosen people are recorded, there are burning traces of the great I AM. Never has He given to the sons and daughters of humanity more open manifestations of His power and glory than when He alone was acknowledged as Israel's ruler, and gave the law to His people. Here was a scepter swayed by no human hand; and the stately goings forth of Israel's invisible King were unspeakably grand and awful.

In all these revelations of the divine presence the glory of God was manifested through Christ. Not alone at the Saviour's advent, but through all the ages after the Fall and the promise of redemption, "God was in Christ, reconciling the world unto Himself." (2 Corinthians 5:19) Christ was the foundation and **center of the sacrificial system** in both the patriarchal and the Jewish age. Since the sin of our first parents there has been no direct communication between God and humanity.

The Father has given the world into the hands of Christ, that through His mediatorial work He may redeem men and women and vindicate the authority and holiness of the law of God. All the communion between heaven and the fallen race has been through Christ. It was the Son of God that gave to our first parents the promise of redemption. It was He who revealed Himself to the patriarchs. Adam, Noah, Abraham, Isaac, Jacob, and Moses understood the gospel.—*Patriarchs and Prophets*, pp. 365, 366.

Further Reflection: *If God made such careful provision for my salvation, reconciling me to Himself through Christ, what can I do to make sure that I do not squander so great a salvation?*

GREAT CHIEF WORKER

But Jesus answered them, "My Father has been working until now, and I have been working."

—John 5:17

Men and women make the work of advancing the truth tenfold harder than it really is by seeking to take God's work out of His hands into their own finite hands. They think that they must be constantly inventing something to make people do things which they suppose these persons ought to do. The time thus spent is all the while making the work more complicated, for the **great chief Worker** is left out of the question in the care of His own heritage. Men and women undertake the job of tinkering up the defective character of others, and only succeed in making the defects much worse. They would better leave God to do His own work, for He does not regard them as capable of reshaping character.

What they need is to be imbued with the spirit of Christ. If they take hold of His strength, they will make peace with Him; then they will be in a fair way to make peace with their fellow laborers. The less of the meekness and lowliness of Christ the human agent has in his spirit and character, the more he sees perfection in his own methods and imperfection in the methods of others. Our only safety is to watch unto prayer, and to counsel together, believing that God will keep our brethren as well as ourselves, for there is no respect of persons with Him. God will work for us when we are faithful students and the doers of His words.

But when there is, on the part of the laborers, so manifest a disregard of Christ's express command that we love one another as He has loved us, how can we expect that brethren will heed the commandments of finite human beings, and the regulations and definite specifications as to how each shall labor? The wisdom that prescribes for us must be supernatural, else it will prove a physician that cannot heal, but will only destroy. We would better seek God with the whole heart, and lay down self-importance; for "all ye are brethren."—*Testimonies to Ministers and Gospel Workers*, pp. 191, 192.

Further Reflection: *What do I do when I become frustrated by the lack of spiritual progress or change in the lives of those to whom I am ministering?*

GALILEAN TEACHER

"And as Moses lifted up the serpent in the wilderness, even so must the Son of Man be lifted up."

—John 3:14

After the death of Stephen there arose against the believers in Jerusalem a persecution so relentless that "they were all scattered abroad throughout the regions of Judea and Samaria." Saul "made havoc of the church, entering into every house, and haling men and women committed them to prison." Of his zeal in this cruel work he said at a later date: "I verily thought with myself, that I ought to do many things contrary to the name of Jesus of Nazareth. Which thing I also did in Jerusalem: and many of the saints did I shut up in prison. . . . And I punished them oft in every synagogue, and compelled them to blaspheme. . . ." That Stephen was not the only one who suffered death may be seen from Saul's own words, "And when they were put to death, I gave my voice against them." (Acts 26:9–11)

At this time of peril Nicodemus came forward in fearless avowal of his faith in the crucified Saviour. Nicodemus was a member of the Sanhedrin and with others had been stirred by the teaching of Jesus. As he had witnessed Christ's wonderful works, the conviction had fastened itself upon his mind that this was the Sent of God. Too proud openly to acknowledge himself in sympathy with the **Galilean Teacher**, he had sought a secret interview. In this interview Jesus had unfolded to him the plan of salvation and His mission to the world, yet still Nicodemus had hesitated. He hid the truth in his heart, and for three years there was little apparent fruit. But while Nicodemus had not publicly acknowledged Christ, he had in the Sanhedrin council repeatedly thwarted the schemes of the priests to destroy Him. When at last Christ had been lifted up on the cross, Nicodemus remembered the words that He had spoken to him in the night interview on the Mount of Olives, "As Moses lifted up the serpent in the wilderness, even so must the Son of man be lifted up" (John 3:14); and he saw in Jesus the world's Redeemer.

With Joseph of Arimathea, Nicodemus had borne the expense of the burial of Jesus. The disciples had been afraid to show themselves openly as Christ's followers, but Nicodemus and Joseph had come boldly to their aid. The help of these rich and honored men was greatly needed in that hour of darkness.—*The Acts of the Apostles,* pp. 103, 104.

Further Reflection: *How can I avoid discounting those who may not openly confess Christ?*

LIVING VINE

"Abide in Me, and I in you. As the branch cannot bear fruit of itself, unless it abides in the vine, neither can you, unless you abide in Me."
—John 15:4

John's affection for his Master was not a mere human friendship, but the love of a repentant sinner, who felt that he had been redeemed by the precious blood of Christ. He esteemed it the highest honor to work and suffer in the service of his Lord. His love for Jesus led him to love all for whom Christ died. His religion was of a practical character. He reasoned that love to God would be manifested in love to his children. He was heard again and again to say, "Beloved, if God so loved us, we ought also to love one another." "We love Him because He first loved us. If a man say, I love God, and hateth his brother, he is a liar; for he that loveth not his brother, whom he hath seen, how can he love God, whom he hath not seen?" The apostle's life was in harmony with his teachings. The love which glowed in his heart for Christ, led him to put forth the most earnest, untiring labor for his fellow human beings, especially for his brethren in the Christian church. He was a powerful preacher, fervent, and deeply in earnest, and his words carried with them a weight of conviction.

The confiding love and unselfish devotion manifested in the life and character of John, present lessons of untold value to the Christian church. Some may represent him as possessing this love independent of divine grace; but John had, by nature, serious defects of character; he was proud and ambitious, and quick to resent slight and injury.

The depth and fervor of John's affection for the Master was not the cause of Christ's love for him, but the effect of that love. John desired to become like Jesus, and under the transforming influence of the love of Christ, he became meek and lowly of heart. Self was hid in Jesus. He was closely united to the **Living Vine**, and thus became a partaker of the divine nature. Such will ever be the result of communion with Christ. This is true sanctification.

There may be marked defects in the character; evil temper, irritable disposition, envy, and jealousy may bear sway; yet if the person becomes a true disciple of Jesus, the power of divine grace will make them a new creature.—*Review and Herald*, February 15, 1881.

Further Reflection: *Have I given Jesus permission today to remove the defects in my character and continue His transformation of my life?*

DIVINE INSTRUCTOR

I will instruct you and teach you in the way you should go;
I will guide you with My eye.

—Psalm 32:8

The last like the first sentence of the Lord's Prayer, points to our Father as above all power and authority and every name that is named. The Saviour beheld the years that stretched out before His disciples, not, as they had dreamed, lying in the sunshine of worldly prosperity and honor, but dark with the tempests of human hatred and satanic wrath. Amid national strife and ruin, the steps of the disciples would be beset with perils, and often their hearts would be oppressed by fear. They were to see Jerusalem a desolation, the temple swept away, its worship forever ended, and Israel scattered to all lands, like wrecks on a desert shore. Jesus said, "Ye shall hear of wars and rumors of wars." "Nation shall rise against nation, and kingdom against kingdom: and there shall be famines, and pestilences, and earthquakes, in divers places. All these are the beginning of sorrows." (Matthew 24:6–8)

Yet Christ's followers were not to fear that their hope was lost or that God had forsaken the earth. The power and the glory belong unto Him whose great purposes would still move on unthwarted toward their consummation. In the prayer that breathes their daily wants, the disciples of Christ were directed to look above all the power and dominion of evil, unto the Lord their God, whose kingdom ruleth over all and who is their Father and everlasting Friend.

The ruin of Jerusalem was a symbol of the final ruin that shall overwhelm the world. The prophecies that received a partial fulfillment in the overthrow of Jerusalem have a more direct application to the last days. We are now standing on the threshold of great and solemn events. A crisis is before us, such as the world has never witnessed. And sweetly to us, as to the first disciples, comes the assurance that God's kingdom ruleth over all. The program of coming events is in the hands of our Maker. The Majesty of heaven has the destiny of nations, as well as the concerns of His church, in His own charge. The **divine Instructor** is saying to every agent in the accomplishment of His plans, as He said to Cyrus, "I girded thee, though thou hast not known Me." (Isaiah 45:5)
—*Thoughts From the Mount of Blessing*, pp. 120, 121.

Further Reflection: *How comforting is it to know that Jesus sees all that I will face in life and offers me the wisdom and power I need to meet my every challenge?*

ENLIGHTENER

Who being the brightness of His glory and the express image of His person, and upholding all things by the word of His power, when He had by Himself purged our sins, sat down at the right hand of the Majesty on high.

—Hebrews 1:3

As a personal Being, God has revealed Himself in His Son. Jesus, the outshining of the Father's glory, "and the express image of His person," (Hebrews 1:3), was on earth found in fashion as a man. As a personal Saviour He came to the world. As a personal Saviour He ascended on high. As a personal Saviour He intercedes in the heavenly courts. Before the throne of God in our behalf ministers "One like unto the Son of man." (Revelation 1:13)

Christ, the Light of the world, veiled the dazzling splendor of His divinity and came to live as a man among human beings, that they might, without being consumed, become acquainted with their Creator. No person has seen God at any time except as He is revealed through Christ. . . .

Christ came to teach human beings what God desires them to know. In the heavens above, in the earth, in the broad waters of the ocean, we see the handiwork of God. All created things testify to His power, His wisdom, His love. But not from the stars or the ocean or the cataract can we learn of the personality of God as it is revealed in Christ.

God saw that a clearer revelation than nature was needed to portray both His personality and His character. He sent His Son into the world to reveal, so far as could be endured by human sight, the nature and the attributes of the invisible God.

Had God desired to be represented as dwelling personally in the things of nature—in the flower, the tree, the spire of grass—would not Christ have spoken of this to His disciples when He was on the earth? But never in the teaching of Christ is God thus spoken of. Christ and the apostles taught clearly the truth of the existence of a personal God.

Christ revealed all of God that sinful human beings could bear without being destroyed. He is the divine Teacher, the **Enlightener**. Had God thought us in need of revelations other than those made through Christ and in His written word, He would have given them.—*Testimonies for the Church,* vol. 8, pp. 265, 266.

Further Reflection: *If Jesus revealed all of God that sinful human beings could bear, what kinds of things will He teach human beings about God throughout eternity?*

MARCH 14

CREATOR OF HEAVEN AND EARTH

For since the creation of the world His invisible attributes are clearly seen, being understood by the things that are made, even His eternal power and Godhead, so that they are without excuse.

—Romans 1:20

There was a certain man in Caesarea called Cornelius, a centurion of the band called the Italian band, a devout man, and one that feared God with all his house, which gave much alms to the people, and prayed to God always." Though Cornelius was a Roman, he had become acquainted with the true God, and had renounced idolatry. He was obedient to the will of God, and worshiped Him with a true heart. He had not connected himself with the Jews, but was acquainted with, and obedient to, the moral law. He had not been circumcised, nor did he take part in the sacrificial offerings; he was therefore accounted by the Jews as unclean. He, however, sustained the Jewish cause by liberal donations, and was known far and near for his deeds of charity and benevolence. His righteous life made him of good repute, among both Jews and Gentiles.

Cornelius had not an understanding faith in Christ, although he believed the prophecies, and was looking for Messiah to come. Through his love and obedience to God, he was brought nigh unto Him, and was prepared to receive the Saviour when He should be revealed to him. Condemnation comes by rejecting the light given. The centurion was a man of noble family, and held a position of high trust and honor; but these circumstances had not tended to subvert the noble attributes of his character. True goodness and greatness united to make him a man of moral worth. His influence was beneficial to all with whom he was brought in contact.

He believed in the one God, the **Creator of Heaven and Earth**. He revered Him, acknowledged His authority, and sought counsel of Him in all the business of his life. He was faithful in his home duties as well as in his official responsibilities, and had erected the altar of God in his family. He dared not venture to carry out his plans, and bear the burden of his weighty responsibilities, without the help of God; therefore he prayed much and earnestly for that help. Faith marked all his works, and God regarded him for the purity of his actions, and his liberalities.—*The Spirit of Prophecy*, vol. 3, pp. 324, 325.

Further Reflection: *Am I ready to reach those who Jesus has prepared to receive Him?*

GIFT EVERY DAY

Through the LORD's mercies we are not consumed,
Because His compassions fail not.
They are new every morning;
Great is Your faithfulness.
—Lamentations 3:22, 23

How would human beings live if the gifts and blessings of heaven were not constantly flowing to them? God gives constantly that humans may give constantly. There is no time when gifts and offerings should not come in accordance with the resources which God has provided.

It is not our own money that we are handling. It is God's, and His work cannot advance unless His treasury is supplied by gifts and offerings. God has lent us means that we may return His own to him. And if we faithfully do our duty, there will always be enough for home and foreign missions.

All that we do is to be done willingly. We are to bring our offerings with joy and gratitude. . . . The most costly service we can render is but meager compared to the gift of God to our world. Christ is a **gift every day**. God gave Him to the world, and He graciously takes the gifts entrusted to His human agents for the advancement of His work in the world. Thus we show that we recognize and acknowledge that everything belongs to God, absolutely and entirely.

God calls upon us to be laborers together with Him. This is the message that He sends to us through various means. The truth is to be presented to those who know not God. The Bible is to be read to those who will hear it. The Holy Spirit co-operates with him who opens the Scriptures to others. The minister who is a true shepherd gives the Word to the people. He engages earnestly in personal labor, and makes supplication to God. This is all the human agent can do. He sows the seed, but he knows not which shall prosper, either this or that: but God giveth the increase. He draws, He leads, He searches the heart.

Work must be done at home and in the regions beyond. This work requires God's entrusted money. Those who are truly converted are under obligation to do a work which requires money and consecration. The Lord does not propose to come to this world and lay down gold and silver. . . . It is not returning to God His entrusted gifts that makes individuals poor; withholding them tends to poverty, for the one purpose above all others for which God's gifts should be used is the sustaining of workers in the great harvest field.—Manuscript 124, 1898.

Further Reflection: *Tithe is returned. Offerings are given. How generous am I with God?*

DIVINE ONE

And do not be conformed to this world, but be transformed by the renewing of your mind.

—Romans 12:2

In the life of the disciple John true sanctification is exemplified. During the years of his close association with Christ, he was often warned and cautioned by the Saviour; and these reproofs he accepted. As the character of the **Divine One** was manifested to him, John saw his own deficiencies, and was humbled by the revelation. Day by day, in contrast with his own violent spirit, he beheld the tenderness and forbearance of Jesus, and heard His lessons of humility and patience. Day by day his heart was drawn out to Christ, until he lost sight of self in love for his Master. The power and tenderness, the majesty and meekness, the strength and patience, that he saw in the daily life of the Son of God, filled his soul with admiration. He yielded his resentful, ambitious temper to the molding power of Christ, and divine love wrought in him a transformation of character.

In striking contrast to the sanctification worked out in the life of John is the experience of his fellow disciple, Judas. Like his associate, Judas professed to be a disciple of Christ, but he possessed only a form of godliness. He was not insensible to the beauty of the character of Christ; and often, as he listened to the Saviour's words, conviction came to him, but he would not humble his heart or confess his sins. By resisting the divine influence he dishonored the Master whom he professed to love. John warred earnestly against his faults; but Judas violated his conscience and yielded to temptation. . . .

John and Judas are representatives of those who profess to be Christ's followers. Both these disciples had the same opportunities to study and follow the divine Pattern. Both were closely associated with Jesus and were privileged to listen to His teaching. Each possessed serious defects of character; and each had access to the divine grace that transforms character. But while one in humility was learning of Jesus, the other revealed that he was not a doer of the word, but a hearer only. One, daily dying to self and overcoming sin, was sanctified through the truth; the other, resisting the transforming power of grace and indulging selfish desires, was brought into bondage to Satan.—*The Acts of the Apostles*, pp. 557, 558.

Further Reflection: *Am I resisting God's transformation in any area of my life?*

CO-WORKER

"The One to be Ruler in Israel, whose goings forth are from of old, from everlasting."

—Micah 5:2

The history of the great conflict between good and evil, from the time it first began in heaven to the final overthrow of rebellion and the total eradication of sin, is also a demonstration of God's unchanging love.

The Sovereign of the universe was not alone in His work of beneficence. He had an associate—a **co-worker** who could appreciate His purposes, and could share His joy in giving happiness to created beings. "In the beginning was the Word, and the Word was with God, and the Word was God. The same was in the beginning with God." (John 1:1, 2) Christ, the Word, the only begotten of God, was one with the eternal Father—one in nature, in character, in purpose—the only being that could enter into all the counsels and purposes of God. "His name shall be called Wonderful, Counselor, The mighty God, The everlasting Father, The Prince of Peace." (Isaiah 9:6) His "goings forth have been from of old, from everlasting." (Micah 5:2) And the Son of God declares concerning Himself: "The Lord possessed Me in the beginning of His way, before His works of old. I was set up from everlasting. . . . When He appointed the foundations of the earth: then I was by Him, as one brought up with Him: and I was daily His delight, rejoicing always before Him." (Proverbs 8:22–30)

The Father wrought by His Son in the creation of all heavenly beings. "By Him were all things created, . . . whether they be thrones, or dominions, or principalities, or powers: all things were created by Him, and for Him." (Colossians 1:16) Angels are God's ministers, radiant with the light ever flowing from His presence and speeding on rapid wing to execute His will. But the Son, the anointed of God, the "express image of His person," "the brightness of His glory," "upholding all things by the word of His power," holds supremacy over them all. (Hebrews 1:3) "A glorious high throne from the beginning," was the place of His sanctuary (Jeremiah 17:12); "a scepter of righteousness," the scepter of His kingdom. (Hebrews 1:8) "Honor and majesty are before Him: strength and beauty are in His sanctuary." (Psalm 96:6)—*Patriarchs and Prophets*, pp. 33, 34.

Further Reflection: *If I was to give Jesus a name or title based on what He has meant to me, what would it be?*

MEEK AND LOWLY ONE

But made Himself of no reputation, taking the form of a bondservant, and coming in the likeness of men.

—Philippians 2:7

By coming to dwell with us, Jesus was to reveal God both to humans and to angels. He was the Word of God—God's thought made audible. In His prayer for His disciples He says, "I have declared unto them Thy name,"—"merciful and gracious, long-suffering, and abundant in goodness and truth,"—"that the love wherewith Thou hast loved Me may be in them, and I in them." But not alone for His earth-born children was this revelation given. Our little world is the lesson book of the universe. God's wonderful purpose of grace, the mystery of redeeming love, is the theme into which "angels desire to look," and it will be their study throughout endless ages. Both the redeemed and the unfallen beings will find in the cross of Christ their science and their song. It will be seen that the glory shining in the face of Jesus is the glory of self-sacrificing love. In the light from Calvary it will be seen that the law of self-renouncing love is the law of life for earth and heaven; that the love which "seeketh not her own" has its source in the heart of God; and that in the **meek and lowly One** is manifested the character of Him who dwelleth in the light which no person can approach unto.

In the beginning, God was revealed in all the works of creation. It was Christ that spread the heavens, and laid the foundations of the earth. It was His hand that hung the worlds in space, and fashioned the flowers of the field. "His strength setteth fast the mountains." "The sea is His, and He made it." (Psalm 65:6; 95:5) It was He that filled the earth with beauty, and the air with song. And upon all things in earth, and air, and sky, He wrote the message of the Father's love.

Now sin has marred God's perfect work, yet that handwriting remains. Even now all created things declare the glory of His excellence. There is no leaf of the forest, or lowly blade of grass, but has its ministry. Every tree and shrub and leaf pours forth that element of life without which neither human beings nor animal could live; and human and animal, in turn, minister to the life of tree and shrub and leaf. The flowers breathe fragrance and unfold their beauty in blessing to the world.—*The Desire of Ages*, pp. 19–21.

Further Reflection: *In today's world, meekness is seen as weakness. How can I exemplify the meekness of Christ in today's hardscrabble world and not become a doormat?*

SAVIOUR-SHEPHERD

"My sheep hear My voice, and I know them, and they follow Me."
—John 10:27

As the shepherd leads his flock over the rocky hills, through forest and wild ravines, to grassy nooks by the riverside; as he watches them on the mountains through the lonely night, shielding from robbers, caring tenderly for the sickly and feeble, his life comes to be one with theirs. A strong and tender attachment unites him to the objects of his care. However large the flock, the shepherd knows every sheep. Every one has its name, and responds to the name at the shepherd's call.

As an earthly shepherd knows his sheep, so does the Divine know His flock that are scattered throughout the world. "Ye My flock, the flock of My pasture, are men, and I am your God, saith the Lord God." Jesus says, "I have called thee by thy name; thou art Mine." "I have graven thee upon the palms of My hands." (Ezekiel 34:31; Isaiah 43:1; 49:16)

Jesus knows us individually, and is touched with the feeling of our infirmities. He knows us all by name. He knows the very house in which we live, the name of each occupant. He has at times given directions to His servants to go to a certain street in a certain city, to such a house, to find one of His sheep.

Every soul is as fully known to Jesus as if he were the only one for whom the Saviour died. The distress of every one touches His heart. The cry for aid reaches His ear. He came to draw all men and women unto Himself. He bids them, "Follow Me," and His Spirit moves upon their hearts to draw them to come to Him. Many refuse to be drawn. Jesus knows who they are. He also knows who gladly hear His call, and are ready to come under His pastoral care. He says, "My sheep hear My voice, and I know them, and they follow Me." He cares for each one as if there were not another on the face of the earth.

"He calleth His own sheep by name, and leadeth them out. . . . And the sheep follow Him: for they know His voice." The Eastern shepherd does not drive his sheep. He depends not upon force or fear; but going before, he calls them. They know his voice, and obey the call. So does the **Saviour-Shepherd** with His sheep.—*The Desire of Ages*, pp. 479, 480.

Further Reflection: *When Jesus calls me, do I come to Him? When He asks me to do something, do I hasten or hesitate to obey?*

DIVINE SOWER

"The sower sows the word."

—Mark 4:14

The prophet Isaiah bears striking testimony to Christ: "Unto us a Child is born, unto us a Son is given; and the government shall be upon His shoulder; and His name shall be called Wonderful, Counselor, The mighty God, The everlasting Father, The Prince of Peace." . . .

Christ reproached His disciples with their slowness of comprehension. They were influenced by maxims and traditionary lore, so that the truths spoken by the greatest Teacher the world has ever known were often lost truths to them. Christ led them to realize that He had put them in possession of truth of which they little suspected the value. After His resurrection, as He was walking to Emmaus with two of the disciples, He opened their understanding, that they might understand the Scriptures, so explaining the Old Testament to them that they saw in its teaching a meaning that the writers themselves had not seen.

Christ's words are represented as being bread from heaven. As the disciples ate the words of Christ, their understanding was quickened. As they diligently sought for the truth as for hidden treasure, they understood better the value of the grace and righteousness of Christ. In their comprehension of His teaching, they stepped from the obscurity of dawn to the radiance of noon.

The work of no human author is perfect. The depth of human intellect may be measured. The richest mines of human production are not inexhaustible. But the highest, deepest, broadest flight of the imagination cannot find out God. There is infinity beyond all that we in our own strength can comprehend; the Holy Spirit must reveal Him to us. Many are too well satisfied with the surface truths of revelation. Precious gems of truth are passed by because their value is not seen. Let the Bible student tax his mind as he studies God's Word; for the meaning often lies hidden beneath the surface. The knowledge thus gained will be like heavenly seed planted by the **divine Sower**.—*The Signs of the Times*, December 22, 1898.

Further Reflection: *If the Holy Spirit is required to help me process the seed sown by the Divine Sower, how often do I pray for this mind-opening Gift?*

HEALER OF THE SOUL

When Jesus saw their faith, He said to the paralytic, "Son, be of good cheer; your sins are forgiven you."
—Matthew 9:2

There are today thousands suffering from physical disease, who, like the paralytic, are longing for the message, "Thy sins are forgiven." The burden of sin, with its unrest and unsatisfied desires, is the foundation of their maladies. They can find no relief until they come to the **Healer of the soul**. The peace which He alone can give, would impart vigor to the mind, and health to the body.

Jesus came to "destroy the works of the devil." "In Him was life," and He says, "I am come that they might have life, and that they might have it more abundantly." He is "a quickening spirit." (1 John 3:8; John 1:4; 10:10; 1 Corinthians 15:45) And He still has the same life-giving power as when on earth He healed the sick, and spoke forgiveness to the sinner. . . .

The effect produced upon the people by the healing of the paralytic was as if heaven had opened, and revealed the glories of the better world. As the man who had been cured passed through the multitude, blessing God at every step, and bearing his burden as if it were a feather's weight, the people fell back to give him room, and with awe-stricken faces gazed upon him, whispering softly among themselves, "We have seen strange things today."

The Pharisees were dumb with amazement and overwhelmed with defeat. They saw that here was no opportunity for their jealousy to inflame the multitude. The wonderful work wrought upon the man whom they had given over to the wrath of God had so impressed the people that the rabbis were for the time forgotten. They saw that Christ possessed a power which they had ascribed to God alone; yet the gentle dignity of His manner was in marked contrast to their own haughty bearing. They were disconcerted and abashed, recognizing, but not confessing, the presence of a superior being. The stronger the evidence that Jesus had power on earth to forgive sins, the more firmly they entrenched themselves in unbelief. From the home of Peter, where they had seen the paralytic restored by His word, they went away to invent new schemes for silencing the Son of God.—*The Desire of Ages*, pp. 270, 271.

Further Reflection: *How do I feel when Jesus does something miraculous for someone other than me?*

GREAT HEALER

"They will lay hands on the sick, and they will recover."
—Mark 16:18

This world is a vast lazar house, but Christ came to heal the sick, to proclaim deliverance to the captives of Satan. He was in Himself health and strength. He imparted His life to the sick, the afflicted, those possessed of demons. He turned away none who came to receive His healing power. He knew that those who petitioned Him for help had brought disease upon themselves; yet He did not refuse to heal them. And when virtue from Christ entered into these poor souls, they were convicted of sin, and many were healed of their spiritual disease, as well as of their physical maladies. The gospel still possesses the same power, and why should we not today witness the same results?

Christ feels the woes of every sufferer. When evil spirits rend a human frame, Christ feels the curse. When fever is burning up the life current, He feels the agony. And He is just as willing to heal the sick now as when He was personally on earth. Christ's servants are His representatives, the channels for His working. He desires through them to exercise His healing power.

In the Saviour's manner of healing there were lessons for His disciples. On one occasion He anointed the eyes of a blind man with clay, and bade him, "Go, wash in the pool of Siloam. . . . He went his way therefore, and washed, and came seeing." (John 9:7) The cure could be wrought only by the power of the **Great Healer**, yet Christ made use of the simple agencies of nature. While He did not give countenance to drug medication, He sanctioned the use of simple and natural remedies.

To many of the afflicted ones who received healing, Christ said, "Sin no more, lest a worse thing come unto thee." (John 5:14) Thus He taught that disease is the result of violating God's laws, both natural and spiritual. The great misery in the world would not exist did human beings but live in harmony with the Creator's plan.

Christ had been the guide and teacher of ancient Israel, and He taught them that health is the reward of obedience to the laws of God.—*The Desire of Ages*, pp. 823, 824.

Further Reflection: *How does Christ feel the pains of billions of suffering human beings, yet respond to each as though they were the only one on earth?*

DIVINE WORKER

"I must work the works of Him who sent Me while it is day."
—John 9:4

God has a purpose in sending trial to His children. He never leads them otherwise than they would choose to be led if they could see the end from the beginning, and discern the glory of the purpose which they are fulfilling. He subjects them to discipline to humble them—to lead them, through trial and affliction, to see their weakness and to draw near unto Him. As they cry to Him for help, He responds, saying, "Here am I."

Christians are Christ's jewels. They are to shine brightly for Him, shedding forth the light of His loveliness. Their luster depends on the polishing they receive. They may choose to be polished or to remain unpolished. But every one who is pronounced worthy of a place in the Lord's temple must submit to the polishing process. Without the polishing that the Lord gives they can reflect no more light than a common pebble.

Christ says to men and women, "You are Mine. I have bought you. You are now only a rough stone, but if you will place yourself in My hands, I will polish you, and the luster with which you shall shine will bring honor to My name. No person shall pluck you out of My hand. I will make you My peculiar treasure. On My coronation day, you will be a jewel in My crown of rejoicing."

The **divine Worker** spends little time on worthless material. Only the precious jewels does He polish after the similitude of a palace, cutting away all the rough edges. This process is severe and trying; it hurts human pride. Christ cuts deep into the experience that human beings in their self-sufficiency have regarded as complete, and takes away self-uplifting from the character. He cuts away the surplus surface, and putting the stone to the polishing wheel, presses it close, that all roughness may be worn away. Then, holding the jewel up to the light, the Master sees in it a reflection of Himself, and He pronounces it worthy of a place in His casket.

"In that day, saith the Lord of hosts, will I take thee . . . and will make thee as a signet: for I have chosen thee, saith the Lord of hosts." Blessed be the experience, however severe, that gives new value to the stone, and causes it to shine with living brightness.—*Review and Herald*, December 19, 1907.

Further Reflection: *Where is Jesus polishing you right now? How do you deal with the hurt that you feel as He removes the rough edges from your life?*

TEACHER SENT FROM GOD

"You call Me Teacher and Lord, and you say well, for so I am."
—John 13:13

In the **Teacher sent from God,** heaven gave to us its best and greatest. He who had stood in the councils of the Most High, who had dwelt in the innermost sanctuary of the Eternal, was the One chosen to reveal in person to humanity the knowledge of God.

Through Christ had been communicated every ray of divine light that had ever reached our fallen world. It was He who had spoken through everyone that throughout the ages had declared God's word to humanity. Of Him all the excellences manifest in the earth's greatest and noblest souls were reflections. The purity and beneficence of Joseph, the faith and meekness and long-suffering of Moses, the steadfastness of Elisha, the noble integrity and firmness of Daniel, the ardor and self-sacrifice of Paul, the mental and spiritual power manifest in all these men, and in all others who had ever dwelt on the earth, were but gleams from the shining of His glory. In Him was found the perfect ideal.

To reveal this ideal as the only true standard for attainment; to show what every human being might become; what, through the indwelling of humanity by divinity, all who received Him would become—for this, Christ came to the world. He came to show how people are to be trained as befits the sons of God; how on earth they are to practice the principles and to live the life of heaven.

God's greatest gift was bestowed to meet humanity's greatest need. The Light appeared when the world's darkness was deepest. Through false teaching the minds of human beings had long been turned away from God. In the prevailing systems of education, human philosophy had taken the place of divine revelation. Instead of the heaven-given standard of truth, men and women had accepted a standard of their own devising. From the Light of life they had turned aside to walk in the sparks of the fire which they had kindled.—*Education,* pp. 73, 74.

Further Reflection: *"Of Him all the excellences manifest in the earth's greatest and noblest souls were reflections." If humanity's greatest and noblest men and women are but reflections of Jesus, what concrete step can I take today to better reflect Christ?*

ELDER BROTHER

"Take My yoke upon you and learn from Me, for I am gentle and lowly in heart, and you will find rest for your souls. For My yoke is easy and My burden is light."
—Matthew 11:29, 30

In these words Christ is speaking to every human being. Whether they know it or not, all are weary and heavy-laden. All are weighed down with burdens that only Christ can remove. The heaviest burden that we bear is the burden of sin. If we were left to bear this burden, it would crush us. But the Sinless One has taken our place. "The Lord hath laid on Him the iniquity of us all." (Isaiah 53:6) He has borne the burden of our guilt. He will take the load from our weary shoulders. He will give us rest. The burden of care and sorrow also He will bear. He invites us to cast all our care upon Him; for He carries us upon His heart.

The **Elder Brother** of our race is by the eternal throne. He looks upon every soul who is turning his face toward Him as the Saviour. He knows by experience what are the weaknesses of humanity, what are our wants, and where lies the strength of our temptations; for He was in all points tempted like as we are, yet without sin. He is watching over you, trembling child of God. Are you tempted? He will deliver. Are you weak? He will strengthen. Are you ignorant? He will enlighten. Are you wounded? He will heal. The Lord "telleth the number of the stars;" and yet "He healeth the broken in heart, and bindeth up their wounds." (Psalm 147:4, 3) "Come unto Me," is His invitation. Whatever your anxieties and trials, spread out your case before the Lord. Your spirit will be braced for endurance. The way will be opened for you to disentangle yourself from embarrassment and difficulty. The weaker and more helpless you know yourself to be, the stronger will you become in His strength. The heavier your burdens, the more blessed the rest in casting them upon the Burden Bearer. The rest that Christ offers depends upon conditions, but these conditions are plainly specified. They are those with which all can comply. He tells us just how His rest is to be found.

"Take My yoke upon you," Jesus says. The yoke is an instrument of service. Cattle are yoked for labor, and the yoke is essential that they may labor effectually. By this illustration Christ teaches us that we are called to service as long as life shall last. We are to take upon us His yoke, that we may be co-workers with Him.—*The Desire of Ages*, pp. 328, 329.

Further Reflection: *What burden must I put down to take up Christ's yoke of service?*

MARCH 26

MISSIONARY-IN-CHIEF

"For the Son of Man has come to seek and to save that which was lost."
—Luke 19:10

Let every sincere Christian who has a connection with our schools, be determined to be a faithful servant in the cause of Christ, and help every student to be faithful, pure, and holy in life. Let everyone who loves God seek to win those who have not yet confessed Christ. Every day they may exert a silent, prayerful influence, and co-operate with Jesus Christ, the **missionary-in-chief** to our world. Let every soul—man, woman, and youth—grow in excellence of character and devotion, in purity and holiness, and live with an eye single to the glory of God, that the enemies of our faith may not triumph. Let there be such a binding together in the bonds of our holy faith, that our united influence may be wholly on the Lord's side, and may work for the transformation of those with whom we associate. Let it be made manifest that you have a living connection with God, and are ambitious for the Master's glory, seeking to cultivate in yourselves every grace of character by which you may honor Him who gave His life for you. May the love of Christ exercise a constraining power to draw others into the path cast up for the ransomed of the Lord to walk in. When the students in our schools shall learn to like God's will, they will find it comparatively easy to do it.

If students see defects of character in others, let them be thankful that they have discerned these defects, and therefore may be put on their guard against them. You will, no doubt, see persons who are not learning the meekness and lowliness of Christ, but who love display, and are vain, frivolous, and worldly. The only remedy for such is to behold Jesus, and by studying His character they will come to despise everything that is vain and frivolous, weak and mean. The character of Christ is full of forbearance, patience, goodness, mercy, and unexampled love. By beholding such a character, they will rise above the littleness of that which has fashioned and molded them, and made them unholy and unlovely. They will say, "I will not sit with vain persons, neither will I go with dissemblers." They will realize that "he that walketh with wise men shall be wise; but a companion of fools shall be destroyed."—*Review and Herald*, January 16, 1894.

Further Reflection: *What does it mean for me to be ambitious for the Master's glory?*

EVER-LIVING SAVIOUR

He always lives to make intercession for them.
—Hebrews 7:25

Christ has said, "Ye shall be witnesses unto Me." You are to hold forth the word of life, to let your light so shine before men that they, seeing your good works, may glorify your Father who is in heaven. The confession of the church, the declaration of the evidences of God's truth, love, faithfulness, and power, are chosen agencies of heaven to reveal Christ's pardoning love to the world. The testimonies of the people of God, when impressed by His Spirit, convict men and women of the sin of neglecting so great salvation. While individuals who are converted to God acknowledge His power through patriarchs and prophets, they have a more interesting testimony to bear concerning the miracles of the grace of Christ, the **ever-living Saviour**, in their present and personal experiences. These precious acknowledgments of the goodness, forbearance, and love of God, when accompanied by a consistent life, carry with them an irresistible power, that results in the salvation of souls. Says the apostle, "Ye are a chosen generation, a royal priesthood, a holy nation, a peculiar people; that ye should show forth the praises of Him who hath called you out of darkness into His marvelous light."

Every important truth received into the heart must find expression in the life. It is in proportion to the reception of the love of Christ that men and women desire to proclaim its power to others; and the very act of proclaiming it, deepens and intensifies its value to their own souls. Those whose souls are full of the love of Christ, are full of eagerness to make disclosures of the comfort, hope, and peace that pervade their hearts. They feel as did Paul when he said, "Unto me, which am less than the least of all saints, is this grace given, that I should preach among the Gentiles the unsearchable riches of Christ; and to make all men see what is the fellowship of the mystery, which from the beginning of the world hath been hid in God, who created all things by Jesus Christ: to the intent that now unto the principalities and powers in heavenly places might be known to the church, the manifold wisdom of God, according to the eternal purpose which He purposed in Christ Jesus our Lord."—*Review and Herald,* February 19, 1889.

Further Reflection: *The desire to proclaim the love of Christ comes in proportion to the reception of that love. When was the last time that I told someone about the love of Christ?*

MARCH 28

EXALTED ONE

"If anyone desires to be first, he shall be last of all and servant of all."
—Mark 9:35

There was in these words a solemnity and impressiveness which the disciples were far from comprehending. That which Christ discerned they could not see. They did not understand the nature of Christ's kingdom, and this ignorance was the apparent cause of their contention. But the real cause lay deeper. By explaining the nature of the kingdom, Christ might for the time have quelled their strife; but this would not have touched the underlying cause. Even after they had received the fullest knowledge, any question of precedence might have renewed the trouble. Thus disaster would have been brought to the church after Christ's departure.

The strife for the highest place was the outworking of that same spirit which was the beginning of the great controversy in the worlds above, and which had brought Christ from heaven to die. There rose up before Him a vision of Lucifer, the "son of the morning," in glory surpassing all the angels that surround the throne, and united in closest ties to the Son of God. Lucifer had said, "I will be like the Most High" (Isaiah 14:12, 14); and the desire for self-exaltation had brought strife into the heavenly courts, and had banished a multitude of the hosts of God. Had Lucifer really desired to be like the Most High, he would never have deserted his appointed place in heaven; for the spirit of the Most High is manifested in unselfish ministry. Lucifer desired God's power, but not His character. He sought for himself the highest place, and every being who is actuated by his spirit will do the same. Thus alienation, discord, and strife will be inevitable. Dominion becomes the prize of the strongest. The kingdom of Satan is a kingdom of force; every individual regards every other as an obstacle in the way of his own advancement, or a steppingstone on which he himself may climb to a higher place.

While Lucifer counted it a thing to be grasped to be equal with God, Christ, the **Exalted One**, "made Himself of no reputation, and took upon Him the form of a servant, and was made in the likeness of men: and being found in fashion as a man, He humbled Himself, and became obedient unto death, even the death of the cross." (Philippians 2:7, 8)—*The Desire of Ages*, pp. 435, 436.

Further Reflection: *Do I seek high positions out of a sense of service or pride? How can I be sure that I my motives are pure when seeking the highest place?*

PERFECT PATTERN

Let your speech always be with grace, seasoned with salt, that you may know how you ought to answer each one.
—Colossians 4:6

By diligent effort all may acquire the power to read intelligibly, and to speak in a full, clear, round tone, in a distinct and impressive manner. By doing this we may greatly increase our efficiency as workers for Christ.

Every Christian is called to make known to others the unsearchable riches of Christ; therefore he should seek for perfection in speech. He should present the word of God in a way that will commend it to the hearers. God does not design that His human channels shall be uncouth. It is not His will that men and women shall belittle or degrade the heavenly current that flows through them to the world.

We should look to Jesus, the **perfect pattern**; we should pray for the aid of the Holy Spirit, and in His strength we should seek to train every organ for perfect work.

Especially is this true of those who are called to public service. Every minister and every teacher should bear in mind that he is giving to the people a message that involves eternal interests. The truth spoken will judge them in the great day of final reckoning. And with some souls the manner of the one delivering the message will determine its reception or rejection. Then let the word be so spoken that it will appeal to the understanding and impress the heart. Slowly, distinctly, and solemnly should it be spoken, yet with all the earnestness which its importance demands.

The right culture and use of the power of speech has to do with every line of Christian work; it enters into the home life, and into all our intercourse with one another. We should accustom ourselves to speak in pleasant tones, to use pure and correct language, and words that are kind and courteous. Sweet, kind words are as dew and gentle showers to the soul. The Scripture says of Christ that grace was poured into His lips that He might "know how to speak a word in season to him that is weary." (Psalm 45:2; Isaiah 50:4)—*Christ's Object Lessons*, pp. 335, 336.

Further Reflection: *How does God use my voice to offer hope and healing to others? Have I consecrated my gift of speech to God?*

FAITHFUL HOUSEHOLDER

Then He said to them, "Therefore every scribe instructed concerning the kingdom of heaven is like a householder who brings out of his treasure things new and old."

—Matthew 13:52

This is life eternal," Christ said, "that they might know Thee the only true God, and Jesus Christ, whom Thou hast sent." (John 17:3) Why is it that we do not realize the value of this knowledge? Why are not these glorious truths glowing in our hearts, trembling upon our lips, and pervading our whole being?

In giving us His word, God has put us in possession of every truth essential for our salvation. Thousands have drawn water from these wells of life, yet there is no diminishing of the supply. Thousands have set the Lord before them, and by beholding have been changed into the same image. Their spirit burns within them as they speak of His character, telling what Christ is to them, and what they are to Christ. But these searchers have not exhausted these grand and holy themes. Thousands more may engage in the work of searching out the mysteries of salvation. As the life of Christ and the character of His mission are dwelt upon, rays of light will shine forth more distinctly at every attempt to discover truth. Each fresh search will reveal something more deeply interesting than has yet been unfolded. The subject is inexhaustible. The study of the incarnation of Christ, His atoning sacrifice and mediatorial work, will employ the mind of the diligent student as long as time shall last; and looking to heaven with its unnumbered years he will exclaim, "Great is the mystery of godliness."

In eternity we shall learn that which, had we received the enlightenment it was possible to obtain here, would have opened our understanding. The themes of redemption will employ the hearts and minds and tongues of the redeemed through the everlasting ages. They will understand the truths which Christ longed to open to His disciples, but which they did not have faith to grasp. Forever and forever new views of the perfection and glory of Christ will appear. Through endless ages will the **faithful Householder** bring forth from His treasure things new and old.—*Christ's Object Lessons*, pp. 133, 134.

Further Reflection: *During the ceaseless ages of Eternity, Jesus will give me precious treasures from His storehouse of truth. What treasure do I want Him to unfold first?*

SAVIOUR OF THE WORLD

"In My Father's house are many mansions; if it were not so, I would have told you. I go to prepare a place for you."
—John 14:2

Jesus remained with His disciples forty days, causing them joy and gladness of heart as He opened to them more fully the realities of the kingdom of God. He commissioned them to bear testimony to the things which they had seen and heard concerning His sufferings, death, and resurrection, that He had made a sacrifice for sin, and that all who would might come unto Him and find life. With faithful tenderness He told them that they would be persecuted and distressed; but they would find relief in recalling their experience and remembering the words which He had spoken to them. He told them that He had overcome the temptations of Satan and obtained the victory through trials and suffering. Satan could have no more power over Him, but would bring his temptations to bear more directly upon them and upon all who should believe in His name. But they could overcome as He had overcome.

Jesus endowed His disciples with power to work miracles, and told them that although they should be persecuted by wicked people, He would from time to time send His angels to deliver them; their lives could not be taken until their mission should be accomplished; then they might be required to seal with their blood the testimonies which they had borne.

His anxious followers gladly listened to His teachings, eagerly feasting upon every word which fell from His holy lips. Now they certainly knew that He was the **Saviour of the world**. His words sank deep into their hearts, and they sorrowed that they must soon be parted from their heavenly Teacher and no longer hear comforting, gracious words from His lips. But again their hearts were warmed with love and exceeding joy, as Jesus told them that He would go and prepare mansions for them and come again and receive them, that they might be ever with Him. He promised also to send the Comforter, the Holy Spirit, to guide them into all truth. "And He lifted up His hands, and blessed them."—*Early Writings*, pp. 189, 190.

Further Reflection: *How can I extend the comforting heart of Jesus to those I meet today?*

APRIL

BRANCH

There shall come forth a Rod from the stem of Jesse, and a Branch shall grow out of his roots.

—Isaiah 11:1

The Messiah was to be of the royal line, for in the prophecy uttered by Jacob the Lord said, "The scepter shall not depart from Judah, nor a lawgiver from between his feet, until Shiloh come; and unto Him shall the gathering of the people be." (Genesis 49:10)

Isaiah prophesied: "There shall come forth a rod out of the stem of Jesse, and a **Branch** shall grow out of his roots." "Incline your ear, and come unto Me: hear, and your soul shall live; and I will make an everlasting covenant with you, even the sure mercies of David. Behold, I have given Him for a witness to the people, a leader and commander to the people. Behold, thou shalt call a nation that thou knowest not, and nations that knew not thee shall run unto thee because of the Lord thy God, and for the Holy One of Israel; for He hath glorified thee." (Isaiah 11:1; 55:3–5)

Jeremiah also bore witness of the coming Redeemer as a Prince of the house of David: "Behold, the days come, saith the Lord, that I will raise unto David a righteous Branch and a King shall reign and prosper, and shall execute judgment and justice in the earth. In His days Judah shall be saved, and Israel shall dwell safely: and this is His name whereby He shall be called, The Lord Our Righteousness." And again: "Thus saith the Lord: David shall never want a man to sit upon the throne of the house of Israel; neither shall the priests the Levites want a man before Me to offer burnt offerings, and to kindle meat offerings, and to do sacrifice continually." (Jeremiah 23:5, 6; 33:17, 18)

Even the birthplace of the Messiah was foretold: "Thou, Bethlehem Ephratah, though thou be little among the thousands of Judah, yet out of thee shall He come forth unto Me that is to be Ruler in Israel; whose goings forth have been from of old, from everlasting." (Micah 5:2)—*The Acts of the Apostles*, pp. 223, 224.

Further Reflection: *Would I have recognized Jesus as the Messiah of Bible prophecy if I was alive during the time of His arrival? Have I accepted Him today as my Savior?*

FIRST GREAT TEACHER

And it so it was, when Jesus had ended these sayings, that the people were astonished at His teaching.
—Matthew 7:28

It has been the custom to exalt books and authors that do not present the proper foundation for true education. From what source did these authors obtain their wisdom, a large share of which does not deserve our respect, even if the authors are regarded as being wise people? Have they taken their lessons from the greatest Teacher that the world ever knew? If not, they are decidedly in the fault. Those who are preparing for the heavenly abodes should be recommended to make the Bible their chief book of study.

These popular authors have not pointed out to the students the way that leads to eternal life. "And this is life eternal, that they might know thee the only true God, and Jesus Christ, whom thou hast sent." (John 17:3) The authors of the books current in our schools are recommended and exalted as learned persons; their education is in every way deficient, unless they themselves have been educated in the school of Christ, and by practical knowledge bear witness to the word of God as the most essential study for children and youth. "The fear of the Lord is the beginning of wisdom." Books should have been prepared to place in the hands of students that would educate them to have a sincere, reverent love for truth and steadfast integrity. The class of studies which are positively essential in the formation of character to give them a preparation for the future life should be kept ever before them. Christ should be uplifted as the **first great teacher**, the only begotten Son of God, who was with the Father from eternal ages. The Son of God was the Great Teacher sent into the world as the light of the world. "The Word was made flesh, and dwelt among us." The Father was represented in Christ, and the attention in education must be of that character that they will look to Him and believe in Him as the likeness of God. He had a most wonderful mission to this world, and His work was not in a line to give a full relation of His personal claims to deity, but His humiliation was a concealment of His claims. . . .

. . . His character was a life of obedience to all God's commandments, and was to be a sample for all human beings upon the earth. His life was the living of the law in humanity.—*Special Testimonies on Education*, pp. 229–231.

Further Reflection: *How much time do I spend each day studying God's Word?*

COVENANT ANGEL

And the Angel of the LORD appeared to him, and said to him, "The LORD is with you, you mighty man of valor!"
—Judges 6:12

Gideon desired some token that the one now addressing him was the **Covenant Angel**, who in time past had wrought for Israel. Hastening to his tent, he prepared from his scanty store a kid and unleavened cakes which he brought forth and set before Him. But the Angel bade him, "Take the flesh and the unleavened cakes, and lay them upon this rock, and pour out the broth." Gideon did so, and then the sign he desired was given: with the staff in His hand, the Angel touched the flesh and the unleavened cakes, and a flame bursting from the rock consumed the sacrifice. Then the Angel vanished. . . .

Gideon's father, Joash, who shared in the apostasy of his countrymen, had erected at Ophrah a large altar to Baal. Gideon was commanded to destroy this altar and to erect an altar to Jehovah over the rock on which the offering had been consumed, and there present a sacrifice to the Lord. The offering of sacrifice had been committed to the priests and restricted to the altar at Shiloh; but He who had established the ritual service had power to change its requirements. Gideon must declare war on idolatry before going out to battle with the enemies of his people.

Gideon performed the work in secret, with the aid of his servants accomplishing the whole in one night. Great was the rage of the men of Ophrah when they came next morning to pay their devotions to Baal. Joash, who had been told of the Angel's visit, stood in defense of his son. "Will ye plead for Baal? Will ye save him? He that will plead for him, let him be put to death whilst it is yet morning." If Baal could not defend his own altar, how could he be trusted to protect his worshipers?

All thoughts of violence toward Gideon were dismissed. When he sounded the trumpet of war, the men of Ophrah were among the first to gather to his standard. Heralds were dispatched to his own tribe of Manasseh, and also to Asher, Zebulun, and Naphtali, and all answered the call.—*Patriarchs and Prophets*, pp. 547, 548.

Further Reflection: *How do I respond to my family members who are living in opposition to the will of God?*

MESSIAH

And she brought forth her firstborn Son, and wrapped Him in swaddling cloths, and laid Him in a manger, because there was no room for them in the inn.

—Luke 2:7

The angels had wondered at the glorious plan of redemption. They watched to see how the people of God would receive His Son, clothed in the garb of humanity. Angels came to the land of the chosen people. Other nations were dealing in fables and worshiping false gods. To the land where the glory of God had been revealed, and the light of prophecy had shone, the angels came. They came unseen to Jerusalem, to the appointed expositors of the Sacred Oracles, and the ministers of God's house. Already to Zacharias the priest, as he ministered before the altar, the nearness of Christ's coming had been announced. Already the forerunner was born, his mission attested by miracle and prophecy. The tidings of his birth and the wonderful significance of his mission had been spread abroad. Yet Jerusalem was not preparing to welcome her Redeemer.

With amazement the heavenly messengers beheld the indifference of that people whom God had called to communicate to the world the light of sacred truth. The Jewish nation had been preserved as a witness that Christ was to be born of the seed of Abraham and of David's line; yet they knew not that His coming was now at hand. In the temple the morning and the evening sacrifice daily pointed to the Lamb of God; yet even here was no preparation to receive Him. The priests and teachers of the nation knew not that the greatest event of the ages was about to take place. They rehearsed their meaningless prayers, and performed the rites of worship to be seen by men and women, but in their strife for riches and worldly honor they were not prepared for the revelation of the **Messiah**. The same indifference pervaded the land of Israel. Hearts selfish and world-engrossed were untouched by the joy that thrilled all heaven. Only a few were longing to behold the Unseen. To these heaven's embassy was sent. . . .

Men and women know it not, but the tidings fill heaven with rejoicing. With a deeper and more tender interest the holy beings from the world of light are drawn to the earth. The whole world is brighter for His presence.—*The Desire of Ages*, pp. 43–47.

Further Reflection: *Is my heart prepared today to receive Jesus, the Messiah?*

BENEFACTOR

For I know the thoughts that I think toward you, says the LORD, thoughts of peace and not of evil, to give you a future and a hope.
—Jeremiah 29:11

The leaders at Jerusalem had sent out spies to find some pretext for putting Christ to death. He responded by giving them an evidence of His love for humanity, His respect for the law, and His power to deliver from sin and death. Thus He bore witness of them: "They have rewarded Me evil for good, and hatred for My love." (Psalm 109:5) He who on the mount gave the precept, "Love your enemies," Himself exemplified the principle, not rendering "evil for evil, or railing for railing: but contrariwise blessing." (Matthew 5:44; 1 Peter 3:9)

The same priests who condemned the leper to banishment certified his cure. This sentence, publicly pronounced and registered, was a standing testimony for Christ. And as the healed man was reinstated in the congregation of Israel, upon the priests' own assurance that there was not a taint of the disease upon him, he himself was a living witness for his **Benefactor**. Joyfully he presented his offering, and magnified the name of Jesus. The priests were convinced of the divine power of the Saviour. Opportunity was granted them to know the truth and to be profited by the light. Rejected, it would pass away, never to return. By many the light was rejected; yet it was not given in vain. Many hearts were moved that for a time made no sign. During the Saviour's life, His mission seemed to call forth little response of love from the priests and teachers; but after His ascension "a great company of the priests were obedient to the faith." (Acts 6:7)

The work of Christ in cleansing the leper from his terrible disease is an illustration of His work in cleansing the soul from sin. The man who came to Jesus was "full of leprosy." Its deadly poison permeated his whole body. The disciples sought to prevent their Master from touching him; for he who touched a leper became himself unclean. But in laying His hand upon the leper, Jesus received no defilement. His touch imparted life-giving power. The leprosy was cleansed. Thus it is with the leprosy of sin—deep-rooted, deadly, and impossible to be cleansed by human power.—*The Desire of Ages*, pp. 265, 266.

Further Reflection: *How comforting is it to know that no matter my sin, Jesus still offers me His healing, cleansing touch? Have I accepted it?*

GREATEST EDUCATOR

And when it was day, He called His disciples to Himself; and from them He chose twelve whom He also named apostles.

—Luke 6:13

The first pupils of Jesus were chosen from the ranks of the common people. They were humble, unlettered men, these fishers of Galilee; men unschooled in the learning and customs of the rabbis, but trained by the stern discipline of toil and hardship. They were men of native ability and of teachable spirit; men who could be instructed and molded for the Saviour's work. In the common walks of life there is many a toiler patiently treading the round of his daily tasks, unconscious of latent powers that, roused to action, would place him among the world's great leaders. Such were the men who were called by the Saviour to be His colaborers. And they had the advantage of three years' training by the **greatest educator** this world has ever known.

In these first disciples was presented a marked diversity. They were to be the world's teachers, and they represented widely varied types of character. There were Levi Matthew the publican, called from a life of business activity, and subservience to Rome; the zealot Simon, the uncompromising foe of the imperial authority; the impulsive, self-sufficient, warmhearted Peter, with Andrew his brother; Judas the Judean, polished, capable, and mean-spirited; Philip and Thomas, faithful and earnest, yet slow of heart to believe; James the less and Jude, of less prominence among the brethren, but men of force, positive both in their faults and in their virtues; Nathanael, a child in sincerity and trust; and the ambitious, loving-hearted sons of Zebedee.

In order successfully to carry forward the work to which they had been called, these disciples, differing so widely in natural characteristics, in training, and in habits of life, needed to come into unity of feeling, thought, and action. This unity it was Christ's object to secure. To this end He sought to bring them into unity with Himself. The burden of His labor for them is expressed in His prayer to the Father, "that they all may be one; as Thou, Father, art in Me, and I in Thee, that they also may be one in Us . . . that the world may know that Thou hast sent Me, and hast loved them, as Thou hast loved Me." (John 17:21–23)—*Education,* pp. 85, 86.

Further Reflection: *Do I respect the diverse gifts and talents of those with whom I serve Christ? How can I affirm the giftedness of someone today?*

FOUNTAIN OF BLESSING

"But whoever drinks of the water that I shall give him will never thirst."
—John 4:14

He who seeks to quench his thirst at the fountains of this world will drink only to thirst again. Everywhere people are unsatisfied. They long for something to supply the need of the soul. Only One can meet that want. The need of the world, "The Desire of all nations," is Christ. The divine grace which He alone can impart, is as living water, purifying, refreshing, and invigorating. . . .

Jesus did not convey the idea that merely one draft of the water of life would suffice the receiver. He who tastes of the love of Christ will continually long for more; but he seeks for nothing else. The riches, honors, and pleasures of the world do not attract him. The constant cry of his heart is, More of Thee. And He who reveals to the soul its necessity is waiting to satisfy its hunger and thirst. Every human resource and dependence will fail. The cisterns will be emptied, the pools become dry; but our Redeemer is an inexhaustible fountain. We may drink, and drink again, and ever find a fresh supply. He in whom Christ dwells has within himself the **Fountain of Blessing**—"a well of water springing up into everlasting life." From this source he may draw strength and grace sufficient for all his needs.

As Jesus spoke of the living water, the woman looked upon Him with wondering attention. He had aroused her interest, and awakened a desire for the gift of which He spoke. She perceived that it was not the water of Jacob's well to which He referred; for of this she used continually, drinking, and thirsting again. "Sir," she said, "give me this water, that I thirst not, neither come hither to draw." . . .

As the woman talked with Jesus, she was impressed with His words. Never had she heard such sentiments from the priests of her own people or from the Jews. As the past of her life had been spread out before her, she had been made sensible of her great want. She realized her soul thirst, which the waters of the well of Sychar could never satisfy. Nothing that had hitherto come in contact with her had so awakened her to a higher need. . . . The question arose in her mind, Might not this be the long-looked-for Messiah? She said to Him, "I know that Messias cometh, which is called Christ: when He is come, He will tell us all things." Jesus answered, "I that speak unto thee am He."—*The Desire of Ages*, pp. 187, 189, 190.

Further Reflection: *What thirst might I be seeking to quench from broken fountains?*

BEST BELOVED

And suddenly a voice came from heaven, saying,
"This is My beloved Son, in whom I am well pleased."
—Matthew 3:17

The result of hastening or hindering the gospel, we think of, if at all, in relation to ourselves and to the world. Few think of its relation to God. Few give thought to the suffering that sin has caused our Creator. All heaven suffered in Christ's agony; but that suffering did not begin or end with His manifestation in humanity. The cross is a revelation to our dull senses of the pain that sin, from its very inception, has brought to the heart of God. Every departure from the right, every deed of cruelty, every failure of humanity to reach God's ideal, brings grief to Him. When there came upon Israel the calamities that inevitably followed separation from God—subjugation by their enemies, oppression, cruelty, and death—it is said of God, that "His soul was grieved for the misery of Israel." (Judges 10:16) "In all their affliction He was afflicted . . . and He bare them, and carried them all the days of old." (Isaiah 63:9)

His Spirit "maketh intercession for us with groanings, which cannot be uttered." (Romans 8:26) As the "whole creation groaneth and travaileth together in pain" (Romans 8:26, 22), the heart of the infinite Father is pained in sympathy. Our world is a vast lazar-house, a scene of misery that no pen can picture, misery that we dare not allow even our thoughts to dwell upon. Did we realize it as it is, the burden would be too terrible. Yet God feels it all. In order to destroy sin and its results He gave His **best Beloved**, and He has put it in our power, by co-operation with Him, to bring this scene of misery to an end. "This gospel of the kingdom shall be preached in all the world for a witness unto all nations; and then shall the end come." (Matthew 24:14)—*Education*, pp. 263, 264.

Further Reflection: *When God broke through the atmosphere that day to declare that Jesus was His beloved Son in whom He was well pleased, He knew what lay ahead for Jesus—a life of suffering and death. As Ellen White noted, all of heaven suffered with Jesus. If I was in heaven during the time when Jesus was suffering on earth to save fallen humanity from sin, what might I say or do to comfort God the Father?*

FOUNTAIN OF LIFE

That you may be filled with the knowledge of His will in all wisdom and spiritual understanding.

—Colossians 1:9

The letter to the Colossians is filled with lessons of highest value to all who are engaged in the service of Christ, lessons that show the singleness of purpose and the loftiness of aim which will be seen in the life of him who rightly represents the Saviour.

Renouncing all that would hinder him from making progress in the upward way or that would turn the feet of another from the narrow path, the believer will reveal in his daily life mercy, kindness, humility, meekness, forbearance, and the love of Christ.

The power of a higher, purer, nobler life is our great need. The world has too much of our thought, and the kingdom of heaven too little.

In his efforts to reach God's ideal for him, the Christian is to despair of nothing. Moral and spiritual perfection, through the grace and power of Christ, is promised to all. Jesus is the source of power, the **fountain of life**. He brings us to His word, and from the tree of life presents to us leaves for the healing of sin-sick souls. He leads us to the throne of God, and puts into our mouth a prayer through which we are brought into close contact with Himself. In our behalf He sets in operation the all-powerful agencies of heaven. At every step we touch His living power.

God fixes no limit to the advancement of those who desire to be "filled with the knowledge of His will in all wisdom and spiritual understanding." Through prayer, through watchfulness, through growth in knowledge and understanding, they are to be "strengthened with all might, according to His glorious power." Thus they are prepared to work for others. It is the Saviour's purpose that human beings, purified and sanctified, shall be His helping hand. For this great privilege let us give thanks to Him who "hath made us meet to be partakers of the inheritance of the saints in light: who hath delivered us from the power of darkness, and hath translated us into the kingdom of His dear Son."—*The Acts of the Apostles*, pp. 477, 478.

Further Reflection: *How committed am I to experiencing the limitless advancement offered by Jesus to me? Do I earnestly desire to be "filled with the knowledge of His will in all wisdom and spiritual understanding?"*

SOURCE OF ALL VITALITY

For since by man came death, by Man also came the resurrection of the dead. For as in Adam all die, even so in Christ all shall be made alive.
—1 Corinthians 15:21, 22

While life is the inheritance of the righteous, death is the portion of the wicked.

The soul that sinneth it shall die an everlasting death—a death that will last forever, from which there will be no hope of a resurrection; and then the wrath of God will be appeased.

It was a marvel to me that Satan could succeed so well in making people believe that the words of God, "The soul that sinneth, it shall die," mean that the soul that sinneth it shall not die, but live eternally in misery. Said the angel, "Life is life, whether it is in pain or happiness. Death is without pain, without joy, without hatred."

Christ endured an agonizing death under the most humiliating circumstances that we might have life. He gave up His precious life that He might vanquish death. But He rose from the tomb, and the myriads of angels who came to behold Him take up the life He had laid down heard His words of triumphant joy as He stood above Joseph's rent sepulcher proclaiming: "I am the resurrection, and the life." (John 11:25)

The question, "If a man die, shall he live again?" has been answered. By bearing the penalty of sin, by going down into the grave, Christ has brightened the tomb for all who die in faith. God in human form has brought life and immortality to light through the gospel. In dying, Christ secured eternal life for all who believe in Him. In dying, He condemned the originator of sin and disloyalty to suffer the penalty of sin—eternal death.

The possessor and giver of eternal life, Christ was the only one who could conquer death. He is our Redeemer.

Christ is life itself. He who passed through death to destroy him that had the power of death is the **Source of all vitality**. There is balm in Gilead, and a Physician there.—*The Faith I Live By*, p. 177.

Further Reflection: *If Jesus Christ is "life itself," what happens to me when I am not one with Him, when I become disconnected from Him?*

UNCONDEMNED

Now as they led Him away, they laid hold of a certain man, Simon a Cyrenian, who was coming from the country, and on him they laid the cross that he might bear it after Jesus.

—Luke 23:26

The crowd that followed the Saviour saw His weak and staggering steps, but they manifested no compassion. They taunted and reviled Him because He could not carry the heavy cross. Again the burden was laid upon Him, and again He fell fainting to the ground. His persecutors saw that it was impossible for Him to carry His burden farther. They were puzzled to find anyone who would bear the humiliating load. The Jews themselves could not do this, because the defilement would prevent them from keeping the Passover. None even of the mob that followed Him would stoop to bear the cross.

At this time a stranger, Simon a Cyrenian, coming in from the country, meets the throng. He hears the taunts and ribaldry of the crowd; he hears the words contemptuously repeated, Make way for the King of the Jews! He stops in astonishment at the scene; and as he expresses his compassion, they seize him and place the cross upon his shoulders.

Simon had heard of Jesus. His sons were believers in the Saviour, but he himself was not a disciple. The bearing of the cross to Calvary was a blessing to Simon, and he was ever after grateful for this providence. It led him to take upon himself the cross of Christ from choice, and ever cheerfully stand beneath its burden.

Not a few women are in the crowd that follow the **Uncondemned** to His cruel death. Their attention is fixed upon Jesus. Some of them have seen Him before. Some have carried to Him their sick and suffering ones. Some have themselves been healed. The story of the scenes that have taken place is related. They wonder at the hatred of the crowd toward Him for whom their own hearts are melting and ready to break. And notwithstanding the action of the maddened throng, and the angry words of the priests and rulers, these women give expression to their sympathy. As Jesus falls fainting beneath the cross, they break forth into mournful wailing.

This was the only thing that attracted Christ's attention.—*The Desire of Ages*, pp. 742, 743.

Further Reflection: *Why does Jesus, an innocent Person who did many good works, inspire such hatred in some?*

FRIEND AT THE HEAVENLY COURT

For as by one man's disobedience many were made sinners, so also by one Man's obedience many will be made righteous.

—Romans 5:19

Blessed be the God and Father of our Lord Jesus Christ, which according to His abundant mercy hath begotten us again unto a lively hope by the resurrection of Jesus Christ from the dead." Is there any reason why this lively hope should not give us as much confidence and joy at this time, as it gave the disciples in the early church? Christ is not enclosed in Joseph's new tomb. He is risen, and has ascended up on high, and we are to act out our faith, that the world may see that we have a lively hope, and may know that we have a **Friend at the heavenly court**.

We are begotten again unto a lively hope, and to an inheritance incorruptible, and undefiled, and that fadeth not away, reserved in heaven for us. Our hope is not without foundation; our inheritance is not corruptible. It is not the subject of imagination, but it is reserved in heaven for us "who are kept by the power of God through faith unto salvation ready to be revealed in the last time. Wherein ye greatly rejoice, though now for a season, if need be, ye are in heaviness through manifold temptations: that the trial of your faith, being much more precious than of gold that perisheth, though it be tried with fire, might be found unto praise and honor and glory at the appearing of Jesus Christ."

In seasons of temptations we seem to lose sight of the fact that God tests us that our faith may be tried, and be found unto praise and honor and glory at the appearing of Jesus. The Lord places us in different positions to develop us. If we have defects of character of which we are not aware, He gives us discipline that will bring those defects to our knowledge, that we may overcome them. It is His providence that brings us into varying circumstances. In each new position, we meet a different class of temptations. How many times, when we are placed in some trying situation, we think, "This is a wonderful mistake. How I wish I had stayed where I was before." But why is it that you are not satisfied? . . . What should you do when you are tried by the providences of the Lord?—You should rise to the emergency of the case, and overcome your defects of character.—*Review and Herald*, August 6, 1889.

Further Reflection: *What is the incorruptible inheritance awaiting me in heaven?*

PATTERN OF HOLINESS

Pursue peace with all people, and holiness, without which no one will see the Lord.

—Hebrews 12:14

People in responsible positions, who are proclaiming the truth of God in the name of Jesus without the spiritual energy given by the quickening power of God, are doing an unreal work, and cannot be certain whether success or defeat will attend their labors. . . . It is not the great services and lofty aspirations which receive the approval of God, but the love and consecration through which the service is performed, be it great or little. Storms of opposition and rebuffs are God's providences to drive us under the shelter of His wing. When the cloud envelops us, His voice is heard: "Peace I leave with you, my peace I give unto you; not as the world giveth . . ."

The act of Christ in breathing upon His disciples the Holy Ghost, and in imparting His peace to them, was as a few drops before the plentiful shower to be given on the day of Pentecost. Jesus impressed this fact upon His disciples, that as they should proceed in the work entrusted to them, they would the more fully comprehend the nature of that work, and the manner in which the kingdom of Christ was to be set up on earth. They were appointed to be witnesses for the Saviour; they were to testify what they had seen and heard of His resurrection; they were to repeat the gracious words which proceeded from His lips. They were acquainted with His holy character; He was as an angel standing in the sun, yet casting no shadow. It was the sacred work of the apostles to present the spotless character of Christ to men and women, as the standard for their lives. The disciples had been so intimately associated with this **Pattern of holiness** that they were in some degree assimilated to Him in character, and were specially fitted to make known to the world His precepts and example.

The more that the minister of Christ associates with his Master, through contemplation of His life and character, the more closely will he resemble Him, and the better qualified will he be to teach His truths. Every feature in the life of the great Example should be studied with care, and close converse should be held with Him through the prayer of living faith. Thus will the defective human character be transformed into the image of His glorious character. Thus will the teacher of the truth be prepared to lead souls to Christ.—*The Spirit of Prophecy*, vol. 3, pp. 242–244.

Further Reflection: *What aspect of Christ's character should I study and seek to live?*

FRIEND OF THE HELPLESS

Therefore I take pleasure in infirmities, in reproaches, in needs, in persecutions, in distresses, for Christ's sake. For when I am weak, then I am strong.

—2 Corinthians 12:10

"Casting down imaginations, and every high thing that exalteth itself against the knowledge of God, and bringing into captivity every thought to the obedience of Christ." (2 Corinthians 10:5) The first work of those who would reform is, to purify the imagination. If the mind is led out in a vicious direction, it must be restrained to dwell only upon pure and elevated subjects. When tempted to yield to a corrupt imagination, then flee to the throne of grace, and pray for strength from Heaven. In the strength of God the imagination can be disciplined to dwell upon things which are pure and heavenly. . . .

Those who would have that wisdom which is from God, must become fools in the sinful knowledge of this age, in order to be wise. They should shut their eyes, that they may see and learn no evil. They should close their ears, lest they hear that which is evil, and obtain that knowledge which would stain their purity of thoughts and acts. And they should guard their tongues, lest they utter corrupt communications, and guile be found in their mouths.

All are accountable for their actions while upon probation in this world. All have power to control their actions. If they are weak in virtue and purity of thoughts and acts, they can obtain help from the **Friend of the helpless**. Jesus is acquainted with all the weaknesses of human nature, and, if entreated, will give strength to overcome the most powerful temptations. All can obtain this strength if they seek for it in humility. Jesus gives all a blessed invitation who are burdened, and laden with sin, to come to Him, the sinner's friend. "Come unto Me, all ye that labor, and are heavy laden, and I will give you rest. Take My yoke upon you, and learn of Me; for I am meek and lowly in heart; and ye shall find rest unto your souls. For My yoke is easy, and My burden is light." (Matthew 11:28–30)

Here the most inquisitive may safely learn in the school of Christ that which will prove for their present and everlasting good. The uneasy and dissatisfied will here find rest. With their thoughts and affections centered in Christ, they will obtain true wisdom, which will be worth more to them than the richest earthly treasures.—*A Solemn Appeal*, pp. 76–78.

Further Reflection: *How pure are my thoughts? Furthermore, how can I "learn no evil?"*

CONQUERING PRINCE

"I am He who lives, and was dead, and behold, I am alive forevermore. Amen. And I have the keys of Hades and of Death."
—Revelation 1:18

The captives brought up from the graves at the time of the resurrection of Jesus were His trophies as a **conquering Prince**. Thus He attested His victory over death and the grave; thus He gave a pledge and an earnest of the resurrection of all the righteous dead. Those who were called from their graves went into the city, and appeared unto many in their resurrected forms, and testified that Jesus had indeed risen from the dead, and that they had risen with Him. The voice that cried, "It is finished," was heard among the dead. It pierced the walls of sepulchers, and summoned the sleepers to arise. Thus shall it be when God's voice shall be heard shaking the heavens and earth. That voice will penetrate the graves and unbar the tombs. A mighty earthquake will then cause the world to reel to and fro like a drunkard. Then Christ, the King of Glory, shall appear, attended by all the heavenly angels. The trumpet shall sound, and the Life-giver shall call forth the righteous dead to immortal life.

It was well known to the priests and rulers that certain persons who were dead had risen at the resurrection of Jesus. Authentic reports were brought to them of different ones who had seen and conversed with these resurrected ones, and heard their testimony that Jesus, the Prince of life, whom the priests and rulers had slain, was risen from the dead. The false report that the disciples had robbed the sepulcher of the body of their Master was so diligently circulated that very many believed it. But the priests, in manufacturing their false report, overreached themselves, and all thinking persons, not blinded by bigotry, detected the falsehood. . . .

The priests and rulers were in continual dread lest, in walking the streets, or within the privacy of their own homes, they should meet face to face with the resurrected Christ. They felt that there was no safety for them; bolts and bars seemed but poor protection against the risen Son of God.—*The Spirit of Prophecy*, vol. 3, pp. 223–225.

Further Reflection: *How would my spiritual life change if I saw someone whom Jesus had raised from the dead? Am I more moved by spectacular manifestations of Jesus' power or the everyday blessings that He bestows upon me?*

DIVINE HELPER

Bear one another's burdens, and so fulfill the law of Christ.
—Galatians 6:2

The power of love was in all Christ's healing, and only by partaking of that love, through faith, can we be instruments for His work. If we neglect to link ourselves in divine connection with Christ, the current of life-giving energy cannot flow in rich streams from us to the people. There were places where the Saviour Himself could not do many mighty works because of their unbelief. So now unbelief separates the church from her **divine Helper**. Her hold upon eternal realities is weak. By her lack of faith, God is disappointed, and robbed of His glory.

It is in doing Christ's work that the church has the promise of His presence. Go teach all nations, He said; "and, lo, I am with you alway, even unto the end of the world." To take His yoke is one of the first conditions of receiving His power. The very life of the church depends upon her faithfulness in fulfilling the Lord's commission. To neglect this work is surely to invite spiritual feebleness and decay. Where there is no active labor for others, love wanes, and faith grows dim.

Christ intends that His ministers shall be educators of the church in gospel work. They are to teach the people how to seek and save the lost. But is this the work they are doing? Alas, how many are toiling to fan the spark of life in a church that is ready to die! How many churches are tended like sick lambs by those who ought to be seeking for the lost sheep! And all the time millions upon millions without Christ are perishing.

Divine love has been stirred to its unfathomable depths for the sake of humanity, and angels marvel to behold in the recipients of so great love a mere surface gratitude. Heaven stands indignant at the neglect shown to the souls of human beings. Would we know how Christ regards it? How would a father and mother feel, did they know that their child, lost in the cold and the snow, had been passed by, and left to perish, by those who might have saved it? Would they not be terribly grieved, wildly indignant? Would they not denounce those murderers with wrath hot as their tears, intense as their love? The sufferings of every person are the sufferings of God's child, and those who reach out no helping hand to their perishing fellow beings provoke His righteous anger. This is the wrath of the Lamb.—*The Desire of Ages*, p. 825.

Further Reflection: *Do I lack the presence of Jesus because I neglect the work of Jesus?*

MIGHTY GENERAL OF THE ARMIES OF HEAVEN

"I am the LORD, and there is no other; there is no God besides Me."
—Isaiah 45:5

Our Lord is cognizant of the conflict of His people in these last days with the satanic agencies combined with evil men and women who neglect and refuse this great salvation. With the greatest simplicity and candor our Saviour, the **Mighty General of the armies of Heaven**, does not conceal the stern conflict which they will experience. He points out the dangers, He shows us the plan of the battle, and the hard and hazardous work to be done, and then lifts His voice before entering the conflict to count the cost while at the same time He encourages all to take up the weapons of their warfare and expect the heavenly host to compose the armies to war in defense of truth and righteousness.

Humanity's weakness shall find supernatural strength and help in every stern conflict to do the deeds of Omnipotence, and perseverance in faith and perfect trust in God will ensure success. While the vast confederacy of evil is arrayed against them He bids them to be brave and strong and fight valiantly, for they have a heaven to win, and they have more than an angel in their ranks, the mighty General of armies leads on the armies of heaven. As on the occasion of the taking of Jericho, not one of the armies of Israel could boast of exercising their finite strength to overthrow the walls of this city, but the Captain of the Lord's Host planned that battle in the greatest simplicity, that the Lord God alone should receive the glory and human beings should not be exalted. God has promised us all power. "For the promise is unto you and your children, and to all that are afar off, even as many as the Lord our God shall call." (Acts 2:39)

It is not great talent that we want now, it is humble hearts and direct, consecrated, personal effort, watching, praying, working with all perseverance. The sins of the people may seem so offensive to God as to be invincible, but Christ has sent His representative, the Holy Spirit, surrounding His living agents who are employed to pierce the ignorance with the bright beams of the Son of Righteousness. His voice will give assurance, "Lo I am with you alway, even to the end of the world." (Matthew 28:20) The fact is to be ever kept before us, we are carrying forward the warfare in the presence of an invisible world.—Letter 51, 1895.

Further Reflection: *My weakness will find supernatural strength in every stern conflict to do the deeds of Omnipotence. What deeds of Omnipotence do I want to do for God today?*

GREATEST GIFT

But God demonstrates His own love toward us,
in that while we were still sinners, Christ died for us.
—Romans 5:8

A man might pass over the place where treasure had been concealed. In dire necessity he might sit down to rest at the foot of a tree, not knowing of the riches hidden at its roots. So it was with the Jews. As a golden treasure, truth had been entrusted to the Hebrew people. The Jewish economy, bearing the signature of Heaven, had been instituted by Christ Himself. In types and symbols the great truths of redemption were veiled. Yet when Christ came, the Jews did not recognize Him to whom all these symbols pointed. They had the word of God in their hands; but the traditions which had been handed down from generation to generation, and the human interpretation of the Scriptures, hid from them the truth as it is in Jesus. The spiritual import of the sacred writings was lost. The treasure house of all knowledge was open to them, but they knew it not.

God does not conceal His truth from human beings. By their own course of action they make it obscure to themselves. Christ gave the Jewish people abundant evidence that He was the Messiah; but His teaching called for a decided change in their lives. They saw that if they received Christ, they must give up their cherished maxims and traditions, their selfish, ungodly practices. It required a sacrifice to receive changeless, eternal truth. Therefore they would not admit the most conclusive evidence that God could give to establish faith in Christ. They professed to believe the Old Testament Scriptures, yet they refused to accept the testimony contained therein concerning Christ's life and character. They were afraid of being convinced lest they should be converted and be compelled to give up their preconceived opinions. The treasure of the gospel, the Way, the Truth, and the Life, was among them, but they rejected the **greatest gift** that Heaven could bestow.

Among the chief rulers also many believed on Him," we read; "but because of the Pharisees they did not confess Him, lest they should be put out of the synagogue." (John 12:42) They were convinced; they believed Jesus to be the Son of God; but it was not in harmony with their ambitious desires to confess Him.—*Christ's Object Lessons*, pp. 104–106.

Further Reflection: *What am I willing to sacrifice to receive changeless, eternal truth?*

DIVINE MODEL

"I will no longer talk much with you, for the ruler of this world is coming, and he has nothing in Me."

—John 14:30

The "time of trouble, such as never was," is soon to open upon us; and we shall need an experience which we do not now possess and which many are too indolent to obtain. It is often the case that trouble is greater in anticipation than in reality; but this is not true of the crisis before us. The most vivid presentation cannot reach the magnitude of the ordeal. In that time of trial, every soul must stand for himself before God. "Though Noah, Daniel, and Job" were in the land, "as I live, saith the Lord God, they shall deliver neither son nor daughter; they shall but deliver their own souls by their righteousness." (Ezekiel 14:20)

Now, while our great High Priest is making the atonement for us, we should seek to become perfect in Christ. Not even by a thought could our Saviour be brought to yield to the power of temptation. Satan finds in human hearts some point where he can gain a foothold; some sinful desire is cherished, by means of which his temptations assert their power. But Christ declared of Himself: "The prince of this world cometh, and hath nothing in Me." (John 14:30) Satan could find nothing in the Son of God that would enable him to gain the victory. He had kept His Father's commandments, and there was no sin in Him that Satan could use to his advantage. This is the condition in which those must be found who shall stand in the time of trouble.

It is in this life that we are to separate sin from us, through faith in the atoning blood of Christ. Our precious Saviour invites us to join ourselves to Him, to unite our weakness to His strength, our ignorance to His wisdom, our unworthiness to His merits. God's providence is the school in which we are to learn the meekness and lowliness of Jesus. The Lord is ever setting before us, not the way we would choose, which seems easier and pleasanter to us, but the true aims of life. It rests with us to co-operate with the agencies which Heaven employs in the work of conforming our characters to the **divine model**. None can neglect or defer this work but at the most fearful peril to their souls.—*The Great Controversy*, pp. 622, 623.

Further Reflection: *What cherished sin must I give up? How can I unite my weakness in this area of my life with the strength offered by Jesus?*

GIVER OF EVERY GOOD AND PERFECT GIFT

You open Your hand and satisfy the desire of every living thing.
—Psalm 145:16

The tender mercies and loving-kindnesses of the Lord have been toward us all the days of our life, and the whole world should be filled with thankful voices, proclaiming the benevolence and love of God. The psalmist says: "The eyes of all wait upon Thee; and Thou givest them their meat in due season. Thou openest Thine hand, and satisfiest the desire of every living thing." When we were sold under sin, He who was rich in glory, for our sake became poor, that we through His poverty might be rich. Well may we ask our souls, "How much owest thou unto my Lord?" The benevolence of Christ is exercised every day in the year. He gives daily His gifts unto us. His Holy Spirit is constantly at work, drawing the hearts of men and women, guiding them into all truth. Before the crucifixion of Christ, He told His sorrowing disciples that He would send them another Comforter, which should abide with them forever. The grace of Christ is multiplied toward us, and given without stint. The streams of salvation are continually flowing for us.

In view of what Christ has done and is doing for the children of humanity, should we not bring gratitude offerings to Him? Should our gifts flow only to one another, and the **Giver of every good and perfect gift** be forgotten? The Lord has said, "Them that honor Me, I will honor." We should not wait to make an offering to God until we are out of debt. His cause demands the means that He has given to us in trust, and we should present a portion on the altar of God as freely as the infinite sacrifice was made for us. We have no time to lose in passing our treasures on to the bank of heaven. Whatever we may do, let us not forget God. If we love Him with all the heart, we shall remember His claims upon us. God requires that we shall be like Him, that we shall imitate the self-sacrificing example of Christ, and live a life of self-denial. We should prayerfully consider the question, "How much owest thou unto the Lord?"

Are there those who are robbing God in tithes and offerings? Seek to make your accounts straight; do not leave your obligation to God as the last thing to be settled.—*The Signs of the Times*, January 6, 1890.

Further Reflection: *When has God miraculously returned money that I sacrificially gave to His cause? In what other ways does God repay that which we wager for Him?*

TRUE SHEPHERD

"I am the good shepherd. The good shepherd gives His life for the sheep."

—John 10:11

There is a work that must be done for the wealthy, to arouse them to a realization of their relationship to and their accountability to God. They must be awakened to the fact that they are to give an account to Him who shall judge the living and the dead at His appearing and His kingdom. Those who are rich are put under responsibility to labor for others in the love and fear of God. But many of the rich trust in their riches, and do not realize the danger in which they are placed. God has something to give them of vastly more value than gold or silver or precious jewels. The soul needs to be attracted by the things that are of enduring value. They need to understand the value of true goodness. Jesus says unto them, "Come unto Me, all ye that labor and are heavy laden, and I will give you rest." He asks them to exchange the yoke of their own manufacturing for His yoke, which is easy, and for His burden, which is light. He says, "Learn of Me; for I am meek and lowly in heart; and ye shall find rest unto your souls." He is calling: "If any man thirst, let him come unto Me and drink." "Him that cometh unto Me I will in nowise cast out."

Those who will listen to the voice of Christ, will recognize the voice of superior goodness, the voice of the **true Shepherd**. Oh, that the wealthy might feel their responsibility to be faithful stewards of the means which God has entrusted to their care! Oh, that they might understand that they must be agents for God, if they would meet His approval! Oh, that they might know that they were standing upon holy ground, and might be distinguished workers, engaging with Christ in the grand work of elevating those whom Christ died to save! . . .

. . . He [God] has entrusted riches to the wealthy in order that they may bless humanity, by relieving the wants of the suffering and needy. This is the work that has been committed to them, and in doing this work they are not to feel that they have done some wonderful thing. . . .

. . . He does not intend that one shall have all the luxuries of life, and that others shall cry for bread. All the means entrusted to humanity over and above what is required to supply their own necessities, is entrusted to them for the blessing of humanity.—*The Signs of the Times*, July 30, 1894.

Further Reflection: *Do I see wealthy people as possible candidates for heaven whom God has called me to reach, or do I see a group rich with goods and in need of nothing?*

GLORIFIED HEAD

"That the love with which You loved Me may be in them, and I in them."

—John 17:26

Christ declares the mission He had in coming to the earth. He says in His last public prayer, "O righteous Father, the world hath not known Thee: but I have known Thee, and these have known that Thou hast sent Me. And I have declared unto them Thy name, and will declare it; that the love wherewith Thou hast loved Me may be in them, and I in them." (John 17:25, 26) When Moses asked the Lord to show him His glory, the Lord said, "I will make all My goodness pass before thee." (Exodus 33:19) "And the Lord passed by before him, and proclaimed, The Lord, The Lord God, merciful and gracious, long suffering, and abundant in goodness and truth, keeping mercy for thousands, forgiving iniquity and transgression and sin, and that will by no means clear the guilty. . . . And Moses made haste, and bowed his head toward the earth, and worshiped." (Exodus 34:6–8) When we are able to comprehend the character of God as did Moses, we too shall make haste to bow in adoration and praise. Jesus contemplated nothing less than "that the love wherewith Thou hast loved Me" (John 17:26) should be in the hearts of His children, that they might impart the knowledge of God to others.

O what an assurance is this, that the love of God may abide in the hearts of all who believe in Him! O what salvation is provided; for He is able to save unto the uttermost all that come unto God by Him. . . . Those who are partakers of His sufferings here, of His humiliation, enduring for His name's sake, are to have the love of God bestowed upon them as it was upon the Son. One who knows, has said, "The Father Himself loveth you." . . . This love is ours through faith in the Son of God, therefore a connection with Christ means everything to us. We are to be one with Him as He is one with the Father, and then we are beloved by the infinite God as members of the body of Christ, as branches of the living Vine. We are to be attached to the parent stock, and to receive nourishment from the Vine. Christ is our **glorified Head**, and the divine love flowing from the heart of God, rests in Christ, and is communicated to those who have been united to Him. This divine love entering the soul inspires it with gratitude, frees it from its spiritual feebleness, from pride, vanity, and selfishness, and from all that would deform the Christian character.—*Fundamentals of Christian Education*, pp. 177–179.

Further Reflection: *How can I experience divine love if I am disconnected from Christ?*

GOOD SHEPHERD

"And when he brings out his own sheep, he goes before them; and the sheep follow him, for they know his voice."

—John 10:4

Near Bethsaida, at the northern end of the Sea of Galilee, was a lonely region, beautiful with the fresh green of spring, that offered a welcome retreat to Jesus and His disciples. For this place they set out, going in their boat across the lake. Here they could rest, apart from the confusion of the multitude. Here the disciples could listen to the words of Christ, undisturbed by the retorts and accusations of the Pharisees. Here they hoped to enjoy a short season of fellowship in the society of their Lord.

Only a short time did Jesus have alone with His beloved ones, but how precious to them were those few moments. They talked together regarding the work of the gospel and the possibility of making their labor more effective in reaching the people. As Jesus opened to them the treasures of truth, they were vitalized by divine power and inspired with hope and courage.

But soon He was again sought for by the multitude. Supposing that He had gone to His usual place of retirement, the people followed Him thither. His hope to gain even one hour of rest was frustrated. But in the depth of His pure, compassionate heart the **Good Shepherd** of the sheep had only love and pity for these restless, thirsting souls. All day He ministered to their needs, and at evening dismissed them to go to their homes and rest.

In a life wholly devoted to the good of others, the Saviour found it necessary to turn aside from ceaseless activity and contact with human needs, to seek retirement and unbroken communion with His Father. As the throng that had followed Him depart, He goes into the mountains, and there, alone with God, pours out His soul in prayer for these suffering, sinful, needy ones.

When Jesus said to His disciples that the harvest was great and the laborers were few, He did not urge upon them the necessity of ceaseless toil, but bade them, "Pray ye therefore the Lord of the harvest, that He will send forth laborers into His harvest." (Matthew 9:38) To His toil-worn workers today as really as to His first disciples He speaks these words of compassion, "Come ye yourselves apart . . . and rest awhile." —*The Ministry of Healing*, pp. 56–58.

Further Reflection: *Do I sometimes cherish the rest God offers more than His call to labor?*

APRIL 24

ISRAEL'S RULER

Nathanael answered and said to Him, "Rabbi, You are the Son of God! You are the King of Israel!"

—John 1:49

In the Jewish age, all the revealings of God to His people, everything relating to His worship, was closely connected with the sanctuary—with the tabernacle in the wilderness, and afterward with the temple. Here God was worshiped; here the sacrificial offerings were presented before Him. Here was the breastplate of the high priest, set with precious stones, from which messages from Jehovah were received. Here, in the holy of holies, overshadowed by the wings of cherubim, dwelt the perpetual token of the presence of the Holy One, the Creator of the heavens and the earth. Here was the ark of the covenant, containing the tables of the law—the ark which was to Israel the symbol of the divine presence, and the pledge of victory in battle. . . .

All through the pages of sacred history, where the dealings of God with His chosen people are recorded, there are burning traces of the great I AM. Never has He given to the sons of humanity more open manifestations of His power and glory than when He alone was acknowledged as **Israel's Ruler**, and gave the law to His people. Here was a scepter swayed by no human hand; and the stately goings forth of Israel's invisible King were unspeakably grand and awful.

Truly this was a wonderful dispensation, and those who speak derisively of the old Jewish law and the Dark Ages, should remember that they are treading on holy ground. While we rejoice today that our Saviour has appeared on earth, and that the offering for sin typified in the ceremonial law has become a reality, we are not excusable in harboring feelings of disrespect for that period when Christ Himself was the leader of His people. Those who do this may not know what they are doing; but they are showing themselves ignorant both of the Scriptures and of the power of God. They show that they need divine enlightenment, a more intelligent knowledge of God and His word.

The Christ typified in the rites and ceremonies of the Jewish law is the very same Christ that is revealed in the gospel. The clouds that enshrouded His divine form have rolled back; the mists and shades have disappeared; and Jesus, the world's Redeemer, stands revealed.—*The Signs of the Times*, June 3, 1886.

Further Reflection: *Why didn't Jesus simply reveal Himself without types and symbols?*

HEAD OF HUMANITY

He is the image of the invisible God, the firstborn over all creation.
—Colossians 1:15

This is a time when every person in a responsible position, and every member of the church, should bring every feature of his work into close accord with the teachings of the word of God. By untiring vigilance, by fervent prayer, by Christlike words and deeds, we are to show the world what God desires His church to be.

From His high position, Christ, the King of glory, the Majesty of heaven, saw the condition of men and women. He pitied human beings in their weakness and sinfulness, and came to this earth to reveal what God is to humanity. Leaving the royal courts, and clothing His divinity with humanity, He came to the world Himself, in our behalf to work out a perfect character. He did not choose His dwelling among the rich of the earth. He was born in poverty, of lowly parentage, and lived in the despised village of Nazareth. As soon as He was old enough to handle tools, He shared the burden of caring for the family.

Christ humbled Himself to stand at the **Head of humanity**, to meet the temptations and endure the trials that humanity must meet and endure. He must know what humanity has to meet from the fallen foe, that He might know how to succor those who are tempted.

And Christ has been made our Judge. The Father is not the Judge. The angels are not. He who took humanity upon Himself, and in this world lived a perfect life, is to judge us. He only can be our Judge. Will you remember this, brethren? Will you remember it, ministers? Will you remember it, fathers and mothers? Christ took humanity that He might be our Judge. No one of you has been appointed to be a judge of others. It is all that you can do to discipline yourselves. In the name of Christ I entreat you to heed the injunction that He gives you never to place yourselves on the judgment seat. From day to day this message has been sounded in my ears: "Come down from the judgment seat. Come down in humility."

Never was there a time when it was more important that we should deny ourselves and take up the cross daily than now. How much self-denial are we willing to practice?—*Testimony Treasures* vol. 3, pp. 382, 383.

Further Reflection: *What is my cross? What will I pick up today as I follow Christ?*

GREAT BURDEN BEARER

Casting all your care upon Him, for He cares for you.
—1 Peter 5:7

When in trouble, many think they must appeal to some earthly friend, telling him their perplexities, and begging for help. Under trying circumstances unbelief fills their hearts, and the way seems dark. And all the time there stands beside them the mighty Counselor of the ages, inviting them to place their confidence in Him. Jesus, the **great Burden Bearer**, is saying, "Come unto Me, and I will give you rest." Shall we turn from Him to uncertain human beings, who are as dependent upon God as we ourselves are?

You may feel the deficiency of your character and the smallness of your ability in comparison with the greatness of the work. But if you had the greatest intellect ever given to human beings, it would not be sufficient for your work. "Without Me ye can do nothing," says our Lord and Saviour. (John 15:5) The result of all we do rests in the hands of God. Whatever may betide, lay hold upon Him with steady, persevering confidence.

In your business, in companionship for leisure hours, and in alliance for life, let all the associations you form be entered upon with earnest, humble prayer. You will thus show that you honor God, and God will honor you. Pray when you are fainthearted. When you are desponding, close the lips firmly to men and women; do not shadow the path of others; but tell everything to Jesus. Reach up your hands for help. In your weakness lay hold of infinite strength. Ask for humility, wisdom, courage, increase of faith, that you may see light in God's light and rejoice in His love.—*The Ministry of Healing*, pp. 512, 513.

If we will walk humbly with God, if we will work in the spirit of Christ, none of us will carry heavy burdens. We shall lay them upon the Great Burden Bearer. Then we may expect triumphs in the presence of God, in the communion of His love. From the beginning to the end every camp meeting may be a love feast, because God's presence is with His people.

All heaven is interested in our salvation. The angels of God, thousands upon thousands, and ten thousand times ten thousand, are commissioned to minister to those who shall be heirs of salvation. They guard us against evil and press back the powers of darkness that are seeking our destruction.—*Testimonies for the Church*, vol. 6, p. 63.

Further Reflection: *How often do I pray before entering into friendships with others?*

SACRIFICIAL VICTIM

He was led as a lamb to the slaughter, and as a sheep before its shearers is silent, so He opened not His mouth.

—Isaiah 53:7

The Son of God Himself descended from heaven in the garb of humanity that He might give power to men and women, enabling them to be partakers of the divine nature, and to escape the corruption which is in the world through lust. His long human arm encircled the race, while with His divine arm He grasped the throne of the Infinite. By living, not to please Himself, but to please His heavenly Father, by spending His life in work for others, by doing good, and seeking to save suffering humanity, Christ gave practical lessons of self-denial and self-sacrifice.

But Satan, working through disobedient elements, was counterworking the work of God. By one desperate act he determined to cut off every ray of light that was shining amid the moral darkness of the world, and thus cut off the communication coming from the throne of God. He determined to defy God the Father, who sent His Son into the world. This is the heir, said the wicked husbandman; come, let us kill Him, and the inheritance shall be ours. And they crucified the Lord of life and glory.

Before He offered Himself as the **sacrificial Victim**, Christ sought for the most essential and complete gift to bestow upon the world, which would act in His place, and bring the boundless resources of grace within the reach of His followers. "I will pray the Father," He said, "and He shall give you another Comforter, that He may abide with you forever; even the Spirit of truth; whom the world cannot receive, because it seeth Him not, neither knoweth Him; but ye know Him for He dwelleth with you, and shall be in you." (John 14:16, 17)

The striking feature of divine operations is the accomplishment of the greatest work that can be done in our world by very simple means. It is God's plan that every part of His government shall depend on every other part, the whole as a wheel within a wheel, working with entire harmony. He moves upon human forces, causing His Spirit to touch invisible cords, and the vibration rings to the extremity of the universe.

The prince of the power of evil can only be held in check by the power of God in the third person of the Godhead, the Holy Spirit.—Manuscript 22, 1897.

Further Reflection: *What act of self-denial or self-sacrifice will I do today?*

MIGHTY COUNSELOR OF THE AGES

If any of you lacks wisdom, let him ask of God, who gives to all liberally and without reproach, and it will be given to him.

—James 1:5

Do not think that the Christian life is a life free from temptation. Temptations will come to every Christian. Both the Christian and the one who does not accept Christ as his leader will have trials. The difference is that the latter is serving a tyrant, doing his mean drudgery, while the Christian is serving the One who died to give him eternal life. Do not look upon trial as something strange, but as the means by which we are to be purified and strengthened. "Count it all joy when ye fall into divers temptations." James declares, "Knowing this, that the trying of your faith worketh patience."

Our sea will not always be smooth. We shall have storm and tempest. Meeting difficulties is a part of our education, necessary to the formation of a strong, symmetrical character.

In the future life we shall understand things that here greatly perplex us. We shall realize how strong a Helper we had, and how angels of God were commissioned to guard us as we followed the counsel of the Word of God.

To all who receive Him Christ will give power to become the sons of God. He is a present help in every time of need. Let us be ashamed of our wavering faith. Those who are overcome have only themselves to blame for their failure to resist the enemy. All who choose can come to Christ and find the help they need.

The world is enshrouded in the darkness of error. Satan and his angels are urging on their warfare against the truth. We must have help. But the help we need will not come from human beings. We must look to Him who has said, "All power is given unto Me in heaven and in earth," "Lo, I am with you alway, even unto the end of the world."

There stands among you the **mighty Counselor of the ages** inviting you to place your confidence in Him. Shall we turn away from Him to uncertain human beings, who are as wholly dependent on God as we ourselves are?—*The Signs of the Times*, January 3, 1906.

Further Reflection: *If God sometimes uses other people to counsel me, how can I avoid making them my confidants instead of God?*

GREAT CENTER OF ATTRACTION

"And I, if I am lifted up from the earth, will draw all peoples to Myself."
—John 12:32

The third angel's message calls for the presentation of the Sabbath of the fourth commandment, and this truth must be brought before the world; but the **great Center of attraction**, Jesus Christ, must not be left out of the third angel's message. By many who have been engaged in the work for this time, Christ has been made secondary, and theories and arguments have had first place. . . .

A veil has seemed to be before the eyes of many who have labored in the cause, so that when they presented the law, they have not had views of Jesus, and have not proclaimed the fact that, where sin abounded, grace doth much more abound. It is at the cross of Calvary that mercy and truth meet together, where righteousness and peace kiss each other. The sinner must ever look toward Calvary; and with the simple faith of a little child, he must rest in the merits of Christ, accepting His righteousness and believing in His mercy. Laborers in the cause of truth should present the righteousness of Christ, not as new light but as precious light that has for a time been lost sight of by the people. We are to accept Christ as our personal Saviour, and He imputes unto us the righteousness of God in Christ. Let us repeat and make prominent the truth that John has portrayed: "Herein is love, not that we loved God, but that He loved us, and sent His Son to be the propitiation for our sins." (1 John 4:10)

In the love of God has been opened the most marvelous vein of precious truth, and the treasures of the grace of Christ are laid open before the church and the world. "For God so loved the world, that He gave His only begotten Son." (John 3:16) What love is this—what marvelous, unfathomable love—that would lead Christ to die for us while we were yet sinners! What a loss it is to the soul who understands the strong claims of the law, and who yet fails to understand the grace of Christ which doth much more abound! It is true that the law of God reveals the love of God when it is preached as the truth in Jesus; for the gift of Christ to this guilty world must be largely dwelt upon in every discourse. It is no wonder that hearts have not been melted by the truth, when it has been presented in a cold and lifeless manner.—*Selected Messages*, book 1, pp. 383, 384.

Further Reflection: *What does it mean to share biblical truth "as it is in Jesus?"*

DIVINE HEALER

"And he set him on his own animal, brought him to an inn and took care of him."

—Luke 10:34

The spirit of the good Samaritan has not been largely represented in our churches. Many in need of help have been passed by, as the priest and Levite passed by the wounded and bruised stranger who had been left to die by the wayside. The very ones who needed the power of the **divine Healer** to cure their wounds have been left uncared for and unnoticed. Many have acted as if it were enough to know that Satan had his trap all set for a soul, and they could go home and care not for the lost sheep. It is evident that those who manifest such a spirit have not been partakers of the divine nature, but of the attributes of the enemy of God.

Someone must fulfill the commission of Christ; someone must carry on the work which He began to do on earth; and the church has been given this privilege. For this purpose it has been organized. Why, then, have not church members accepted the responsibility? There are those who have seen this great neglect; they have seen the needs of many who are in suffering and want; they have recognized in these poor souls those for whom Christ gave His life, and their hearts have been stirred with pity, every energy has been roused to action. . . . Those who have been engaged in this Christian help work have been doing what the Lord desires to have done, and He has accepted their labors. That which has been done in this line is a work which every Seventh-day Adventist should heartily sympathize with and endorse, and take hold of earnestly. In neglecting this work which is within their own borders, in refusing to bear these burdens, the church is meeting with great loss. . . .

Because of their neglect the Lord has looked with disfavor upon the church. A love of ease and selfish indulgence has been shown by many. Some who have had the privilege of knowing Bible truth have not brought it into the inner sanctuary of the soul. God holds all these accountable for the talents which they have not returned to Him in honest, faithful service in making every effort possible to seek and to save those who were lost.—*Testimonies for the Church*, vol. 6, pp. 294–296.

Further Reflection: *Why does God ask me to care for the lost when I am also struggling to make ends meet? How does helping others help me?*

MAY

GREAT COMMANDER IN HEAVEN AND EARTH

When the enemy comes in like a flood, the Spirit of the LORD will lift up a standard against him.

—Isaiah 59:19

I was shown that God's true people are the salt of the earth and the light of the world. God requires of them continual advancement in the knowledge of the truth, and in the way of holiness. Then will they understand the coming in of Satan, and in the strength of Jesus will resist him. Satan will call to his aid legions of his angels to oppose the advance of even one soul, and, if possible, wrest it from the hand of Christ.

I saw evil angels contending for souls, and angels of God resisting them. . . . Evil angels were corrupting the atmosphere with their poisonous influence, and crowding about these souls to stupefy their sensibilities. Holy angels were anxiously watching and waiting to drive back Satan's host. But it is not the work of good angels to control the minds of human beings against their will. If they yield to the enemy, and make no effort to resist him, then the angels of God can do but little more than hold in check the host of Satan, that they shall not destroy, until further light be given to those in peril, to move them to arouse and look to heaven for help. Jesus will not commission holy angels to extricate those who make no effort to help themselves.

If Satan sees that he is in danger of losing one soul, he will exert himself to the utmost to keep that one. And when the individual is aroused to his danger, and, with distress and fervor, looks to Jesus for strength, Satan fears that he will lose a captive, and he calls a reinforcement of his angels to hedge in the poor soul, and form a wall of darkness around him, that heaven's light may not reach him. But if the one in danger perseveres, and in his helplessness casts himself upon the merits of the blood of Christ, our Saviour listens to the earnest prayer of faith, and sends a reinforcement of those angels that excel in strength to deliver him. . . . At the sound of fervent prayer, Satan's whole host trembles. . . . And when angels, all-powerful, clothed with the armory of heaven, come to the help of the fainting, pursued soul, Satan and his host fall back, well knowing that their battle is lost. . . . And although they hate and war with one another, yet they improve every opportunity. . . . But the **great Commander in heaven and earth** has limited Satan's power.—*Testimonies for the Church*, vol. 1, pp. 345, 346.

Further Reflection: *Have I brought my all to the battle with Satan? Have I resisted him?*

CROWN OF REJOICING

And not only that, but we also rejoice in God through our Lord Jesus Christ, through whom we have now received the reconciliation.

—Romans 5:11

As Moses lifted up the serpent in the wilderness," even so was "the Son of man lifted up: that whosoever believeth in Him should not perish, but have eternal life." (John 3:14, 15) If you are conscious of your sins, do not devote all your powers to mourning over them, but look and live. Jesus is our only Saviour; and although millions who need to be healed will reject His offered mercy, not one who trusts in His merits will be left to perish. While we realize our helpless condition without Christ, we must not be discouraged; we must rely upon a crucified and risen Saviour. Poor, sin-sick, discouraged soul, look and live. Jesus has pledged His word; He will save all who come unto Him.

Come to Jesus, and receive rest and peace. You may have the blessing even now. Satan suggests that you are helpless and cannot bless yourself. It is true; you are helpless. But lift up Jesus before him: "I have a risen Saviour. In Him I trust, and He will never suffer me to be confounded. In His name I triumph. He is my righteousness and my **crown of rejoicing**." Let no one here feel that his case is hopeless, for it is not. You may see that you are sinful and undone, but it is just on this account that you need a Saviour. If you have sins to confess, lose no time. These moments are golden. "If we confess our sins, He is faithful and just to forgive us our sins, and to cleanse us from all unrighteousness." (1 John 1:9) Those who hunger and thirst after righteousness will be filled, for Jesus has promised it. Precious Saviour! His arms are open to receive us, and His great heart of love is waiting to bless us.

Some seem to feel that they must be on probation and must prove to the Lord that they are reformed, before they can claim His blessing. But these dear souls may claim the blessing even now. They must have His grace, the Spirit of Christ, to help their infirmities, or they cannot form a Christian character. Jesus loves to have us come to Him, just as we are—sinful, helpless, dependent.—*Selected Messages*, book 1, pp. 352, 353.

Further Reflection: *How can I experience the joy of rejoicing in Jesus today, even as I hunger and thirst for righteousness?*

WATCHER WHO NEVER SLUMBERS

Behold, He who keeps Israel shall neither slumber nor sleep.
—Psalm 121:4

God has not been unmindful of the good deeds, the self-denying acts, of the church in the past. All are registered on high. But these are not enough. These will not save the church when she ceases to fulfill her mission. Unless the cruel neglect and indifference manifested in the past shall cease, the church, instead of going from strength to strength, will continue to degenerate into weakness and formality. Shall we let this be? Is the dull torpor, the mournful deterioration in love and spiritual zeal, which exists today, to be perpetuated? Is this the condition in which Christ is to find His church?

Brethren, your own lamps will surely flicker and become dim, until they go out in darkness, unless you shall make decided efforts to reform. "Remember therefore from whence thou art fallen, and repent, and do thy first works." The opportunity now presented may be short. If this season of grace and repentance passes unimproved, the warning is given, "I will come unto thee quickly, and will remove thy candlestick out of his place." These words are uttered by the long-suffering, forbearing One. They are a solemn warning to churches and to individuals, that the **Watcher who never slumbers** is measuring their course of action. It is only by reason of His marvelous patience that they are not cut down as cumberers of the ground. But His Spirit will not always strive. His patience will wait but little longer.

At the last day the final decision by the Judge of all the earth will turn upon our interest in, and practical labor for, the needy, the oppressed, the tempted. You cannot always pass these by on the other side, and yourselves find entrance as redeemed sinners into the city of God. "Inasmuch," says Christ, "as ye did it not unto one of the least of these, ye did it not to me."

But it is not yet too late to redeem the neglects of the past. Let there be a revival of the first love, the first ardor. Search out the ones you have driven away; bind up by confession the wounds you have made. Come close to the great Heart of pitying love, and let the current of that divine compassion flow into your heart, and from you into the hearts of others.—*Review and Herald*, November 30, 1886.

Further Reflection: *Is there anything preventing you from witnessing to those whom you see from day to day?*

COMPLETE SAVIOUR

For in Him dwells all the fullness of the Godhead bodily; and you are complete in Him, who is the head of all principality and power.
—Colossians 2:9, 10

How are you to know that you are accepted of God? Study His word prayerfully. Lay it not aside for any other book. This Book convinces of sin. It plainly reveals the way of salvation. It brings to view a bright and glorious reward. It reveals to you a **complete Saviour**, and teaches you that through His boundless mercy alone can you expect salvation. Do not neglect secret prayer, for it is the soul of religion. With earnest, fervent prayer, plead for purity of soul. Plead as earnestly, as eagerly, as you would for your mortal life, were it at stake. Remain before God until unutterable longings are begotten within you for salvation, and the sweet evidence is obtained of pardoned sin.

Jesus has not left you to be amazed at the trials and difficulties you meet. He has told you all about them, and He has told you also not to be cast down and oppressed when trials come. Look to Jesus, your Redeemer, and be cheerful and rejoice. The trials hardest to bear are those that come from our brethren, our own familiar friends; but even these trials may be borne with patience. Jesus is not lying in Joseph's new tomb. He has risen and has ascended to heaven, there to intercede in our behalf. We have a Saviour who so loved us that He died for us, that through Him we might have hope and strength and courage, and a place with Him upon His throne. He is able and willing to help you whenever you call upon Him.

Do you feel your insufficiency for the position of trust that you occupy? Thank God for this. The more you feel your weakness, the more you will be inclined to seek for a helper. "Draw nigh to God, and He will draw nigh to you." (James 4:8) Jesus wants you to be happy, to be cheerful. He wants you to do your best with the ability that God has given you and then trust the Lord to help you and to raise up those who will be your helpers in carrying burdens.—*Counsels for the Church*, pp. 55, 56.

Further Reflection: *How can I be more thankful when I go through difficulties and trials? How can I encourage someone today who is experiencing a difficult time?*

DIVINE SUFFERER

The chastisement for our peace was upon Him,
and by His stripes we are healed.

—Isaiah 53:5

As humanity's substitute and surety, the iniquity of men and women was laid upon Christ; He was counted a transgressor that He might redeem them from the curse of the law. The guilt of every descendant of Adam of every age was pressing upon His heart; and the wrath of God, and the terrible manifestation of His displeasure because of iniquity, filled the soul of His Son with consternation. The withdrawal of the divine countenance from the Saviour, in this hour of supreme anguish, pierced His heart with a sorrow that can never be fully understood by humanity. Every pang endured by the Son of God upon the cross, the blood drops that flowed from His head, His hands, and feet, the convulsions of agony which racked His frame, and the unutterable anguish that filled His soul at the hiding of His Father's face from Him, speak to men and women, saying, "It is for love of thee that the Son of God consents to have these heinous crimes laid upon Him; for thee He spoils the domain of death, and opens the gates of Paradise and immortal life. He who stilled the angry waves by His word, and walked the foam-capped billows, who made devils tremble, and disease flee from His touch, who raised the dead to life and opened the eyes of the blind—offers Himself upon the cross as the last sacrifice for humanity. . . .

Satan, with his fierce temptations, wrung the heart of Jesus. Sin, so hateful to His sight, was heaped upon Him till He groaned beneath its weight. No wonder that His humanity trembled in that fearful hour. Angels witnessed with amazement the despairing agony of the Son of God, so much greater than His physical pain that the latter was hardly felt by Him. . . .

Inanimate nature expressed a sympathy with its insulted and dying Author. The sun refused to look upon the awful scene. Its full, bright rays were illuminating the earth at midday, when suddenly it seemed to be blotted out. . . . The dense blackness was an emblem of the soul-agony and horror that encompassed the Son of God. He had felt it in the garden of Gethsemane, when from His pores were forced drops of blood, and where He would have died had not an angel been sent from the courts of Heaven to invigorate the **divine sufferer**, that He might tread His blood-stained path to Calvary.—*The Spirit of Prophecy*, vol. 3, pp. 162–164.

Further Reflection: *What more must Jesus suffer to convince me to surrender to Him?*

GREAT INTERCESSOR

"I have prayed for you, that your faith should not fail."
—Luke 22:32

Who can estimate the result of the prayers of the world's Redeemer? When Christ shall see of the travail of His soul and shall be satisfied, then will be seen and realized the value of His earnest prayers while His divinity was veiled with humanity.

Jesus pleaded, not for one only, but for all His disciples: "Father, I will that they also whom Thou hast given Me, be with Me where I am." His eye pierced the dark veil of the future and read the life history of every son and daughter of Adam. He felt the burdens and sorrows of every tempest-tossed soul, and that earnest prayer included with His living disciples all His followers to the close of time. "Neither pray I for these alone, but for them also which shall believe on Me through their word." Yes; that prayer of Christ embraces even us. We should be comforted by the thought that we have a **great intercessor** in the heavens, presenting our petitions before God. "If any man sin, we have an advocate with the Father, Jesus Christ the righteous." In the hour of greatest need, when discouragement would overwhelm the soul, it is then that the watchful eye of Jesus sees that we need His help. The hour of humanity's necessity is the hour of God's opportunity. When all human support fails, then Jesus comes to our aid, and His presence scatters the darkness and lifts the cloud of gloom.

In their little boat upon the Sea of Galilee, amid the storm and darkness, the disciples toiled hard to reach the shore, but found all their efforts unsuccessful. As despair seized them, Jesus was seen walking upon the foam-capped billows. Even the presence of Christ they did not at first discern, and their terror increased, until His voice, saying, "It is I; be not afraid," dispelled their fears and gave them hope and joy. Then how willingly the poor, wearied disciples ceased their efforts and trusted all to the Master.

This striking incident illustrates the experience of the followers of Christ. How often do we tug at the oars, as though our own strength and wisdom were sufficient, until we find our efforts useless. . . . Our compassionate Redeemer pities our weakness; and when, in answer to the cry of faith, He takes up the work we ask Him to do, how easily He accomplishes that which seemed to us so difficult.—*Testimonies for the Church*, vol. 4, pp. 529, 530.

Further Reflection: *What do you need Jesus to pray for today on your behalf?*

CARETAKER

By this we know love, because He laid down His life for us. And we also ought to lay down our lives for the brethren.
—1 John 3:16

The Son of man came not to be ministered unto, but to minister, and to give His life a ransom for many." Among His disciples Christ was in every sense a **caretaker**, a burden bearer. He shared their poverty, He practiced self-denial on their account, He went before them to smooth the more difficult places, and soon He would consummate His work on earth by laying down His life. The principle on which Christ acted is to actuate the members of the church which is His body. The plan and ground of salvation is love. In the kingdom of Christ those are greatest who follow the example He has given, and act as shepherds of His flock.

The words of Paul reveal the true dignity and honor of the Christian life: "Though I be free from all men, yet have I made myself servant unto all," "not seeking mine own profit, but the profit of many, that they may be saved." (1 Corinthians 9:19; 10:33)

In matters of conscience the soul must be left untrammeled. No one is to control another's mind, to judge for another, or to prescribe his duty. God gives to every soul freedom to think, and to follow his own convictions. "Every one of us shall give account of himself to God." No one has a right to merge his own individuality in that of another. In all matters where principle is involved, "let every man be fully persuaded in his own mind." (Romans 14:12, 5) In Christ's kingdom there is no lordly oppression, no compulsion of manner. The angels of heaven do not come to the earth to rule, and to exact homage, but as messengers of mercy, to co-operate with human beings in uplifting humanity.

The principles and the very words of the Saviour's teaching, in their divine beauty, dwelt in the memory of the beloved disciple. To his latest days the burden of John's testimony to the churches was, "This is the message that ye heard from the beginning, that we should love one another." "Hereby perceive we the love of God, because He laid down His life for us: and we ought to lay down our lives for the brethren." (1 John 3:11, 16)—*The Desire of Ages*, pp. 550, 551.

Further Reflection: *Jesus practiced a love that always sought to uplift the lost. Does my love for Jesus lift anyone other than myself?*

UNERRING PATTERN

Blessed is every one who fears the LORD, who walks in His ways.
—Psalm 128:1

If there was ever a people in need of constantly increasing light from heaven, it is the people that, in this time of peril, God has called to be the depositaries of His holy law and to vindicate His character before the world. Those to whom has been committed a trust so sacred must be spiritualized, elevated, vitalized, by the truths they profess to believe.

The Lord is now dealing with His people who believe present truth. He designs to bring about momentous results, and while in His providence He is working toward this end, He says to His people: "Go forward." True, the path is not yet opened; but when they move on in the strength of faith and courage, God will make the way plain before their eyes. There are ever those who will complain, as did ancient Israel, and charge the difficulties of their position upon those whom God has raised up for the special purpose of advancing His cause. They fail to see that God is testing them by bringing them into strait places, from which there is no deliverance except by His hand.

There are times when the Christian life seems beset by dangers, and duty seems hard to perform. The imagination pictures impending ruin before, and bondage or death behind. Yet the voice of God speaks clearly above all discouragements: "Go forward." We should obey this command, let the result be what it may, even though our eyes cannot penetrate the darkness and though we feel the cold waves about our feet.

In a divided, halfhearted life, you will find doubt and darkness. You cannot enjoy the consolations of religion, neither the peace which the world gives. Do not sit down in Satan's easy chair of do-little, but arise, and aim at the elevated standard which it is your privilege to attain. It is a blessed privilege to give up all for Christ. Look not at the lives of others and imitate them and rise no higher. You have only one true, **unerring Pattern**. It is safe to follow Jesus only.—*Counsels for the Church*, pp. 345, 346.

Further Reflection: *How many of my doubts are the result of a failure to enlist fully in the cause of God? What assurances are missed by failing to go forward with Christ?*

DIVINE COUNSELOR

"Prepare the way of the Lord; make His paths straight."
—Mark 1:3

The whole treasures of heaven are at our hand for the work of preparing the way of the Lord. Providence has prepared sufficient power in the universe of heavenly agencies to make the missionary work a wonderful success, if human agencies will qualify and fully equip themselves for the great work. Our success thus far has been fully proportioned to our efforts. God lays every soul who claims to believe in Jesus under tribute to employ his capabilities in His service.

There is no need of despondency, of vain apprehension, if those who have an experience in and a knowledge of the truth will keep themselves beneath the bright beams of the Sun of Righteousness, for the Lord is gracious and the prayer of Christ for His disciples was that they may be one as He was one with the Father. "That the world may believe that Thou hast sent Me. And the glory which Thou gavest Me I have given them; that they may be one, even as We are one." (John 17:21, 22) . . .

There will be an accumulation of divine agencies to combine with human effort that there may be the accomplishment of the work for the last time. The work will most assuredly be cut short in a most unexpected manner. . . .

The accessions to the truth will be of a rapidity which will surprise the church. God's name alone will be glorified. Finite human beings will wonder and adore. The church is now highly privileged to bear a vigorous part as active agents with heavenly instrumentalities. Every Christian now should become men and women of intercession with God. They will evidence how much they love Jesus and the soul that He has purchased with His own blood.

Men and women in the church are privileged with the golden opportunity now to obtain an experience higher and holier, beautified with the attributes of Christ. . . . He must be their **divine Counselor**, and there must be by the church as a whole and by its individual members a spirit of intercession and wrestling with our covenant-keeping God in behalf of themselves and also for the watchmen on the walls of Zion and the workers in the cause of God, that they may be clothed with the garments of salvation and may have at this time power to prevail with God, that many souls may be the fruits of their ministry.—Letter 43a, 1890.

Further Reflection: *What will I do today to help lead someone to Christ?*

THE ROOT AND THE OFFSPRING OF DAVID

"I, Jesus, have sent My angel to testify to you these things in the churches. I am the Root and the Offspring of David, the Bright and Morning Star."

—Revelation 22:16

The third angel's message is to be given with power. The power of the proclamation of the first and second messages is to be intensified in the third. In the Revelation John says of the heavenly messenger who unites with the third angel: "I saw another angel come down from heaven, having great power; and the earth was lightened with His glory. And He cried mightily with a strong voice." (Revelation 18:1, 2) We are in danger of giving the third angel's message in so indefinite a manner that it does not impress the people. So many other interests are brought in that the very message which should be proclaimed with power becomes tame and voiceless. At our camp meetings a mistake has been made. The Sabbath question has been touched upon, but has not been presented as the great test for this time. While the churches profess to believe in Christ, they are violating the law which Christ Himself proclaimed from Sinai. The Lord bids us: "Show My people their transgression, and the house of Jacob their sins." (Isaiah 58:1) The trumpet is to give a certain sound. . . .

Our message is a life-and-death message, and we must let it appear as it is, the great power of God. We are to present it in all its telling force. Then the Lord will make it effectual. . . .

The perils of the last days are upon us, and in our work we are to warn the people of the danger they are in. Let not the solemn scenes which prophecy has revealed be left untouched. If our people were half awake, if they realized the nearness of the events portrayed in the Revelation, a reformation would be wrought in our churches, and many more would believe the message. We have no time to lose; God calls upon us to watch for souls as they that must give an account. Advance new principles, and crowd in the clear-cut truth. It will be as a sword cutting both ways. But be not too ready to take a controversial attitude. There will be times when we must stand still and see the salvation of God. Let Daniel speak, let the Revelation speak, and tell what is truth. But whatever phase of the subject is presented, uplift Jesus as the center of all hope, "**the Root and the Offspring of David**, and the bright and morning Star." (Revelation 22:16)—*Testimonies for the Church*, vol. 6, pp. 60–62.

Further Reflection: *Do I share the third angel's message with people I know?*

GREAT PHYSICIAN

Then Jesus went about all the cities and villages, teaching in their synagogues, preaching the gospel of the kingdom, and healing every sickness and every disease among the people.

—Matthew 9:35

Christ's servants are to follow His example. As He went from place to place, He comforted the suffering and healed the sick. Then He placed before them the great truths in regard to His kingdom. This is the work of His followers. As you relieve the sufferings of the body, you will find ways for ministering to the wants of the soul. You can point to the uplifted Saviour, and tell of the love of the **great Physician**, who alone has power to restore.

Tell the poor desponding ones who have gone astray that they need not despair. Though they have erred, and have not been building a right character, God has joy to restore them, even the joy of His salvation. He delights to take apparently hopeless material, those through whom Satan has worked, and make them the subjects of His grace. He rejoices to deliver them from the wrath which is to fall upon the disobedient. Tell them there is healing, cleansing for every soul. . . .

Those who go into the byways and hedges will find others of a widely different character, who need their ministry. There are those who are living up to all the light they have, and are serving God the best they know how. But they realize that there is a great work to be done for themselves and for those about them. . . . They are praying with tears that God will send them the blessing which by faith they discern afar off. In the midst of the wickedness of the great cities many of these souls are to be found. Many of them are in very humble circumstances, and because of this they are unnoticed by the world. There are many of whom ministers and churches know nothing. But in lowly, miserable places they are the Lord's witnesses. They may have had little light and few opportunities for Christian training, but in the midst of nakedness, hunger, and cold they are seeking to minister to others. Let the stewards of the manifold grace of God seek out these souls, visit their homes, and through the power of the Holy Spirit minister to their needs. Study the Bible with them and pray with them with that simplicity which the Holy Spirit inspires. Christ will give His servants a message that will be as the bread of heaven to the soul.—*Christ's Object Lessons*, pp. 233–235.

Further Reflection: *How can I "see" those in my community who are yearning for truth?*

CAPTAIN OF OUR SALVATION

"Be strong and of good courage, do not fear nor be afraid of them; for the LORD your God, He is the One who goes with you. He will not leave you nor forsake you."
—Deuteronomy 31:6

In vision I saw two armies in terrible conflict. One army was led by banners bearing the world's insignia; the other was led by the blood-stained banner of Prince Emmanuel. Standard after standard was left to trail in the dust, as company after company from the Lord's army joined the foe, and tribe after tribe from the ranks of the enemy united with the commandment-keeping people of God. An angel flying in the midst of heaven put the standard of Emmanuel into many hands, while a mighty general cried out with a loud voice: "Come into line. Let those who are loyal to the commandments of God and the testimony of Christ now take their position. Come out from among them, and be ye separate, and touch not the unclean, and I will receive you, and will be a Father unto you, and ye shall be My sons and daughters. Let all who will, come up to the help of the Lord, to the help of the Lord against the mighty."

The battle raged. Victory alternated from side to side. Now the soldiers of the cross gave way, "as when a standard-bearer fainteth." (Isaiah 10:18) But their apparent retreat was but to gain a more advantageous position. Shouts of joy were heard. A song of praise to God went up, and angel voices united in the song, as Christ's soldiers planted His banner on the walls of fortresses till then held by the enemy. The **Captain of our salvation** was ordering the battle, and sending support to His soldiers. His power was mightily displayed, encouraging them to press the battle to the gates. He taught them terrible things in righteousness as He led them on step by step, conquering and to conquer.

At last the victory was gained. The army following the banner with the inscription, "The commandments of God, and the faith of Jesus," was gloriously triumphant. The soldiers of Christ were close beside the gates of the city, and with joy the city received her King. The kingdom of peace and joy and everlasting righteousness was established.—*Christian Experience and Teachings of Ellen G. White*, pp. 228, 229.

Further Reflection: *How does it feel to know that Jesus is leading me in my battle against the enemy of my soul? How can I make His efforts on my behalf effectual?*

HEAVENLY MESSENGER

And He said, "Let Me go, for the day breaks."
But he said, "I will not let You go unless You bless me!"
—Genesis 32:26

Jacob's experience during that night of wrestling and anguish represents the trial through which the people of God must pass just before Christ's second coming. The prophet Jeremiah, in holy vision looking down to this time, said, "We have heard a voice of trembling, of fear, and not of peace. . . . All faces are turned into paleness. Alas! for that day is great, so that none is like it: it is even the time of Jacob's trouble; but he shall be saved out of it." (Jeremiah 30:5–7)

When Christ shall cease His work as Mediator in humanity's behalf, then this time of trouble will begin. Then the case of every soul will have been decided, and there will be no atoning blood to cleanse from sin. When Jesus leaves His position as humanity's intercessor before God, the solemn announcement is made, "He that is unjust, let him be unjust still: and he which is filthy, let him be filthy still: and he that is righteous, let him be righteous still: and he that is holy, let him be holy still." (Revelation 22:11) Then the restraining Spirit of God is withdrawn from the earth. As Jacob was threatened with death by his angry brother, so the people of God will be in peril from the wicked who are seeking to destroy them. And as the patriarch wrestled all night for deliverance from the hand of Esau, so the righteous will cry to God day and night for deliverance from the enemies that surround them.

Satan had accused Jacob before the angels of God, claiming the right to destroy him because of his sin; he had moved upon Esau to march against him; and during the patriarch's long night of wrestling, Satan endeavored to force upon him a sense of his guilt, in order to discourage him, and break his hold upon God. When in his distress Jacob laid hold of the Angel, and made supplication with tears, the **heavenly Messenger**, in order to try his faith, also reminded him of his sin, and endeavored to escape from him. But Jacob would not be turned away. He had learned that God is merciful, and he cast himself upon His mercy. He pointed back to his repentance for his sin, and pleaded for deliverance. As he reviewed his life, he was driven almost to despair; but he held fast the Angel, and with earnest, agonizing cries urged his petition until he prevailed.—*Patriarchs and Prophets*, pp. 201, 202.

Further Reflection: *What am I wrestling with Jesus about right now in my life?*

MASTER WORKMAN

"Go out into the highways and hedges, and compel them to come in, that my house may be filled."

—Luke 14:23

Those who in response to the call of the hour have entered the service of the **Master Workman** may well study His methods of labor. During His earthly ministry the Saviour took advantage of the opportunities to be found along the great thoroughfares of travel. It was at Capernaum that Jesus dwelt at the intervals of His journeys to and fro, and it came to be known as "His own city." This city was well adapted to be the center of the Saviour's work. Being on the highway from Damascus to Jerusalem and Egypt, and to the Mediterranean Sea, it was a great thoroughfare of travel. People from many lands passed through the city or tarried for rest on their journeyings to and fro. Here Jesus could meet all nations and all ranks, the rich and great, as well as the poor and lowly; and His lessons would be carried to other countries and into many households. . . .

In these days of travel the opportunities for coming in contact with men and women of all classes and of many nationalities are much greater than in the days of Israel. The thoroughfares of travel have multiplied a thousand-fold. God has wonderfully prepared the way. The agency of the printing press, with its manifold facilities, is at our command. Bibles, and publications in many languages, setting forth the truth for this time, are at our hand and can be swiftly carried to every part of the world.

Christians who are living in the great centers of commerce and travel have special opportunities. Believers in these cities can work for God in the neighborhood of their homes.

In the world-renowned health resorts and centers of tourist traffic, crowded with many thousands of seekers after health and pleasure, there should be stationed ministers and canvassers capable of arresting the attention of the multitudes. Let these workers watch their chance for presenting the message for this time, and hold meetings as they have opportunity. Let them be quick to seize opportunities to speak to the people. Accompanied by the power of the Holy Spirit . . . the word of God is to be presented with clearness and power, that those who have ears to hear may hear the truth.—*Testimonies for the Church*, vol. 9, pp. 121, 122.

Further Reflection: *How can the Holy Spirit empower me to work as Jesus did?*

SUPPORTER OF ETERNAL, SPIRITUAL LIFE

And they were astonished at His teaching,
for His word was with authority.

—Luke 4:32

Verily, verily, I say unto you," Christ said, "Ye seek Me, not because ye saw the miracle, but because ye did eat of the loaves, and were filled. Labour not for the meat that perisheth, but for that meat which endureth unto everlasting life, which the Son of man shall give unto you; for Him hath the Father sealed. Then said they unto Him, What shall we do, that we might work the works of God? Jesus answered and said unto them, This is the work of God, That ye believe on Him whom He hath sent." (John 6:26–29)

He assured them that Moses gave them not the bread from heaven. "My Father," He said, "giveth you the true bread from heaven. For the bread of God is He which cometh down from heaven, and giveth life unto the world." (Verses 32, 33)

We have the result of this plain discourse. What was it? They would not receive the truth. They refused to hear and turned away from Christ. And their rejection of Christ, the Bread of life, was, to them, a final rejection of the truth. They walked no more with Him.

"I am the Bread of Life," the author, nourisher, and **supporter of eternal, spiritual life**. In the thirty-fifth verse of the sixth chapter of John, Christ represents Himself under the similitude of heavenly bread. To eat His flesh and to drink His blood means to receive Him as a heaven-sent teacher. Belief in Him is essential to spiritual life. Those who feast on the Word never hunger, never thirst, never desire any higher or more exalted good. "In righteousness shalt thou be established; thou shalt be far from oppression; for thou shalt not fear; and from terror; for it shall not come near thee. Behold, they shall surely gather together but not by Me; whosoever shall gather together against thee shall fall for thy sake. . . . No weapon that is formed against thee shall prosper, and every tongue that shall rise against thee in judgment thou shalt condemn. This is the heritage of the servants of the Lord, and their righteousness is of Me, saith the Lord." (Isaiah 54:14, 15, 17)—Manuscript 81, 1906.

Further Reflection: *What is the eternal, spiritual life that Christ is seeking to nourish now in my life?*

YOUNG GALILEAN

Now so it was that after three days they found Him in the temple, sitting in the midst of the teachers, both listening to them and asking them questions.

—Luke 2:46

It was the last day of Christ's teaching in the temple. Of the vast throngs that were gathered at Jerusalem, the attention of all had been attracted to Him; the people had crowded the temple courts, watching the contest that had been in progress, and they eagerly caught every word that fell from His lips. Never before had such a scene been witnessed. There stood the **young Galilean**, bearing no earthly honor or royal badge. Surrounding Him were priests in their rich apparel, rulers with robes and badges significant of their exalted station, and scribes with scrolls in their hands, to which they made frequent reference. Jesus stood calmly before them, with the dignity of a king. As one invested with the authority of heaven, He looked unflinchingly upon His adversaries, who had rejected and despised His teachings, and who thirsted for His life. They had assailed Him in great numbers, but their schemes to ensnare and condemn Him had been in vain. Challenge after challenge He had met, presenting the pure, bright truth in contrast to the darkness and errors of the priests and Pharisees. He had set before these leaders their real condition, and the retribution sure to follow persistence in their evil deeds. The warning had been faithfully given. Yet another work remained for Christ to do. Another purpose was still to be accomplished.

The interest of the people in Christ and His work had steadily increased. They were charmed with His teaching, but they were also greatly perplexed. They had respected the priests and rabbis for their intelligence and apparent piety. In all religious matters they had ever yielded implicit obedience to their authority. Yet they now saw these men trying to cast discredit upon Jesus, a teacher whose virtue and knowledge shone forth the brighter from every assault. They looked upon the lowering countenances of the priests and elders, and there saw discomfiture and confusion. They marveled that the rulers would not believe on Jesus, when His teachings were so plain and simple. They themselves knew not what course to take. With eager anxiety they watched the movements of those whose counsel they had always followed.—*The Desire of Ages*, pp. 610, 611.

Further Reflection: *How is my faith in Jesus affected by the actions of spiritual leaders?*

GREAT MASTER WORKER

Then I went down to the potter's house, and there he was, making something at the wheel.

—Jeremiah 18:3

It is because God is leading them that these things come upon them. Trials and obstacles are the Lord's chosen methods of discipline and His appointed conditions of success. He who reads the hearts of human beings knows their characters better than they themselves know them. He sees that some have powers and susceptibilities which, rightly directed, might be used in the advancement of His work. In His providence He brings these persons into different positions and varied circumstances that they may discover in their character the defects which have been concealed from their own knowledge. He gives them opportunity to correct these defects and to fit themselves for His service. Often He permits the fires of affliction to assail them that they may be purified.

The fact that we are called upon to endure trial shows that the Lord Jesus sees in us something precious which He desires to develop. If He saw in us nothing whereby He might glorify His name, He would not spend time in refining us. He does not cast worthless stones into His furnace. It is valuable ore that He refines. The blacksmith puts the iron and steel into the fire that he may know what manner of metal they are. The Lord allows His chosen ones to be placed in the furnace of affliction to prove what temper they are of and whether they can be fashioned for His work.

The potter takes the clay and molds it according to his will. He kneads it and works it. He tears it apart and presses it together. He wets it and then dries it. He lets it lie for a while without touching it. When it is perfectly pliable, he continues the work of making of it a vessel. He forms it into shape and on the wheel trims and polishes it. He dries it in the sun and bakes it in the oven. Thus it becomes a vessel fit for use. So the **great Master Worker** desires to mold and fashion us. And as the clay is in the hands of the potter, so are we to be in His hands. We are not to try to do the work of the potter. Our part is to yield ourselves to be molded by the Master Worker.—*The Ministry of Healing,* pp. 471, 472.

Further Reflection: *How have I delayed the completion of my vessel by removing myself from the hands of the Great Master Worker?*

FOUNDATION STONE

"He is the Rock, His work is perfect;
For all His ways are justice,
A God of truth and without injustice;
Righteous and upright is He."

—Deuteronomy 32:4

Carried down in prophetic vision to the first advent, the prophet is shown that Christ is to bear trials and tests of which the treatment of the chief cornerstone in the temple of Solomon was symbolic. . . .

In infinite wisdom, God chose the **foundation stone**, and laid it Himself. He called it "a sure foundation." The entire world may lay upon it their burdens and griefs; it can endure them all. With perfect safety they may build upon it. Christ is a "tried stone." Those who trust in Him, He never disappoints. He has borne every test. He has endured the pressure of Adam's guilt, and the guilt of his posterity, and has come off more than conqueror of the powers of evil. He has borne the burdens cast upon Him by every repenting sinner. In Christ the guilty heart has found relief. He is the sure foundation. All who make Him their dependence rest in perfect security.

In Isaiah's prophecy, Christ is declared to be both a sure foundation and a stone of stumbling. The apostle Peter, writing by inspiration of the Holy Spirit, clearly shows to whom Christ is a foundation stone, and to whom a rock of offense:

"If so be ye have tasted that the Lord is gracious. To whom coming, as unto a living stone, disallowed indeed of men, but chosen of God, and precious, ye also, as lively stones, are built up a spiritual house, an holy priesthood, to offer up spiritual sacrifices, acceptable to God by Jesus Christ. Wherefore also it is contained in the Scripture, Behold, I lay in Zion a chief cornerstone, elect, precious: and he that believeth on Him shall not be confounded. Unto you therefore which believe He is precious: but unto them which be disobedient, the stone which the builders disallowed, the same is made the head of the corner, and a stone of stumbling, and a rock of offense, even to them which stumble at the word, being disobedient." (1 Peter 2:3–8)

To those who believe, Christ is the sure foundation. These are they who fall upon the Rock and are broken.—*The Desire of Ages*, pp. 598, 599.

Further Reflection: *Jesus is a sure foundation for all who fall upon the Rock and are broken, but what happens if I choose not to be broken? (Matthew 21:44)*

ROCK OF OUR SALVATION

"Trust in the LORD forever, for in YAH, the LORD, is everlasting strength."
—Isaiah 26:4

God will again move mightily upon chosen servants to make terrible charges upon the hosts of Satan. The people whom He will accept to carry forward His work, to fight His battles, must be people of principle, brave and firm and true. The customs, traditions, and doctrines, even of professedly great and good people, must have no weight, until first brought to the infallible test of the law and the testimony. "If they speak not according to this word, it is because there is no light in them." To this test, popes and prelates refused to submit, knowing that it would overthrow at once all their pretended power. It was to maintain this great truth that Luther battled so firmly and fearlessly. His words echo down the line to all the tried and tempted defenders of the truth—stand fast. "In the Lord Jehovah is everlasting strength."

The Reformer found in Christ a hiding-place from the storms of opposition, wrath, and hatred that threatened to overwhelm him. In Christ alone was peace and strength and security. Such will be the experience of every Christian. Amid all the changes and agitations of the world, the **Rock of our salvation** stands firm. It has been assailed by the combined hosts of earth and hell. For centuries have active minds planned, and strong hands labored, to remove this great cornerstone, and lay another foundation for the faith of the world. The papal power most nearly succeeded in this blasphemous work. But God raised up Luther to cry day and night, as he built upon the walls of Zion. "Other foundation can no man lay than that is laid, which is Jesus Christ." That great cornerstone, the Rock of Ages, stands today unshaken. Amid all the tumults and conflicts of the world, Christ still offers rest to the weary, and the water of life to the thirsting soul. Through the ages His words come down to us—"I am the way, the truth and the life."—*The Signs of the Times*, July 26, 1883.

Further Reflection: *What contemporary forces are attempting to undermine my faith in Jesus Christ?*

GREAT MINISTER IN THE WORK OF REDEMPTION

He has sent redemption to His people; He has commanded His covenant forever: Holy and awesome is His name.

—Psalm 111:9

In this language is represented the omnipotence of the Lord Jesus. He is introduced to the Bible student as the Creator of the world, and as its rightful Ruler. . . .

This first chapter of Hebrews contrasts the position of the angels and the position of Christ. God has spoken words concerning Christ that are not to be applied to the angels. They are "sent forth to minister for them who shall be heirs of salvation," but Christ, as Mediator, is the **great Minister in the work of redemption**. The Holy Spirit is His representative in our world, to execute the divine purpose of bringing to fallen human beings power from above, that they may be overcomers.

All who enter into a covenant with Jesus Christ become by adoption the children of God. They are cleansed by the regenerating power of the Word, and angels are commissioned to minister unto them. They are baptized in the name of the Father, of the son, and of the Holy Ghost. They pledge themselves to become active members of His church in the earth. They are to be dead to all the allurements of worldly desires; but in conversation and godliness, they are, through sanctification of the Spirit, to exert a living influence for God.

"Heirs of God, and joint-heirs with Jesus Christ" (Romans 8:17)—what an exalted, dignified position! Separate and distinct from the world, secure from the wily snares of Satan! By their baptismal vows, God's professed followers have pledged themselves to stand in opposition to evil. The enemy of souls will work with all craft to corrupt their minds. He will seek to introduce his methods into their service for the Master. But there is safety for them if they will heed the injunction: "Finally, my brethren, be strong in the Lord, and in the power of His might. Put on the whole armor of God, that ye may be able to stand against the wiles of the devil."(Ephesians 6:10, 11)—Manuscript 57, 1907.

Further Reflection: *What a blessing it is to know that God's people are safe from Satan's devices when they lean on the power of His might! What are some of the privileges of being heirs together with Christ?*

GREAT ANTITYPE

"Behold! The Lamb of God who takes away the sin of the world!"
—John 1:29

If the follower of Christ will believe His word and practice it, there is no science in the natural world that he will not be able to grasp and appreciate. There is nothing but that will furnish him means for imparting the truth to others. Natural science is a treasure house of knowledge from which every student in the school of Christ may draw. As we contemplate the beauty of nature, as we study its lessons in the cultivation of the soil, in the growth of the trees, in all the wonders of earth and sea and sky, there will come to us a new perception of truth. And the mysteries connected with God's dealings with humanity, the depths of His wisdom and judgment as seen in human life—these are found to be a storehouse rich in treasure.

But it is in the written word that a knowledge of God is most clearly revealed to fallen humanity. This is the treasure house of the unsearchable riches of Christ.

The word of God includes the Scriptures of the Old Testament as well as of the New. One is not complete without the other. Christ declared that the truths of the Old Testament are as valuable as those of the New. Christ was as much humanity's Redeemer in the beginning of the world as He is today. Before He clothed His divinity with humanity and came to our world, the gospel message was given by Adam, Seth, Enoch, Methuselah, and Noah. Abraham in Canaan and Lot in Sodom bore the message, and from generation to generation faithful messengers proclaimed the Coming One. The rites of the Jewish economy were instituted by Christ Himself. He was the foundation of their system of sacrificial offerings, the **great antitype** of all their religious service. The blood shed as the sacrifices were offered pointed to the sacrifice of the Lamb of God. All the typical offerings were fulfilled in Him.

Christ as manifested to the patriarchs, as symbolized in the sacrificial service, as portrayed in the law, and as revealed by the prophets, is the riches of the Old Testament. Christ in His life, His death, and His resurrection, Christ as He is manifested by the Holy Spirit, is the treasure of the New Testament. Our Saviour, the outshining of the Father's glory, is both the Old and the New.—*Christ's Object Lessons*, pp. 125, 126.

Further Reflection: *Am I more drawn to the Jesus of the New Testament than the Jesus foreshadowed in the Old? How can I better appreciate the Great Antitype of the Old Testament?*

HEALER OF ALL MALADIES

"Therefore I say to you, whatever things you ask when you pray, believe that you receive them, and you will have them."

—Mark 11:24

The Saviour knows that in humanity we shall find no solace for our woe, and He pities us because we are so needy, and yet so unwilling to make Him our confidant, our burden-bearer. Of the poor, fainting soul, tired of looking to humanity only to be betrayed and forgotten, Christ says, "Let him take hold of My strength, that he may make peace with Me; and he shall make peace with Me."

Do not take your sorrows and difficulties to human beings. Present yourself to Him who is able to do "exceeding abundantly." He knows just how to help you. Do not turn from the loving, compassionate Redeemer to human friends, who, though they may give you the best they have, may lead you into wrong paths. Take all your troubles to Jesus. He will receive and strengthen and comfort you. He is the great **healer of all maladies**. His great heart of infinite love yearns over you. He sends you the message that you may recover yourself from the snare of the enemy. You may regain your self-respect. You may stand where you regard yourself, not as a failure, but as a conqueror, in and through the uplifting influence of the Spirit of God.

There are many who live under such a pressure of worry that they taste but little of the sweetness of God's love. They do not know the meaning of the words, "That My joy might remain in you, and that your joy might be full." Let us do our best, and then leave everything in the hands of the Lord, saying, I believe Thy promises. Wilt Thou not give evidence of Thy working? He will hear and answer.

"All things, whatsoever ye shall ask in prayer, believing, ye shall receive." These words are the pledge that all that an omnipotent Saviour can bestow will be given to those who trust in Him. As stewards of the grace of heaven, we are to ask in faith, and then wait trustingly for the salvation of God. We are not to step in before Him, trying in our own strength to bring about that which we desire. In His name we are to ask, and then we are to act as if we trusted His efficiency.—*The Signs of the Times*, February 14, 1906.

Further Reflection: *How can I know when to put forth personal effort to bring about that which I may desire and when to wait on God?*

DIVINE SUBSTITUTE

For when we were still without strength, in due time Christ died for the ungodly.

—Romans 5:6

The world's Redeemer possessed the power to draw people to Himself, to quiet their fears, to dispel their gloom, to inspire them with hope and courage, to enable them to believe in the willingness of God to receive them through the merits of the **divine Substitute**. As subjects of the love of God we ever should be grateful that we have a mediator, an advocate, an intercessor in the heavenly courts, who pleads in our behalf before the Father.

We have everything we could ask to inspire us with faith and trust in God. In earthly courts, when a king would make his greatest pledge to assure people of his truth, he gives his child as a hostage, to be redeemed on the fulfillment of his promise; and behold what a pledge of the Father's faithfulness; for when He would assure humanity of the immutability of His council, He gave His only-begotten Son to come to earth, to take the nature of human beings, not only for the brief years of life, but to retain His nature in the heavenly courts, an everlasting pledge of the faithfulness of God. O the depth of the riches both of the wisdom and love of God! "Behold, what manner of love the Father hath bestowed upon us, that we should be called the sons of God." (1 John 3:1)

Through faith in Christ we become members of the royal family, heirs of God, and joint heirs with Jesus Christ. In Christ we are one. As we come in sight of Calvary, and view the royal Sufferer who in humanity's nature bore the curse of the law in their behalf, all national distinctions, all sectarian differences are obliterated; all honor of rank, all pride of caste is lost.

The light shining from the throne of God upon the cross of Calvary forever puts an end to human-made separations between class and race. People of every class become members of one family, children of the heavenly King, not through earthly power, but through the love of God who gave Jesus to a life of poverty, affliction, and humiliation, to a death of shame and agony, that He might bring many sons and daughters unto glory.—*Selected Messages*, book 1, p. 258.

Further Reflection: *In a world in which differences are often a source of tension, how can I help bring divided people to the unifying ground of the Cross?*

HEART SEARCHER

"I, the LORD, search the heart,
I test the mind,
Even to give every man according to his ways,
According to the fruit of his doings."
—Jeremiah 17:10

I have been tempted, sorely tempted, as I see how little many who profess to love God are really loving Him. Our obedience to His commandments testifies whether we are indeed children of God. We are inclined to worry at the outlook of things transpiring in our world. All the forces of the powers of darkness are working against the human race to restrict religious liberty and to compel service and the worshiping of an idol sabbath. God knows all about the outcome.

I am so glad the Father understands every phase of the difficulties we shall have to meet. Believing Him and knowing Him to be God, we know that He sees with a larger vision than is possible for us. His ideals are higher than any of our conceptions. He can read every purpose of hearts that are leaguing against God and co-operating with the evil angels to overthrow the righteous. All the forces of evil angels combined with evil men and women will be in action to suppress truth, and liberty to believe truth. We will not fail now in our work; we will not be discouraged. Every question is open as the day to the **Heart Searcher**. He sees the effort made to influence a child in the wrong direction. The high and lofty One who inhabiteth eternity will not overlook the one who would work counter to His will in tainting and corrupting human minds. We must consider that God knows, God understands.

Keep in view the high standard. We are as God's chosen, working out His plans, accomplishing His purposes. Self is under control to God. We must keep looking unto Jesus, trusting in Him, and not disappoint the hope and expectation of God. We must want to do and want to be just what God would have us to be. And the lesson we have to learn daily is to be meek and lowly of heart. Then can we raise the standard higher and still higher. My children, every day hide in the cleft of the Rock where you may not be seen but where you can see, and where you can hear the proclamation of God's character. This is worth everything to us.—Letter 141, 1896.

Further Reflection: *If I fail to stand against those who work to corrupt human minds, how will God view me?*

MAY 25

COVERT FROM THE TEMPEST

"He is my refuge and my fortress; my God, in Him I will trust."
—Psalm 91:2

Angels, cherubim, and seraphim bow in holy reverence before God. "Ten thousand times ten thousand and thousands of thousands" of angels are round about the throne, and are sent to minister to those who shall be heirs of salvation. The ruling principles of God's throne are justice and mercy. It is called the throne of grace. Would you have divine enlightenment?—Go to the throne of grace. You will be answered from the mercy seat. A covenant has been entered into by the Father and by the Son to save the world through Christ. . . . The rainbow above the throne is a token that God through Christ binds Himself to save all who believe in Him. The covenant is as sure as the throne, and His throne is established in righteousness. Then why are we so unbelieving, so distrustful? Why doubt so frequently, and trust God so fitfully? Whenever we come to the throne of God to ask His mercy, we may look up, and behold the rainbow of promise, and find in it assurance that our prayers shall be answered.

But let no one flatter himself that he may transgress the commandments, and yet receive the favor of God. In the government of God, justice and grace stand side by side. The law cannot be transgressed with impunity. Justice and judgment are the habitation of His throne. In Christ mercy and truth have met together; righteousness and peace have kissed each other. Christ Himself gave the law from Mount Sinai, and He has not lessened a jot or tittle of its claims. He has given His own life to atone for humanity's transgression of the law, and to enable them to obey its precepts. . . .

Christ knows the sinner's trials; He knows His temptations. He has taken upon Himself our nature; He was tempted in all points like as we are, and He knows how to succor those who are tempted. He has wept, and He knows our sorrows; He has experienced all our griefs. To all who believe and trust in Him, He will be a hiding-place from the wind, and a **covert from the tempest**. As a man, Christ ascended to heaven. As a man, He is the substitute for humanity. As a man, He liveth to make intercession for us. He is preparing a place for all who love Him.—*The Signs of the Times*, October 10, 1892.

Further Reflection: *If Jesus is touched by my sorrows and pains and offers me a shelter from the tempest, how can I offer this Shelter to someone who needs it today?*

HEAVENLY BENEFACTOR

Oh, that men would give thanks to the LORD for His goodness, and for His wonderful works to the children of men!
—Psalm 107:8

If Christians would associate together, speaking to each other of the love of God and of the precious truths of redemption, their own hearts would be refreshed and they would refresh one another. We may be daily learning more of our heavenly Father, gaining a fresh experience of His grace; then we shall desire to speak of His love; and as we do this, our own hearts will be warmed and encouraged. If we thought and talked more of Jesus, and less of self, we should have far more of His presence.

If we would but think of God as often as we have evidence of His care for us we should keep Him ever in our thoughts and should delight to talk of Him and to praise Him. We talk of temporal things because we have an interest in them. We talk of our friends because we love them; our joys and our sorrows are bound up with them. Yet we have infinitely greater reason to love God than to love our earthly friends; it should be the most natural thing in the world to make Him first in all our thoughts, to talk of His goodness and tell of His power. The rich gifts He has bestowed upon us were not intended to absorb our thoughts and love so much that we should have nothing to give to God; they are constantly to remind us of Him and to bind us in bonds of love and gratitude to our **heavenly Benefactor**. We dwell too near the lowlands of earth. Let us raise our eyes to the open door of the sanctuary above, where the light of the glory of God shines in the face of Christ, who "is able also to save them to the uttermost that come unto God by Him." (Hebrews 7:25)

We need to praise God more "for His goodness, and for His wonderful works to the children of men." (Psalm 107:8) Our devotional exercises should not consist wholly in asking and receiving. Let us not be always thinking of our wants and never of the benefits we receive. We do not pray any too much, but we are too sparing of giving thanks. We are the constant recipients of God's mercies, and yet how little gratitude we express, how little we praise Him for what He has done for us.—*Prayer*, p. 287.

Further Reflection: *Is there any correlation between the things I love to talk about and the God whom I claim to love?*

CREATOR OF THE WORLD

Yet for us there is one God, the Father, of whom are all things,
and we for Him; and one Lord Jesus Christ,
through whom are all things.

—1 Corinthians 8:6

Silas and Timothy had "come from Macedonia" to help Paul, and together they labored for the Gentiles. To the heathen, as well as to the Jews, Paul and his companions preached Christ as the Saviour of the fallen race. Avoiding complicated, far-fetched reasoning, the messengers of the cross dwelt upon the attributes of the **Creator of the world**, the Supreme Ruler of the universe. Their hearts aglow with the love of God and of His Son, they appealed to the heathen to behold the infinite sacrifice made in humanity's behalf. They knew that if those who had long been groping in the darkness of heathenism could but see the light streaming from Calvary's cross, they would be drawn to the Redeemer. . . .

The gospel workers in Corinth realized the terrible dangers threatening the souls of those for whom they were laboring; and it was with a sense of the responsibility resting on them that they presented the truth as it is in Jesus. Clear, plain, and decided was their message—a savor of life unto life, or of death unto death. And not only in their words, but in the daily life, was the gospel revealed. . . .

The hatred with which the Jews had always regarded the apostles was now intensified. The conversion and baptism of Crispus had the effect of exasperating instead of convincing these stubborn opposers. They could not bring arguments to disprove Paul's preaching, and for lack of such evidence they resorted to deception and malignant attack. They blasphemed the gospel and the name of Jesus. In their blind anger no words were too bitter, no device too low, for them to use. They could not deny that Christ had worked miracles; but they declared that He had performed them through the power of Satan; and they boldly affirmed that the wonderful works wrought by Paul were accomplished through the same agency.—*The Acts of the Apostles*, pp. 248, 249.

Further Reflection: *How do I share Christ with those who may be hostile to religion?*

DIVINE COMPANION

"I am with you always, even to the end of the age." Amen.
—Matthew 28:20

We bear about in our body the dying of the Lord Jesus, which is life and salvation and righteousness to us. Wherever we go, there is the recollection of One dear to us. We are abiding in Christ by a living faith. He is abiding in our hearts by our individual appropriating of faith. We have the companionship of the divine presence, and as we realize this presence, our thoughts are brought into captivity to Jesus Christ. Our spiritual exercises are in accordance with the vividness of our sense of this companionship. Enoch walked with God in this way; and Christ is dwelling in our hearts by faith when we will consider what He is to us, and what a work He has wrought out for us in the plan of redemption. We shall be most happy in cultivating a sense of this great gift of God to our world and to us personally.

These thoughts have a controlling power upon the whole character. I want to impress upon your mind that you may have a **divine companion** with you, if you will, always. "And what agreement hath the temple of God with idols? for ye are the temple of the living God; as God hath said, I will dwell in them, and walk in them; and I will be their God, and they shall be My people." As the mind dwells upon Christ, the character is molded after the divine similitude. The thoughts are pervaded with a sense of His goodness, His love. We contemplate His character, and thus He is in all our thoughts. His love encloses us. If we gaze even a moment upon the sun in its meridian glory, when we turn away our eyes, the image of the sun will appear in everything upon which we look.

Thus it is when we behold Jesus; everything we look upon reflects His image, the Sun of Righteousness. We cannot see anything else, or talk of anything else. His image is imprinted upon the eye of the soul and affects every portion of our daily life, softening and subduing our whole nature. By beholding, we are conformed to the divine similitude, even the likeness of Christ. To all with whom we associate we reflect the bright and cheerful beams of His righteousness. We have become transformed in character; for heart, soul, mind, are irradiated by the reflection of Him who loved us and gave Himself for us.—*Testimonies to Ministers and Gospel Workers*, pp. 388, 389.

Further Reflection: *When today will I make time for a sustained look at Jesus?*

HEAVENLY MERCHANTMAN

"Again, the kingdom of heaven is like a merchant seeking beautiful pearls."

—Matthew 13:45

The gospel of Christ is a blessing that all may possess. The poorest are as well able as the richest to purchase salvation; for no amount of worldly wealth can secure it. It is obtained by willing obedience, by giving ourselves to Christ as His own purchased possession. Education, even of the highest class, cannot of itself bring a person nearer to God. . . .

We are to seek for the pearl of great price, but not in worldly marts or in worldly ways. The price we are required to pay is not gold or silver, for this belongs to God. Abandon the idea that temporal or spiritual advantages will win for you salvation. God calls for your willing obedience. He asks you to give up your sins. . . .

There are some who seem to be always seeking for the heavenly pearl. But they do not make an entire surrender of their wrong habits. They do not die to self that Christ may live in them. Therefore they do not find the precious pearl. They have not overcome unholy ambition and their love for worldly attractions. They do not take up the cross and follow Christ in the path of self-denial and sacrifice. Almost Christians, yet not fully Christians, they seem near the kingdom of heaven, but they cannot enter there. Almost but not wholly saved, means to be not almost but wholly lost.

The parable of the merchantman seeking goodly pearls has a double significance: it applies not only to people as seeking the kingdom of heaven, but to Christ as seeking His lost inheritance. Christ, the **heavenly merchantman** seeking goodly pearls, saw in lost humanity the pearl of price. In human beings, defiled and ruined by sin, He saw the possibilities of redemption. Hearts that have been the battleground of the conflict with Satan, and that have been rescued by the power of love, are more precious to the Redeemer than are those who have never fallen. God looked upon humanity, not as vile and worthless; He looked upon it in Christ, saw it as it might become through redeeming love. He collected all the riches of the universe, and laid them down in order to buy the pearl.—*Christ's Object Lessons*, pp. 117, 118.

Further Reflection: *If salvation can be purchased through willing obedience to God, what prevents human beings from totally surrendering their wills to God?*

EVERLASTING FRIEND

"But lay up for yourselves treasures in heaven."
—Matthew 6:20

Every opportunity to help a brother in need, or to aid the cause of God in the spread of the truth, is a pearl that you can send beforehand and deposit in the bank of heaven for safekeeping. God is testing and proving you. He has been giving His blessings to you with a lavish hand and is now watching to see what use you are making of them, to see if you will help those who need help and if you will feel the worth of souls and do what you can with the means that He has entrusted to you. Every such opportunity improved adds to your heavenly treasure. But love of self has led you to prefer earthly possessions even at the sacrifice of the heavenly. . . . It is your privilege to exercise tender compassion and to bless others; but your eyes are so blinded by the god of this world that you cannot discern this precious gem—the blessing to be received by doing good, by being rich in good works, ready to distribute, willing to communicate, laying up for yourself a good foundation against the time to come, that you may lay hold on eternal life. . . .

Your only hope is to humble your heart before God. "For what shall it profit a man, if he shall gain the whole world, and lose his own soul? or what shall a man give in exchange for his soul?" I entreat of you: Do not close your eyes to your danger. Do not be blind to the higher interests of the soul, to the blessed and glorious prospects for the better life. The anxious, burdened seekers for worldly gain are blind and insane. They turn from the immortal, imperishable treasure, to this world. The glitter and tinsel of this world captivate their senses, and eternal things are not valued. They labor for that which satisfieth not and spend their money for that which is not bread, when Jesus offers them peace and hope and infinite blessings, for a life of obedience. All the treasures of the earth would not be rich enough to buy these precious gifts. . . .

The long night of watching, of toil and hardship, is nearly past. Christ is soon to come. Get ready. The angels of God are seeking to attract you from yourself and from earthly things. Let them not labor in vain. Faith, living faith, is what you need; faith that works by love and purifies the soul. Remember Calvary and the awful, the infinite sacrifice there made for human beings. Jesus now invites you to come to Him just as you are and make Him your strength and **everlasting Friend.**—*Testimonies for the Church*, vol. 3, pp. 249–251.

Further Reflection: *Am I using the resources entrusted to me to bless those in need?*

CHIEF SHEPHERD

Shepherd the flock of God which is among you, serving as overseers, not by compulsion but willingly, not for dishonest gain but eagerly.
—1 Peter 5:2

God's care for His heritage is unceasing. He suffers no affliction to come upon His children but such as is essential for their present and eternal good. He will purify His church, even as Christ purified the temple during His ministry on earth. All that He brings upon His people in test and trial comes that they may gain deeper piety and greater strength to carry forward the triumphs of the cross.

There had been a time in Peter's experience when he was unwilling to see the cross in the work of Christ. When the Saviour made known to the disciples His impending sufferings and death, Peter exclaimed, "Be it far from Thee, Lord: this shall not be unto Thee." (Matthew 16:22) Self-pity, which shrank from fellowship with Christ in suffering, prompted Peter's remonstrance. It was to the disciple a bitter lesson, and one which he learned but slowly, that the path of Christ on earth lay through agony and humiliation. But in the heat of the furnace fire he was to learn its lesson. Now, when his once active form was bowed with the burden of years and labors, he could write, "Beloved, think it not strange concerning the fiery trial which is to try you, as though some strange thing happened unto you: but rejoice, inasmuch as ye are partakers of Christ's sufferings; that, when His glory shall be revealed, ye may be glad also with exceeding joy."

Addressing the church elders regarding their responsibilities as undershepherds of Christ's flock, the apostle wrote: "Feed the flock of God which is among you, taking the oversight thereof, not by constraint, but willingly; not for filthy lucre, but of a ready mind; neither as being lords over God's heritage, but being ensamples to the flock. And when the **Chief Shepherd** shall appear, ye shall receive a crown of glory that fadeth not away."

Those who occupy the position of undershepherds are to exercise a watchful diligence over the Lord's flock. This is not to be a dictatorial vigilance, but one that tends to encourage and strengthen and uplift. —*The Acts of the Apostles*, pp. 524–526.

Further Reflection: *How can I affirm the leaders in my life who help to shepherd God's flock?*

JUNE

HEAVENLY VISITOR

Then fear came upon all, and they glorified God, saying, "A great prophet has risen up among us"; and, "God has visited His people."

—Luke 7:16

There is a work for all to do to open the door of the heart to the **heavenly visitor**. The Lord of glory, who has redeemed us by His own blood, seeks admittance; but too often we do not welcome Him in. Worldliness does not incline us to throw wide open the door of the heart at the knock of Him who is seeking entrance. Some open the door slightly, and permit a little light from His presence to enter; but they do not bid Him hearty welcome. There is no room for Jesus; the place which should have been reserved for Him is occupied with other things. He entreats, and for a time they feel inclined to hear and open the door; but even this inclination departs, and they fail to secure the communion with the heavenly guest which it was their privilege to have.

"Behold, I stand at the door and knock," says the Saviour. The mansions in glory are His, and the joy of that heavenly abode; yet He humbles Himself to seek an entrance at the door of the heart, that He may bless us with His light, and make us to rejoice in His glory. His work is to seek and to save that which is lost and ready to perish. He will redeem from sin and death all who will come to Him; and will elevate them to His throne, and give them everlasting life.

Jesus will not force open the door of the heart. We must open it ourselves, and show that we desire His presence by giving Him a sincere welcome. If all would make thorough work of clearing away the world's rubbish, and preparing a place for Jesus, He would enter, and abide with them, and would do a great work through them for the salvation of others. But many receive not the tokens of God's mercy and loving-kindness with thankful hearts; they do not bend their energies and unite their interests in His work, and they do not share in the blessing that He is waiting to bestow.

"If *any man* hear My voice," says Christ, "and open the door, I will come in to him, and will sup with him, and he with Me." These words are not addressed simply to the more intelligent and refined, but to all, without respect of persons.—*The Signs of the Times*, February 10, 1887.

Further Reflection: *The opening of the heart to Jesus is something that each of us must do before He can enter. What areas of my heart remain closed to Jesus?*

COMMANDER OF THE HEAVENLY HOST

For you know the grace of our Lord Jesus Christ, that though He was rich, yet for your sakes He became poor, that you through His poverty might become rich.

—2 Corinthians 8:9

There is a world to be warned. To us has been entrusted this work. At any cost we must practice the truth. We are to stand as self-sacrificing minutemen, willing to suffer the loss of life itself, if need be, in the service of God. There is a great work to be done in a short time. We need to understand our work, and to do it with fidelity. Everyone who is finally crowned victor will, by noble, determined effort to serve God, have earned the right to be clothed with Christ's righteousness. To enter the crusade against Satan, bearing aloft the blood-stained banner of the cross of Christ—this is the duty of every Christian.

This work calls for self-sacrifice. Self-denial and the cross stand all along the way of life. "He that will come after Me," Christ said, "let him deny himself, and take up his cross, and follow Me." Those who secure the treasures of this world are obliged to toil and sacrifice. Should those who are seeking for an eternal reward think that they need make no sacrifices?

The most difficult sermon to preach and the hardest to practice is self-denial. The greedy sinner, self, closes the door to the good which might be done, but which is not done because money is invested for selfish purposes. But it is impossible for anyone to retain the favor of God and enjoy communion with the Saviour, and at the same time be indifferent to the interests of his fellow beings who have no life in Christ, who are perishing in their sins. Christ has left us a wonderful example of self-sacrifice. He pleased not Himself, but spent His life in the service of others. He made sacrifices at every step, sacrifices which none of His followers can ever make, because they have never occupied the position He occupied before He came to this earth. He was **Commander of the Heavenly Host**, but He came here to suffer for sinners. He was rich, yet for our sakes He became poor, that through His poverty we might be made rich. Because He loved us, He laid aside His glory and took upon Him the form of a Servant.—*Review and Herald*, January 31, 1907.

Further Reflection: *Who in home, church, or community needs my selfless service today?*

TRUE COUNSELOR

Nevertheless I have this against you, that you have left your first love.
—Revelation 2:4

Let us not flatter ourselves that we are the children of God, when our lack of Christ's love is made manifest by our indifference to the souls for whom He died. "In this the children of God are manifest, and the children of the Devil: whosoever doeth not righteousness is not of God, neither he that loveth not his brother. For this is the message that ye heard from the beginning, that we should love one another. . . . We know that we have passed from death unto life, because we love the brethren. He that loveth not his brother abideth in death. Whosoever hateth his brother is a murderer: and ye know that no murderer hath eternal life abiding in him. Hereby perceive we the love of God, because He laid down His life for us: and we ought to lay down our lives for the brethren. But whoso hath this world's good, and seeth his brother have need, and shutteth up his bowels of compassion from him, how dwelleth the love of God in him? My little children, let us not love in word, neither in tongue; but in deed and in truth."

A spirit of careless indifference toward our brethren has been coming into our churches, and the religion of many has become cold, selfish, loveless Phariseeism. The **True Counselor** has spoken words of the utmost importance to all our souls—"Thou hast left thy first love." What a loss is this! "Remember therefore from whence thou art fallen, and repent, and do the first works." O, how many have failed to grow up into Christ, their living head! Instead of growing up into Christ, they have grown away from Christ, and have nourished the elements of character that have been like those of Satan. These characteristics of evil excluded Satan from the royal courts above, and they will exclude you from the family of God, "except thou repent." Your heart must be softened and made susceptible to the influence of the Spirit of God, that you may grow up into a spiritual temple in Christ. The saints on earth must love as Christ loved, or they will not be saints in heaven. If your sympathies have become dried up, turn to God, humble your proud heart before Him, fall on the Rock and be broken, and then Christ will mold you after His own similitude, and make you a vessel unto honor.—*Review and Herald*, February 10, 1891.

Further Reflection: *What is the proof that the Holy Spirit has softened my heart?*

ONE ALTOGETHER LOVELY

Let the wicked forsake his way,
And the unrighteous man his thoughts;
Let him return to the LORD,
And He will have mercy on him.

—Isaiah 55:7

Have you, reader, chosen your own way? Have you wandered far from God? Have you sought to feast upon the fruits of transgression, only to find them turn to ashes upon your lips? And now, your life plans thwarted and your hopes dead, do you sit alone and desolate? That voice which has long been speaking to your heart, but to which you would not listen, comes to you distinct and clear, "Arise ye, and depart; for this is not your rest: because it is polluted, it shall destroy you, even with a sore destruction." (Micah 2:10) . . .

Do not listen to the enemy's suggestion to stay away from Christ until you have made yourself better, until you are good enough to come to God. If you wait until then you will never come. When Satan points to your filthy garments, repeat the promise of the Saviour, "Him that cometh to Me I will in no wise cast out." (John 6:37) Tell the enemy that the blood of Jesus Christ cleanses from all sin. Make the prayer of David your own: "Purge me with hyssop, and I shall be clean: wash me, and I shall be whiter than snow." (Psalm 51:7)

The exhortations of the prophet to Judah to behold the living God, and to accept His gracious offers, were not in vain. There were some who gave earnest heed, and who turned from their idols to the worship of Jehovah. They learned to see in their Maker love and mercy and tender compassion. And in the dark days that were to come in the history of Judah, when only a remnant were to be left in the land, the prophet's words were to continue bearing fruit in decided reformation. "At that day," declared Isaiah, "shall a man look to his Maker, and his eyes shall have respect to the Holy One of Israel. And he shall not look to the altars, the work of his hands, neither shall respect that which his fingers have made, either the groves, or the images." (Isaiah 17:7, 8)

Many were to behold the **One Altogether Lovely**, the Chiefest among ten thousand.—*Prophets and Kings*, pp. 319–321.

Further Reflection: *Why does God plead so fervently for my repentance? How can I avoid taking His grace for granted?*

MIGHTY CONQUEROR

His glory covered the heavens, and the earth was full of His praise.
—Habakkuk 3:3

The voice of God is heard from heaven, declaring the day and hour of Jesus' coming, and delivering the everlasting covenant to His people. Like peals of loudest thunder, His words roll through the earth. The Israel of God stand listening, with their eyes fixed upward. Their countenances are lighted up with His glory, and shine as did the face of Moses when he came down from Sinai. The wicked cannot look upon them. And when the blessing is pronounced on those who have honored God by keeping His Sabbath holy, there is a mighty shout of victory.

Soon there appears in the east a small black cloud, about half the size of a man's hand. It is the cloud which surrounds the Saviour, and which seems in the distance to be shrouded in darkness. The people of God know this to be the sign of the Son of man. In solemn silence they gaze upon it as it draws nearer the earth, becoming lighter and more glorious, until it is a great white cloud, its base a glory like consuming fire, and above it the rainbow of the covenant. Jesus rides forth as a **Mighty Conqueror**. Not now a "man of sorrows," to drink the bitter cup of shame and woe, He comes, victor in heaven and earth, to judge the living and the dead. "Faithful and True," "in righteousness He doth judge and make war." And "the armies in Heaven follow Him." (Revelation 19:11, 14)

With anthems of celestial melody the holy angels, a vast, unnumbered throng, attend Him on His way. The firmament seems filled with radiant forms,—"ten thousand times ten thousand, and thousands of thousands." No human pen can portray the scene, nor mortal mind is adequate to conceive its splendor. "His glory covered the heavens, and the earth was full of His praise. And His brightness was as the light." (Habakkuk 3:3, 4) As the living cloud comes still nearer, every eye beholds the Prince of life. No crown of thorns now mars that sacred head, but a diadem of glory rests on His holy brow. His countenance outshines the dazzling brightness of the noonday sun. "And He hath on His vesture and on His thigh a name written, *King of kings, and Lord of lords*." (Revelation 19:16)—*The Great Controversy*, pp. 640, 641.

Further Reflection: *Perhaps I celebrate Jesus as the Suffering Savior who rescued me from sin, but can I recount a time when Jesus has been a Mighty Conqueror for me?*

SAVIOUR OF THE WORLD

For it was fitting for Him, for whom are all things and by whom are all things, in bringing many sons to glory, to make the captain of their salvation perfect through sufferings.

—Hebrews 2:10

Who can comprehend the love here displayed! The angelic host beheld with wonder and with grief Him who had been the Majesty of heaven, and who had worn the crown of glory, now wearing the crown of thorns, a bleeding victim to the rage of an infuriated mob, fired to insane madness by the wrath of Satan. Behold the Patient Sufferer! Upon His head is the thorny crown. His lifeblood flows from every lacerated vein. All this in consequence of sin! Nothing could have induced Christ to leave His honor and majesty in heaven, and come to a sinful world, to be neglected, despised, and rejected by those He came to save, and finally to suffer upon the cross, but eternal, redeeming love, which will ever remain a mystery.

Wonder, O heavens, and be astonished, O earth! Behold the oppressor and the oppressed! A vast multitude enclose the **Saviour of the world**. Mockings and jeerings are mingled with the coarse oaths of blasphemy. His lowly birth and humble life are commented upon by unfeeling wretches. His claim to be the Son of God is ridiculed by the chief priests and elders, and vulgar jests and insulting derision are passed from lip to lip. Satan was having full control of the minds of his servants. In order to do this effectually, he commences with the chief priests and elders, and imbues them with religious frenzy. They are actuated by the same satanic spirit which moves the most vile and hardened wretches. There is a corrupt harmony in the feelings of all, from the hypocritical priests and elders down to the most debased. Christ, the precious Son of God, was led forth, and the cross was laid upon His shoulders. At every step was left blood which flowed from His wounds. . . .

Not one word did Jesus answer to all this. While the nails were being driven through His hands, and the sweat drops of agony were forced from His pores, from the pale, quivering lips of the innocent Sufferer a prayer of pardoning love was breathed for His murderers: "Father, forgive them; for they know not what they do"—*Testimonies for the Church*, vol. 2, pp. 207–209.

Further Reflection: *If Jesus bore so much for me, why do I find it so difficult to suffer for Him?*

HUMBLE NAZARENE

And Nathanael said to him, "Can anything good come out of Nazareth?" Philip said to him, "Come and see."

—John 1:46

In humility Christ began His mighty work for the uplifting of the fallen race. Passing by the cities and the renowned seats of learning, He made His home in the humble and obscure village of Nazareth. In this place, from which it was commonly supposed that no good could come, the world's Redeemer passed the greater part of His life working at His trade as a carpenter. His home was among the poor; His family was not distinguished by learning, riches, or position. In the path which the poor, the neglected, the sorrowing, must tread, He walked while on earth, taking upon Him all the woes which the afflicted must bear.

It was the proud boast of the Jews that the Messiah was to come as a king, conquering His enemies and treading down the heathen in His wrath. But it was not the mission of Christ to exalt men and women by ministering to their pride. He, the **Humble Nazarene**, might have poured contempt upon the world's pride, for He was commander in the heavenly courts; but He came in humility, showing that it is not riches or position or authority that the God of heaven respects, but that He honors a contrite heart made noble by the power of the grace of Christ.

Christ closed His life of toil and denial in our behalf by a crowning sacrifice for us. . . .

Christ is a living Savior. Today He sits at the right hand of God as our Advocate, making intercession for us; and He calls upon us to look unto Him and be saved. But it has ever been the tempter's determined purpose to eclipse Jesus from the view, that we may be led to lean upon the arm of humanity for help and strength; and he has so well accomplished his purpose that we, turning our eyes from Jesus, in whom all hope of eternal life is centered, look to our fellow human beings for aid and guidance. . . .

As the serpent was lifted up in the wilderness by Moses, that all who had been bitten by the fiery serpents might look and live, so must the Son of Man be lifted up before the world by His servants.—*Review and Herald*, September 29, 1896.

Further Reflection: *How do I resist the pull of the world's temptations to power, wealth, and fame?*

MIGHTY HEALER OF THE SIN-SICK SOUL

"Those who are well have no need of a physician, but those who are sick."

—Matthew 9:12

May the Lord increase our faith and help us to see that He desires us all to become acquainted with His ministry of healing and with the mercy seat. He desires the light of His grace to shine forth from many places. He who understands the necessities of the situation arranges that advantages shall be brought to the workers in various places to enable them more effectually to arouse the attention of the people to the truths that make for deliverance from both physical and spiritual ills.

The tender sympathies of our Saviour were aroused for fallen and suffering humanity. If you would be His follower, you must cultivate compassion and sympathy. Indifference to human woes must give place to lively interest in the sufferings of others. The widow, the orphan, the sick and dying, will always need help. Here is an opportunity to proclaim the gospel—to hold up Jesus, the hope and consolation of all men. When the suffering body has been relieved the heart is opened, and you can pour in the heavenly balm. If you are looking to Jesus and drawing from Him knowledge and strength and grace, you can impart His consolation to others, because the Comforter is with you.

You will meet with much prejudice, a great deal of false zeal and miscalled piety; but in both the home and the foreign field you will find more hearts that God has been preparing for the seed of truth than you imagine, and they will hail with joy the divine message when it is presented to them.

Many are suffering from maladies of the soul far more than from diseases of the body, and they will find no relief until they come to Christ, the wellspring of life. The burden of sin, with its unrest and unsatisfied desires, lies at the foundation of a large share of the maladies the sinner suffers. Christ is the **Mighty Healer of the sin-sick soul**. These poor, afflicted ones need to have a clearer knowledge of Him whom to know aright is life eternal. They need to be patiently and kindly yet earnestly taught how to throw open the windows of the soul and let the sunlight of God's love come in. . . . Satisfying joys will give vigor to the mind and health and vital energy to the body.—*Counsels on Health*, pp. 501, 502.

Further Reflection: *If I had to choose healing of body or soul, which would I choose?*

GREAT GIFT

He who did not spare His own Son, but delivered Him up for us all, how shall He not with Him also freely give us all things?
—Romans 8:32

The Lord looks with pity on those who allow themselves to be burdened with household cares and business perplexities. They are cumbered with much serving, and neglect the one thing essential. "Seek ye first the kingdom of God, and His righteousness," the Saviour says; "and all these things shall be added unto you." That is, look away from this world to the eternal. Put forth your most earnest endeavors to obtain those things upon which God places value, and which Christ gave His precious life that you might secure. His sacrifice has thrown open wide to you the gates of heavenly commerce. Lay up your treasure beside the throne of God, by doing with His entrusted capital the work that He desires done in the winning of souls to a knowledge of the truth. This will secure you eternal riches. . . .

When we think of the **great gift** of heaven for the redemption of a sinful world, and then consider the offerings that we can make, we shrink from drawing a comparison. The demands that might be made upon a whole universe could not compare with that one gift. Immeasurable love was expressed when One equal with the Father came to pay the price for the souls of men, and bring to them eternal life. Shall those who profess the name of Christ see no attraction in the world's Redeemer, be indifferent to the possession of truth and righteousness, and turn from the heavenly treasure to the earthly?

"And this is the condemnation, that light is come into the world, and men loved darkness rather than light, because their deeds were evil. But everyone that doeth evil hateth the light, neither cometh to the light, lest his deeds should be reproved. But he that doeth truth cometh to the light, that his deeds may be made manifest, that they are wrought in God."—*Counsels on Stewardship*, pp. 225, 226.

Further Reflection: *How would the current things I value change if the things that Jesus values become my highest priority?*

SOURCE OF SPIRITUAL POWER

They are abundantly satisfied with the fullness of Your house, and You give them drink from the river of Your pleasures.
—Psalm 36:8

When His words of instruction have been received, and have taken possession of us, Jesus is to us an abiding presence, controlling our thoughts and ideas and actions. We are imbued with the instruction of the greatest Teacher the world ever knew. A sense of human accountability and of human influence gives character to our views of life and of daily duties. Jesus Christ is everything to us—the first, the last, the best in everything. Jesus Christ, His Spirit, His character, colors everything; it is the warp and the woof, the very texture of our entire being. The words of Christ are spirit and life. Self is dead, but Christ is a living Saviour. Continuing to look unto Jesus, we reflect His image to all around us. We cannot stop to consider our disappointments, or even to talk of them; for a more pleasant picture attracts our sight—the precious love of Jesus. . . .

What said Christ to the Samaritan woman at Jacob's well? "If thou knewest the gift of God, and who it is that saith to thee, Give Me to drink; thou wouldest have asked of Him, and He would have given thee living water." "Whosoever drinketh of this water shall thirst again: but whosoever drinketh of the water that I shall give him shall never thirst; but the water that I shall give him shall be in him a well of water springing up into everlasting life." The water that Christ referred to was the revelation of His grace in His word; His Spirit, His teaching, is as a satisfying fountain to every soul. . . . In Christ is fullness of joy forevermore. The desires and pleasures and amusements of the world are never satisfying nor healing to the soul. . . .

Christ's gracious presence in His word is ever speaking to the soul, representing Him as the well of living water to refresh the thirsting soul. It is our privilege to have a living, abiding Saviour. He is the **Source of spiritual power** implanted within us, and His influence will flow forth in words and actions, refreshing all within the sphere of our influence, begetting in them desires and aspirations for strength and purity, for holiness and peace, and for that joy which brings no sorrow with it. This is the result of an indwelling Saviour.—*Testimonies to Ministers and Gospel Workers*, pp. 389, 390.

Further Reflection: *What counterfeit sources of spiritual power am I tempted to try?*

GREAT CENTER FROM WHOM RADIATES ALL GLORY

"I am the light of the world."

—John 8:12

With prophetic eye Christ traced the scenes to take place in His last great conflict. He knew that when He should exclaim, "It is finished," all heaven would triumph. His ear caught the distant music and the shouts of victory in the heavenly courts. He knew that the knell of Satan's empire would then be sounded. . . .

Christ rejoiced that He could do more for His followers than they could ask or think. He spoke with assurance, knowing that an almighty decree had been given before the world was made. He knew that truth, armed with the omnipotence of the Holy Spirit, would conquer in the contest with evil; and that the bloodstained banner would wave triumphantly over His followers. . . .

"These things I have spoken unto you," He said, "that in Me ye might have peace. In the world ye shall have tribulation: but be of good cheer; I have overcome the world." Christ did not fail, neither was He discouraged, and His followers are to manifest a faith of the same enduring nature. They are to live as He lived, and work as He worked, because they depend on Him as the great Master Worker. Courage, energy, and perseverance they must possess. Though apparent impossibilities obstruct their way, by His grace they are to go forward. Instead of deploring difficulties, they are called upon to surmount them. . . . It is His purpose that the highest influence in the universe, emanating from the source of all power, shall be theirs. They are to have power to resist evil, power that neither earth, nor death, nor hell can master, power that will enable them to overcome as Christ overcame.

Christ designs that heaven's order, heaven's plan of government, heaven's divine harmony, shall be represented in His church on earth. Thus in His people He is glorified. Through them the Sun of Righteousness will shine in undimmed luster to the world. . . . The church, endowed with the righteousness of Christ, is His depositary, in which the riches of His mercy, His grace, and His love, are to appear in full and final display. Christ looks upon His people in their purity and perfection, as the reward of His humiliation, and the supplement of His glory—Christ, the **great Center, from whom radiates all glory**.—*The Desire of Ages*, pp. 679, 680.

Further Reflection: *How do I see Jesus revealing His glory in my life?*

LORD OF HEAT AND COLD

"I see four men loose, walking in the midst of the fire; and they are not hurt, and the form of the fourth is like the Son of God."
—Daniel 3:25

As the three Hebrews stood before the king, he was convinced that they possessed something the other wise men of his kingdom did not have. They had been faithful in the performance of every duty. He would give them another trial. If only they would signify their willingness to unite with the multitude in worshiping the image, all would be well with them; "but if ye worship not," he added, "ye shall be cast the same hour into the midst of a burning fiery furnace." Then with his hand stretched upward in defiance, he demanded, "Who is that God that shall deliver you out of my hands?"

In vain were the king's threats. He could not turn the men from their allegiance to the Ruler of the universe. From the history of their fathers they had learned that disobedience to God results in dishonor, disaster, and death; and that the fear of the Lord is the beginning of wisdom, the foundation of all true prosperity. Calmly facing the furnace, they said, "O Nebuchadnezzar, we are not careful to answer thee in this matter. If it be so [if this is your decision], our God whom we serve is able to deliver us from the burning fiery furnace, and He will deliver us out of thine hand, O king." Their faith strengthened as they declared that God would be glorified by delivering them, and with triumphant assurance born of implicit trust in God, they added, "But if not, be it known unto thee, O king, that we will not serve thy gods, nor worship the golden image which thou hast set up."

The king's wrath knew no bounds. "Full of fury," "the form of his visage was changed against Shadrach, Meshach, and Abednego," representatives of a despised and captive race. Directing that the furnace be heated seven times hotter than its wont, he commanded the mighty men of his army to bind the worshipers of Israel's God, preparatory to summary execution. . . .

But the Lord did not forget His own. As His witnesses were cast into the furnace, the Saviour revealed Himself to them in person, and together they walked in the midst of the fire. In the presence of the **Lord of heat and cold**, the flames lost their power to consume.—*Prophets and Kings*, pp. 507–509.

Further Reflection: *When was it that Jesus met me in the fires of trial and oppression?*

HOPE OF ISRAEL

"Rabbi, we know that You are a teacher come from God; for no one can do these signs that You do unless God is with him."

—John 3:2

If there is nothing more in all the Scriptures which point out definitely the way to heaven, we have it here in these words. [John 3:1–16] They tell us what conversion is. They tell us what we must do in order to be saved. And, my friends, I want to tell you that this strikes directly at the root of the surface work in the religious world. It strikes directly against the idea that you can become a child of God without any particular change. There is a decided change wrought in us if the truth of God has found a place in our hearts, for it has a sanctifying power upon life and upon character. When we see the fruits of righteousness in those who claim to have advanced truth, as we claim to have it, then there will be a course of action which testifies that we have learned of Christ.

When Christ, the **Hope of Israel**, was hung upon the cross and was lifted up as He told Nicodemus He would be, the disciples' hope died with Jesus. They could not explain the matter. They could not understand all that Christ had told them about it beforehand.

But after the Resurrection their hopes and faith were resurrected, and they went forth proclaiming Christ and Him crucified. They told how by wicked hands the Lord of life and glory had been taken and crucified, but He had risen from the dead. And thus with great boldness they spoke the words of life at which the people were much astonished.

The Pharisees and those who heard the disciples boldly proclaim Jesus as the Messiah interpreted it that they had been with Jesus and learned of Him. They talked just as Jesus talked. This settled it in their minds that they had learned of Jesus. How has it been with His disciples in all ages of the world? Why, they have learned of Jesus; they have been in His school; they have been His students and have learned the lessons of Christ in regard to the living connection that the soul has with God. That living faith is essential for our salvation that we should lay hold upon the merits of the blood of the crucified and risen Saviour, on Christ, our righteousness.—*Faith and Works*, pp. 63, 64.

Further Reflection: *If someone who did not know me observed me for a week, would they conclude that I have "learned of Jesus"?*

MAN OF CALVARY

"If anyone desires to come after Me, let him deny himself, and take up his cross daily, and follow Me."

—Luke 9:23

In order to be purified and to remain pure, Seventh-day Adventists must have the Holy Spirit in their hearts and in their homes. The Lord has given me light that when the Israel of today humble themselves before Him, and cleanse the soul-temple from all defilement, He will hear their prayers in behalf of the sick and will bless in the use of His remedies for disease. When in faith the human agent does all he can to combat disease, using the simple methods of treatment that God has provided, his efforts will be blessed of God.

If, after so much light has been given, God's people will cherish wrong habits, indulging self and refusing to reform, they will suffer the sure consequences of transgression. If they are determined to gratify perverted appetite at any cost, God will not miraculously save them from the consequences of their indulgence. They "shall lie down in sorrow." (Isaiah 50:11) . . .

Oh, how many lose the richest blessings that God has in store for them in health and spiritual endowments! There are many souls who wrestle for special victories and special blessings that they may do some great thing. To this end they are always feeling that they must make an agonizing struggle in prayer and tears. When these persons search the Scriptures with prayer to know the expressed will of God, and then do His will from the heart without one reservation or self-indulgence, they will find rest. All the agonizing, all the tears and struggles, will not bring them the blessing they long for. Self must be entirely surrendered. They must do the work that presents itself, appropriating the abundance of the grace of God which is promised to all. . . .

"If any man will come after Me," said Jesus, "let him deny himself, and take up his cross daily, and follow Me." (Luke 9:23) Let us follow the Saviour in His simplicity and self-denial. Let us lift up the **Man of Calvary** by word and by holy living. The Saviour comes very near to those who consecrate themselves to God. If ever there was a time when we needed the working of the Spirit of God upon our hearts and lives, it is now. Let us lay hold of this divine power for strength to live a life of holiness and self-surrender.—*Testimonies for the Church*, vol. 9, pp. 164–166.

Further Reflection: *What cross will I take up today as I seek to live a holy life?*

STRONG AND MIGHTY DELIVERER

You are my hiding place; You shall preserve me from trouble;
You shall surround me with songs of deliverance.
—Psalm 32:7

I have been shown that we must be guarded on every side and perseveringly resist the insinuations and devices of Satan. He has transformed himself into an angel of light and is deceiving thousands and leading them captive. The advantage he takes of the science of the human mind, is tremendous. Here, serpent-like, he imperceptibly creeps in to corrupt the work of God. The miracles and works of Christ he would make appear as the result of human skill and power. If he should make an open, bold attack upon Christianity, it would bring the Christian in distress and agony to the feet of his Redeemer, and his **strong and mighty Deliverer** would put the bold adversary to flight. He therefore transforms himself into an angel of light and works upon the mind to allure from the only safe and right path. . . .

I was directed to the power of God manifested through Moses when the Lord sent him in before Pharaoh. Satan understood his business and was upon the ground. He well knew that Moses was chosen of God to break the yoke of bondage upon the children of Israel, and that in his work he prefigured Christ's first advent to break Satan's power over the human family and deliver those who were made captives by his power. Satan knew that when Christ should appear, mighty works and miracles would be wrought by Him, that the world might know that the Father had sent Him. He trembled for his power. He consulted with his angels how to accomplish a work which should answer a twofold purpose: 1. To destroy the influence of the work wrought by God through His servant Moses, by working through his agents, and thus counterfeiting the true work of God; 2. To exert an influence by his work through the magicians which would reach down through all ages and destroy in the minds of many true faith in the mighty miracles and works to be performed by Christ when He should come to this world. He knew that his kingdom would suffer, for the power which he held over humanity would be subject to Christ. . . . Those signs and wonders were wrought through Moses to convince Pharaoh that the great "I AM" sent him to command Pharaoh to let Israel go that they might serve Him.—*Testimonies for the Church*, vol. 1, pp. 290–292.

Further Reflection: *How does the Holy Spirit help me prepare for Satan's nefarious attacks?*

DYING VICTIM

"Worthy is the Lamb who was slain to receive power and riches and wisdom, and strength and honor and glory and blessing!"
—Revelation 5:12

Christ was the foundation of the whole Jewish economy. The death of Abel was in consequence of Cain's refusing to accept God's plan in the school of obedience to be saved by the blood of Jesus Christ typified by the sacrificial offerings pointing to Christ. Cain refused the shedding of blood which symbolized the blood of Christ to be shed for the world. This whole ceremony was prepared by God, and Christ became the foundation of the whole system. This is the beginning of its work as the schoolmaster to bring sinful human agents to a consideration of Christ the Foundation of the whole Jewish economy.

All who did service in connection with the sanctuary were being educated constantly in regard to the intervention of Christ in behalf of the human race. This service was designed to create in every heart a love for the law of God, which is the law of His kingdom. The sacrificial offering was to be an object lesson of the love of God revealed in Christ—in the suffering, **dying victim**, who took upon Himself the sin of which human beings were guilty. . . .

In the contemplation of this great theme of salvation we see Christ's work. Not only the promised gift of the Spirit, but also the nature and character of this sacrifice and intervention are subjects which should create in our hearts elevated, sacred, high ideas of the law of God, which holds its claims upon every human agency. The violation of that law in the small act of eating of the forbidden fruit, brought upon humanity and upon the earth the consequence of disobedience to the holy law of God. The nature of the intervention should ever make men and women afraid to do the smallest action in disobedience to God's requirement.

There should be a clear understanding of that which constitutes sin, and we should avoid the least approach to step over the boundaries from obedience to disobedience.

God would have every member of His creation understand the great work of the infinite Son of God in giving His life for the salvation of the world. "Behold, what manner of love the Father hath bestowed upon us, that we should be called the sons of God: therefore the world knoweth us not, because it knew Him not." (1 John 3:1)—*Selected Messages*, book 1, pp. 233, 234.

Further Reflection: *Does the sacrifice of Jesus make me afraid to sin?*

ORIGINATOR

And beginning at Moses and all the Prophets, He expounded to them in all the Scriptures the things concerning Himself.

—Luke 24:27

Christ in His teaching presented old truths of which He Himself was the **originator**, truths which He had spoken through patriarchs and prophets; but He now shed upon them a new light. How different appeared their meaning! A flood of light and spirituality was brought in by His explanation. And He promised that the Holy Spirit should enlighten the disciples, that the word of God should be ever unfolding to them. They would be able to present its truths in new beauty.

Ever since the first promise of redemption was spoken in Eden, the life, the character, and the mediatorial work of Christ have been the study of human minds. Yet every mind through whom the Holy Spirit has worked has presented these themes in a light that is fresh and new. The truths of redemption are capable of constant development and expansion. Though old, they are ever new, constantly revealing to the seeker for truth a greater glory and a mightier power.

In every age there is a new development of truth, a message of God to the people of that generation. The old truths are all essential; new truth is not independent of the old, but an unfolding of it. It is only as the old truths are understood that we can comprehend the new. When Christ desired to open to His disciples the truth of His resurrection, He began "at Moses and all the prophets" and "expounded unto them in all the scriptures the things concerning Himself." (Luke 24:27) But it is the light which shines in the fresh unfolding of truth that glorifies the old. He who rejects or neglects the new does not really possess the old. For him it loses its vital power and becomes but a lifeless form.

There are those who profess to believe and to teach the truths of the Old Testament, while they reject the New. But in refusing to receive the teachings of Christ, they show that they do not believe that which patriarchs and prophets have spoken. "Had ye believed Moses," Christ said, "ye would have believed Me; for he wrote of Me." (John 5:46) Hence there is no real power in their teaching of even the Old Testament. —*Christ's Object Lessons*, pp. 127, 128.

Further Reflection: *What ancient truth has God adapted and made effectual to meet a present need in my life?*

IDEAL OF ALL TRUTH

And we know that the Son of God has come and has given us an understanding, that we may know Him who is true; and we are in Him who is true, in His Son Jesus Christ. This is the true God and eternal life.
—1 John 5:20

Christ, the great Medical Missionary, came to our world as the **ideal of all truth**. Truth never languished on His lips, never suffered in His hands. Words of truth fell from His lips with the freshness and power of a new revelation. He unfolded the mysteries of the kingdom of heaven, bringing forth jewel after jewel of truth.

Christ spoke with authority. Every truth essential for the people to know He proclaimed with the unfaltering assurance of certain knowledge. He uttered nothing fanciful or sentimental. He presented no sophistries, no human opinions. No idle tales, no false theories clothed in beautiful language, came from His lips. The statements that He made were truths established by personal knowledge. He foresaw the delusive doctrines that would fill the world, but He did not unfold them. In His teachings He dwelt upon the unchangeable principles of God's word. He magnified the simple, practical truths that the common people could understand and bring into the daily experience.

Christ might have opened to men the deepest truths of science. He might have unlocked mysteries that have required centuries of toil and study to penetrate. He might have made suggestions in scientific lines that would have afforded food for thought and stimulus for invention to the close of time. But He did not do this. He said nothing to gratify curiosity or to satisfy humanity's ambitions by opening doors to worldly greatness. In all His teaching, Christ brought the minds of men in contact with the Infinite Mind. He did not direct the people to study men's theories about God, His word, or His works. He taught them to behold God as manifested in His works, in His word, and by His providences. —*Testimonies for the Church*, vol. 8, pp. 201, 202.

Further Reflection: *If Jesus said nothing to gratify the curiosities of His hearers nor to satisfy human ambition, what does that say to me about how I should speak and act?*

GREAT SOURCE OF ILLUMINATION

That was the true Light which gives light to every man coming into the world.

—John 1:9

No other light ever has shone or ever will shine upon fallen humanity save that which emanates from Christ. Jesus, the Saviour, is the only light that can illuminate the darkness of a world lying in sin. Of Christ it is written, "In Him was life; and the life was the light of men." (John 1:4) It was by receiving of His life that His disciples could become light bearers. The life of Christ in the soul, His love revealed in the character, would make them the light of the world.

Humanity has in itself no light. Apart from Christ we are like an unkindled taper, like the moon when her face is turned away from the sun; we have not a single ray of brightness to shed into the darkness of the world. But when we turn toward the Sun of Righteousness, when we come in touch with Christ, the whole soul is aglow with the brightness of the divine presence.

Christ's followers are to be more than a light in the midst of humanity. They are the light of the world. Jesus says to all who have named His name, You have given yourselves to Me, and I have given you to the world as My representatives. . . . As Christ is the channel for the revelation of the Father, so we are to be the channel for the revelation of Christ. While our Saviour is the **great source of illumination**, forget not, O Christian, that He is revealed through humanity. God's blessings are bestowed through human instrumentality. Christ Himself came to the world as the Son of man. Humanity, united to the divine nature, must touch humanity. The church of Christ, every individual disciple of the Master, is heaven's appointed channel for the revelation of God to human beings. Angels of glory wait to communicate through you heaven's light and power to souls that are ready to perish. Shall the human agent fail of accomplishing his appointed work? Oh, then to that degree is the world robbed of the promised influence. . . .

But Jesus did not bid the disciples, "Strive to *make* your light shine;" He said, "*Let* it shine." If Christ is dwelling in the heart, it is impossible to conceal the light of His presence. If those who profess to be followers of Christ are not the light of the world, it is because the vital power has left them; if they have no light to give, it is because they have no connection with the Source of light.—*Thoughts From the Mount of Blessing*, pp. 39–41.

Further Reflection: *Am I glowing? Whose path will Jesus illumine through me today?*

DIVINE PILOT

"Who can this be, that even the winds and the sea obey Him?"
—Matthew 8:27

Every ship sailing the sea of life needs to have the **divine Pilot** on board; but when storms arise, when tempests threaten, many persons push their Pilot overboard, and commit their bark into the hand of finite humans, or try to steer it themselves. Then disaster and wreckage generally follow, and the Pilot is blamed for running them into such dangerous waters. Do not commit yourselves into the keeping of people, but say, "The Lord is my helper;" I will seek His counsel, I will be a doer of His will. All the advantages you may have cannot be a blessing to you, neither can the highest-class education qualify you to become a channel of light, unless you have the co-operation of the Divine Spirit. It is as impossible for us to receive qualification from men and women, without the divine enlightenment, as it was for the gods of Egypt to deliver those who trusted in them. Students must not suppose that every suggestion for them to prolong their studies is in harmony with God's plan. Let every such suggestion be taken to the Lord in prayer, and seek earnestly for His guidance—not only once, but again and again. Plead with Him, until you are convinced whether the counsel is of God or humanity. Do not trust yourself to men and women. Act under the Divine Guide.

You have been chosen by Christ. You have been redeemed by the precious blood of the Lamb. Plead before God the efficacy of that blood. Say unto Him: "I am Thine by creation; I am Thine by redemption. I respect human authority, and the advice of my brethren; but I cannot depend wholly upon these. I want Thee, O God, to teach me. I have covenanted with Thee to adopt the divine standard of character, and make Thee my Counselor and Guide—a party to every plan of my life; therefore teach me." Let the glory of the Lord be your first consideration. Repress every desire for worldly distinction, every ambition to secure the first place. Encourage heart purity and holiness, that you may represent the true principles of the gospel. Let every act of your life be sanctified by a holy endeavor to do the Lord's will, that your influence may not lead others into forbidden paths. When God is the Leader, His righteousness shall go before thee, and the glory of the Lord shall be thy rereward. —*Fundamentals of Christian Education*, pp. 348, 349.

Further Reflection: *How does distrusting self affect my image of myself as a Christian?*

TRUE ROCK

For they drank of that spiritual Rock that followed them, and that Rock was Christ.

—1 Corinthians 10:4

From the smitten rock in Horeb first flowed the living stream that refreshed Israel in the desert. During all their wanderings, wherever the need existed, they were supplied with water by a miracle of God's mercy. The water did not, however, continue to flow from Horeb. Wherever in their journeyings they wanted water, there from the clefts of the rock it gushed out beside their encampment.

It was Christ, by the power of His word, that caused the refreshing stream to flow for Israel. "They drank of that spiritual Rock that followed them: and that Rock was Christ." (1 Corinthians 10:4) He was the source of all temporal as well as spiritual blessings. Christ, the **true Rock**, was with them in all their wanderings. "They thirsted not when He led them through the deserts: He caused the waters to flow out of the rock for them; He clave the rock also, and the waters gushed out." "They ran in the dry places like a river." (Isaiah 48:21; Psalm 105:41)

The smitten rock was a figure of Christ, and through this symbol the most precious spiritual truths are taught. As the life-giving waters flowed from the smitten rock, so from Christ, "smitten of God," "wounded for our transgressions," "bruised for our iniquities" (Isaiah 53:4, 5), the stream of salvation flows for a lost race. As the rock had been once smitten, so Christ was to be "once offered to bear the sins of many." (Hebrews 9:28) Our Saviour was not to be sacrificed a second time; and it is only necessary for those who seek the blessings of His grace to ask in the name of Jesus, pouring forth the heart's desire in penitential prayer. Such prayer will bring before the Lord of hosts the wounds of Jesus, and then will flow forth afresh the life-giving blood, symbolized by the flowing of the living water for Israel.—*Patriarchs and Prophets*, p. 411.

Further Reflection: *The life-giving power of Christ is still available for any and all who would drink of Him. What will I miss today if I fail to drink from the True Rock, Christ Jesus?*

DIVINE LEADER

Your ears shall hear a word behind you, saying,
"This is the way, walk in it."

—Isaiah 30:21

Those who undertake to carry forward the work in their own strength will certainly fail. Education alone will not fit a person for a place in the work, will not enable him to obtain a knowledge of God. Hear what Paul has to say on this matter: "For Christ sent me not to baptize, but to preach the gospel: not with wisdom of words, lest the cross of Christ should be made of none effect. For the preaching of the cross is to them that perish foolishness; but unto us which are saved it is the power of God. For it is written, I will destroy the wisdom of the wise, and will bring to nothing the understanding of the prudent. . . . For after that in the wisdom of God the world by wisdom knew not God, it pleased God by the foolishness of preaching to save them that believe."

Through successive ages of darkness, in the midnight of heathenism, God permitted people to try the experiment of finding out God by their own wisdom, not to demonstrate their inability to His satisfaction, but that humans themselves might see that they could not obtain a knowledge of God and of Jesus Christ His Son, save through the revelation of His word by the Holy Spirit. When Christ came to the world, the experiment had been fully tried, and the result made it evident that the world by wisdom knew not God. Even in the church God has allowed people to test their own wisdom in this matter, but when a crisis has been brought about through human fallibility, God has risen mightily to defend His people. When the church has been brought low, when trial and oppression have come upon His people, He more abundantly exalted them by signal deliverance. When unfaithful teachers came among the people, weakness followed, and the faith of God's people seemed to wane; but God arose and purged His floor. . . .

There are times when apostasy comes into the ranks, when piety is left out of the heart by those who should have kept step with their **divine Leader**. . . . There are idols within and idols without; but God sends the Comforter as a reprover of sin, that His people may be warned of their apostasy and rebuked for their backsliding. When the more precious manifestations of His love shall be gratefully acknowledged and appreciated, the Lord will pour in the balm of comfort and the oil of joy.—*Fundamentals of Christian Education*, pp. 196, 197.

Further Reflection: *What good thing am I attempting to do today without Jesus?*

LIGHT

The Lord *is my light and my salvation;*
Whom shall I fear?
The Lord *is the strength of my life;*
Of whom shall I be afraid?

—Psalm 27:1

Those who honor God and keep His commandments are subject to the accusations of Satan. The enemy works with all his energy to lead persons into sin. Then he pleads that on account of their past sins, he should be allowed to exercise his hellish cruelty on them as his own subjects. Of this work Zechariah has written. "And he shewed me Joshua the high priest"—a representative of the people who keep the commandments of God—"standing before the angel of the Lord, and Satan standing at his right hand to resist him." (Zechariah 3:1)

Christ is our High Priest. Satan stands before Him night and day as an accuser of the brethren. With his masterly power he presents every objectionable feature of character as sufficient reason for the withdrawal of Christ's protecting power, thus allowing Satan to discourage and destroy those whom he has caused to sin. But Christ has made atonement for every sinner. Can we by faith hear our Advocate saying, "The Lord rebuke thee, O Satan; even the Lord that hath chosen Jerusalem rebuke thee: is not this a brand plucked out of the fire?" (Verse 2)

"Now Joshua was clothed with filthy garments." (Verse 3) Thus sinners appear before the enemy who by his masterly, deceptive power has led them away from allegiance to God. With garments of sin and shame the enemy clothes those who have been overpowered by his temptations, and then he declares that it is unfair for Christ to be their **Light**, their Defender.

But, poor, repentant mortals, hear the words of Jesus, and believe as you hear: "And He answered (the accusing charge of Satan) and spake unto those (angels) that stood before Him (to do his bidding), saying, Take away the filthy garments from him." I will blot out his transgressions. I will cover his sins. I will impute to him My righteousness. "And unto him He said, Behold, I have caused thine iniquity to pass from thee, and I will clothe thee with change of raiment." (Verse 4)—Manuscript 125, 1901.

Further Reflection: *How can I avoid internalizing Satan's accusations against me, especially those that come from people who have allowed him to use them?*

JUDGE OF ALL THE EARTH

That He might present her to Himself a glorious church,
not having spot or wrinkle or any such thing,
but that she should be holy and without blemish.
—Ephesians 5:27

The deepest interest manifested among human beings in the decisions of earthly tribunals but faintly represents the interest evinced in the heavenly courts when the names entered in the book of life come up in review before the **Judge of all the earth**. The divine Intercessor presents plea that all who have overcome through faith in His blood be forgiven their transgressions, that they be restored to their Eden home, and crowned as joint heirs with Himself to "the first dominion." (Micah 4:8) Satan in his efforts to deceive and tempt our race had thought to frustrate the divine plan in humanity's creation; but Christ now asks that this plan be carried into effect as if human beings had never fallen. He asks for His people not only pardon and justification, full and complete, but a share in His glory and a seat upon His throne.

While Jesus is pleading for the subjects of His grace, Satan accuses them before God as transgressors. The great deceiver has sought to lead them into skepticism, to cause them to lose confidence in God, to separate themselves from His love, and to break His law. Now he points to the record of their lives, to the defects of character, the unlikeness to Christ, which has dishonored their Redeemer, to all the sins that he has tempted them to commit, and because of these he claims them as his subjects.

Jesus does not excuse their sins, but shows their penitence and faith, and, claiming for them forgiveness, He lifts His wounded hands before the Father and the holy angels, saying: I know them by name. I have graven them on the palms of My hands. The sacrifices of God are a broken spirit: a broken and a contrite heart, O God, Thou wilt not despise." (Psalm 51:17) And to the accuser of His people He declares: "The Lord rebuke thee, O Satan; even the Lord that hath chosen Jerusalem rebuke thee: is not this a brand plucked out of the fire?" (Zechariah 3:2) Christ will clothe His faithful ones with His own righteousness, that He may present them to His Father "a glorious church, not having spot, or wrinkle, or any such thing." (Ephesians 5:27)—*The Great Controversy*, pp. 483, 484.

Further Reflection: *If Christ is on my side in the judgment, why do I sometimes fear it?*

LOWLY TEACHER

And He taught in their synagogues, being glorified by all.
—Luke 4:15

In the interview with Nicodemus, Jesus unfolded the plan of salvation, and His mission to the world. In none of His subsequent discourses did He explain so fully, step by step, the work necessary to be done in the hearts of all who would inherit the kingdom of heaven. At the very beginning of His ministry He opened the truth to a member of the Sanhedrin, to the mind that was most receptive, and to an appointed teacher of the people. But the leaders of Israel did not welcome the light. Nicodemus hid the truth in his heart, and for three years there was little apparent fruit.

But Jesus was acquainted with the soil into which He cast the seed. The words spoken at night to one listener in the lonely mountain were not lost. For a time Nicodemus did not publicly acknowledge Christ, but he watched His life, and pondered His teachings. In the Sanhedrin council he repeatedly thwarted the schemes of the priests to destroy Him. When at last Jesus was lifted up on the cross, Nicodemus remembered the teaching upon Olivet: "As Moses lifted up the serpent in the wilderness, even so must the Son of man be lifted up: that whosoever believeth in Him should not perish, but have eternal life." The light from that secret interview illumined the cross upon Calvary, and Nicodemus saw in Jesus the world's Redeemer.

After the Lord's ascension, when the disciples were scattered by persecution, Nicodemus came boldly to the front. He employed his wealth in sustaining the infant church that the Jews had expected to be blotted out at the death of Christ. In the time of peril he who had been so cautious and questioning was firm as a rock, encouraging the faith of the disciples, and furnishing means to carry forward the work of the gospel. He was scorned and persecuted by those who had paid him reverence in other days. He became poor in this world's goods; yet he faltered not in the faith which had its beginning in that night conference with Jesus.

Nicodemus related to John the story of that interview, and by his pen it was recorded for the instruction of millions. The truths there taught are as important today as they were on that solemn night in the shadowy mountain, when the Jewish ruler came to learn the way of life from the **lowly Teacher** of Galilee.—*The Desire of Ages*, pp. 176, 177.

Further Reflection: *Can I lead someone step by step through the plan of salvation?*

HEAD OVER ALL

Heal me, O LORD, and I shall be healed; save me, and I shall be saved, for You are my praise.
—Jeremiah 17:14

The medical missionary work has never been presented to me in any other way than as bearing the same relation to the work as a whole as the arm does to the body. The gospel ministry is an organization for the proclamation of the truth and the carrying forward of the work for sick and well. This is the body, the medical missionary work is the arm, and Christ is the **head over all**. Thus the matter has been presented to me.

It has been urged that because the medical missionary work is the arm of the body, there should be a oneness of respect shown. This is so. The medical missionary work is the arm of the body, and God wants us to take a decided interest in this work.

Christ was bound up in all branches of the work. He did not make any division. He did not feel that He was infringing on physicians when He healed the sick. He proclaimed the truth, and when the sick came to Him for healing, He asked them if they believed that He could make them whole. He was just as ready to lay His hands in healing on the sick and afflicted as He was to preach the gospel. He was just as much at home in this work as in proclaiming the truth; for healing the sick is a part of the gospel.

To take people right where they are, whatever their position, whatever their condition, and help them in every way possible—this is gospel ministry. It may be necessary for ministers to go into the homes of the sick and say, "I am ready to help you, and I will do the best I can. I am not a physician, but I am a minister, and I like to minister to the sick and afflicted." Those who are sick in body are nearly always sick in soul, and when the soul is sick, the body is made sick.—*Medical Ministry*, pp. 237, 238.

Further Reflection: *As Jesus ministered on earth, His healing and preaching benefited all who came in contact with Him, whether they were believers or not. Do I sometimes avoid ministering to sick people who may not share my beliefs?*

OMEGA OF REVELATION

When I saw Him, I fell at His feet as dead.
But He laid His right hand on me, saying to me,
"Do not be afraid; I am the First and the Last."

—Revelation 1:17

The very same Jesus who has given us the Sabbath, and has directed us how to keep it holy, is the Alpha of Genesis, and carries us step by step through the ages, through the incarnation, through His offering of Himself as a living sacrifice for the redemption of a fallen world. He was tried, but was not condemned, because there was nothing to condemn. After the trial Pilate said, "I find no fault in Him." Yet He gave Himself up to be murdered because His own nation was jealous of Him, and hated Him. Christ died as a malefactor on the cross of Calvary. He was laid in the grave. The third day He rose from the dead, and proclaimed, over the rent sepulcher of Joseph: "I am the resurrection, and the life." He ascended to His Father, and today He is our Advocate in the courts of heaven.

We trace Christ all through the Old Testament and the New. "And, behold, I come quickly; and My reward is with me, to give every man according as his work shall be. I am Alpha and Omega, the beginning and the end, the first and the last. Blessed are they that do His commandments, that they may have right to the tree of life, and may enter in through the gates into the city. For without are dogs, and sorcerers, and whoremongers, and murderers, and idolaters, and whosoever loveth and maketh a lie. I, Jesus, have sent Mine angel to testify unto you these things in the churches. I am the root and the offspring of David, and the bright and morning star. And the Spirit and the bride say, Come. And let him that heareth say, Come. And let him that is athirst come. And whosoever will, let him take the water of life freely."

Here we have the Alpha of Genesis and the **Omega of Revelation**. The blessing is promised to all those who keep the commandments of God, and who co-operate with Him in the proclamation of the third angel's message. "I Jesus have sent Mine angel to testify unto you these things in the churches. I am the root and the offspring of David, and the bright and morning star." That which Christ has spoken in the Old Testament is for all the world.—*Review and Herald,* June 8, 1897.

Further Reflection: *How is the fact that Jesus is the first and the last relevant to my life today?*

DIVINE REMEDY

How shall we escape if we neglect so great a salvation,
which at the first began to be spoken by the Lord,
and was confirmed to us by those who heard Him.
—Hebrews 2:3

When people are not under the control of the Word and the Spirit of God, they are captives of Satan, and we know not to what lengths he may lead them in sin. The patriarch Jacob beheld those who take pleasure in wickedness. He saw what would be the result of association with them, and in the Spirit he exclaimed, "O my soul, come not thou into their secret; unto their assembly, mine honour, be not thou united." (Genesis 49:6) He lifts up the danger signal, to warn every soul against such associations. The apostle Paul echoes the warning: "Have no fellowship with the unfruitful works of darkness." (Ephesians 5:11) "Be not deceived: Evil company doth corrupt good manners." (1 Corinthians 15:33, R.V.)

The soul is deceived when it trusts to worldly policy and human inventions instead of trusting in the Lord God of Israel. Can humans find a better guide than the Lord Jesus? a better counselor in doubt and trial? a better defense in danger? To set aside the wisdom of God for human wisdom is a soul-destroying delusion.

If you would see what humanity will do when it rejects the influence of the grace of God, look to that scene in the judgment hall, when the infuriated mob, headed by Jewish priests and elders, clamored for the life of the Son of God. See the divine Sufferer standing by the side of Barabbas, and Pilate asking which he should release unto them. The hoarse cry, swelled by hundreds of passionate, Satan-inspired voices, is, "Away with this man, and release unto us Barabbas"! (Luke 23:18) And when Pilate asked what was to be done with Jesus they cried, "Crucify Him, crucify Him"! (Luke 23:21)

Human nature then is human nature now. When the **divine Remedy** that would have saved and exalted human nature is despised, the same spirit still lives in the hearts of human beings, and we cannot trust to their guidance and maintain our loyalty to Christ.—*Selected Messages*, book 2, pp. 129, 130.

Further Reflection: *How can I distinguish those who have the spirit of Christ from those who do not?*

ANOINTED OF THE LORD

So they cried out again, "Crucify Him!"
Then Pilate said to them, "Why, what evil has He done?"
But they cried out all the more, "Crucify Him!"
—Mark 15:13, 14

At the crucifixion of Christ, those who had thus been healed did not join with the rabble throng in crying, "Crucify Him, crucify Him." Their sympathies were with Jesus; for they had felt His great sympathy and wonderful power. They knew Him to be their Saviour; for He had given them health of body and soul. They listened to the preaching of the apostles, and the entrance of God's word into their hearts gave them understanding. They became agents of God's mercy, and instruments of His salvation.

The crowd that had fled from the temple court after a time slowly drifted back. They had partially recovered from the panic that had seized them, but their faces expressed irresolution and timidity. They looked with amazement on the works of Jesus, and were convicted that in Him the prophecies concerning the Messiah were fulfilled. The sin of the desecration of the temple rested, in a great degree, upon the priests. It was by their arrangement that the court had been turned into a market place. The people were comparatively innocent. They were impressed by the divine authority of Jesus; but with them the influence of the priests and rulers was paramount. They regarded Christ's mission as an innovation, and questioned His right to interfere with what was permitted by the authorities of the temple. They were offended because the traffic had been interrupted, and they stifled the convictions of the Holy Spirit.

Above all others the priests and rulers should have seen in Jesus the **anointed of the Lord**; for in their hands were the sacred scrolls that described His mission, and they knew that the cleansing of the temple was a manifestation of more than human power. Much as they hated Jesus, they could not free themselves from the thought that He might be a prophet sent by God to restore the sanctity of the temple. With a deference born of this fear, they went to Him with the inquiry, "What sign showest Thou unto us, seeing that Thou doest these things?"—*The Desire of Ages*, pp. 163, 164.

Further Reflection: *When have I allowed my doubts or preconceived notions to block clear manifestations of God's working in my life? How can I evaluate and benefit from God's providential moving?*

SANCTIFIER

"Surely My Sabbaths you shall keep, for it is a sign between Me and you throughout your generations, that you may know that I am the LORD who sanctifies you."

—Exodus 31:13

As the Sabbath was the sign that distinguished Israel when they came out of Egypt to enter the earthly Canaan, so it is the sign that now distinguishes God's people as they come out from the world to enter the heavenly rest. The Sabbath is a sign of the relationship existing between God and His people, a sign that they honor His law. It distinguishes between His loyal subjects and transgressors.

From the pillar of cloud Christ declared concerning the Sabbath: "Verily My Sabbaths ye shall keep: for it is a sign between Me and you throughout your generations; that ye may know that I am the Lord that doth sanctify you." (Exodus 31:13) The Sabbath given to the world as the sign of God as the Creator is also the sign of Him as the **Sanctifier**. The power that created all things is the power that re-creates the soul in His own likeness. To those who keep holy the Sabbath day it is the sign of sanctification. True sanctification is harmony with God, oneness with Him in character. It is received through obedience to those principles that are the transcript of His character. And the Sabbath is the sign of obedience. He who from the heart obeys the fourth commandment will obey the whole law. He is sanctified through obedience.

To us as to Israel the Sabbath is given "for a perpetual covenant." To those who reverence His holy day the Sabbath is a sign that God recognizes them as His chosen people. It is a pledge that He will fulfill to them His covenant. Every soul who accepts the sign of God's government places himself under the divine, everlasting covenant. He fastens himself to the golden chain of obedience, every link of which is a promise.

The fourth commandment alone of all the ten contains the seal of the great Lawgiver, the Creator of the heavens and the earth. Those who obey this commandment take upon themselves His name, and all the blessings it involves are theirs.—*Testimonies for the Church*, vol. 6, pp. 349, 350.

Further Reflection: *If sanctification is the process of being made holy, how does Jesus use the Sabbath to sanctify me? Is my Sabbath observance making me more holy?*

JULY

MASTER

But Jesus did not commit Himself to them, because He knew all men.
—John 2:24

Those only who are constantly receiving fresh supplies of grace, will have power proportionate to their daily need and their ability to use that power. Instead of looking forward to some future time when, through a special endowment of spiritual power, they will receive a miraculous fitting up for soul winning, they are yielding themselves daily to God, that He may make them vessels meet for His use. Daily they are improving the opportunities for service that lie within their reach. Daily they are witnessing for the **Master** wherever they may be, whether in some humble sphere of labor in the home, or in a public field of usefulness.

To the consecrated worker there is wonderful consolation in the knowledge that even Christ during His life on earth sought His Father daily for fresh supplies of needed grace; and from this communion with God He went forth to strengthen and bless others. Behold the Son of God bowed in prayer to His Father! Though He is the Son of God, He strengthens His faith by prayer, and by communion with heaven gathers to Himself power to resist evil and to minister to the needs of human beings. As the Elder Brother of our race He knows the necessities of those who, compassed with infirmity and living in a world of sin and temptation, still desire to serve Him. He knows that the messengers whom He sees fit to send are weak, erring persons; but to all who give themselves wholly to His service He promises divine aid. His own example is an assurance that earnest, persevering supplication to God in faith—faith that leads to entire dependence upon God, and unreserved consecration to His work—will avail to bring to human beings the Holy Spirit's aid in the battle against sin.

Every worker who follows the example of Christ will be prepared to receive and use the power that God has promised to His church for the ripening of earth's harvest. Morning by morning, as the heralds of the gospel kneel before the Lord and renew their vows of consecration to Him, He will grant them the presence of His Spirit, with its reviving, sanctifying power. As they go forth to the day's duties, they have the assurance that the unseen agency of the Holy Spirit enables them to be "laborers together with God."—*The Acts of the Apostles*, pp. 55, 56.

Further Reflection: *If Jesus wants to address my deepest needs, what area of my life should I open to Him today?*

UNFAILING HELPER

"MENE, MENE, TEKEL, UPHARSIN."

—Daniel 5:25

The hand was gone, but four terrible words were left. With bated breath the people waited as Daniel announced their meaning: *"Mene, Mene, Tekel, Upharsin:"* "God hath numbered thy kingdom, and finished it;" "thou art weighed in the balances, and art found wanting;" "thy kingdom is divided, and given to the Medes and Persians." (Daniel 5:25-28)

Just as surely as there was a Witness at the feast of Belshazzar, there is also a Witness in every scene of sacrilegious mirth, and just as surely is the recording angel writing, "Thou art weighed in the balances, and art found wanting."

Intemperance is on the increase, in spite of the efforts made to control it. We cannot be too earnest in seeking to hinder its progress, to raise the fallen, and shield the weak from temptation. With our feeble human hands we can do but little, but we have an **unfailing Helper**. We must not forget that the arm of Christ can reach to the very depths of human woe and degradation. He can give us help to conquer even this terrible demon of intemperance.

But it is in the home that the real work must begin. The greatest burden rests upon those who have the responsibility of educating the youth, of forming their character. Here is a work for mothers, in helping their children to form correct habits and pure tastes, to develop moral stamina, true moral worth. Teach them that they are not to be swayed by others, that they are not to yield to wrong influences, but to influence others for good, to ennoble and elevate those with whom they associate. Teach them that if they connect themselves with God, they will have strength from Him to resist the fiercest temptations.

In the Babylonian court, Daniel was surrounded by allurements to sin, but by the help of Christ he maintained his integrity. He who cannot resist temptation, with every facility which has been placed within his reach, is not registered in the books of heaven as a man. The Lord never places men in positions so trying that it is beyond their power to withstand evil. Divine power is ever ready to protect and strengthen him who has been made a partaker of the divine nature.—*Christian Temperance and Bible Hygiene*, pp. 21, 22.

Further Reflection: *How can I avoid giving in to Satan's many allurements to sin?*

CHAMPION OF TRUTH

Yes, and all who desire to live godly in Christ Jesus will suffer persecution.

—2 Timothy 3:12

Satan's enmity against the human race is kindled because, through Christ, they are the objects of God's love and mercy. He desires to thwart the divine plan for man's redemption, to cast dishonor upon God, by defacing and defiling His handiwork; he would cause grief in heaven and fill the earth with woe and desolation. And he points to all this evil as the result of God's work in creating human beings.

It is the grace that Christ implants in the soul which creates in men and women enmity against Satan. Without this converting grace and renewing power, human beings would continue the captives of Satan, servants ever ready to do his bidding. But the new principle in the soul creates conflict where hitherto had been peace. The power which Christ imparts enables men and women to resist the tyrant and usurper. Whoever is seen to abhor sin instead of loving it, whoever resists and conquers those passions that have held sway within, displays the operation of a principle wholly from above.

The antagonism that exists between the spirit of Christ and the spirit of Satan was most strikingly displayed in the world's reception of Jesus. It was not so much because He appeared without worldly wealth, pomp, or grandeur that the Jews were led to reject Him. They saw that He possessed power which would more than compensate for the lack of these outward advantages. But the purity and holiness of Christ called forth against Him the hatred of the ungodly. His life of self-denial and sinless devotion was a perpetual reproof to a proud, sensual people. It was this that evoked enmity against the Son of God. Satan and evil angels joined with evil human beings. All the energies of apostasy conspired against the **Champion of truth**.

The same enmity is manifested toward Christ's followers as was manifested toward their Master. Whoever sees the repulsive character of sin, and in strength from above resists temptation, will assuredly arouse the wrath of Satan and his subjects.—*The Great Controversy*, pp. 506, 507.

Further Reflection: *What is my current attitude towards sin? Do I find it repulsive and abhorrent, or have I become desensitized to its destructive power?*

STAR OF HOPE

But when the fullness of the time had come, God sent forth His Son.
—Galatians 4:4

The rebellion of Israel against the law and authority of God, caused their destruction. The honor God had given them of being thus conducted by His Son, increased their sin. The charges of the Jews that Christ did not regard the law of Moses, was without the least foundation. Christ was a Jew, and, to the hour of His death upon the cross, observed the law binding upon the Jews. But when type met antitype, at the death of Christ, then the offering of the blood of beasts became valueless. Christ made the one great offering in giving His own life, which all their former offerings had foreshadowed, which terminated the value of all the sacrificial offerings of the Jewish law.

Since the fall, no immediate communication could exist between God and humanity, only through Christ, and God committed to His Son, in a special sense, the case of the fallen race. Christ has undertaken the work of redemption. He purposes to maintain the full honor of God's law, notwithstanding the human family have transgressed it. He will redeem from its curse all the obedient who will embrace the offer of mercy by accepting the atonement so wonderfully provided. . . .

Adam and Eve at their creation had knowledge of the original law of God. It was imprinted upon their hearts, and they were acquainted with the claims of law upon them. When they transgressed the law of God, and fell from their state of happy innocence, and became sinners, the future of the fallen race was not relieved by a single ray of hope. God pitied them and Christ devised the plan for their salvation by Himself bearing the guilt. When the curse was pronounced upon the earth and upon humanity in connection with the curse was a promise that through Christ there was hope and pardon for the transgression of God's law. Although gloom and darkness hung, like the pall of death, over the future, yet in the promise of the Redeemer, the **star of hope** lighted up the dark future. The gospel was first preached to Adam by Christ. Adam and Eve felt sincere sorrow and repentance for their guilt. They believed the precious promise of God, and were saved from utter ruin.—*Review and Herald*, April 29, 1875.

Further Reflection: *If I was Adam, how would it feel to know that God had made a way to save the world that my sin had so terribly damaged?*

WISE AND MIGHTY COUNSELOR

"As the heavens are higher than the earth, so are My ways higher than your ways, and My thoughts than your thoughts."
—Isaiah 55:9

God would have you trust in His love, and be constantly guarding your soul by locking the gate of your thoughts, that they shall not become unmanageable, for when you allow your mind to indulge these thoughts of self-pity, the enemy comes in to suggest the most unkind and unreasonable things in regard to those who would do you good, and only good.

The Lord is to be your Helper, and you will find comfort of mind and strength in considering the very things He would have you think upon. Consider the ways of the Lord toward you that your human life may be an exposition and a witness to His ways. You are a child of God; ever act toward your heavenly Father as you wish your children to act toward you. You cannot measure God; you cannot by searching find out God. "Canst thou find out the Almighty unto perfection? It is as high as heaven; what canst thou do? Deeper than hell; what canst thou know?" (Job 11:7, 8)

The Bible is to be to you practical and useful in every phase of your life. In every perplexity, go to God; keep your tongue as in a bridle while with men and women, but talk with God. A life guarded and controlled by the Word of God develops purity and nobility of character, comparable to fine gold, yea, even the golden wedge of Ophir. Jesus bids you come to Him in the night of trial, and you will find rest for your soul. He says, "Take My yoke upon you; and learn of Me; for I am meek and lowly in heart, and ye shall find rest unto your soul. For My yoke is easy, and My burden is light." (Matthew 11:29, 30)

Listen to Jesus, follow His counsel, and you will not go astray from the **wise and mighty Counselor**, the only true Guide, the only One who can give you peace, happiness, and fullness of joy. Is not Jesus, everything to you? Can you not hide your life with Christ in God? One with Christ, you are one with the Father. You may have deep and solemn earnestness, but be careful to have all your powers under the control of the Holy Spirit, that your work may be done in simplicity, and without friction.—Letter 10, 1894.

Further Reflection: *What does it mean to hide my life with Christ in God?*

ROCK OF AGES

Coming to Him as to a living stone, rejected indeed by men, but chosen by God and precious, you also, as living stones, are being built up a spiritual house.

—1 Peter 2:4, 5

The apostles built upon a sure foundation, even the **Rock of ages**. To this foundation they brought the stones that they quarried from the world. Not without hindrance did the builders labor. Their work was made exceedingly difficult by the opposition of the enemies of Christ. They had to contend against the bigotry, prejudice, and hatred of those who were building upon a false foundation. Many who wrought as builders of the church could be likened to the builders of the wall in Nehemiah's day, of whom it is written: "They which builded on the wall, and they that bare burdens, with those that laded, everyone with one of his hands wrought in the work, and with the other hand held a weapon." (Nehemiah 4:17)

Kings and governors, priests and rulers, sought to destroy the temple of God. But in the face of imprisonment, torture, and death, faithful people carried the work forward; and the structure grew, beautiful and symmetrical. At times the workmen were almost blinded by the mists of superstition that settled around them. At times they were almost overpowered by the violence of their opponents. But with unfaltering faith and unfailing courage they pressed on with the work.

One after another the foremost of the builders fell by the hand of the enemy. Stephen was stoned; James was slain by the sword; Paul was beheaded; Peter was crucified; John was exiled. Yet the church grew. New workers took the place of those who fell, and stone after stone was added to the building. Thus slowly ascended the temple of the church of God.

Centuries of fierce persecution followed the establishment of the Christian church, but there were never wanting people who counted the work of building God's temple dearer than life itself. Of such it is written: "Others had trial of cruel mockings and scourgings, yea, moreover of bonds and imprisonment: they were stoned, they were sawn asunder, were tempted, were slain with the sword: they wandered about in sheepskins and goatskins; being destitute, afflicted, tormented; (of whom the world was not worthy:) they wandered in deserts, and in mountains, and in dens and caves of the earth." (Hebrews 11:36–38)—*The Acts of the Apostles*, pp. 596–598.

Further Reflection: *What am I willing to sacrifice to continue building up God's church?*

PATTERN

Therefore be imitators of God as dear children.
—Ephesians 5:1

If the people who lived before the Flood had been obedient to the Word of God they would not have perished by the waters of the Flood. If the Israelites had been obedient to the words of God, He would have bestowed upon them special blessings. But they fell in consequence of the indulgence of appetite and passion. They would not be obedient to the words of God. Indulgence of perverted appetite led them into numerous and grievous sins. If they had made the requirements of God their first consideration, and their physical wants secondary, in submission to God's choice of proper food for them, not one of them would have fallen in the wilderness. They would have been established in the goodly land of Canaan, a holy, happy people with not a feeble one in all their tribes.

The Saviour of the world became sin for the race. In becoming humanity's substitute Christ did not manifest His power as the Son of God, but ranked Himself among the sons of men and women. He was to bear the trial of temptation as a man, in our behalf, under the most trying circumstances, and leave an example of faith and perfect trust in His heavenly Father. Christ knew that His Father would supply Him food when it would be for His glory. He would not in this severe ordeal, when hunger pressed Him beyond measure, prematurely diminish one particle of the trial allotted to Him by exercising His divine power.

Fallen human beings when brought into straightened places could not have the power to work miracles on their own behalf, to save themselves from pain or anguish, or to give themselves victory over their enemies. It was the purpose of God to test and prove the race, and give them an opportunity to develop character by bringing them frequently into trying positions to test their faith and confidence in His love and power. The life of Christ was a perfect **pattern**. He was ever, by His example and teachings, teaching men and women that God was their dependence, and that in Him should be their faith and firm trust.—*Confrontation*, pp. 43, 44.

Further Reflection: *Jesus willingly chose to experience every human challenge and extremity that He might help me develop character in life's difficult moments. Have I given Jesus permission to make today a character-building day?*

BELOVED TEACHER AND FRIEND

Simon Peter said to Him, "Lord, where are You going?"
Jesus answered him, "Where I am going you cannot follow Me now,
but you shall follow Me afterward."

—John 13:36

Looking upon His disciples with divine love and with the tenderest sympathy, Christ said, "Now is the Son of man glorified, and God is glorified in Him."

Judas had left the upper chamber, and Christ was alone with the eleven. He was about to speak of His approaching separation from them; but before doing this He pointed to the great object of His mission. It was this that He kept ever before Him. It was His joy that all His humiliation and suffering would glorify the Father's name. To this He first directs the thoughts of His disciples.

Then addressing them by the endearing term, "Little children," He said, "Yet a little while I am with you. Ye shall seek Me: and as I said unto the Jews, Whither I go, ye cannot come; so now I say to you."

The disciples could not rejoice when they heard this. Fear fell upon them. They pressed close about the Saviour. Their Master and Lord, their **beloved Teacher and Friend**, He was dearer to them than life. To Him they had looked for help in all their difficulties, for comfort in their sorrows and disappointments. Now He was to leave them, a lonely, dependent company. Dark were the forebodings that filled their hearts.

But the Saviour's words to them were full of hope. He knew that they were to be assailed by the enemy, and that Satan's craft is most successful against those who are depressed by difficulties. Therefore He pointed them away from "the things which are seen," to "the things which are not seen." (2 Corinthians 4:18) From earthly exile He turned their thoughts to the heavenly home.—*The Desire of Ages*, p. 662.

Further Reflection: *If Jesus is building me a mansion in hopes of spending eternity with me, what traits of character am I building in preparation for eternity?*

AUTHOR OF TRUTH

"Sanctify them by Your truth. Your word is truth."
—John 17:17

Through nature, through types and symbols, through patriarchs and prophets, God had spoken to the world. Lessons must be given to humanity in the language of humanity. The Messenger of the covenant must speak. His voice must be heard in His own temple. Christ must come to utter words which should be clearly and definitely understood. He, the **author of truth**, must separate truth from the chaff of humanity's utterance, which had made it of no effect. The principles of God's government and the plan of redemption must be clearly defined. The lessons of the Old Testament must be fully set before men and women.

Among the Jews there were yet steadfast souls, descendants of that holy line through whom a knowledge of God had been preserved. These still looked for the hope of the promise made unto the fathers. They strengthened their faith by dwelling upon the assurance given through Moses, "A Prophet shall the Lord your God raise up unto you of your brethren, like unto me; Him shall ye hear in all things whatsoever He shall say unto you." (Acts 3:22) Again, they read how the Lord would anoint One "to preach good tidings unto the meek," "to bind up the brokenhearted, to proclaim liberty to the captives," and to declare the "acceptable year of the Lord." (Isaiah 61:1, 2) They read how He would "set judgment in the earth," how the isles should "wait for His law," how the Gentiles should come to His light, and kings to the brightness of His rising. (Isaiah 42:4; 60:3)

The dying words of Jacob filled them with hope: "The scepter shall not depart from Judah, nor a lawgiver from between his feet, until Shiloh come." (Genesis 49:10) The waning power of Israel testified that the Messiah's coming was at hand. The prophecy of Daniel pictured the glory of His reign over an empire which should succeed all earthly kingdoms; and, said the prophet, "It shall stand forever." (Daniel 2:44) While few understood the nature of Christ's mission, there was a widespread expectation of a mighty prince who should establish his kingdom in Israel, and who should come as a deliverer to the nations.

The fullness of the time had come. Humanity, becoming more degraded through ages of transgression, called for the coming of the Redeemer.—*The Desire of Ages*, p. 34.

Further Reflection: *Do I know how to distinguish truth from error?*

OUR RIGHTEOUSNESS

But of Him you are in Christ Jesus, who became for us wisdom from God—and righteousness and sanctification and redemption.
—1 Corinthians 1:30

The thought that the righteousness of Christ is imputed to us, not because of any merit on our part, but as a free gift from God, is a precious thought. The enemy of God and human beings is not willing that this truth should be clearly presented; for he knows that if the people receive it fully, his power will be broken. If he can control minds so that doubt and unbelief and darkness shall compose the experience of those who claim to be the children of God, he can overcome them with temptation.

That simple faith which takes God at His word should be encouraged. God's people must have that faith which will lay hold of divine power; "for by grace are ye saved through faith; and that not of yourselves: it is the gift of God." (Ephesians 2:8) Those who believe that God for Christ's sake has forgiven their sins, should not, through temptation, fail to press on to fight the good fight of faith. Their faith should grow stronger until their Christian life, as well as their words, shall declare, "The blood of Jesus Christ . . . cleanseth us from all sin." (1 John 1:7)

If we would have the spirit and power of the third angel's message, we must present the law and the gospel together, for they go hand in hand. As a power from beneath is stirring up the children of disobedience to make void the law of God, and to trample upon the truth that Christ is **our righteousness**, a power from above is moving upon the hearts of those who are loyal, to exalt the law, and to lift up Jesus as a complete Saviour. Unless divine power is brought into the experience of the people of God, false theories and ideas will take minds captive, Christ and His righteousness will be dropped out of the experience of many, and their faith will be without power or life.

Ministers are to present Christ in His fullness both in the churches and in new fields, that the hearers may have an intelligent faith. The people must be instructed that Christ is unto them salvation and righteousness.—*Gospel Workers*, pp. 161, 162.

Further Reflection: *How does Christ's righteousness break Satan's power in my life?*

GREAT ADVOCATE

"Until now you have asked nothing in My name.
Ask, and you will receive, that your joy may be full."
—John 16:24

God's appointments and grants in our behalf are without limit. The throne of grace is itself the highest attraction because it is occupied by One who permits us to call Him Father. But God did not deem the principle of salvation complete while invested only with His own love. By His appointment He has placed at His altar an Advocate clothed with our nature. As our Intercessor, His office work is to introduce us to God as His sons and daughters. Christ intercedes in behalf of those who have received Him. To them He gives power, by virtue of His own merits, to become members of the royal family, children of the heavenly King. And the Father demonstrates His infinite love for Christ, who paid our ransom with His blood, by receiving and welcoming Christ's friends as His friends. He is satisfied with the atonement made. He is glorified by the incarnation, the life, death, and mediation of His Son.

No sooner does the child of God approach the mercy seat than he becomes the client of the **great Advocate**. At his first utterance of penitence and appeal for pardon Christ espouses his case and makes it His own, presenting the supplication before the Father as His own request.

As Christ intercedes in our behalf, the Father lays open all the treasures of His grace for our appropriation, to be enjoyed and to be communicated to others. "Ask in My name," Christ says; "I do not say that I will pray the Father for you; for the Father Himself loveth you, because you have loved Me. Make use of My name. This will give your prayers efficiency, and the Father will give you the riches of His grace; wherefore, 'ask, and ye shall receive, that your joy may be full.' " (John 16:24.)

God desires His obedient children to claim His blessing and to come before Him with praise and thanksgiving. God is the Fountain of life and power. He can make the wilderness a fruitful field for the people that keep His commandments, for this is for the glory of His name. He has done for His chosen people that which should inspire every heart with thanksgiving, and it grieves Him that so little praise is offered. —*Testimonies for the Church*, vol. 6, pp. 363, 364.

Further Reflection: *What blessings does God have for me that I have yet to claim?*

JULY 12

BREAD OF LIFE

"Most assuredly, I say to you, Moses did not give you the bread from heaven, but My Father gives you the true bread from heaven."
—John 6:32

Verily, verily, I say unto you," Christ said, "Ye seek Me, not because ye saw the miracle, but because ye did eat of the loaves, and were filled. Labour not for the meat that perisheth, but for that meat which endureth unto everlasting life, which the Son of man shall give unto you; for Him hath the Father sealed. Then said they unto Him, What shall we do, that we might work the works of God? Jesus answered and said unto them, This is the work of God, That ye believe on Him whom He hath sent." (John 6:26–29)

He assured them that Moses gave them not the bread from heaven. "My Father," He said, "giveth you the true bread from heaven. For the bread of God is He which cometh down from heaven, and giveth life unto the world." (Verses 32, 33)

We have the result of this plain discourse. What was it? They would not receive the truth. They refused to hear and turned away from Christ. And their rejection of Christ, the Bread of life, was, to them, a final rejection of the truth. They walked no more with Him.

"I am the **Bread of life**," the author, nourisher, and supporter of eternal, spiritual life. In the thirty-fifth verse of the sixth chapter of John, Christ represents Himself under the similitude of heavenly bread. To eat His flesh and to drink His blood means to receive Him as a heaven-sent teacher. Belief in Him is essential to spiritual life. Those who feast on the Word never hunger, never thirst, never desire any higher or more exalted good. "In righteousness shalt thou be established; thou shalt be far from oppression; for thou shalt not fear; and from terror; for it shall not come near thee. Behold, they shall surely gather together but not by Me; whosoever shall gather together against thee shall fall for thy sake. . . . No weapon that is formed against thee shall prosper, and every tongue that shall rise against thee in judgment thou shalt condemn. This is the heritage of the servants of the Lord, and their righteousness is of Me, saith the Lord." (Isaiah 54:14, 15, 17)—Manuscript 81, 1906.

Further Reflection: *If I knew that someone was rejecting Jesus in a certain area of their lives, how would I approach them to help them?*

DIVINE LEGISLATOR

For the L*ORD* *is our Judge,*
The L*ORD* *is our Lawgiver,*
The L*ORD* *is our King;*
He will save us.

—Isaiah 33:22

The Lord's day mentioned by John was the Sabbath, the day on which Jehovah rested after the great work of creation, and which He blessed and sanctified because He had rested upon it. The Sabbath was as sacredly observed by John upon the Isle of Patmos as when he was among the people, preaching upon that day. By the barren rocks surrounding him, John was reminded of rocky Horeb, and how, when God spoke His law to the people there, He said, "Remember the sabbath day, to keep it holy."

The Son of God spoke to Moses from the mountaintop. God made the rocks His sanctuary. His temple was the everlasting hills. The **Divine Legislator** descended upon the rocky mountain to speak His law in the hearing of all the people, that they might be impressed by the grand and awful exhibition of His power and glory, and fear to transgress His commandments. God spoke His law amid thunders and lightnings and the thick cloud upon the top of the mountain, and His voice was as the voice of a trumpet exceeding loud. The law of Jehovah was unchangeable, and the tablets upon which He wrote that law were solid rock, signifying the immutability of His precepts. Rocky Horeb became a sacred spot to all who loved and revered the law of God.

While John was contemplating the scenes of Horeb, the Spirit of Him who sanctified the seventh day, came upon him. He contemplated the sin of Adam in transgressing the divine law, and the fearful results of that transgression. The infinite love of God, in giving His Son to redeem a lost race, seemed too great for language to express. As he presents it in his epistle, he calls upon the church and the world to behold it.—*The Sanctified Life*, pp. 74, 75.

All who regard the Sabbath as a sign between them and God . . . will represent the principles of His government. They will bring into daily practice the laws of His kingdom.—*My Life Today*, p. 259.

Further Reflection: *What message is Jesus sending me each time I keep the Sabbath?*

FOUNTAIN OF HEALING MERCY FOR THE WORLD

"For the Son of Man did not come to destroy men's lives but to save them."

—Luke 9:56

Jesus carried into His labor cheerfulness and tact. It requires much patience and spirituality to bring Bible religion into the home life and into the workshop, to bear the strain of worldly business, and yet keep the eye single to the glory of God. This is where Christ was a helper. He was never so full of worldly care as to have no time or thought for heavenly things. Often He expressed the gladness of His heart by singing psalms and heavenly songs. Often the dwellers in Nazareth heard His voice raised in praise and thanksgiving to God. He held communion with heaven in song; and as His companions complained of weariness from labor, they were cheered by the sweet melody from His lips. His praise seemed to banish the evil angels, and, like incense, fill the place with fragrance. The minds of His hearers were carried away from their earthly exile, to the heavenly home.

Jesus was the **fountain of healing mercy for the world**; and through all those secluded years at Nazareth, His life flowed out in currents of sympathy and tenderness. The aged, the sorrowing, and the sin-burdened, the children at play in their innocent joy, the little creatures of the groves, the patient beasts of burden—all were happier for His presence. He whose word of power upheld the worlds would stoop to relieve a wounded bird. There was nothing beneath His notice, nothing to which He disdained to minister.

Thus as He grew in wisdom and stature, Jesus increased in favor with God and human beings. He drew the sympathy of all hearts by showing Himself capable of sympathizing with all. The atmosphere of hope and courage that surrounded Him made Him a blessing in every home. And often in the synagogue on the Sabbath day He was called upon to read the lesson from the prophets, and the hearts of the hearers thrilled as a new light shone out from the familiar words of the sacred text.

Yet Jesus shunned display. During all the years of His stay in Nazareth, He made no exhibition of His miraculous power. He sought no high position and assumed no titles.—*The Desire of Ages*, pp. 73, 74.

Further Reflection: *How will I perpetuate Jesus' legacy of healing mercy for the world? How can I open my heart today so His current of love flows through me?*

DYING AUTHOR

"O My Father, if it is possible, let this cup pass from Me; nevertheless, not as I will, but as You will."
—Matthew 26:39

Satan with his fierce temptations wrung the heart of Jesus. The Saviour could not see through the portals of the tomb. Hope did not present to Him His coming forth from the grave a conqueror, or tell Him of the Father's acceptance of the sacrifice. He feared that sin was so offensive to God that Their separation was to be eternal. Christ felt the anguish which the sinner will feel when mercy shall no longer plead for the guilty race. It was the sense of sin, bringing the Father's wrath upon Him as humanity's substitute, that made the cup He drank so bitter, and broke the heart of the Son of God.

With amazement angels witnessed the Saviour's despairing agony. The hosts of heaven veiled their faces from the fearful sight. Inanimate nature expressed sympathy with its insulted and **dying Author**. The sun refused to look upon the awful scene. Its full, bright rays were illuminating the earth at midday, when suddenly it seemed to be blotted out. Complete darkness, like a funeral pall, enveloped the cross. "There was darkness over all the land unto the ninth hour." There was no eclipse or other natural cause for this darkness, which was as deep as midnight without moon or stars. It was a miraculous testimony given by God that the faith of after generations might be confirmed.

In that thick darkness God's presence was hidden. He makes darkness His pavilion, and conceals His glory from human eyes. God and His holy angels were beside the cross. The Father was with His Son. Yet His presence was not revealed. Had His glory flashed forth from the cloud, every human beholder would have been destroyed. And in that dreadful hour Christ was not to be comforted with the Father's presence. He trod the wine press alone, and of the people there was none with Him.

In the thick darkness, God veiled the last human agony of His Son. All who had seen Christ in His suffering had been convicted of His divinity. That face, once beheld by humanity, was never forgotten. As the face of Cain expressed his guilt as a murderer, so the face of Christ revealed innocence, serenity, benevolence—the image of God.—*The Desire of Ages*, pp. 753, 754.

Further Reflection: *In what ways did creation "weep" on the day that Jesus died?*

MEEK PATTERN

"Is this not the carpenter's son?"

—Matthew 13:55

A large portion of those who profess to be looking for Christ would be as forward as the Pharisees were to have the disciples silenced, and they would doubtless raise the cry, "Fanaticism! Mesmerism! Mesmerism!" And the disciples, spreading their garments and branches of palm trees in the way, would be thought extravagant and wild. But God will have a people on the earth who will not be so cold and dead but that they can praise and glorify Him. He will receive glory from some people, and if those of His choice, those who keep His commandments, should hold their peace, the very stones would cry out.

Jesus is coming, but not as at His first advent, a babe in Bethlehem; not as He rode into Jerusalem, when the disciples praised God with a loud voice and cried, "Hosanna"; but in the glory of the Father and with all the retinue of holy angels to escort Him on His way to earth. All heaven will be emptied of the angels, while the waiting saints will be looking for Him and gazing into heaven, as were the people of Galilee when He ascended from the Mount of Olivet. Then only those who are holy, those who have followed fully the **meek Pattern**, will with rapturous joy exclaim as they behold Him, "Lo, this is our God; we have waited for Him, and He will save us." And they will be changed "in a moment, in the twinkling of an eye, at the last trump"—that trump which wakes the sleeping saints, and calls them forth from their dusty beds, clothed with glorious immortality, and shouting, "Victory! Victory over death and the grave!" The changed saints are then caught up together with the angels to meet the Lord in the air, never more to be separated from the object of their love.

With such a prospect as this before us, such a glorious hope, such a redemption that Christ has purchased for us by His own blood, shall we hold our peace? Shall we not praise God even with a loud voice, as did the disciples when Jesus rode into Jerusalem? Is not our prospect far more glorious than was theirs? Who dare then forbid us glorifying God, even with a loud voice, when we have such a hope, big with immortality, and full of glory? We have tasted of the powers of the world to come, and long for more. My whole being cries out after the living God, and I shall not be satisfied until I am filled with all His fullness.—*Early Writings*, pp. 109, 110.

Further Reflection: *How loudly do I praise God for the blessed hope I have in Jesus?*

BELOVED OF HEAVEN

"As the Father loved Me, I also have loved you; abide in My love."
—John 15:9

For more than a thousand years the Jewish people had awaited the Saviour's coming. Upon this event they had rested their brightest hopes. In song and prophecy, in temple rite and household prayer, they had enshrined His name. And yet at His coming they knew Him not. The **Beloved of heaven** was to them "as a root out of a dry ground;" He had "no form nor comeliness;" and they saw in Him no beauty that they should desire Him. "He came unto His own, and His own received Him not." (Isaiah 53:2; John 1:11)

Yet God had chosen Israel. He had called them to preserve among men and women the knowledge of His law, and of the symbols and prophecies that pointed to the Saviour. He desired them to be as wells of salvation to the world. What Abraham was in the land of his sojourn, what Joseph was in Egypt, and Daniel in the courts of Babylon, the Hebrew people were to be among the nations. They were to reveal God to humanity.

In the call of Abraham the Lord had said, "I will bless thee . . . and thou shalt be a blessing . . . and in thee shall all families of the earth be blessed." (Genesis 12:2, 3) The same teaching was repeated through the prophets. Even after Israel had been wasted by war and captivity, the promise was theirs, "The remnant of Jacob shall be in the midst of many people as a dew from the Lord, as the showers upon the grass, that tarrieth not for man, nor waiteth for the sons of men." (Micah 5:7) Concerning the temple at Jerusalem, the Lord declared through Isaiah, "Mine house shall be called an house of prayer for all peoples." (Isaiah 56:7, R. V.)

But the Israelites fixed their hopes upon worldly greatness. From the time of their entrance to the land of Canaan, they departed from the commandments of God, and followed the ways of the heathen. It was in vain that God sent them warning by His prophets. In vain they suffered the chastisement of heathen oppression. Every reformation was followed by deeper apostasy.

Had Israel been true to God, He could have accomplished His purpose through their honor and exaltation.—*The Desire of Ages*, pp. 27, 28.

Further Reflection: *If I am a citizen of "spiritual Israel," how can I succeed where ancient Israel failed? How can I reveal God to those with whom I come in contact today?*

CHRIST OF THE GOSPEL DISPENSATION

But as many as received Him, to them He gave the right to become children of God, to those who believe in His name.
—John 1:12

From Paul's day to the present time, God by His Holy Spirit has been calling after the Jew as well as the Gentile. "There is no respect of persons with God," declared Paul. The apostle regarded himself as "debtor both to the Greeks, and to the barbarians," as well as to the Jews; but he never lost sight of the decided advantages possessed by the Jews over others, "chiefly, because that unto them were committed the oracles of God." "The gospel," he declared, "is the power of God unto salvation to everyone that believeth; to the Jew first, and also to the Greek. For therein is the righteousness of God revealed from faith to faith: as it is written, The just shall live by faith." It is of this gospel of Christ, equally efficacious for Jew and Gentile, that Paul in his epistle to the Romans declared he was not ashamed.

When this gospel shall be presented in its fullness to the Jews, many will accept Christ as the Messiah. Among Christian ministers there are only a few who feel called upon to labor for the Jewish people; but to those who have been often passed by, as well as to all others, the message of mercy and hope in Christ is to come.

In the closing proclamation of the gospel, when special work is to be done for classes of people hitherto neglected, God expects His messengers to take particular interest in the Jewish people whom they find in all parts of the earth. As the Old Testament Scriptures are blended with the New in an explanation of Jehovah's eternal purpose, this will be to many of the Jews as the dawn of a new creation, the resurrection of the soul. As they see the **Christ of the gospel dispensation** portrayed in the pages of the Old Testament Scriptures, and perceive how clearly the New Testament explains the Old, their slumbering faculties will be aroused, and they will recognize Christ as the Saviour of the world. Many will by faith receive Christ as their Redeemer. To them will be fulfilled the words, "As many as received Him, to them gave He power to become the sons of God, even to them that believe on His name." (John 1:12)—*The Acts of the Apostles*, pp. 380, 381.

Further Reflection: *What do I have in common with Jews that might serve as a bridge for sharing biblical truths about the Messiahship of Jesus with them?*

JUDGE OF ALL LIVING

For we must all appear before the judgment seat of Christ, that each one may receive the things done in the body, according to what he has done, whether good or bad.
—2 Corinthians 5:10

Under the inspiration of Satan, the Jews had chosen a robber and a murderer in the place of Christ, and with this company they had bound themselves for the judgment of the last day. Pilate had said, pointing to Christ, "Behold your King." But with determined voice the chief priests and rulers cried out, "Away with Him, away with Him, crucify Him." Pilate said, "Shall I crucify your King?" and the chief priests answered, "We have no King but Caesar." (John 19:14, 15) And Pilate delivered Him, in whom he declared he could find no fault at all, to be scourged—the most cruel, unmerciful punishment that can be given to a human being.

But He who submitted to the humiliation and suffering of the cross here, in the council of God was to have the fullest compensation and ascend the throne, acknowledged by all the heavenly universe to be the King of saints. He had undertaken the work of salvation, and He showed before the worlds unfallen and the heavenly family that the work He had begun He was able to complete.

The heavenly universe, and the fallen world, both saints and sinners, should recognize in Him who was crucified the **Judge of all living**. Every crown that is given to the saints of the Most High will be bestowed by the hands of Christ—those hands that cruel priests and rulers condemned to be nailed to the cross. The marks of those wounds will be as bright beams coming forth from His hands. It is Christ who gives men the grace of repentance. His merits were accepted by the Father in behalf of every soul that will help to compose the family of God. His bruised and wounded hands alone can give them the consolation of life, eternal life.

A solemn time will be the day of final decision. . . . Then is it not of tremendous importance to us individually that our works be right works?—Manuscript 39, 1898.

Further Reflection: *How can Jesus be both my Advocate and Judge?*

ETERNAL ROCK

The stone which the builders rejected has become the chief cornerstone.

—Psalm 118:22

To those who believe, Christ is the sure foundation. These are they who fall upon the Rock and are broken. Submission to Christ and faith in Him are here represented. To fall upon the Rock and be broken is to give up our self-righteousness and to go to Christ with the humility of a child, repenting of our transgressions, and believing in His forgiving love. And so also it is by faith and obedience that we build on Christ as our foundation.

Upon this living stone, Jews and Gentiles alike may build. This is the only foundation upon which we may securely build. It is broad enough for all, and strong enough to sustain the weight and burden of the whole world. And by connection with Christ, the living stone, all who build upon this foundation become living stones. Many persons are by their own endeavors hewn, polished, and beautified; but they cannot become "living stones," because they are not connected with Christ. Without this connection, no person can be saved. Without the life of Christ in us, we cannot withstand the storms of temptation. Our eternal safety depends upon our building upon the sure foundation. Multitudes are today building upon foundations that have not been tested. When the rain falls, and the tempest rages, and the floods come, their house will fall, because it is not founded upon the **eternal Rock**, the chief cornerstone Christ Jesus.

"To them which stumble at the word, being disobedient," Christ is a rock of offense. But "the stone which the builders disallowed, the same is made the head of the corner." Like the rejected stone, Christ in His earthly mission had borne neglect and abuse. He was "despised and rejected of men; a man of sorrows, and acquainted with grief. . . . He was despised, and we esteemed Him not." (Isaiah 53:3) But the time was near when He would be glorified. By the resurrection from the dead He would be declared "the Son of God with power." (Romans 1:4) At His second coming He would be revealed as Lord of heaven and earth. Those who were now about to crucify Him would recognize His greatness. Before the universe the rejected stone would become the head of the corner.—*The Desire of Ages*, pp. 599, 600.

Further Reflection: *Can I point to a time in my life when Jesus proved to be my Eternal Rock, a sure foundation in a time of storm?*

GREAT VENDOR OF SPIRITUAL RICHES

Oh, the depth of the riches both of the wisdom and knowledge of God!

—Romans 11:33

Victory will come to all who are loyal, steadfast in their allegiance to the cause of truth. "Blessed is the man that endureth temptation; for when he is tried, he shall receive the crown of life, which the Lord hath promised to them that love Him." (James 1:12) Let all inquire, Are we individually faithful stewards in trust of the last message of mercy to be given to the world, the message that decided their eternal destiny? Are we faithful to closely examine self, to see what manner of spirit we are of? Are we constantly aiming to represent the truth as it is in Jesus, or is it molded by the peculiarities of the human worker? Will the fires of the last conflagration consume our work?

Fidelity, thorough wholeness to God, is essential for every worker now if we would receive from Christ the benediction, "Well done, good and faithful servant." (Matthew 25:23) The exhortation to Timothy from his father in the gospel was, "Take heed unto thyself and unto the doctrine." (1 Timothy 4:16) The great question is: How shall we meet the future? Our only safety is in doing our work for each day as it comes, working, watching, waiting, every moment relying on the strength of Him who was dead and who is alive again, who lives forevermore. Every step must be guarded; as we advance, our tread may be firm, and then we may move solidly onward and upward.

But many are Laodiceans, living in a spiritual self-deception. They clothe themselves in the garments of their own righteousness, imagining themselves to be rich and increased with goods and in the need of nothing, when they need daily to learn of Jesus His meekness and lowliness, else they find themselves bankrupt, their whole life being a lie. Shall not we who bear the last message of mercy to a guilty world represent Jesus in purity in self-denial, that the word may be sounded from human lips inspired by the Holy Spirit of God, "Open the door of your heart, and let Jesus in?" The **great Vendor of spiritual riches** is inviting your recognition. He says, "I counsel thee to buy of Me gold tried in the fire, that thou mayest be rich; and white raiment, that thou mayest be clothed, and that the shame of thy nakedness do not appear: and anoint thine eyes with eyesalve, that thou mayest see." (Revelation 3:18)—Letter 66, 1894.

Further Reflection: *What spiritual riches has Jesus bestowed on me?*

FRIEND OF SINNERS

"When I say to the wicked, 'O wicked man, you shall surely die!' and you do not speak to warn the wicked from his way, that wicked man shall die in his iniquity; but his blood I will require at your hand."

—Ezekiel 33:8

Every indignity, reproach, and cruelty that Satan can instigate human hearts to devise, has been visited upon the followers of Jesus. And it will be fulfilled in a yet more marked manner; for the carnal mind is still at enmity with the law of God, and will not be subject to its commands. We have been highly favored in living under a government where we can worship God according to the dictates of our conscience. But human nature is no more in harmony with the principles of Christ today than it has been in ages past. The world is still in opposition to Jesus. The same hatred that prompted the cry, "Crucify Him, crucify Him," still works in the children of disobedience. The same satanic spirit that in the Dark Ages consigned men and women to prison, to exile, and to the stake, that conceived the exquisite torture of the Inquisition, produced the massacre of St. Bartholomew, and kindled the fires of Smithfield, is still at work with malignant energy in unregenerate hearts.

We are required to be Christ-like toward those who are our enemies; but we must not, in order to have peace, cover up the faults of those we see in error. The world's Redeemer never purchased peace by covering iniquity, or by anything like compromise. Though His heart was constantly overflowing with love for the human race, He was never indulgent to their sins. He was the **friend of sinners**, and He would not remain silent while they were pursuing a course that would ruin their souls—the souls that He had purchased with His own blood. He was a stern reprove of all vice. He labored that men and women should be true to themselves in being all that God would have them, and true to their higher and eternal interest. Living in a world marred and seared with the curse brought upon it by disobedience, He could not be at peace with it if He left it unwarned, uninstructed, unrebuked. This would be to purchase peace at the neglect of duty. His peace was the consciousness of having done the will of His Father, rather than a condition of things that existed as the result of not having done His duty.—*Review and Herald*, January 16, 1900.

Further Reflection: *How do I relate to people who are engaged in open sin?*

BUILDER OF THE CHURCH OF GOD

"And He shall build the temple of the Lord."
—Zechariah 6:12

In the temple in heaven, the dwelling place of God, His throne is established in righteousness and judgment. In the most holy place is His law, the great rule of right by which all humanity are tested. The ark that enshrines the tables of the law is covered with the mercy seat, before which Christ pleads His blood in the sinner's behalf. Thus is represented the union of justice and mercy in the plan of human redemption. This union infinite wisdom alone could devise and infinite power accomplish; it is a union that fills all heaven with wonder and adoration. The cherubim of the earthly sanctuary, looking reverently down upon the mercy seat, represent the interest with which the heavenly host contemplate the work of redemption. This is the mystery of mercy into which angels desire to look—that God can be just while He justifies the repenting sinner and renews His communion with the fallen race; that Christ could stoop to raise unnumbered multitudes from the abyss of ruin and clothe them with the spotless garments of His own righteousness to unite with angels who have never fallen and to dwell forever in the presence of God.

The work of Christ as humanity's intercessor is presented in that beautiful prophecy of Zechariah concerning Him "whose name is the Branch." Says the prophet: "He shall build the temple of the Lord; and He shall bear the glory, and shall sit and rule upon His [the Father's] throne; and He shall be a priest upon His throne: and the *counsel of peace* shall be between Them both." (Zechariah 6:12, 13) . . .

. . . By His sacrifice and mediation Christ is both the foundation and the **builder of the church of God**. The apostle Paul points to Him as "the chief Cornerstone; in whom all the building fitly framed together groweth into an holy temple in the Lord: in whom ye also," he says, "are builded together for an habitation of God through the Spirit." (Ephesians 2:20–22)

"He shall bear the glory." To Christ belongs the glory of redemption for the fallen race.—*The Great Controversy*, pp. 415, 416.

Further Reflection: *Jesus has created me to be a holy temple for His dwelling. Have I opened the door to let Him come in?*

JULY 24

COMING REDEEMER

Arise for our help, and redeem us for Your mercies' sake.
—Psalm 44:26

How unmistakably plain were Isaiah's prophecies of Christ's sufferings and death! "Who hath believed our report?" the prophet inquires, "and to whom is the arm of the Lord revealed? For He shall grow up before Him as a tender plant, and as a root out of a dry ground: He hath no form nor comeliness; and when we shall see Him, there is no beauty that we should desire Him. He is despised and rejected of men; a man of sorrows, and acquainted with grief: and we hid as it were our faces from Him; He was despised, and we esteemed Him not.

"Surely He hath borne our griefs, and carried our sorrows: yet we did esteem Him stricken, smitten of God, and afflicted. But He was wounded for our transgressions, He was bruised for our iniquities: the chastisement of our peace was upon Him; and with His stripes we are healed.

"All we like sheep have gone astray; we have turned everyone to his own way; and the Lord hath laid on Him the iniquity of us all. He was oppressed, and He was afflicted, yet He opened not His mouth: He is brought as a lamb to the slaughter, and as a sheep before her shearers is dumb, so He openeth not His mouth. He was taken from prison and from judgment: and who shall declare His generation? for He was cut off out of the land of the living: for the transgression of my people was He stricken." (Isaiah 53:1–8)

Even the manner of His death had been shadowed forth. As the brazen serpent had been uplifted in the wilderness, so was the **coming Redeemer** to be lifted up, "that whosoever believeth in Him should not perish, but have everlasting life." (John 3:16)

"One shall say unto Him, What are these wounds in Thine hands? Then He shall answer, Those with which I was wounded in the house of My friends." (Zechariah 13:6)

"He made His grave with the wicked, and with the rich in His death; because He had done no violence, neither was any deceit in His mouth. Yet it pleased the Lord to bruise Him; He hath put Him to grief." (Isaiah 53:9, 10)

But He who was to suffer death at the hands of evil human beings was to rise again as a conqueror over sin and the grave.—*The Acts of the Apostles*, pp. 225–227.

Further Reflection: *Does my commitment to accept Christ's sacrifice for me match His commitment to save me? In other words, am I as vested in my salvation as Christ is?*

GREAT PATTERN

"Let your light so shine before men, that they may see your good works and glorify your Father in heaven."

—Matthew 5:16

Paul writes, "Do all things without murmurings and disputings that ye may be blameless and harmless, the sons of God, without rebuke in the midst of a crooked and perverse generation, among whom ye shine as lights in the world; holding forth the word of life, that I may rejoice in the day of Christ that I have not run in vain neither labored in vain." (Philippians 2:14–16) . . .

How much do persons who are not themselves under God's control, although professing to be Christians, really contribute to the efficiency of the gospel in their business relations with those who are not converted? There are many against whose names on the record books of heaven will be found written, Not producers, but consumers. They do not bear fruit to the glory of God. The Lord cannot co-operate with them. They are stones which take up room in the building, but emit no light. They cannot shine as living stones, because they do not receive light from the chief Cornerstone. Can they afford to trust their souls any longer to such uncertainty? Christians are either under Christ's rule, heeding His instruction by doing the work they are supposed as God's followers to be doing, or they are under the control of the enemy. They are either doing positive good or incalculable harm. . . .

Christians are to be light-bearers, saying to all with whom they are brought into contact, Follow me as I follow Christ. They are to be examples of piety, representing Christ in word, in spirit, in action, in all business dealing with their brethren and with strangers. They are to show that their actions are a copy of the actions of their **great Pattern**. All this Christ enjoins upon His followers. They are to show the superiority of heaven's principles over the principles of the world. . . .

. . . True Christians will always shine as lights in the world. They are light-bearers, working upon a higher plane of action than those who are not Christians. Their purity and uprightness in every action is a source of illumination. They impart what they receive, making known the duties and privileges of a Christian. The refining, ennobling principles of the gospel are brought into every phase of life.—Letter 148, 1899.

Further Reflection: *What "incalculable harm" might I do if I am unconsecrated to God?*

MINISTER OF THE NEW COVENANT

But Christ came as High Priest of the good things to come,
with the greater and more perfect tabernacle not made with hands,
that is, not of this creation.

—Hebrews 9:11

The sacrificial service that had pointed to Christ passed away; but the eyes of men and women were turned to the true sacrifice for the sins of the world. The earthly priesthood ceased; but we look to Jesus, the **minister of the new covenant**, and "to the blood of sprinkling, that speaketh better things than that of Abel." "The way into the holiest of all was not yet made manifest, while as the first tabernacle was yet standing . . . but Christ being come an high priest of good things to come, by a greater and more perfect tabernacle, not made with hands . . . by His own blood He entered in once into the holy place, having obtained eternal redemption for us." (Hebrews 12:24; 9:8–12)

"Wherefore He is able also to save them to the uttermost that come unto God by Him, seeing He ever liveth to make intercession for them." (Hebrews 7:25) Though the ministration was to be removed from the earthly to the heavenly temple; though the sanctuary and our great high priest would be invisible to human sight, yet the disciples were to suffer no loss thereby. They would realize no break in their communion, and no diminution of power because of the Saviour's absence. While Jesus ministers in the sanctuary above, He is still by His Spirit the minister of the church on earth. He is withdrawn from the eye of sense, but His parting promise is fulfilled, "Lo, I am with you alway, even unto the end of the world." (Matthew 28:20) While He delegates His power to inferior ministers, His energizing presence is still with His church.

"Seeing then that we have a great high priest . . . Jesus, the Son of God, let us hold fast our profession. For we have not an high priest which cannot be touched with the feeling of our infirmities; but was in all points tempted like as we are, yet without sin. Let us therefore come boldly unto the throne of grace, that we may obtain mercy, and find grace to help in time of need." (Hebrews 4:14–16)—*The Desire of Ages*, p. 166.

Further Reflection: *What personal power does Jesus offer me today in my battle with sin, as Minister of the New Covenant?*

BLEEDING VICTIM

And Jesus cried out with a loud voice, and breathed His last.
—Mark 15:37

The priests and rulers were amazed to find that Christ was dead. Death by the cross was a lingering process; it was difficult to determine when life had ceased. It was an unheard-of thing for one to die within six hours of crucifixion. The priests wished to make sure of the death of Jesus, and at their suggestion a soldier thrust a spear into the Saviour's side. From the wound thus made, there flowed two copious and distinct streams, one of blood, the other of water. This was noted by all the beholders, and John states the occurrence very definitely. . . .

After the resurrection the priests and rulers circulated the report that Christ did not die upon the cross, that He merely fainted, and was afterward revived. Another report affirmed that it was not a real body of flesh and bone, but the likeness of a body, that was laid in the tomb. The action of the Roman soldiers disproves these falsehoods. They broke not His legs, because He was already dead. To satisfy the priests, they pierced His side. Had not life been already extinct, this wound would have caused instant death.

But it was not the spear thrust, it was not the pain of the cross, that caused the death of Jesus. That cry, uttered "with a loud voice" (Matthew 27:50; Luke 23:46), at the moment of death, the stream of blood and water that flowed from His side, declared that He died of a broken heart. His heart was broken by mental anguish. He was slain by the sin of the world.

With the death of Christ the hopes of His disciples perished. They looked upon His closed eyelids and drooping head, His hair matted with blood, His pierced hands and feet, and their anguish was indescribable. Until the last they had not believed that He would die; they could hardly believe that He was really dead. Overwhelmed with sorrow, they did not recall His words foretelling this very scene. Nothing that He had said now gave them comfort. They saw only the cross and its **bleeding Victim**. The future seemed dark with despair. Their faith in Jesus had perished; but never had they loved their Lord as now. Never before had they so felt His worth, and their need of His presence.—*The Desire of Ages*, pp. 771, 772.

Further Reflection: *In a world where many still doubt the existence of Jesus and do not value His death, how can my life testify that Jesus is real and lives today?*

HONORED OF HEAVEN

And He put all things under His feet, and gave Him to be head over all things to the church.

—Ephesians 1:22

Day was breaking over the Sea of Galilee. The disciples, weary with a night of fruitless toil, were still in their fishing boats on the lake. Jesus had come to spend a quiet hour by the waterside. In the early morning He hoped for a little season of rest from the multitude that followed Him day after day. But soon the people began to gather about Him. Their numbers rapidly increased, so that He was pressed upon all sides. Meanwhile the disciples had come to land. In order to escape the pressure of the multitude, Jesus stepped into Peter's boat, and bade him pull out a little from the shore. Here Jesus could be better seen and heard by all, and from the boat He taught the multitude on the beach.

What a scene was this for angels to contemplate; their glorious Commander, sitting in a fisherman's boat, swayed to and fro by the restless waves, and proclaiming the good news of salvation to the listening throng that were pressing down to the water's edge! He who was the **Honored of heaven** was declaring the great things of His kingdom in the open air, to the common people. Yet He could have had no more fitting scene for His labors. Take, the mountains, the spreading fields, the sunlight flooding the earth, all furnished objects to illustrate His lessons and impress them upon the mind. And no lesson of Christ's fell fruitless. Every message from His lips came to some soul as the word of eternal life.

Every moment added to the multitude upon the shore. Aged persons leaning upon their staffs, hardy peasants from the hills, fishermen from their toil on the lake, merchants and rabbis, the rich and learned, old and young, bringing their sick and suffering ones, pressed to hear the words of the divine Teacher. To such scenes as this the prophets had looked forward, and they wrote: *"The land of Zebulon and the land of Naphtali, toward the sea, beyond Jordan, Galilee of the Gentiles, the people which sat in darkness saw a great light, and to them which sat in the region and shadow of death, to them did light spring up." R. V.—The Desire of Ages*, pp. 244, 245.

Further Reflection: *Where in my life do I need Jesus to speak peace right now?*

OWNER OF ALL OUR EARTHLY TREASURES

"Do not lay up for yourselves treasures on earth, where moth and rust destroy and where thieves break in and steal."
—Matthew 6:19

The **owner of all our earthly treasures** came to our world in human form. The Word was made flesh, and dwelt among us. We cannot appreciate how deeply interested He must be in the human family. He knows the value of every soul. What grief oppressed Him as He saw His purchased inheritance charmed with Satan's inventions!

The only satisfaction Satan takes in playing the game of life for the souls of men is the satisfaction he takes in hurting the heart of Christ. Though He was rich, for our sake Christ became poor, that we through His poverty might be made rich. Yet in view of this great fact, the majority of the world permit earthly possessions to eclipse heavenly attractions. They set their affections upon earthly things, and turn away from God. What a grievous sin it is that men and women will not come to their senses, and understand how foolish it is to permit inordinate affections for earthly things to expel the love of God from the heart. When the love of God is expelled, the love of the world quickly flows in to supply the vacuum. The Lord alone can cleanse the soul temple from the moral defilement.

Jesus gave His life for the life of the world, and He places an infinite value upon human beings. He desires that men and women shall appreciate themselves, and consider their future well-being. If the eye is kept single, the whole body will be full of light. If the spiritual vision is clear, unseen realities will be looked upon in their true value, and beholding the eternal world will give added enjoyment to this world.

The Christian will be filled with joy in proportion as he or she is a faithful steward of the Lord's goods. Christ yearns to save every son and daughter of Adam. He lifts His voice in warning, in order to break the spell which has bound the soul in captivity to the slavery of sin. He beseeches men to turn from their infatuation. He brings the nobler world before their vision, and says, "Lay not up for yourselves treasure upon the earth."—*Counsels on Stewardship*, pp. 136, 137.

Further Reflection: *How happy am I to share the material blessings that God has entrusted to me?*

HEAVENLY ARCHITECT

"For all those things My hand has made, and all those things exist," says the LORD.

—Isaiah 66:2

We are to love God, not only with all the heart, mind, and soul, but with all the strength. This covers the full, intelligent use of the physical powers.

Christ was a true worker in temporal as well as in spiritual things, and into all His work He brought a determination to do His Father's will. The things of heaven and earth are more closely connected and are more directly under the supervision of Christ than many realize. It was Christ who planned the arrangement for the first earthly tabernacle. He gave every specification in regard to the building of Solomon's temple. The One who in His earthly life worked as a carpenter in the village of Nazareth was the **heavenly architect** who marked out the plan for the sacred building where His name was to be honored.

It was Christ who gave to the builders of the tabernacle wisdom to execute the most skillful and beautiful workmanship. He said, "See, I have called by name Bezaleel the son of Uri, the son of Hur, of the tribe of Judah; and I have filled him with the Spirit of God, in wisdom, and in understanding, and in knowledge, and in all manner of workmanship. . . . And I, behold, I have given with him Aholiab, the son of Ahisamach, of the tribe of Dan; and in the hearts of all that are wise hearted I have put wisdom, that they may make all that I have commanded thee." (Exodus 31:2–6)

God desires that His workers in every line shall look to Him as the Giver of all they possess. All right inventions and improvements have their source in Him who is wonderful in counsel and excellent in working. The skillful touch of the physician's hand, his power over nerve and muscle, his knowledge of the delicate organism of the body, is the wisdom of divine power, to be used in behalf of the suffering. The skill with which the carpenter uses the hammer, the strength with which the blacksmith makes the anvil ring, comes from God. He has entrusted men and women with talents, and He expects them to look to Him for counsel. Whatever we do, in whatever department of the work we are placed, He desires to control our minds that we may do perfect work.—*Christ's Object Lessons*, pp. 348, 349.

Further Reflection: *How do I love God with my physical powers as I go about today's activities?*

DIVINE ADVOCATE

"See, I have inscribed you on the palms of My hands;
Your walls are continually before Me."

—Isaiah 49:16

Satan has an accurate knowledge of the sins that he has tempted God's people to commit, and he urges his accusations against them, declaring, that by their sins they have forfeited divine protection, and claiming that he has the right to destroy them. He pronounces them just as deserving as himself of exclusion from the favor of God. "Are these," he says, "the people who are to take my place in heaven, and the place of the angels who united with me? They profess to obey the law of God; but have they kept its precepts? Have they not been lovers of self more than lovers of God? Have they not placed their own interests above His service? Have they not loved the things of the world? Look at the sins that have marked their lives. Behold their selfishness, their malice, their hatred of one another. Will God banish me and my angels from His presence, and yet reward those who have been guilty of the same sins? Thou canst not do this, O Lord, in justice. Justice demands that sentence be pronounced against them."

But while the followers of Christ have sinned, they have not given themselves up to be controlled by the satanic agencies. They have repented of their sins and have sought the Lord in humility and contrition, and the **divine Advocate** pleads in their behalf. He who has been most abused by their ingratitude, who knows their sin and also their penitence, declares: "The Lord rebuke thee, O Satan. I gave My life for these souls. They are graven upon the palms of My hands. They may have imperfections of character; they may have failed in their endeavors; but they have repented, and I have forgiven and accepted them."

The assaults of Satan are strong, his delusions are subtle; but the Lord's eye is upon His people. Their affliction is great, the flames of the furnace seem about to consume them; but Jesus will bring them forth as gold tried in the fire. Their earthliness will be removed, that through them the image of Christ may be perfectly revealed.—*Prophets and Kings*, pp. 588, 589.

Further Reflection: *Have I repented of my sins and surrendered my life fully to Jesus, my Divine Advocate?*

AUGUST

FOUNTAIN OF WISDOM AND KNOWLEDGE

If any of you lacks wisdom, let him ask of God, who gives to all liberally and without reproach, and it will be given to him.

—James 1:5

As the worker studies the life of Christ, and the character of His mission is dwelt upon, each fresh search will reveal something more deeply interesting than has yet been unfolded. The subject is inexhaustible. The study of the incarnation of Christ, His atoning sacrifice and mediatorial work, will employ the mind of the diligent student as long as time shall last; and looking to heaven with its unnumbered years, he will exclaim, "Great is the mystery of godliness!" (1 Timothy 3:16)

We talk about the first angel's message and the second angel's message, and we think we have some understanding of the third angel's message. But as long as we are content with a limited knowledge, we shall be disqualified to obtain clearer views of truth. He who holds forth the word of life must take time to study the Bible and to search his own heart. Neglecting this, he will not know how to minister to needy souls. The diligent, humble student, seeking by earnest prayer and study for the truth as it is in Jesus, will most assuredly be rewarded. He seeks for help, not from ideas of human writers, but from the **Fountain of wisdom and knowledge**; and under the guidance of holy intelligences he gains a clear understanding of truth.

It is not by the might or power of the human agent that truth is to be impressed upon minds, "but by My Spirit, saith the Lord of hosts." (Zechariah 4:6) It is not the temperament or the eloquence of the one who preaches the word that makes his work successful. Paul may plant and Apollos water, but God gives the increase. It is a minister's familiarity with God's word and his submission to the divine will, that give success to his efforts.

The heart that receives the word of God is not as a pool that evaporates, nor like a broken cistern that loses its treasure. It is like the mountain stream fed by unfailing springs, whose cool, sparkling waters leap from rock to rock, refreshing the weary, the thirsty, the heavy-laden.—*Gospel Workers*, 251, 252.

Further Reflection: *Ellen White writes that Jesus, the Fountain of wisdom and knowledge, wishes to give all a clear understanding of truth. How does my failure to drink from this Fountain affect my spiritual life?*

GREATEST TEACHER

Then He taught them many things by parables.

—Mark 4:2

The religion of Christ never degrades the receiver. It never makes him or her coarse or rough, discourteous or self-important, passionate or hardhearted. On the contrary, it refines the taste, sanctifies the judgment, and purifies and ennobles the thoughts, bringing them into captivity to Jesus Christ.

God's ideal for His children is higher than the highest human thought can reach. The living God has given in His holy law a transcript of His character. The **greatest Teacher** the world has ever known is Jesus Christ; and what is the standard He has given for all who believe in Him? "Be ye therefore perfect, even as your Father which is in heaven is perfect." (Matthew 5:48) As God is perfect in His high sphere of action, so people may be perfect in their human sphere.

The ideal of Christian character is Christlikeness. There is opened before us a path of continual advancement. We have an object to reach, a standard to gain, which includes everything good and pure and noble and elevated. There should be continual striving and constant progress onward and upward toward perfection of character. . . .

Without the divine working, human beings can do no good thing. God calls every person to repentance, yet men and women cannot even repent unless the Holy Spirit works upon the heart. But the Lord wants no one to wait until he thinks he has repented before he takes steps toward Jesus. The Saviour is continually drawing people to repentance; they need only to submit to be drawn, and their hearts will be melted in penitence.

To human beings is allotted a part in this great struggle for everlasting life—he must respond to the working of the Holy Spirit. It will require a struggle to break through the powers of darkness, and the Spirit works in him to accomplish this. But humans are no passive beings, to be saved in indolence. Men and women are called upon to strain every muscle and exercise every faculty in the struggle for immortality, yet it is God that supplies the efficiency. No human being can be saved in indolence. The Lord bids us, "Strive to enter in at the strait gate: for many, I say unto you, will seek to enter in, and shall not be able." (Luke 13:24)—*Counsels to Parents, Teachers, and Students*, pp. 365, 366.

Further Reflection: *If Jesus could teach me today, what one thing would I want to learn?*

CRUCIFIED REDEEMER

Then Agrippa said to Paul, "You almost persuade me to become a Christian."

—Acts 26:28

The whole company had listened spellbound to Paul's account of his wonderful experiences. The apostle was dwelling upon his favorite theme. None who heard him could doubt his sincerity. But in the full tide of his persuasive eloquence he was interrupted by Festus, who cried out, "Paul, thou art beside thyself; much learning doth make thee mad."

The apostle replied, "I am not mad, most noble Festus; but speak forth the words of truth and soberness. For the king knoweth of these things, before whom also I speak freely: for I am persuaded that none of these thing are hidden from him; for this thing was not done in a corner." Then, turning to Agrippa, he addressed him directly, "King Agrippa, believest thou the prophets? I know that thou believest."

Deeply affected, Agrippa for the moment lost sight of his surroundings and the dignity of his position. Conscious only of the truths which he had heard, seeing only the humble prisoner standing before him as God's ambassador, he answered involuntarily, "Almost thou persuadest me to be a Christian."

Earnestly the apostle made answer, "I would to God, that not only thou, but also all that hear me this day, were both almost, and altogether such as I am," adding, as he raised his fettered hands, "except these bonds."

Festus, Agrippa, and Bernice might in justice have worn the fetters that bound the apostle. All were guilty of grievous crimes. These offenders had that day heard the offer of salvation through the name of Christ. One, at least, had been almost persuaded to accept the grace and pardon offered. But Agrippa put aside the proffered mercy, refusing to accept the cross of a **crucified Redeemer**.

The king's curiosity was satisfied, and, rising from his seat, he signified that the interview was at an end. As the assembly dispersed, they talked among themselves, saying, "This man doeth nothing worthy of death or of bonds."—*The Acts of the Apostles*, pp. 437, 438.

Further Reflection: *How many of God's appeals have I "almost" responded to?*

GIVER OF THE LAW

"Do not think that I came to destroy the Law or the Prophets. I did not come to destroy but to fulfill."

—Matthew 5:17

On the mount [of Olives], Jesus was closely watched by spies; and as He unfolded the principles of righteousness, the Pharisees caused it to be whispered about that His teaching was in opposition to the precepts that God had given from Sinai. The Saviour said nothing to unsettle faith in the religion and institutions that had been given through Moses; for every ray of divine light that Israel's great leader communicated to his people was received from Christ. While many are saying in their hearts that He has come to do away with the law, Jesus in unmistakable language reveals His attitude toward the divine statutes. "Think not," He said, "that I am come to destroy the law, or the prophets."

It is the Creator of humanity, the **Giver of the law**, who declares that it is not His purpose to set aside its precepts. Everything in nature, from the mote in the sunbeam to the worlds on high, is under law. And upon obedience to these laws the order and harmony of the natural world depend. So there are great principles of righteousness to control the life of all intelligent beings, and upon conformity to these principles the well-being of the universe depends. Before this earth was called into being, God's law existed. Angels are governed by its principles, and in order for earth to be in harmony with heaven, men and women also must obey the divine statutes. To humanity in Eden Christ made known the precepts of the law. . . . The mission of Christ on earth was not to destroy the law, but by His grace to bring humanity back to obedience to its precepts.

The beloved disciple, who listened to the words of Jesus on the mount, writing long afterward under the inspiration of the Holy Spirit, speaks of the law as of perpetual obligation. He says that "sin is the transgression of the law" and that "whosoever committeth sin transgresseth also the law." (1 John 3:4) He makes it plain that the law to which he refers is "an old commandment which ye had from the beginning." (1 John 2:7) He is speaking of the law that existed at the creation and was reiterated upon Mount Sinai.—*Thoughts From the Mount of Blessing*, pp. 47, 48.

Further Reflection: *How would I begin to explain to an unbeliever that the well-being of the universe depends on the law of God?*

CHRISTIAN'S LIVING HEAD

All Scripture is given by inspiration of God, and is profitable for doctrine, for reproof, for correction, for instruction in righteousness.
—2 Timothy 3:16

I have been shown that those who have a knowledge of the truth, and yet allow all their powers to be absorbed in worldly interests, are unfaithful. They are not, by their good works, letting the light of truth shine to others. Nearly all their ability is devoted to becoming sharp, skillful men of the world. They forget that their talents were given them of God to be used in advancing His cause. If they were faithful to their duty, the result would be great gain of souls to the Master, but many are lost through their neglect. God calls upon those who know His will to be doers of His word. Weakness, half-heartedness, and indecision provoke the assaults of Satan; and those who permit these traits to grow will be borne helplessly down by the surging waves of temptation. Everyone who professes the name of Christ is required to grow up to the full stature of Christ, the **Christian's living head**.

We all need a guide through the many strait places in life as much as the sailor needs a pilot over the sandy bar or up the rocky river, and where is this guide to be found? We point you, dear brethren, to the Bible. Inspired of God, written by holy men, it points out with great clearness and precision the duties of both old and young. It elevates the mind, softens the heart, and imparts gladness and holy joy to the spirit. The Bible presents a perfect standard of character; it is an infallible guide under all circumstances, even to the end of the journey of life. Take it as the person of your counsel, the rule of your daily life.

Every means of grace should be diligently improved that the love of God may abound in the soul more and more, "that ye may approve things that are excellent; that ye may be sincere and without offense till the day of Christ; being filled with the fruits of righteousness." Your Christian life must take on vigorous and stalwart forms. You can attain to the high standard set before you in the Scriptures, and you must if you would be children of God. You cannot stand still; you must either advance or retrograde. You must have spiritual knowledge, that . . . you may "be filled with all the fullness of God."—*Testimonies for the Church*, vol. 5, pp. 263, 264.

Further Reflection: *If weakness, half-heartedness, and indecision attract the assaults of Satan, what do I need to change in my life to withstand Satan's devices?*

ANGEL OF THE COVENANT

"LORD God of Israel, there is no God in heaven or on earth like You, who keep Your covenant and mercy with Your servants who walk before You with all their hearts."

—2 Chronicles 6:14

It was in a lonely, mountainous region, the haunt of wild beasts and the lurking place of robbers and murderers. Solitary and unprotected, Jacob bowed in deep distress upon the earth. It was midnight. All that made life dear to him were at a distance, exposed to danger and death. Bitterest of all was the thought that it was his own sin which had brought this peril upon the innocent. With earnest cries and tears he made his prayer before God. Suddenly a strong hand was laid upon him. He thought that an enemy was seeking his life. . . .

In the darkness the two struggled for the mastery. Not a word was spoken, but Jacob put forth all his strength, and did not relax his efforts for a moment. While he was thus battling for his life, the sense of his guilt pressed upon his soul; his sins rose up before him, to shut him out from God. But in his terrible extremity he remembered God's promises, and his whole heart went out in entreaty for His mercy. The struggle continued until near the break of day, when the Stranger placed his finger upon Jacob's thigh, and he was crippled instantly.

The patriarch now discerned the character of his antagonist. He knew that he had been in conflict with a heavenly messenger, and this was why his almost superhuman effort had not gained the victory. It was Christ, "the **Angel of the covenant**," who had revealed Himself to Jacob. The patriarch was now disabled and suffering the keenest pain, but he would not loosen his hold. All penitent and broken, he clung to the Angel; "he wept, and made supplication" (Hosea 12:4), pleading for a blessing. He must have the assurance that his sin was pardoned. Physical pain was not sufficient to divert his mind from this object. His determination grew stronger, his faith more earnest and persevering, until the very last. The Angel tried to release Himself; He urged, "Let Me go, for the day breaketh;" but Jacob answered, "I will not let Thee go, except Thou bless me." Had this been a boastful, presumptuous confidence, Jacob would have been instantly destroyed; but his was the assurance of one who confesses his own unworthiness, yet trusts the faithfulness of a covenant-keeping God.—*Patriarchs and Prophets*, pp. 196, 197.

Further Reflection: *Do I cling to God until He blesses or am I prone to give up too soon?*

HEIR

"This is the heir. Come, let us kill him and seize his inheritance."
—Matthew 21:38

In the parable of the vineyard Jesus brought before the Jews their real condition. The householder represented God, the vineyard the Jewish nation hedged in by divine law which was calculated to preserve them as a people separate and distinct from all other nations of the earth. The tower built in the vineyard represented their temple. . . .

The Lord of the vineyard required of His husbandmen a due proportion of the fruit; so God required of the Jews a life corresponding with the sacred privileges He had given them. But as the servants who demanded fruit in their master's name were put to death by the unfaithful husbandmen, so had the Jews slain the prophets who had come to them with messages from God. Not only were these rejected, but when He sent His only Son to them, the destined **Heir** to the vineyard, thinking to preserve the vineyard to themselves, and to secure the honor and profit accruing therefrom, the haughty Jews, the unfaithful servants, reasoned among themselves, saying, "This is the Heir; come, let us kill Him." Thus Jesus revealed in His parable the dark purposes of the Jews against Himself.

After Jesus had heard them pronounce sentence upon themselves in their condemnation of the wicked husbandmen, He looked pityingly upon them and continued: "Did ye never read in the Scriptures, the stone which the builders rejected the same has become the head of the corner; this is the Lord's doing, and it is marvelous in our eyes? Therefore say I unto you, The kingdom of God shall be taken from you, and given to a nation bringing forth the fruits thereof. And whosoever shall fall on this stone shall be broken; but on whomsoever it shall fall, it will grind him to powder."

The Jews had often repeated the words of this prophecy while teaching the people in the synagogues, applying it to the coming Messiah. But Jesus connected the heir so cruelly slain with the stone which the builders rejected, but which eventually became the principal stone of the whole building. Christ himself was the originator of the Jewish system, the very foundation of the costly temple, the antitype to whom all the sacrificial services pointed.—*The Spirit of Prophecy*, vol. 3, pp. 34, 35.

Further Reflection: *Could I one day reject the very Son of God, as the Pharisees had?*

KING IN HIS BEAUTY

Behold, He is coming with clouds, and every eye will see Him, even they who pierced Him.

—Revelation 1:7

Oh, how many who have not sought their souls' salvation will soon make the bitter lamentation: "The harvest is past, the summer is ended, and we are not saved"!

We are living in the closing scenes of this earth's history. Prophecy is fast fulfilling. The hours of probation are fast passing. We have no time—not a moment—to lose. Let us not be found sleeping on guard. Let no one say in his heart or by his works: "My Lord delayeth His coming." Let the message of Christ's soon return sound forth in earnest words of warning. Let us persuade men and women everywhere to repent and flee from the wrath to come. Let us arouse them to immediate preparation, for we little know what is before us. Let ministers and lay members go forth into the ripening fields to tell the unconcerned and indifferent to seek the Lord while He may be found. The workers will find their harvest wherever they proclaim the forgotten truths of the Bible. They will find those who will accept the truth and will devote their lives to winning souls to Christ.

The Lord is soon to come, and we must be prepared to meet Him in peace. Let us be determined to do all in our power to impart light to those around us. We are not to be sad, but cheerful, and we are to keep the Lord Jesus ever before us. He is soon coming, and we must be ready and waiting for His appearing. Oh, how glorious it will be to see Him and be welcomed as His redeemed ones! Long have we waited, but our hope is not to grow dim. If we can but see the **King in His Beauty** we shall be forever blessed. I feel as if I must cry aloud: "Homeward bound!" We are nearing the time when Christ will come in power and great glory to take His ransomed ones to their eternal home. . . .

In the great closing work we shall meet with perplexities that we know not how to deal with; but let us not forget that the three great powers of heaven are working, that a divine hand is on the wheel, and that God will bring His promises to pass. He will gather from the world a people who will serve Him in righteousness.—*Testimonies for the Church*, vol. 8, pp. 252–254.

Further Reflection: *Am I excited to see Jesus in all His beauty? Do I live my life with an eye on the soon return of Christ?*

COMMANDER OF HEAVEN

But made Himself of no reputation, taking the form of a bondservant, and coming in the likeness of men.

—Philippians 2:7

Christ was the only sinless one who ever dwelt on earth; yet for nearly thirty years He lived among the wicked inhabitants of Nazareth. This fact is a rebuke to those who think themselves dependent upon place, fortune, or prosperity, in order to live a blameless life. Temptation, poverty, adversity, is the very discipline needed to develop purity and firmness.

Jesus lived in a peasant's home, and faithfully and cheerfully acted His part in bearing the burdens of the household. He had been the **Commander of heaven**, and angels had delighted to fulfill His word; now He was a willing servant, a loving, obedient son. He learned a trade, and with His own hands worked in the carpenter's shop with Joseph. In the simple garb of a common laborer He walked the streets of the little town, going to and returning from His humble work. He did not employ His divine power to lessen His burdens or to lighten His toil.

As Jesus worked in childhood and youth, mind and body were developed. He did not use His physical powers recklessly, but in such a way as to keep them in health, that He might do the best work in every line. He was not willing to be defective, even in the handling of tools. He was perfect as a workman, as He was perfect in character. By His own example He taught that it is our duty to be industrious, that our work should be performed with exactness and thoroughness, and that such labor is honorable. The exercise that teaches the hands to be useful and trains the young to bear their share of life's burdens gives physical strength, and develops every faculty. All should find something to do that will be beneficial to themselves and helpful to others. God appointed work as a blessing, and only the diligent worker finds the true glory and joy of life. The approval of God rests with loving assurance upon children and youth who cheerfully take their part in the duties of the household, sharing the burdens of father and mother. Such children will go out from the home to be useful members of society.—*The Desire of Ages*, p. 72.

Further Reflection: *If Jesus, the Commander of Heaven, was willing to become a human being, sacrifice His life for fallen humanity, setting an example in both character and deportment, what am I willing to give up for Him today?*

ANTITYPE OF THE WAVE SHEAF

But each one in his own order: Christ the firstfruits, afterward those who are Christ's at His coming.

—1 Corinthians 15:23

In the summer of 1844, midway between the time when it had been first thought that the 2300 days would end, and the autumn of the same year, to which it was afterward found that they extended, the message was proclaimed in the very words of Scripture: "Behold, the Bridegroom cometh!"

That which led to this movement was the discovery that the decree of Artaxerxes for the restoration of Jerusalem, which formed the starting point for the period of the 2300 days, went into effect in the autumn of the year 457 B.C., and not at the beginning of the year, as had been formerly believed. Reckoning from the autumn of 457, the 2300 years terminate in the autumn of 1844. . . .

The slaying of the Passover lamb was a shadow of the death of Christ. Says Paul: "Christ our Passover is sacrificed for us." (1 Corinthians 5:7) The sheaf of first fruits, which at the time of the Passover was waved before the Lord, was typical of the resurrection of Christ. Paul says, in speaking of the resurrection of the Lord and of all His people: "Christ the first fruits; afterward they that are Christ's at His coming." (1 Corinthians 15:23) Like the wave sheaf, which was the first ripe grain gathered before the harvest, Christ is the first fruits of that immortal harvest of redeemed ones that at the future resurrection shall be gathered into the garner of God.

These types were fulfilled, not only as to the event, but as to the time. On the fourteenth day of the first Jewish month, the very day and month on which for fifteen long centuries the Passover lamb had been slain, Christ, having eaten the Passover with His disciples, instituted that feast which was to commemorate His own death as "the Lamb of God, which taketh away the sin of the world." That same night He was taken by wicked hands to be crucified and slain. And as the **antitype of the wave sheaf** our Lord was raised from the dead on the third day, "the first fruits of them that slept."—*The Great Controversy*, pp. 398, 399.

Further Reflection: *When studying prophecy, how can I avoid being "sincerely wrong," as were Adventist pioneers who mistakenly believed Jesus would return on October 22, 1844?*

DEARLY BELOVED

He has delivered us from the power of darkness and conveyed us into the kingdom of the Son of His love.
—Colossians 1:13

I have been shown the great love and condescension of God in giving His Son to die that humanity might find pardon and live. I was shown Adam and Eve, who were privileged to behold the beauty and loveliness of the Garden of Eden and were permitted to eat of all the trees in the garden except one. But the serpent tempted Eve, and she tempted her husband, and they both ate of the forbidden tree. They broke God's command, and became sinners. The news spread through heaven, and every harp was hushed. The angels sorrowed, and feared lest Adam and Eve would again put forth the hand and eat of the tree of life and be immortal sinners. . . .

Sorrow filled heaven as it was realized that humanity was lost and that the world which God had created was to be filled with mortals doomed to misery, sickness, and death. . . . The whole family of Adam must die. I then saw the lovely Jesus and beheld an expression of sympathy and sorrow upon His countenance. Soon I saw Him approach the exceeding bright light which enshrouded the Father. Said my accompanying angel, "He is in close converse with His Father." The anxiety of the angels seemed to be intense while Jesus was communing with His Father. Three times He was shut in by the glorious light about the Father, and the third time He came from the Father we could see His person. His countenance was calm, free from all perplexity and trouble, and shone with a loveliness which words cannot describe. He then made known to the angelic choir that a way of escape had been made for lost human beings; that He had been pleading with His Father, and had obtained permission to give His own life as a ransom for the race, to bear their sins, and take the sentence of death upon Himself, thus opening a way whereby they might, through the merits of His blood, find pardon for past transgressions, and by obedience be brought back to the garden from which they were driven. . . .

Then joy, inexpressible joy, filled heaven, and the heavenly choir sang a song of praise and adoration. They touched their harps and sang a note higher than they had done before, because of the great mercy and condescension of God in yielding up His **dearly Beloved** to die for a race of rebels.—*Early Writings*, pp. 125–127.

Further Reflection: *Why would I choose to die for sins already paid for on the cross?*

PATIENT SUFFERER

Surely He has borne our griefs and carried our sorrows.
—Isaiah 53:4

Above the throne is revealed the cross; and like a panoramic view appear the scenes of Adam's temptation and fall, and the successive steps in the great plan of redemption. The Saviour's lowly birth; His early life of simplicity and obedience; His baptism in Jordan; the fast and temptation in the wilderness; His public ministry, unfolding to humans heaven's most precious blessings; the days crowded with deeds of love and mercy, the nights of prayer and watching in the solitude of the mountains; the plottings of envy, hate, and malice which repaid His benefits; the awful, mysterious agony in Gethsemane beneath the crushing weight of the sins of the whole world; His betrayal into the hands of the murderous mob; the fearful events of that night of horror—the unresisting prisoner, forsaken by His best-loved disciples, rudely hurried through the streets of Jerusalem; the Son of God exultingly displayed before Annas, arraigned in the high priest's palace, in the judgment hall of Pilate, before the cowardly and cruel Herod, mocked, insulted, tortured, and condemned to die—all are vividly portrayed.

And now before the swaying multitude are revealed the final scenes—the **patient Sufferer** treading the path to Calvary; the Prince of heaven hanging upon the cross; the haughty priests and the jeering rabble deriding His expiring agony; the supernatural darkness; the heaving earth, the rent rocks, the open graves, marking the moment when the world's Redeemer yielded up His life.

The awful spectacle appears just as it was. Satan, his angels, and his subjects have no power to turn from the picture of their own work. Each actor recalls the part which he performed. Herod, who slew the innocent children of Bethlehem that he might destroy the King of Israel; the base Herodias, upon whose guilty soul rests the blood of John the Baptist; the weak, timeserving Pilate; the mocking soldiers; the priests and rulers and the maddened throng who cried, "His blood be on us, and on our children!"—all behold the enormity of their guilt. They vainly seek to hide from the divine majesty of His countenance, outshining the glory of the sun, while the redeemed cast their crowns at the Saviour's feet, exclaiming: "He died for me!"—*The Great Controversy*, pp. 666, 667.

Further Reflection: *Will the record of my life demonstrate a love for my Suffering Savior?*

PATTERN OF GOODNESS

"So He said to him, 'Why do you call Me good?' "
—Matthew 19:17

The great controversy between the Prince of light and the prince of darkness has not abated one jot or tittle of its fierceness as time has gone on. The stern conflict between light and darkness, between error and truth, is deepening in its intensity. The synagogue of Satan is intensely active, and the deceiving power of the enemy is working in the most subtle way in this age. Every human mind that is not surrendered to God and is not under the control of the Spirit of God will be perverted through satanic agencies.

The enemy is working continually to supplant Jesus Christ in the human heart, and to place his attributes in the human character in the place of the attributes of God. He brings his strong delusions to bear upon the human mind in order that he may have a controlling power and obliterate the truth and abolish the true **Pattern of goodness** and righteousness, in order that the professed Christian world shall be swept to perdition through separation from God. He is working in order that selfishness shall become worldwide, and thus make of no effect the mission and work of Christ.

Christ came to the world in order to bring back the character of God to man, and to retrace on the human soul the divine image. Through His entire life Christ sought by continuous, laborious efforts to call the world's attention to God and to His holy requirements, in order that men might be imbued with the Spirit of God, might be actuated by love, and might reveal in life and character the divine attributes. Christ came to be the light and life of the world, and His life was one of continual self-denial and self-sacrifice. The Lord Jesus valued every human being, and could not endure the thought that one soul should perish. His great heart of love embraced the whole world and led Him to provide complete salvation to all who would believe in Him.

In the character of Christ majesty and humility were blended. Temperance and self-denial were seen in every act of His life. But there was no taint of bigotry, no cold austerity manifested in His manner to lessen His influence over those with whom He came in contact. The world's Redeemer had a greater-than-angelic nature, yet united with His divine majesty was meekness and humility that attracted all to Himself.—Manuscript 39, 1894.

Further Reflection: *Jesus values me and cannot bear the thought that I might be lost.*

ARBITER OF ALL DESTINIES

The L*ORD* *will perfect that which concerns me; Your mercy, O* L*ORD*, *endures forever; do not forsake the works of Your hands.*

—Psalm 138:8

The cross of Christ will be the science and the song of the redeemed through all eternity. In Christ glorified they will behold Christ crucified. Never will it be forgotten that He whose power created and upheld the unnumbered worlds through the vast realms of space, the Beloved of God, the Majesty of heaven, He whom cherub and shining seraph delighted to adore—humbled Himself to uplift fallen human beings; that He bore the guilt and shame of sin, and the hiding of His Father's face, till the woes of a lost world broke His heart and crushed out His life on Calvary's cross. That the Maker of all worlds, the **Arbiter of all destinies**, should lay aside His glory and humiliate Himself from love to human beings will ever excite the wonder and adoration of the universe. As the nations of the saved look upon their Redeemer and behold the eternal glory of the Father shining in His countenance; as they behold His throne, which is from everlasting to everlasting, and know that His kingdom is to have no end, they break forth in rapturous song: "Worthy, worthy is the Lamb that was slain, and hath redeemed us to God by His own most precious blood!"

The mystery of the cross explains all other mysteries. In the light that streams from Calvary the attributes of God which had filled us with fear and awe appear beautiful and attractive. Mercy, tenderness, and parental love are seen to blend with holiness, justice, and power. While we behold the majesty of His throne, high and lifted up, we see His character in its gracious manifestations, and comprehend, as never before, the significance of that endearing title, "Our Father."

It will be seen that He who is infinite in wisdom could devise no plan for our salvation except the sacrifice of His Son. The compensation for this sacrifice is the joy of peopling the earth with ransomed beings, holy, happy, and immortal.—*The Great Controversy*, pp. 651, 652.

Further Reflection: *When will I pause today to thank God for the only means by which He could save me—the sacrifice of His Son, Jesus Christ?*

HOLY SUBSTITUTE

"He Himself took our infirmities and bore our sicknesses."
—Matthew 8:17

With what intense interest was this controversy watched by the heavenly angels and the unfallen worlds, as the honor of the law was being vindicated. Not merely for this world, but for the universe of heaven, was the controversy to be forever settled. The confederacy of darkness was also watching for the semblance of a chance to triumph over the divine and human Substitute of the human race. . . .

But Satan reached only the heel; he could not touch the head. At the death of Christ, Satan saw that he was defeated. He saw that his true character was clearly revealed before all heaven, and that the heavenly beings and the worlds that God had created would be wholly on the side of God. He saw that his prospects of future influence with them would be entirely cut off. Christ's humanity would demonstrate for eternal ages the question which settled the controversy.

In taking upon Himself our nature in its fallen condition, Christ did not in the least participate in its sin. He was subject to the infirmities and weaknesses by which humanity is encompassed, "that it might be fulfilled which was spoken by Esaias the prophet, saying, Himself took our infirmities, and bare our sicknesses." (Matthew 8:17) He was touched with the feeling of our infirmities, and was in all points tempted like as we are. And yet He knew no sin. He was the Lamb "without blemish and without spot." (1 Peter 1:19) Could Satan in the least particular have tempted Christ to sin, he would have bruised the Saviour's head. As it was, he could only touch His heel. Had the head of Christ been touched, the hope of the human race would have perished. Divine wrath would have come upon Christ as it came upon Adam. Christ and the church would have been without hope.

We should have no misgivings in regard to the perfect sinlessness of the human nature of Christ. Our faith must be an intelligent faith, looking unto Jesus in perfect confidence, in full and entire faith in the atoning Sacrifice. This is essential that the soul may not be enshrouded in darkness. This **holy Substitute** is able to save to the uttermost; for He presented to the wondering universe perfect and complete humility in His human character, and perfect obedience to all the requirements of God.—*Selected Messages*, book 1, pp. 255, 256.

Further Reflection: *How can I be as perfect in my sphere as Christ was in His?*

ALL-POWERFUL MEDIATOR

For there is one God and one Mediator between God and men, the Man Christ Jesus.

—1 Timothy 2:5

In the Judgment, the use made of every talent will be scrutinized. . . . Have we improved the powers entrusted us, in hand and heart and brain, to the glory of God and the blessing of the world? How have we used our time, our pen, our voice, our money, our influence? What have we done for Christ, in the person of the poor, the afflicted, the orphan, or the widow? God has made us the depositary of His holy Word; what have we done with the light and truth given us to make people wise unto salvation? No value is attached to a mere profession of faith in Christ; only the love which is shown by works is counted genuine. Yet it is love alone which in the sight of Heaven makes any act of value. Whatever is done from love, however small it may appear in the estimation of human beings, is accepted and rewarded of God.

The hidden selfishness of men and women stands revealed in the books of Heaven. There is the record of unfulfilled duties to their fellow human beings, of forgetfulness of the Saviour's claims. There they will see how often were given to Satan the time, thought, and strength that belonged to Christ. Sad is the record which angels bear to Heaven. Intelligent beings, professed followers of Christ, are absorbed in the acquirement of worldly possessions, or the enjoyment of earthly pleasures. Money, time, and strength are sacrificed for display and self-indulgence; but few are the moments devoted to prayer, to the searching of the Scriptures, to humiliation of soul and confession of sin.

Satan invents unnumbered schemes to occupy our minds that they may not dwell upon the very work with which we ought to be best acquainted. The arch-deceiver hates the great truths that bring to view an atoning sacrifice and an **All-Powerful Mediator**. He knows that with him everything depends on his diverting minds from Jesus and His truth.

Those who would share the benefits of the Saviour's mediation should permit nothing to interfere with their duty to perfect holiness in the fear of God. The precious hours, instead of being given to pleasure, to display, or to gain-seeking, should be devoted to an earnest, prayerful study of the Word of truth.—*The Great Controversy*, pp. 487, 488.

Further Reflection: *Am I knowingly giving any portion of my strength to the cause of Satan?*

CHANNEL

He indeed was foreordained before the foundation of the world, but was manifest in these last times for you.

—1 Peter 1:20

By rebellion and apostasy humanity forfeited the favor of God; not his rights, for he could have no value except as it was invested in God's dear Son. This point must be understood. He forfeited those privileges which God in His mercy presented him as a free gift, a treasure in trust to be used to advance His cause and His glory, to benefit the beings He had made. The moment the workmanship of God refused obedience to the laws of God's kingdom, that moment he became disloyal to the government of God and he made himself entirely unworthy of all the blessings wherewith God had favored him.

This was the position of the human race after they divorced themselves from God by transgression. . . . And the reason why humanity was not annihilated was because God so loved him that He made the gift of His dear Son that He should suffer the penalty of his transgression. Christ proposed to become humanity's surety and substitute, that they, through matchless grace, should have another trial—a second probation—having the experience of Adam and Eve as a warning not to transgress God's law as they did. And inasmuch as men and women enjoy the blessings of God in the gift of the sunshine and the gift of food, there must be on the part of men and women a bowing before God in thankful acknowledgment that all things come of God. . . .

Humans broke God's law, and through the Redeemer new and fresh promises were made on a different basis. All blessings must come through a Mediator. Now every member of the human family is given wholly into the hands of Christ, and whatever we possess—whether it is the gift of money, of houses, of lands, of reasoning powers, of physical strength, of intellectual talents—in this present life, and the blessings of the future life, are placed in our possession as God's treasures to be faithfully expended for the benefit of humanity. Every gift is stamped with the cross and bears the image and superscription of Jesus Christ. All things come of God. From the smallest benefits up to the largest blessing, all flow through the one **Channel**—a superhuman mediation sprinkled with the blood that is of value beyond estimate because it was the life of God in His Son.—*Faith and Works*, pp. 21, 22.

Further Reflection: *What do I need God to send through the Channel for me today?*

ANGEL OF GOD'S PRESENCE

"And we were like grasshoppers in our own sight, and so we were in their sight."

—Numbers 13:33

And all the congregation lifted up their voice, and cried; and the people wept that night." Revolt and open mutiny quickly followed; for Satan had full sway, and the people seemed bereft of reason. They cursed Moses and Aaron, forgetting that God hearkened to their wicked speeches, and that, enshrouded in the pillar of cloud, the **Angel of God's presence** was witnessing their terrible outburst of wrath. In bitterness they cried. "Would God that we had died in the land of Egypt! or would God we had died in this wilderness!" With the utterance of their discontent, their bitterness grew, until they began to reproach God, saying, "And wherefore hath the Lord brought us unto this land, to fall by the sword, that our wives and our children should be a prey? were it not better for us to return into Egypt? And they said to one another, Let us make a captain, and let us return into Egypt."

Cut to the heart by the rebellion of the people, feeling the enormity of their sin. "Moses and Aaron fell on their faces before all the assembly of the congregation of the children of Israel." And again Caleb and Joshua tried to reassure the people. Above the tempest of lamentation and rebellious grief their clear, ringing voices were heard, saying: "The land, which we passed through to search it, is an exceeding good land. If the Lord delight in us, then He will bring us into this land, and give it us; a land which floweth with milk and honey. Only rebel not ye against the Lord, neither fear ye the people of the land; for they are bread for us: their defense is departed from them, and the Lord is with us: fear them not."

But the congregation would not listen to the earnest entreaty. The unfaithful spies were loud in their denunciations of Caleb and Joshua, and the cry was raised to stone them. The insane mob seized missiles with which to slay these faithful men. They rushed forth with yells of madness, when suddenly the stones dropped from their hands, a hush fell upon them, and they shook with fear. God had interposed to check their murderous designs. The glory of His presence, like a flaming light, illuminated the tabernacle. . . . A mightier One than they had revealed Himself, and no one dared continue his resistance.—*Review and Herald,* May 20, 1902.

Further Reflection: *Have I ever grieved the Holy Spirit in a fit of rebellion? Has my anger ever stopped God's blessings for me?*

ETERNAL WORD

"For this cause I was born, and for this cause I have come into the world, that I should bear witness to the truth."

—John 18:37

Christ was the greatest teacher the world has ever known. He came to this earth to shed abroad the bright beams of truth, that humanity might gain a fitness for heaven. "For this cause came I into the world . . . that I should bear witness unto the truth." (John 18:37) He came to reveal the character of the Father, that people might be led to worship Him in spirit and in truth.

Humanity's need for a divine teacher was known in heaven. The pity and sympathy of God were aroused in behalf of human beings, fallen and bound to Satan's chariot car; and when the fullness of time was come, He sent forth His Son. The One appointed in the councils of heaven came to this earth as man's instructor. The rich benevolence of God gave Him to our world, and to meet the necessities of human nature He took humanity upon Himself. To the astonishment of the heavenly host the **eternal Word** came to this world as a helpless babe. Fully prepared, He left the royal courts and mysteriously allied Himself with fallen human beings. . . .

When Christ left His high command, He might have taken upon Him any condition in life that He chose. But greatness and rank were nothing to Him, and He chose the most humble walk of life. No luxury, ease, or self-gratification came into His experience. The truth of heavenly origin was to be His theme; He was to sow the world with truth. . . .

That during His childhood Christ should grow in wisdom and in favor with God and humanity was not a matter of astonishment, for it was according to the laws of His divine appointment that His talents should develop and His faculties strengthen. He did not seek an education in the schools of the rabbis, for God was His instructor. As He grew older He continued to increase in wisdom. He applied Himself diligently to a study of the Scriptures, for He knew them to be full of invaluable instruction. He was faithful in the discharge of His home duties; and the early morning hours, instead of being spent in bed, often found Him in a retired place, searching the Scriptures and praying to His heavenly Father.—*Counsels to Parents, Teachers, and Students*, pp. 259, 260.

Further Reflection: *If Jesus was the eternal Word, why did He need to study the Scriptures?*

LIGHT TO LIGHTEN THE GENTILES

*"The people who sat in darkness have seen a great light,
and upon those who sat in the region and shadow of death
light has dawned."*

—Matthew 4:16

Nicodemus sought an interview with Jesus at night, saying, "Rabbi, we know that Thou art a teacher come from God: for no man can do these miracles that Thou doest, except God be with him." All this was true, as far as it went; but what said Jesus? He "answered and said unto him, Verily, verily, I say unto thee, Except a man be born again, he cannot see the kingdom of God." Here was a man in a high position of trust, a man who was looked up to as one educated in Jewish customs, one whose mind was stored with wisdom. He was indeed in possession of talents of no ordinary character. He would not go to Jesus by day, for this would make him a subject of remark. It would be too humiliating for a ruler of the Jews to acknowledge himself in sympathy with the despised Nazarene. Nicodemus thinks, I will ascertain for myself the mission and claims of this Teacher, whether He is indeed the **Light to lighten the Gentiles**, and the Glory of Israel.

Jesus virtually says to Nicodemus: It is not controversy that will help your case: it is not arguments that will bring light to the soul. You must have a new heart, or you cannot discern the kingdom of heaven. It is not greater evidence that will bring you into a right position, but new purposes, new springs of action. You must be born again. Until this change takes place, making all things new, the strongest evidences that could be presented would be useless. The want is in your own heart; everything must be changed, or you cannot see the kingdom of God.

This was a very humiliating statement to Nicodemus and with a feeling of irritation he takes up the words of Christ, saying, "How can a man be born when he is old?" He was not spiritually minded enough to discern the meaning of the words of Christ. But the Saviour did not meet argument with argument. Raising His hand in solemn, quiet dignity, He presses home the truth with greater assurance: "Verily, verily, I say unto thee, Except a man be born of water and of the Spirit, he cannot enter into the kingdom of God."—*Testimonies to Ministers and Gospel Workers*, pp. 367, 368.

Further Reflection: *When was the last time that you came to Jesus for one thing but received something else, something unexpected?*

REVEALER OF TRUTH

If we say that we have fellowship with Him, and walk in darkness, we lie and do not practice the truth.

—1 John 1:6

Had silver and gold been sufficient to purchase the salvation of men, how easily might it have been accomplished by Him who says, "The silver is Mine, and the gold is Mine." (Haggai 2:8) But only by the precious blood of the Son of God could the transgressor be redeemed. The plan of salvation was laid in sacrifice. The apostle Paul wrote, "Ye know the grace of our Lord Jesus Christ, that, though He was rich, yet for your sakes He became poor, that ye through His poverty might be rich." (2 Corinthians 8:9) Christ gave Himself for us that He might redeem us from all iniquity. And as the crowning blessing of salvation, "the gift of God is eternal life through Jesus Christ our Lord." (Romans 6:23)

"Seeing ye have purified your souls in obeying the truth through the Spirit unto unfeigned love of the brethren," Peter continued, "see that ye love one another with a pure heart fervently." The word of God—the truth—is the channel through which the Lord manifests His Spirit and power. Obedience to the word produces fruit of the required quality—"unfeigned love of the brethren." This love is heaven-born and leads to high motives and unselfish actions.

When truth becomes an abiding principle in the life, the soul is "born again, not of corruptible seed, but of incorruptible, by the word of God, which liveth and abideth forever." This new birth is the result of receiving Christ as the Word of God. When by the Holy Spirit divine truths are impressed upon the heart, new conceptions are awakened, and the energies hitherto dormant are aroused to co-operate with God.

Thus it had been with Peter and his fellow disciples. Christ was the **revealer of truth** to the world. By Him the incorruptible seed—the word of God—was sown in the hearts of men and women. But many of the most precious lessons of the Great Teacher were spoken to those who did not then understand them. When, after His ascension, the Holy Spirit brought His teachings to the remembrance of the disciples, their slumbering senses awoke.—*The Acts of the Apostles*, pp. 519, 520.

Further Reflection: *What is my newest change in attitude or behavior that came as a result of truth revealed by the Holy Spirit?*

AUTHOR OF PHYSICAL LAWS

"Ah, Lord God! Behold, You have made the heavens and the earth by Your great power and outstretched arm. There is nothing too hard for You."

—Jeremiah 32:17

Health is a blessing of which few appreciate the value; yet upon it the efficiency of our mental and physical powers largely depends. Our impulses and passions have their seat in the body, and it must be kept in the best condition physically and under the most spiritual influences in order that our talents may be put to the highest use.

Anything that lessens physical strength enfeebles the mind and makes it less capable of discriminating between right and wrong. We become less capable of choosing the good and have less strength of will to do that which we know to be right.

The misuse of our physical powers shortens the period of time in which our lives can be used for the glory of God. And it unfits us to accomplish the work God has given us to do. By allowing ourselves to form wrong habits, by keeping late hours, by gratifying appetite at the expense of health, we lay the foundation for feebleness. By neglecting physical exercise, by overworking mind or body, we unbalance the nervous system. Those who thus shorten their lives and unfit themselves for service by disregarding nature's laws, are guilty of robbery toward God. And they are robbing their fellow human beings also. The opportunity of blessing others, the very work for which God sent them into the world, has by their own course of action been cut short. And they have unfitted themselves to do even that which in a briefer period of time they might have accomplished. The Lord holds us guilty when by our injurious habits we thus deprive the world of good.

Transgression of physical law is transgression of the moral law; for God is as truly the **Author of physical laws** as He is the Author of the moral law. His law is written with His own finger upon every nerve, every muscle, every faculty, which has been entrusted to human beings. And every misuse of any part of our organism is a violation of that law.

All should have an intelligent knowledge of the human frame that they may keep their bodies in the condition necessary to do the work of the Lord.—*Christ's Object Lessons*, pp. 346–348.

Further Reflection: *Have I robbed God of usefulness by failing to care for my body temple? What health habit do I need to begin today?*

DIVINE MESSENGER

"For I have come down from heaven, not to do My own will, but the will of Him who sent Me."

—John 6:38

Can we not reason from cause to effect? Can we not see that because of our slothfulness in trading on the Lord's goods, because of our selfishness in refusing to return to Him His own portion, His work is retarded?

When Christ made His triumphal entry into Jerusalem, the applause of the multitude was at its height. Hosannas were on the lips of the people; but the Saviour felt no joy. He beheld the city, and wept over it, saying, "If thou hadst known, even thou, at least in this thy day, the things which belong unto thy peace! but now they are hid from thine eyes." He saw the thousands and thousands soon to be involved in the terrible destruction of the doomed city. How deep must His emotion have been as He thought of the nation that had forged its own fetters, sealed its own doom, gathered about it the cloud of Jehovah's wrath. "You have defiantly resisted all My pleadings," He said. "Again and again I have averted the bolts of justice. In love I have waited for your penitence and repentance. I have borne with you as a man beareth with his own son that serveth him. But ye would not come unto Me that ye might have life."

But Christ's agonizing tears were not shed only for Jerusalem. He wept as He thought of the terrible retribution to fall upon an unrepentant world. He is still working in patience and love for the salvation of sinners. Is not the **divine Messenger** knocking at the door of the heart for entrance? Is not the Spirit striving with sinners? Has not Christ invited sin-sick souls to sit at His feet and learn of Him, to wear His yoke of submission and obedience? Has He not traversed the length and breadth of the land, scattering blessings in His path? There is no wearying of His patience, no repressing of His love. Hear His voice speaking to the weak, the weary, the helpless. "Come unto Me, all ye that labor and are heavy laden, and I will give you rest. Take My yoke upon you, and learn of Me; for I am meek and lowly in heart: and ye shall find rest unto your souls." Will you not let grace soften the heart of stone?—*Review and Herald*, December 3, 1901.

Further Reflection: *How tender is the heart of Jesus? Can I hear Him as He knocks at the door of my heart?*

FORBEARING ONE

The LORD *is merciful and gracious, slow to anger, and abounding in mercy.*

—Psalm 103:8

God has done His part of the work for the salvation of men and women, and now He calls for the co-operation of the church. There is the blood of Christ, the Word of truth, the Holy Spirit, and there are the perishing souls. Every follower of Christ has a part to act to bring men and women to accept the blessings Heaven has provided. Let us closely examine ourselves, and see if we have done this work. Let us question the motives, the actions of the life. Are there not many unpleasant pictures hanging in memory's halls? . . .

Have not Christ and His love been shut out from your life, until a mechanical form has taken the place of heart service? Where is the kindling of soul you once felt at the mention of the name of Jesus? In the freshness of your early dedication, how fervent was your love for souls. How earnestly you sought to represent to them the Saviour's love. The absence of that love has made you cold, critical, exacting. Seek to win it back, and then labor to bring souls to Christ. If you refuse to do this, others who have had less light and experience, and fewer opportunities, will come up and take your place, and do that which you have neglected; for the work must be done to save the tempted, the tried, the perishing. Christ offers the service to His church; who will accept it?

God has not been unmindful of the good deeds, the self-denying acts, of the church in the past. All are registered on high. But these are not enough. These will not save the church when she ceases to fulfill her mission. Unless the cruel neglect and indifference manifested in the past shall cease, the church, instead of going from strength to strength, will continue to degenerate into weakness and formality. . . .

Brethren, your own lamps will surely flicker and become dim, until they go out in darkness, unless you shall make decided efforts to reform. "Remember therefore from whence thou art fallen, and repent, and do thy first works." The opportunity now presented may be short. If this season of grace and repentance passes unimproved, the warning is given, "I will come unto thee quickly, and will remove thy candlestick out of his place." These words are uttered by the long-suffering, **Forbearing One**.—*Review and Herald,* November 30, 1886.

Further Reflection: *Do I still get excited about my Savior, and seeing the lost saved?*

CENTER OF ALL TRUE DOCTRINE

Your word is a lamp to my feet and a light to my path.
—Psalm 119:105

Christ is the **center of all true doctrine**. All true religion is found in His word and in nature. He is the One in whom our hopes of eternal life are centered; and the teacher who learns from Him finds a safe anchorage.

All that the mind can grasp is opened before us in the Bible. This is our spiritual food. We are to contemplate the wonderful works of God and repeat to our children the lessons learned, that we may lead them to see His skill, His power, and His grandeur in His created works.

What a God is our God! He rules over His kingdom with diligence and care, and He has built a hedge—the Ten Commandments—about His subjects to preserve them from the results of transgression. In requiring obedience to the laws of His kingdom, God gives His people health and happiness, peace and joy. He teaches them that the perfection of character He requires can be attained only by becoming familiar with His word.

It is written in the prophets: "O thou afflicted, tossed with tempest, and not comforted, behold, I will lay thy stones with fair colors, and lay thy foundations with sapphires. And I will make thy windows of agates, and thy gates of carbuncles, and all thy borders of pleasant stones. And all thy children shall be taught of the Lord; and great shall be the peace of thy children. In righteousness shalt thou be established: thou shalt be far from oppression; for thou shalt not fear: and from terror; for it shall not come near thee." (Isaiah 54:11–14)

"This shall be the covenant that I will make with the house of Israel; After those days, saith the Lord, I will put My law in their inward parts, and write it in their hearts; and will be their God, and they shall be My people. And they shall teach no more every man his neighbor, and every man his brother, saying, Know the Lord: for they shall all know Me, from the least of them unto the greatest of them, saith the Lord: for I will forgive their iniquity, and I will remember their sin no more." (Jeremiah 31:33, 34)—*Counsels to Parents, Teachers, and Students*, pp. 453, 454.

Further Reflection: *If it is not possible to experience perfection of character without spending time in God's Word, how can I change my schedule to spend more time in biblical study?*

AUTHOR AND FINISHER OF OUR FAITH

"I counsel you to buy from Me gold refined in the fire, that you may be rich; and white garments, that you may be clothed, that the shame of your nakedness may not be revealed."

—Revelation 3:18

Jesus pointed out the power of false teaching to destroy the appreciation and desire for truth. "No man," He said, "having drunk old wine straightway desireth new: for he saith, The old is better." All the truth that has been given to the world through patriarchs and prophets shone out in new beauty in the words of Christ. But the scribes and Pharisees had no desire for the precious new wine. Until emptied of the old traditions, customs, and practices, they had no place in mind or heart for the teachings of Christ. . . .

A legal religion can never lead souls to Christ; for it is a loveless, Christ-less religion. Fasting or prayer that is actuated by a self-justifying spirit is an abomination in the sight of God. The solemn assembly for worship, the round of religious ceremonies, the external humiliation, the imposing sacrifice, proclaim that the doer of these things regards himself as righteous, and as entitled to heaven; but it is all a deception. Our own works can never purchase salvation.

As it was in the days of Christ, so it is now; the Pharisees do not know their spiritual destitution. To them comes the message, "Because thou sayest, I am rich, and increased with goods, and have need of nothing; and knowest not that thou art wretched, and miserable, and poor, and blind, and naked: I counsel thee to buy of Me gold tried in the fire, that thou mayest be rich; and white raiment, that thou mayest be clothed, and that the shame of thy nakedness do not appear." (Revelation 3:17, 18) Faith and love are the gold tried in the fire. But with many the gold has become dim, and the rich treasure has been lost. The righteousness of Christ is to them as a robe unworn, a fountain untouched. . . .

Human beings must be emptied of self before they can be, in the fullest sense, believers in Jesus. When self is renounced, then the Lord can make a person a new creature. . . . The love of Christ will animate the believer with new life. In the one who looks unto the **Author and Finisher of our faith** the character of Christ will be manifest.—*The Desire of Ages*, pp. 279, 280.

Further Reflection: *Have I surrendered myself to Christ so that I can be made new?*

STRONGHOLD

"As for you also,
Because of the blood of your covenant,
I will set your prisoners free from the waterless pit.
Return to the stronghold,
You prisoners of hope.
Even today I declare
That I will restore double to you."

—Zechariah 9:11, 12

Every church should labor for the perishing within its own borders and for those outside its borders. The members are to shine as living stones in the temple of God, reflecting heavenly light. No random, haphazard, desultory work is to be done. To get fast hold of souls ready to perish means more than praying for a drunkard, and then, because he weeps and confesses the pollution of his soul, declaring him saved. Over and over again the battle must be fought.

Let the members of every church feel it their special duty to labor for those in their neighborhood. Let each one who claims to stand under the banner of Christ feel that he has entered into covenant relation with God, to do the work of the Saviour. Let not those who take up this work become weary in well-doing. When the redeemed stand before God, precious souls will respond to their names who are there because of the faithful, patient efforts put forth in their behalf, the entreaties and earnest persuasions to flee to the **Stronghold**. Thus those who in this world have been laborers together with God will receive their reward.

The ministers of the popular churches will not allow the truth to be presented to the people from their pulpits. The enemy leads them to resist the truth with bitterness and malice. Falsehoods are manufactured. Christ's experience with the Jewish rulers is repeated. Satan strives to eclipse every ray of light shining from God to His people. He works through the ministers as he worked through the priests and rulers in the days of Christ. Will those who know the truth join his party, to hinder, embarrass, and turn aside those who are trying to work in God's appointed way to advance His work, to plant the standard of truth in the regions of darkness?—*Counsels on Health*, pp. 356, 357.

Further Reflection: *How do I avoid becoming weary in well-doing when working with people who consistently struggle to stay within God's Stronghold?*

ONLY TRUE GUIDE

And God said to Balaam, "You shall not go with them; you shall not curse the people, for they are blessed."
—Numbers 22:12

The Moabites were a degraded, idolatrous people, yet they manifested sincerity and earnestness in their persistent efforts to secure the power of divination against Israel. According to the light which they had received, their guilt was not so great in the sight of Heaven as was that of Balaam. As he professed to be God's prophet, all he should say would be supposed to come from the Lord Jehovah. Hence he was not to be permitted to speak as he chose, but must deliver the message which God should give him. The Lord saw in this pretentious prophet, a man whose heart was defiled with deception and hypocrisy, and dealt with him according to his own perverse and stubborn ways.

This instance is placed on record for the benefit of all succeeding generations. It is dangerous to trifle with God, in order to follow a stubborn, determined will. There are thousands at the present day who are pursuing a course similar to that of Balaam. They follow their own ways, and take counsel of their own hearts, under a pretense of being guided and controlled by the Spirit of God. And the prayers of these willfully deceived ones are answered in accordance with the spirit that prompts them. For wise purposes the Lord often permits them to have their own way. They walk in a thick mist—the atmosphere which Satan breathes about the soul.

Dangers beset the path of every person who, forsaking the **only true Guide**, tries by the light of his own wisdom to find a safe way through the dangers and difficulties of this world. Such a person places himself in a situation far more perilous than that of the traveler climbing along the slippery face of a cliff, where, if he lose his balance for a moment, he will fall and be dashed in pieces. David describes the peril of those who do not walk with God, but for a time seem to be prosperous in an evil way: "Thou didst set them in slippery places, Thou castest them down to destruction in a moment. They are utterly consumed with terror."—*The Signs of the Times*, November 25, 1880.

Further Reflection: *Do I still hear the voice of God? Is He guiding my life? How can I be sure that I am following the heaven's only true Guide?*

HOPED-FOR DELIVERER

The righteous cry out, and the LORD hears,
and delivers them out of all their troubles.

—Psalm 34:17

When the Saviour began His ministry, the popular conception of the Messiah and His work was such as wholly unfitted the people to receive Him. The spirit of true devotion had been lost in tradition and ceremonialism, and the prophecies were interpreted at the dictate of proud, world-loving hearts. The Jews looked for the coming One, not as a Saviour from sin, but as a great prince who should bring all nations under the supremacy of the Lion of the tribe of Judah. In vain had John the Baptist, with the heart-searching power of the ancient prophets, called them to repentance. In vain had he, beside the Jordan, pointed to Jesus as the Lamb of God, that taketh away the sin of the world. God was seeking to direct their minds to Isaiah's prophecy of the suffering Saviour, but they would not hear.

Had the teachers and leaders in Israel yielded to His transforming grace, Jesus would have made them His ambassadors among men and women. In Judea first the coming of the kingdom had been proclaimed, and the call to repentance had been given. In the act of driving out the desecrators from the temple at Jerusalem, Jesus had announced Himself as the Messiah—the One who should cleanse the soul from the defilement of sin and make His people a holy temple unto the Lord. But the Jewish leaders would not humble themselves to receive the lowly Teacher from Nazareth. At His second visit to Jerusalem He was arraigned before the Sanhedrin, and fear of the people alone prevented these dignitaries from trying to take His life. Then it was that, leaving Judea, He entered upon His ministry in Galilee.

His work there had continued some months before the Sermon on the Mount was given. The message He had proclaimed throughout the land, "The kingdom of heaven is at hand" (Matthew 4:17), had arrested the attention of all classes, and had still further fanned the flame of their ambitious hopes. The fame of the new Teacher had spread beyond the limits of Palestine, and, notwithstanding the attitude of the hierarchy, the feeling was widespread that this might be the **hoped-for Deliverer.**—*Thoughts From the Mount of Blessing*, pp. 1–3.

Further Reflection: *Do I yearn for the day when Jesus will deliver me from the presence of sin?*

ADORED OF THE ANGELS

"Do you think that I cannot now pray to My Father, and He will provide Me with more than twelve legions of angels?"
—Matthew 26:53

Many among Christ's hearers who were dwellers at Jerusalem, and who were not ignorant of the plots of the rulers against Him, felt themselves drawn to Him by an irresistible power. The conviction pressed upon them that He was the Son of God. But Satan was ready to suggest doubt; and for this the way was prepared by their own erroneous ideas of the Messiah and His coming. It was generally believed that Christ would be born at Bethlehem, but that after a time He would disappear, and at His second appearance none would know whence He came. There were not a few who held that the Messiah would have no natural relationship to humanity. . . .

While they were thus wavering between doubt and faith, Jesus took up their thoughts and answered them: "Ye both know Me, and ye know whence I am: and I am not come of Myself, but He that sent Me is true, whom ye know not." They claimed a knowledge of what the origin of Christ should be, but they were in utter ignorance of it. If they had lived in accordance with the will of God, they would have known His Son when He was manifested to them.

The hearers could not but understand Christ's words. Clearly they were a repetition of the claim He had made in the presence of the Sanhedrin many months before, when He declared Himself the Son of God. As the rulers then tried to compass His death, so now they sought to take Him; but they were prevented by an unseen power, which put a limit to their rage. . . .

Among the people many believed on Him, and they said, "When Christ cometh, will He do more miracles than these which this Man hath done?" The leaders of the Pharisees, who were anxiously watching the course of events, caught the expressions of sympathy among the throng. Hurrying away to the chief priests, they laid their plans to arrest Him. They arranged, however, to take Him when He was alone; for they dared not seize Him in the presence of the people. Again Jesus made it manifest that He read their purpose. "Yet a little while am I with you," He said, "and then I go unto Him that sent Me. . . ." Soon He would find a refuge beyond the reach of their scorn and hate. He would ascend to the Father, to be again the **Adored of the angels**.—*The Desire of Ages*, pp. 457, 458.

Further Reflection: *How did the angels feel as they beheld the suffering of Jesus?*

COMPASSIONATE PHYSICIAN

Is there no balm in Gilead,
Is there no physician there?
Why then is there no recovery
For the health of the daughter of my people?
—Jeremiah 8:22

The Scripture says that "men ought always to pray, and not to faint;" (Luke 18:1); and if ever there is a time when they feel their need of prayer, it is when strength fails and life itself seems slipping from their grasp. Often those who are in health forget the wonderful mercies continued to them day by day, year after year, and they render no tribute of praise to God for His benefits. But when sickness comes, God is remembered. When human strength fails, men and women feel their need of divine help. And never does our merciful God turn from the soul that in sincerity seeks Him for help. He is our refuge in sickness as in health. . . .

. . . Christ is the same **compassionate physician** now that He was during His earthly ministry. In Him there is healing balm for every disease, restoring power for every infirmity. His disciples in this time are to pray for the sick as verily as the disciples of old prayed. And recoveries will follow; for "the prayer of faith shall save the sick." We have the Holy Spirit's power, the calm assurance of faith, that can claim God's promises. The Lord's promise, "They shall lay hands on the sick, and they shall recover," (Mark 16:18), is just as trustworthy now as in the days of the apostles. It presents the privilege of God's children, and our faith should lay hold of all that it embraces. Christ's servants are the channel of His working, and through them He desires to exercise His healing power. It is our work to present the sick and suffering to God in the arms of our faith. We should teach them to believe in the Great Healer. The Saviour would have us encourage the sick, the hopeless, the afflicted, to take hold upon His strength. . . .

But only as we live in obedience to His word can we claim the fulfillment of His promises. The psalmist says, "If I regard iniquity in my heart, the Lord will not hear me." (Psalm 66:18) If we render to Him only a partial, halfhearted obedience, His promises will not be fulfilled to us.

In the word of God we have instruction relative to special prayer for the recovery of the sick. But the offering of such prayer is a most solemn act, and should not be entered upon without careful consideration.—*The Ministry of Healing*, pp. 225–227.

Further Reflection: *Should I petition God on behalf of those who have brought illness upon themselves due to self-indulgence? Would a restoration of health change their behavior?*

SEPTEMBER

TRUEST FRIEND

"God, be merciful to me a sinner!"

—Luke 18:13

With awakened conscience many a troubled soul, suffering bodily ailments as the result of continued transgression, cries out, "Lord, be merciful to me a sinner; make me Thy child." It is then that the minister, strong in faith, should be ready to tell the sufferer that there is hope for the penitent, that in Jesus everyone who longs for help and acceptance may find deliverance and peace. He who in meekness and love thus brings the gospel to the afflicted soul so much in need of its message of hope, is a mouthpiece for the One who gave Himself for human beings. As he speaks helpful, appropriate words, and as he offers prayer for the one lying on a bed of suffering, Jesus makes the application. God speaks through human lips. The heart is reached. Humanity is brought into touch with divinity.

The minister should understand by experience that the soothing power of the grace of Christ brings health and peace and fulness of joy. He should know Christ as the One who has invited the weary and heavy-laden to come to Him and find rest. Let him never forget that the Saviour's loving presence constantly surrounds every human agent ordained of God for the impartation of spiritual blessing. The remembrance of this will give vitality to his faith and earnestness to his petitions.

Then to those who call upon him for help he can impart the health-giving power of God's truth. He can talk of the works of healing wrought by Christ, and direct the minds of the sick to Him as the great Physician, who is light and life, as well as comfort and peace. He can tell them that they need not despair, that the Saviour loves them, and that if they surrender themselves to Him, they will have His love, His grace, His keeping power. Let him urge them to rest in God's promises, knowing that He who has given these promises is our best and **truest Friend**. As he endeavors to direct the mind heavenward, he will find that the thought of the tender sympathy of the One who knows just how to apply the healing balm, will give the sick a sense of rest and quietude.—*Gospel Workers*, pp. 213, 214.

Further Reflection: *Good friendships require time and attention, sharing and caring. How good is my friendship with Jesus?*

SEPTEMBER 2

LIFE-GIVER

For I know whom I have believed.

—2 Timothy 1:12

The apostle was looking into the great beyond, not with uncertainty or dread, but with joyous hope and longing expectation. As he stands at the place of martyrdom he sees not the sword of the executioner or the earth so soon to receive his blood; he looks up through the calm blue heaven of that summer day to the throne of the Eternal.

This man of faith beholds the ladder of Jacob's vision, representing Christ, who has connected earth with heaven, and finite humanity with the infinite God. His faith is strengthened as he calls to mind how patriarchs and prophets have relied upon the One who is his support and consolation, and for whom he is giving his life. From these holy persons who from century to century have borne testimony for their faith, he hears the assurance that God is true. His fellow apostles, who, to preach the gospel of Christ, went forth to meet religious bigotry and heathen superstition, persecution, and contempt, who counted not their lives dear unto themselves that they might bear aloft the light of the cross amidst the dark mazes of infidelity—these he hears witnessing to Jesus as the Son of God, the Saviour of the world. From the rack, the stake, the dungeon, from dens and caves of the earth, there falls upon his ear the martyr's shout of triumph. He hears the witness of steadfast souls, who, though destitute, afflicted, tormented, yet bear fearless, solemn testimony for the faith. . . . These, yielding up their lives for the faith, declare to the world that He in whom they have trusted is able to save to the uttermost.

Ransomed by the sacrifice of Christ, washed from sin in His blood, and clothed in His righteousness, Paul has the witness in himself that his soul is precious in the sight of his Redeemer. His life is hid with Christ in God, and he is persuaded that He who has conquered death is able to keep that which is committed to His trust. His mind grasps the Saviour's promise, "I will raise him up at the last day." (John 6:40) His thoughts and hopes are centered on the second coming of his Lord. And as the sword of the executioner descends and the shadows of death gather about the martyr, his latest thought springs forward, as will his earliest in the great awakening, to meet the **Life-giver**, who shall welcome him to the joy of the blest.—*The Acts of the Apostles*, pp. 511–513.

Further Reflection: *Do I know Him in whom I have believed, He who is my only hope?*

ONLY HELPER

How God anointed Jesus of Nazareth with the Holy Spirit and with power, who went about doing good and healing all who were oppressed by the devil, for God was with Him.
—Acts 10:38

For three years the Lord of light and glory had gone in and out among His people. He "went about doing good, and healing all that were oppressed of the devil," binding up the brokenhearted, setting at liberty them that were bound, restoring sight to the blind, causing the lame to walk and the deaf to hear, cleansing the lepers, raising the dead, and preaching the gospel to the poor. (Acts 10:38; Luke 4:18; Matthew 11:5) To all classes alike was addressed the gracious call: "Come unto Me, all ye that labor and are heavy-laden, and I will give you rest." (Matthew 11:28)

Though rewarded with evil for good, and hatred for His love (Psalm 109:5), He had steadfastly pursued His mission of mercy. Never were those repelled that sought His grace. A homeless wanderer, reproach and penury His daily lot, He lived to minister to the needs and lighten the woes of men and women, to plead with them to accept the gift of life. The waves of mercy, beaten back by those stubborn hearts, returned in a stronger tide of pitying, inexpressible love. But Israel had turned from her best Friend and **only Helper**. The pleadings of His love had been despised, His counsels spurned, His warnings ridiculed.

The hour of hope and pardon was fast passing; the cup of God's long-deferred wrath was almost full. The cloud that had been gathering through ages of apostasy and rebellion, now black with woe, was about to burst upon a guilty people; and He who alone could save them from their impending fate had been slighted, abused, rejected, and was soon to be crucified. When Christ should hang upon the cross of Calvary, Israel's day as a nation favored and blessed of God would be ended. The loss of even one soul is a calamity infinitely outweighing the gains and treasures of a world; but as Christ looked upon Jerusalem, the doom of a whole city, a whole nation, was before Him—that city, that nation, which had once been the chosen of God, His peculiar treasure.—*The Great Controversy*, pp. 20, 21.

Further Reflection: *When have I resisted Jesus' merciful entreaties, only to see Him return with even greater demonstrations of pitying love?*

LOVED COMMANDER

Behold what manner of love the Father has bestowed on us, that we should be called children of God! Therefore the world does not know us, because it did not know Him.

—1 John 3:1

The rabbis had a saying that there is rejoicing in heaven when one who has sinned against God is destroyed; but Jesus taught that to God the work of destruction is a strange work. That in which all heaven delights is the restoration of God's own image in the souls whom He has made.

When one who has wandered far in sin seeks to return to God, he will encounter criticism and distrust. There are those who will doubt whether his repentance is genuine, or will whisper, "He has no stability; I do not believe that he will hold out." These persons are doing not the work of God but the work of Satan, who is the accuser of the brethren. Through their criticisms the wicked one hopes to discourage that soul, and to drive him still farther from hope and from God. Let the repenting sinner contemplate the rejoicing in heaven over the return of the one that was lost. Let him rest in the love of God and in no case be disheartened by the scorn and suspicion of the Pharisees.

The rabbis understood Christ's parable as applying to the publicans and sinners; but it has also a wider meaning. By the lost sheep Christ represents not only the individual sinner but the one world that has apostatized and has been ruined by sin. This world is but an atom in the vast dominions over which God presides, yet this little fallen world—the one lost sheep—is more precious in His sight than are the ninety and nine that went not astray from the fold. Christ, the **loved Commander** in the heavenly courts, stooped from His high estate, laid aside the glory that He had with the Father, in order to save the one lost world. For this He left the sinless worlds on high, the ninety and nine that loved Him, and came to this earth, to be "wounded for our transgressions" and "bruised for our iniquities." (Isaiah 53:5) God gave Himself in His Son that He might have the joy of receiving back the sheep that was lost. "Behold, what manner of love the Father hath bestowed upon us, that we should be called the sons of God." (1 John 3:1)—*Christ's Object Lessons*, pp. 190, 191.

Further Reflection: *When was the last time that heaven rejoiced over my repentance for sin?*

TRUE SOURCE OF PARDON AND PEACE

For Your name's sake, O LORD, pardon my iniquity, for it is great.

—Psalm 25:11

The Corinthian believers, once so prone to lose sight of their high calling in Christ, had developed strength of Christian character. Their words and acts revealed the transforming power of the grace of God, and they were now a strong force for good in that center of heathenism and superstition. In the society of his beloved companions and these faithful converts the apostle's worn and troubled spirit found rest.

During his sojourn at Corinth, Paul found time to look forward to new and wider fields of service. His contemplated journey to Rome especially occupied his thoughts. To see the Christian faith firmly established at the great center of the known world was one of his dearest hopes and most cherished plans. A church had already been established in Rome, and the apostle desired to secure the co-operation of the believers there in the work to be accomplished in Italy and in other countries. To prepare the way for his labors among these brethren, many of whom were as yet strangers to him, he sent them a letter announcing his purpose of visiting Rome and his hope of planting the standard of the cross in Spain.

In his epistle to the Romans, Paul set forth the great principles of the gospel. He stated his position on the questions which were agitating the Jewish and the Gentile churches, and showed that the hopes and promises which had once belonged especially to the Jews were now offered to the Gentiles also.

With great clearness and power the apostle presented the doctrine of justification by faith in Christ. He hoped that other churches also might be helped by the instruction sent to the Christians at Rome; but how dimly could he foresee the far-reaching influence of his words! Through all the ages the great truth of justification by faith has stood as a mighty beacon to guide repentant sinners into the way of life. It was this light that scattered the darkness which enveloped Luther's mind and revealed to him the power of the blood of Christ to cleanse from sin. The same light has guided thousands of sin-burdened souls to the **true Source of pardon and peace.**—*The Acts of the Apostles*, pp. 372–374.

Further Reflection: *Has the truth of justification by faith in Jesus brought peace to my life?*

AUTHOR OF OUR SALVATION

But we see Jesus, who was made a little lower than the angels, for the suffering of death crowned with glory and honor, that He, by the grace of God, might taste death for everyone.

—Hebrews 2:9

In these perilous times, when a form of godliness is popular in the world, and a profession of Christianity is fashionable, only a few will discern the living way of self-denial and cross-bearing. "Watch and pray" is the injunction of Him who endured temptation in our behalf. Christ knows our danger, for He has contended with our powerful foe. He knows that our enemy is on the track of all who are striving to do the right. With all his specious arts and devices, Satan seeks to ensnare the servants of God, and turn them from Christ into the broad path that leads to destruction. He watches our going out and our coming in, and, although unseen, he works earnestly and diligently, seeking to destroy those who are ignorant of his designs. . . .

Through the influence of the evil one, even the religion of Christ has been perverted to the minds of many who profess to know and obey the truth. But no matter how high is your profession, you will not stand the test unless you are doers of the word of God. Those only who have a living, abiding principle in the heart, who will not turn aside to do anything that has even an appearance of evil, who will not venture to tarnish the soul with impurity, are washing their robes and making them white in the blood of the Lamb. The washing of the robes of character must go on from day to day, that at last we may be found without spot or wrinkle or any such thing, but blameless before Him with whom we have to do. This work of purifying ourselves even as He is pure must be taken up individually. We should examine our motives, our actions, in the light of God's holy law. We should ever ask, "Is this the way of the Lord?" Every earnest, sincere seeker will be answered of the Lord. The petitions of honest inquirers are always heard by the **Author of our salvation**. He has promised, "The meek will He guide in judgment; and the meek will He teach His way." Angels of God are watching to see the development of our character; they are weighing moral worth; and may the great day of God reveal the fact that we have not been weighed in the balances and found wanting.—*The Signs of the Times*, May 25, 1891.

Further Reflection: *When today will I examine the motives behind my actions?*

COMING PRINCE

In those days John the Baptist came preaching in the wilderness of Judea, and saying, "Repent, for the kingdom of heaven is at hand!"
—Matthew 3:1, 2

Amid discord and strife, a voice was heard from the wilderness, a voice startling and stern, yet full of hope: "Repent ye; for the kingdom of heaven is at hand." With a new, strange power it moved the people. Prophets had foretold the coming of Christ as an event far in the future; but here was an announcement that it was at hand. John's singular appearance carried the minds of his hearers back to the ancient seers. . . .

John proclaimed the coming of the Messiah, and called the people to repentance. As a symbol of cleansing from sin, he baptized them in the waters of the Jordan. Thus by a significant object lesson he declared that those who claimed to be the chosen people of God were defiled by sin, and that without purification of heart and life they could have no part in the Messiah's kingdom.

Princes and rabbis, soldiers, publicans, and peasants came to hear the prophet. For a time the solemn warning from God alarmed them. Many were brought to repentance, and received baptism. Persons of all ranks submitted to the requirement of the Baptist, in order to participate in the kingdom he announced.

Many of the scribes and Pharisees came confessing their sins, and asking for baptism. They had exalted themselves as better than other people, and had led the people to entertain a high opinion of their piety; now the guilty secrets of their lives were unveiled. But John was impressed by the Holy Spirit that many of these people had no real conviction of sin. They were timeservers. As friends of the prophet, they hoped to find favor with the **coming Prince**. And by receiving baptism at the hands of this popular young teacher, they thought to strengthen their influence with the people.

John met them with the scathing inquiry, "O generation of vipers, who hath warned you to flee from the wrath to come? Bring forth therefore fruits meet for repentance; and think not to say within yourselves, We have Abraham to our father: for I say unto you, that God is able of these stones to raise up children unto Abraham."—*The Desire of Ages*, pp. 104–106.

Further Reflection: *If scribes and Pharisees during Jesus' time could lose all conviction of sin, how can I avoid this fate in my life?*

DOOR TO THE FOLD OF GOD

He will feed His flock like a shepherd;
He will gather the lambs with His arm,
And carry them in His bosom,
And gently lead those who are with young.

—Isaiah 40:11

Christ applied these prophecies to Himself, and He showed the contrast between His own character and that of the leaders in Israel. The Pharisees had just driven one from the fold, because he dared to bear witness to the power of Christ. They had cut off a soul whom the True Shepherd was drawing to Himself. In this they had shown themselves ignorant of the work committed to them, and unworthy of their trust as shepherds of the flock. Jesus now set before them the contrast between them and the Good Shepherd, and He pointed to Himself as the real keeper of the Lord's flock. Before doing this, however, He speaks of Himself under another figure.

He said, "He that entereth not by the door into the sheepfold, but climbeth up some other way, the same is a thief and a robber. But he that entereth in by the door is the shepherd of the sheep." The Pharisees did not discern that these words were spoken against them. When they reasoned in their hearts as to the meaning, Jesus told them plainly, "I am the door: by Me if any man enter in, he shall be saved, and shall go in and out, and find pasture. The thief cometh not, but for to steal, and to kill, and to destroy: I am come that they might have life, and that they might have it more abundantly."

Christ is the **Door to the Fold of God**. Through this door all His children, from the earliest times, have found entrance. In Jesus, as shown in types, as shadowed in symbols, as manifested in the revelation of the prophets, as unveiled in the lessons given to His disciples, and in the miracles wrought for the sons of men and women, they have beheld "the Lamb of God, which taketh away the sin of the world" (John 1:29), and through Him they are brought within the fold of His grace. . . .

The Pharisees had not entered by the door. They had climbed into the fold by another way than Christ, and they were not fulfilling the work of the true shepherd.—*The Desire of Ages*, p. 477.

Further Reflection: *If Jesus is the door of the fold of God's flock, what is my role as an undershepherd working for and with Him?*

HEAVENLY SOWER

"Behold, a sower went out to sow."

—Matthew 13:3

In the East the state of affairs was so unsettled, and there was so great danger from violence that the people dwelt chiefly in walled towns, and the husbandmen went forth daily to their labor outside the walls. So Christ, the **heavenly Sower**, went forth to sow. He left His home of security and peace, left the glory that He had with the Father before the world was, left His position upon the throne of the universe. He went forth, a suffering, tempted man; went forth in solitude, to sow in tears, to water with His blood, the seed of life for a world lost.

His servants in like manner must go forth to sow. When called to become a sower of the seed of truth, Abraham was bidden, "Get thee out of thy country, and from thy kindred, and from thy father's house, unto a land that I will show thee." (Genesis 12:1) "And he went out, not knowing whither he went." (Hebrews 11:8) So to the apostle Paul, praying in the temple at Jerusalem, came the message from God, "Depart; for I will send thee far hence unto the Gentiles." (Acts 22:21) So those who are called to unite with Christ must leave all, in order to follow Him. Old associations must be broken up, plans of life relinquished, earthly hopes surrendered. In toil and tears, in solitude, and through sacrifice, must the seed be sown.

"The sower soweth the word." Christ came to sow the world with truth. Ever since the fall of humanity, Satan has been sowing the seeds of error. It was by a lie that he first gained control over men and women, and thus he still works to overthrow God's kingdom in the earth and to bring people under his power. A sower from a higher world, Christ came to sow the seeds of truth. He who had stood in the councils of God, who had dwelt in the innermost sanctuary of the Eternal, could bring to humans the pure principles of truth. Ever since the fall of humanity, Christ had been the Revealer of truth to the world. By Him the incorruptible seed, "the word of God, which liveth and abideth forever," is communicated to men and women. (1 Peter 1:23) In that first promise spoken to our fallen race in Eden, Christ was sowing the gospel seed. But it is to His personal ministry among humanity and to the work which He thus established that the parable of the sower especially applies.—*Christ's Object Lessons*, pp. 36–38.

Further Reflection: *What seed can I sow for the kingdom of God today?*

LAMB OF GOD

"And they shall take some of the blood and put it on the two doorposts and on the lintel of the houses where they eat it."

—Exodus 12:7

While the angel of death was passing through Egypt, each family of the Hebrews was to eat the lamb, that they were commanded to roast whole. This lamb was to be without disease or blemish of any kind. It was to be eaten with unleavened bread, and with bitter herbs. This was to keep in their minds the cruel bondage they had suffered in consequence of their sins in forgetting God, and breaking His commandments. Eating bitter herbs was to remind them that they would reap the fruit of their doings however unwelcome it might be to them. The eating of the bitter herbs was also for the purpose of raising an inquiry in the minds of their children as to the reason of their doing this, and then the parents should relate to them their sufferings in Egypt and the wonderful power of God in their deliverance on that memorable night when they were hurried out of Egypt, by the Egyptians themselves. . . .

The striking of the door-post with the blood of the slain lamb was to represent the blood of Christ to which they were to look forward.

Fifteen hundred years after this night, Jesus, the antitype of the paschal lamb, died upon the cross for the sins of the world. The lamb without blemish represented the spotless **Lamb of God**, without the taint of sin. As the houses of Israel were to be sprinkled with blood in order for the avenging angel to pass over them, so it will be necessary for us to repent of our sins and avail ourselves of the virtue of the blood of Christ to guard us from the avenging angel of God in the day of slaughter. Through Christ alone is our pardon to be obtained. His blood will protect us from a sin-avenging God.

While the institution of the passover was pointing backward to the miraculous deliverance of the Hebrews, it likewise pointed forward, showing the death of the Son of God before it transpired. In the last passover our Lord observed with His disciples, He instituted the Lord's supper in place of the passover, to be observed in memory of His death. No longer had they need of the passover, for He, the great antitypical Lamb, was ready to be sacrificed for the sins of the world. Type met antitype in the death of Christ.—*The Youth's Instructor,* May 1, 1873.

Further Reflection: *How many times should I accept Christ's atoning sacrifice for my sins?*

CRUCIFIED NAZARENE

But we preach Christ Crucified.
—1 Corinthians 1:23

Jesus, whom Paul was about to present before the Greeks in Corinth as the Christ, was a Jew of lowly origin, reared in a town proverbial for its wickedness. He had been rejected by His own nation and at last crucified as a malefactor. The Greeks believed that there was need of elevating the human race, but they regarded the study of philosophy and science as the only means of attaining to true elevation and honor. Could Paul lead them to believe that faith in the power of this obscure Jew would uplift and ennoble every power of the being?

To the minds of multitudes living at the present time, the cross of Calvary is surrounded by sacred memories. Hallowed associations are connected with the scenes of the crucifixion. But in Paul's day the cross was regarded with feelings of repulsion and horror. To uphold as the Saviour of humanity one who had met death on the cross, would naturally call forth ridicule and opposition.

Paul well knew how his message would be regarded by both the Jews and the Greeks of Corinth. "We preach Christ crucified," he admitted, "unto the Jews a stumbling block, and unto the Greeks foolishness." (1 Corinthians 1:23) Among his Jewish hearers there were many who would be angered by the message he was about to proclaim. In the estimation of the Greeks his words would be absurd folly. He would be looked upon as weak-minded for attempting to show how the cross could have any connection with the elevation of the race or the salvation of human beings.

But to Paul the cross was the one object of supreme interest. Ever since he had been arrested in his career of persecution against the followers of the **crucified Nazarene** he had never ceased to glory in the cross. At that time there had been given him a revelation of the infinite love of God, as revealed in the death of Christ; and a marvelous transformation had been wrought in his life, bringing all his plans and purposes into harmony with heaven. From that hour he had been a new man in Christ. He knew by personal experience that when a sinner once beholds the love of the Father, as seen in the sacrifice of His Son, and yields to the divine influence, a change of heart takes place, and henceforth Christ is all and in all.—*The Acts of the Apostles*, pp. 244, 245.

Further Reflection: *What new lesson has the cross taught me about the infinite love of God?*

UNITING STONE

Is Christ divided?

—1 Corinthians 1:13

If thy brother trespass against thee, He says, rebuke him: and if he repent, forgive him. Do not hold him off as unworthy of your confidence. Consider thyself lest thou also be tempted. Bear in mind that none but Christ can read the heart. By Him actions are weighed.

The church should avoid that prejudice that rises like a flash when political subjects, which cross the opinions they have cherished, are introduced. National antipathies and sectarian feelings are not to be held by anyone. Those who stand under the banner of Christ are to stand under no other banner. They are to acknowledge the supreme authority of the King of kings and Lord of lords. They are not to appeal to Caesar or Pilate. In His own good time Christ will avenge His own elect which cry day and night unto Him. Christ has been the **uniting stone**, the chief corner stone in all ages.

The patriarchs, the Levitical priesthood, the Christian churches, all find their center in Christ. He is to be all and in all. "The grace of God, that bringeth salvation hath appeared to all men, teaching us that denying ungodliness and worldly lusts, we should live soberly, righteously, and godly, in this present world; looking for that blessed hope, and the glorious appearing of the great God and our Saviour Jesus Christ: who gave Himself for us, that He might redeem us from all iniquity, and purify unto Himself a peculiar people, zealous of good works." (Titus 2:11–14)

Paul asks, "Is Christ divided?" (1 Corinthians 1:13) Have we not one spiritual Head? When my heart is overwhelmed, then pray, "Lead me to the Rock that is higher than I." (Psalm 61:2) Precious is His all atoning sacrifice, His blood shed in our behalf. Precious is His all-atoning merits, precious His sanctifying righteousness. Precious is His infinite fullness and sufficiency. "Ye are complete in Him." (Colossians 2:10) "And of His fulness have all we received, and grace for grace." (John 1:16) All other foundation is shifting sand. In Christ there is neither Jew nor Greek, bond nor free, male nor female. We are all one in Christ Jesus, and Christ is our Head.—Manuscript 89, 1898.

Further Reflection: *What can I do today to help foster the Christian unity that Christ came to bring, in my home, church, and community?*

TEACHER AND SAVIOUR OF HUMANITY

"Let my teaching drop as the rain,
My speech distill as the dew,
As raindrops on the tender herb,
And as showers on the grass."
—Deuteronomy 32:2

To His children today the Lord declares, "Be strong . . . and work: for I am with you." The Christian always has a strong helper in the Lord. The way of the Lord's helping we may not know; but this we do know: He will never fail those who put their trust in Him. Could Christians realize how many times the Lord has ordered their way, that the purposes of the enemy concerning them might not be accomplished, they would not stumble along complainingly. Their faith would be stayed on God, and no trial would have power to move them. They would acknowledge Him as their wisdom and efficiency, and He would bring to pass that which He desires to work out through them.

The earnest pleadings and the encouragements given through Haggai were emphasized and added to by Zechariah, whom God raised up to stand by his side in urging Israel to carry out the command to arise and build. Zechariah's first message was an assurance that God's word never fails and a promise of blessing to those who would hearken to the sure word of prophecy.

With fields lying waste, with their scant store of provisions rapidly failing, and surrounded as they were by unfriendly peoples, the Israelites nevertheless moved forward by faith in response to the call of God's messengers, and labored diligently to restore the ruined temple. It was a work requiring firm reliance upon God. As the people endeavored to do their part, and sought for a renewal of God's grace in heart and life, message after message was given them through Haggai and Zechariah, with assurances that their faith would be richly rewarded and that the word of God concerning the future glory of the temple whose walls they were rearing would not fail. In this very building would appear, in the fullness of time, the Desire of all nations as the **Teacher and Saviour of humanity**.

Thus the builders were not left to struggle alone; "with them were the prophets of God helping them;" and the Lord of hosts Himself had declared, "Be strong . . . and work: for I am with you." (Ezra 5:2; Haggai 2:4)—*Prophets and Kings*, pp. 576, 577.

Further Reflection: *Do I still cherish directions from God that were given through prophets of old?*

FOUNTAIN OF HAPPINESS

The fear of the LORD leads to life, and he who has it will abide in satisfaction.

—Proverbs 19:23

The opinion which prevails in some classes of society, that religion is not conducive to health or to happiness in this life, is one of the most mischievous of errors. The Scripture says: "The fear of the Lord tendeth to life: and he that hath it shall abide satisfied." (Proverbs 19:23) "What man is he that desireth life, and loveth many days, that he may see good? Keep thy tongue from evil, and thy lips from speaking guile. Depart from evil, and do good; seek peace, and pursue it." (Psalm 34:12–14) . . .

True religion brings men and women into harmony with the laws of God, physical, mental, and moral. It teaches self-control, serenity, temperance. Religion ennobles the mind, refines the taste, and sanctifies the judgment. It makes the soul a partaker of the purity of heaven. Faith in God's love and overruling providence lightens the burdens of anxiety and care. It fills the heart with joy and contentment in the highest or the lowliest lot. Religion tends directly to promote health, to lengthen life, and to heighten our enjoyment of all its blessings. It opens to the soul a never-failing **Fountain of happiness**. Would that all who have not chosen Christ might realize that He has something vastly better to offer them that they are seeking for themselves. People are doing the greatest injury and injustice to their soul when they think and act contrary to the will of God. No real joy can be found in the path forbidden by Him who knows what is best, and who plans for the good of His creatures. The path of transgression leads to misery and destruction; but wisdom's "ways are ways of pleasantness, and all her paths are peace." (Proverbs 3:17)

The physical as well as the religious training practiced in the schools of the Hebrews may be profitably studied. The worth of such training is not appreciated. There is an intimate relation between the mind and the body, and in order to reach a high standard of moral and intellectual attainment the laws that control our physical being must be heeded. To secure a strong, well-balanced character, both the mental and the physical powers must be exercised and developed. What study can be more important for the young than that which treats of this wonderful organism that God has committed to us, and of the laws by which it may be preserved in health?—*Patriarchs and Prophets*, pp. 600, 601.

Further Reflection: *How intentional am I in developing my physical and mental powers?*

COMING ONE

And he sent forth and put to death all the male children who were in Bethlehem and in all its districts.

—Matthew 2:16

At the birth of Christ, Satan saw the plains of Bethlehem illuminated with the brilliant glory of a multitude of heavenly angels. He heard their song, "Glory to God in the highest, and on earth peace, good will toward men." The prince of darkness saw the amazed shepherds filled with fear as they beheld the illuminated plains. They trembled before the exhibitions of bewildering glory which seemed to entrance their senses. The rebel chief himself trembled at the proclamation of the angel to the shepherds, "Fear not: for behold, I bring you good tidings of great joy, which shall be to all people. For unto you is born this day in the city of David a Saviour, which is Christ the Lord." He had met with good success in devising a plan to ruin men and women, and he had become bold and powerful. He had controlled the minds and bodies of men and women from Adam down to the first appearing of Christ. But now Satan was troubled and alarmed for his kingdom and his life.

The song of the heavenly messengers proclaiming the advent of the Saviour to a fallen world, and the joy expressed at this great event, Satan knew boded no good to himself. Dark forebodings were awakened in his mind as to the influence this advent to the world would have upon his kingdom. He queried if this was not the **coming One** who would contest his power and overthrow his kingdom. He looked upon Christ from His birth as his rival. He stirred the envy and jealousy of Herod to destroy Christ by insinuating to him that his power and his kingdom were to be given to this new King. Satan imbued Herod with the very feelings and fears that disturbed his own mind. He inspired the corrupt mind of Herod to slay all the children in Bethlehem who were two years old and under, which plan he thought would succeed in ridding the earth of the infant King.

But against his plans, Satan sees a higher power at work. Angels of God protected the life of the infant Redeemer. Joseph was warned in a dream to flee into Egypt, that in a heathen land he might find an asylum for the world's Redeemer.—*Confrontation*, pp. 27, 28.

Further Reflection: *Do I give Satan opportunity to imbue my mind with his feelings? How can I protect my mind from evil influences?*

HEAVENLY BRIDEGROOM

"Give us some of your oil, for our lamps are going out."
—Matthew 25:8

It is not a matter of little consequence to us as to how we hear and how we treat the truth of God. To misunderstand the truth, or fail to appreciate it, because we do not cherish light that comes to us, will be to build upon the sand. The wise builder builds upon the Rock Christ Jesus, no matter what may be the inconvenience. He builds not upon human, but upon divine merit, accepting the righteousness of Christ as his own, and as his only hope of salvation. The foolish builder built upon the sand, and through his carelessness, or prejudice, or through the deceptions of the natural heart, he cherishes a self-righteous spirit, and places human wisdom in the place where God's wisdom should have the supremacy; and how terrible are the consequences!

There are many unwise builders, and when the storm of temptation comes and beats upon them, it is made evident that their foundation is only sliding sand. They are left in gross darkness, without faith, without principles, and without foundation. The five foolish virgins had a real interest in the gospel. They knew what was the perfect standard of righteousness; but their energies were paralyzed with self-love; for they lived to please and glorify themselves, and had not the oil of grace in their vessels with which to replenish their lamps. They were often distressed by the enemy, who knew their weakness, and placed darkness before them in the semblance of light. Truth, precious, life-giving truth, appeared to them as unessential, and Satan took advantage of their blindness, ignorance, and weakness of faith, and they had a fluctuating experience, based on uncertain principles.

All who wait for the **heavenly Bridegroom** are represented in the parable as slumbering because their Lord delayed His coming; but the wise roused themselves at the message of His approach, and responded to the message, and their spiritual life was replenished. Their spiritual discernment was not all gone, and they sprang into line. As they took hold of the grace of Christ, their religious experience became vigorous and abundant, and their affections were set on things above.—*The Bible Echo,* November 5, 1894.

Further Reflection: *The wise virgins had light when they needed it most. What responsibility do we have to keep our lights burning for those in gross moral darkness?*

KING IN RIGHTEOUSNESS

"In His days Judah will be saved,
And Israel will dwell safely;
Now this is His name by which He will be called:
THE LORD OUR RIGHTEOUSNESS."

—Jeremiah 23:6

Isaiah's rapt portrayals of the Messiah's glory were his study by day and by night—the Branch from the root of Jesse; a King to reign in righteousness, judging "with equity for the meek of the earth;" "a covert from the tempest . . . the shadow of a great rock in a weary land;" Israel no longer to be termed "Forsaken," nor her land "Desolate," but to be called of the Lord, "My Delight," and her land "Beulah." (Isaiah 11:4; 32:2; 62:4, margin) The heart of the lonely exile was filled with the glorious vision.

He looked upon the King in His beauty, and self was forgotten. He beheld the majesty of holiness, and felt himself to be inefficient and unworthy. He was ready to go forth as Heaven's messenger, unawed by the human, because he had looked upon the Divine. He could stand erect and fearless in the presence of earthly monarchs, because he had bowed low before the King of kings.

John did not fully understand the nature of the Messiah's kingdom. He looked for Israel to be delivered from her national foes; but the coming of a **King in righteousness**, and the establishment of Israel as a holy nation, was the great object of his hope. Thus he believed would be accomplished the prophecy given at his birth—

"To remember His holy covenant. . . . that we being delivered out of the hand of our enemies might serve Him without fear, in holiness and righteousness before Him, all the days of our life."

He saw his people deceived, self-satisfied, and asleep in their sins. He longed to rouse them to a holier life. The message that God had given him to bear was designed to startle them from their lethargy, and cause them to tremble because of their great wickedness. Before the seed of the gospel could find lodgment, the soil of the heart must be broken up. Before they would seek healing from Jesus, they must be awakened to their danger from the wounds of sin.—*The Desire of Ages,* pp. 103, 104.

Further Reflection: *How would looking at Jesus change how I see my fellow human beings? How would it change my desire to serve Christ?*

MAJESTY OF HEAVEN

His work is honorable and glorious,
and His righteousness endures forever.

—Psalm 111:3

It was at the ordination of the Twelve that the first step was taken in the organization of the church that after Christ's departure was to carry on His work on the earth. Of this ordination the record says, "He goeth up into a mountain, and calleth unto Him whom He would: and they came unto Him. And He ordained twelve, that they should be with Him, and that He might send them forth to preach." (Mark 3:13, 14)

Look upon the touching scene. Behold the **Majesty of heaven** surrounded by the Twelve whom He has chosen. He is about to set them apart for their work. By these feeble agencies, through His word and Spirit, He designs to place salvation within the reach of all.

With gladness and rejoicing, God and the angels beheld this scene. The Father knew that from these persons the light of heaven would shine forth; that the words spoken by them as they witnessed for His Son, would echo from generation to generation till the close of time.

The disciples were to go forth as Christ's witnesses, to declare to the world what they had seen and heard of Him. Their office was the most important to which human beings had ever been called, second only to that of Christ Himself. They were to be workers together with God for the saving of humanity. As in the Old Testament the twelve patriarchs stood as representatives of Israel, so the twelve apostles stand as representatives of the gospel church.

During His earthly ministry Christ began to break down the partition wall between Jew and Gentile, and to preach salvation to all humanity. Though He was a Jew, He mingled freely with the Samaritans, setting at naught the Pharisaic customs of the Jews with regard to this despised people. He slept under their roofs, ate at their tables, and taught in their streets

The Saviour longed to unfold to His disciples the truth regarding the breaking down of the "middle wall of partition" between Israel and the other nations—the truth that "the Gentiles should be fellow heirs" with the Jews and "partakers of His promise in Christ by the gospel." (Ephesians 2:14; 3:6)—*The Acts of the Apostles*, pp. 18, 19.

Further Reflection: *Do I fully grasp the reality that the Majesty of heaven wants to have a personal relationship with me?*

GREAT EXEMPLAR

Therefore be imitators of God as dear children. And walk in love, as Christ also has loved us and given Himself for us.
—Ephesians 5:1, 2

You may say you have been taken in and have bestowed your means upon those unworthy of your charity, and therefore have become discouraged in trying to help the needy. I present Jesus before you. He came to save fallen humanity, to bring salvation to His own nation; but they would not accept Him. They treated His mercy with insult and contempt, and at length they put to death Him who came for the purpose of giving them life. Did our Lord turn from the fallen race because of this? Though your efforts for good have been unsuccessful ninety-nine times, and you received only insult, reproach, and hate, yet if the one-hundredth time proves a success, and one soul is saved, oh, what a victory is achieved! One soul wrenched from Satan's grasp, one soul benefited, one soul encouraged. This will a thousand times repay you for all your efforts. To you will Jesus say: "Inasmuch as ye have done it unto one of the least of these My brethren, ye have done it unto Me." Should we not gladly do all we can to imitate the life of our divine Lord? Many shrink at the idea of making any sacrifice for others' good. They are not willing to suffer for the sake of helping others. They flatter themselves that it is not required of them to disadvantage themselves for the benefit of others. To such we say: Jesus is our example.

When the request was made for the two sons of Zebedee to sit the one on His right hand and the other on His left in His kingdom, Jesus answered: "Ye know not what ye ask. Are ye able to drink of the cup that I shall drink of, and to be baptized with the baptism that I am baptized with? They say unto Him, We are able. And He saith unto them, Ye shall drink indeed of My cup, and be baptized with the baptism that I am baptized with: but to sit on My right hand, and on My left, is not Mine to give, but it shall be given to them for whom it is prepared of My Father." How many can answer: We can drink of the cup; we can be baptized with the baptism; and make the answer understandingly? How many imitate the **great Exemplar**? All who have professed to be followers of Christ have, in taking this step, pledged themselves to walk even as He walked.—*Testimonies for the Church*, vol. 2, pp. 31, 32.

Further Reflection: *How can I better handle the insults and hatred that I will encounter while seeking to share Christ?*

RISEN SAVIOUR

"But he who received seed on the good ground is he who hears the word and understands it, who indeed bears fruit and produces: some a hundredfold, some sixty, some thirty."

—Matthew 13:23

When Christ gave His disciples the promise of the Spirit, He was nearing the close of His earthly ministry. He was standing in the shadow of the cross, with a full realization of the load of guilt that was to rest upon Him as the Sin Bearer. Before offering Himself as the sacrificial victim, He instructed His disciples regarding a most essential and complete gift which He was to bestow upon His followers—the gift that would bring within their reach the boundless resources of His grace. "I will pray the Father," He said, "and He shall give you another Comforter, that He may abide with you forever; even the Spirit of truth; whom the world cannot receive, because it seeth Him not, neither knoweth Him: but ye know Him; for He dwelleth with you, and shall be in you." (John 14:16, 17) The Saviour was pointing forward to the time when the Holy Spirit should come to do a mighty work as His representative. The evil that had been accumulating for centuries was to be resisted by the divine power of the Holy Spirit.

What was the result of the outpouring of the Spirit on the Day of Pentecost? The glad tidings of a **risen Saviour** were carried to the uttermost parts of the inhabited world. As the disciples proclaimed the message of redeeming grace, hearts yielded to the power of this message. The church beheld converts flocking to her from all directions. Backsliders were reconverted. Sinners united with believers in seeking the pearl of great price. Some who had been the bitterest opponents of the gospel became its champions. The prophecy was fulfilled, "He that is feeble . . . shall be as David; and the house of David . . . as the angel of the Lord." (Zechariah 12:8) Every Christian saw in his brother a revelation of divine love and benevolence. One interest prevailed; one subject of emulation swallowed up all others. The ambition of the believers was to reveal the likeness of Christ's character and to labor for the enlargement of His kingdom.

"With great power gave the apostles witness of the resurrection of the Lord Jesus: and great grace was upon them all." (Acts 4:33) Under their labors were added to the church chosen men, who, receiving the word of truth, consecrated their lives to the work of giving to others the hope that filled their hearts with peace and joy.—*The Acts of the Apostles*, pp. 47, 48.

Further Reflection: *Is the Holy Spirit currently being poured on me?*

DELIVERER FOR HIS PEOPLE

This beginning of signs Jesus did in Cana of Galilee, and manifested His glory; and His disciples believed in Him.

—John 2:11

The wine which Christ provided for the feast, and that which He gave to the disciples as a symbol of His own blood, was the pure juice of the grape. To this the prophet Isaiah refers when he speaks of the new wine "in the cluster," and says, "Destroy it not; for a blessing is in it." (Isaiah 65:8)

It was Christ who in the Old Testament gave the warning to Israel, "Wine is a mocker, strong drink is raging: and whosoever is deceived thereby is not wise." (Proverbs 20:1) And He Himself provided no such beverage. Satan tempts human beings to indulgence that will becloud reason and benumb the spiritual perceptions, but Christ teaches us to bring the lower nature into subjection. His whole life was an example of self-denial. In order to break the power of appetite, He suffered in our behalf the severest test that humanity could endure. It was Christ who directed that John the Baptist should drink neither wine nor strong drink. It was He who enjoined similar abstinence upon the wife of Manoah. And He pronounced a curse upon the person who should put the bottle to his neighbor's lips. Christ did not contradict His own teaching. The unfermented wine which He provided for the wedding guests was a wholesome and refreshing drink. Its effect was to bring the taste into harmony with a healthful appetite.

As the guests at the feast remarked upon the quality of the wine, inquiries were made that drew from the servants an account of the miracle. The company were for a time too much amazed to think of Him who had performed the wonderful work. When at length they looked for Him, it was found that He had withdrawn so quietly as to be unnoticed even by His disciples.

The attention of the company was now turned to the disciples. For the first time they had the opportunity of acknowledging their faith in Jesus. They told what they had seen and heard at the Jordan, and there was kindled in many hearts the hope that God had raised up a **deliverer for His people.** The news of the miracle spread through all that region, and was carried to Jerusalem. With new interest the priests and elders searched the prophecies pointing to Christ's coming.—*The Desire of Ages*, pp. 149, 150.

Further Reflection: *What miracle do I need Jesus to perform in my family today?*

SOLID ROCK

"The Lord lives!
Blessed be my Rock!
Let God be exalted,
The Rock of my salvation!"

—2 Samuel 22:47

Your letters I have read with interest and sympathy. I would say your son now needs a father as he has never needed one before. He has erred; you know it, and he knows that you know it; and words that you would have spoken to him in his innocency with safety, and which would not have produced any bad results, would now seem like unkindness and be sharp as a knife. . . . I know that parents feel the shame of the wrongdoing of a child that has dishonored them very keenly, but does the erring one wound and bruise the heart of the earthly parent any more than we as the children of God bruise our heavenly Parent, who has given us and is still giving us His love, inviting us to return and repent of our sins and iniquities and He will pardon our transgression?

Do not withdraw your love now. That love and sympathy is needed now as never before. When others look with coldness and put the worst construction upon the misdeeds of your boy, should not the father and mother in pitying tenderness seek to guide his footsteps into safe paths? I do not know the character of your son's sins, but I am safe in saying, whatever they may be, Let no comments from human lips, no pressure from human actions, of those who think they are doing justice, lead you to pursue a course which can be interpreted by your son that you feel too much mortified and dishonored to ever take him back into confidence and to forget his transgressions. Let nothing cause you to lose hope, nothing to cut off your love and tenderness for the erring one. Just because he is erring, he needs you, and he wants a father and a mother to help him to recover himself from the snare of Satan. Hold him fast by faith and love, and cling to the all-pitying Redeemer, remembering that he has One who has an interest in him, even above your own. . . .

Do not talk discouragement and hopelessness. Talk courage. Tell him he can redeem himself, that you, his father and mother, will help him to take hold from above to plant his feet on the **solid Rock**, Christ Jesus, to find a sure support and unfailing strength in Jesus.—*Child Guidance*, pp. 266, 267.

Further Reflection: *Why should I never take the grace and mercy of God for granted?*

GUIDE

Show me Your ways, O Lord; teach me Your paths.
—Psalm 25:4

The Lord says, "Call upon Me in the day of trouble." (Psalm 50:15) He invites us to present to Him our perplexities and necessities, and our need of divine help. He bids us be instant in prayer. As soon as difficulties arise, we are to offer to Him our sincere, earnest petitions. By our importunate prayers we give evidence of our strong confidence in God. The sense of our need leads us to pray earnestly, and our heavenly Father is moved by our supplications.

Often those who suffer reproach or persecution for their faith are tempted to think themselves forsaken by God. In the eyes of men and women they are in the minority. To all appearance their enemies triumph over them. But let them not violate their conscience. He who has suffered in their behalf, and has borne their sorrows and afflictions, has not forsaken them.

The children of God are not left alone and defenseless. Prayer moves the arm of Omnipotence. Prayer has "subdued kingdoms, wrought righteousness, obtained promises, stopped the mouths of lions, quenched the violence of fire"—we shall know what it means when we hear the reports of the martyrs who died for their faith—"turneth to flight the armies of the aliens." (Hebrews 11:33, 34)

If we surrender our lives to His service, we can never be placed in a position for which God has not made provision. Whatever may be our situation, we have a **Guide** to direct our way; whatever our perplexities, we have a sure Counselor; whatever our sorrow, bereavement, or loneliness, we have a sympathizing Friend. If in our ignorance we make missteps, Christ does not leave us. His voice, clear and distinct, is heard saying, "I am the Way, the Truth, and the Life." (John 14:6) "He shall deliver the needy when he crieth; the poor also, and him that hath no helper." (Psalm 72:12)

The Lord declares that He will be honored by those who draw nigh to Him, who faithfully do His service.—*Christ's Object Lessons*, pp. 172, 173.

Further Reflection: *I can "never be placed in a position for which God has not made provision." If this is true, why do I become anxious when facing difficult circumstances?*

PRINCE OF PREACHERS

The officers answered, "No man ever spoke like this Man!"
—John 7:46

After the ordination of the disciples, Christ gave the sermon on the mount. This discourse was given to humanity to be to them the law of duty and the light of heaven, their hope and consolation in despondency. It is heaven's benediction to the world—a voice from the throne of God. Here the **Prince of preachers**, the Master-teacher, utters the words that the Father gave Him to speak. He is the Eternal Wisdom, who was with the Father before the world was created. He knows the Father; for He is one with Him.

The beatitudes are Christ's greeting, not only to those who believe, but to the whole human family. He seems to have forgotten for a moment that He is in the world, not in heaven; and He uses the familiar salutation of the world of light. Blessings flow from His lips as the gushing forth of a long-sealed current of rich life.

Christ leaves us in no doubt as to the traits of character that He will always recognize and bless. From the ambitious favorites of the world, He turns to those whom they disown, pronouncing all blessed who receive His light and life. To the poor in spirit, the meek, the lowly, and sorrowful, the despised, the persecuted, He opens His arms of refuge, saying, "Come unto Me . . . and I will give you rest." (Matthew 11:28)

Christ can look on the misery of the world without a shade of sorrow for having created human beings. In the human heart He sees more than sin, more than misery. In His infinite wisdom, He sees humanity's possibilities, the height to which they may attain. He knows that even though human beings have abused their mercies, and destroyed their God-given dignity, yet the Creator is to be glorified by their redemption.

The discourse is an example of how we are to teach. What pains Christ has taken to make mysteries no longer mysteries, but plain, simple truths. There is in His instruction nothing vague, nothing hard to understand.

"He opened His mouth, and taught them." (Matthew 5:2) His words were spoken in no whispered tones, nor yet with harsh, disagreeable utterance. His voice was as a voice from the throne of God. He spoke with clear, emphatic utterance, and with solemn, convincing force.—Letter 96, 1902.

Further Reflection: *What can I learn from the way in which Jesus shared truth?*

GREAT KING

"He will be great, and will be called the Son of the Highest; and the Lord God will give Him the throne of His father David."

—Luke 1:32

We are to compare our characters with the infallible standard of God's law. In order to do this, we must search the Scriptures, measuring our attainments by the Word of God. Through the grace of Christ, the highest attainments in character are possible; for every soul who comes under the molding influence of the Spirit of God, may be transformed in mind and heart. In order to understand your condition, it is necessary to study the Bible, and to watch unto prayer. The apostle says, "Examine yourselves, whether ye be in the faith; prove your own selves. Know ye not your own selves, how that Jesus Christ is in you, except ye be reprobates?" Let not those who are ignorant remain in ignorance. They cannot remain in ignorance, and meet the mind of God. They are to look to the cross of Calvary, and estimate the soul by the value of the offering there made. Jesus says to all believers, "Ye are My witnesses." "Ye are laborers together with God." This being true, how earnestly should each one strive to make use of every power to improve every opportunity for becoming efficient that he may be "not slothful in business; fervent in spirit; serving the Lord."

Every talent that has been given to men and women is to be exercised that it may increase in value, and all the improvement must be rendered back to God. If you are defective in manner, in voice, in education, you need not always remain in this condition. You must continually strive that you may reach a higher standard both in education and in religious experience, that you may become teachers of good things. As servants of the **Great King**, you should individually realize that you are under obligation to improve yourselves by observation, study, and by communion with God. The word of God is able to make you wise, to guide and make you perfect in Christ. The blessed Saviour was a faultless pattern for all His followers to imitate. It is the privilege of the child of God to understand spiritual things, to be able wisely to manage that which may be entrusted to his charge.—*Fundamentals of Christian Education*, p. 214.

Further Reflection: *If I imitated Christ in the development of every talent given to me by God, how would it change my personal and professional life?*

LONG-PROMISED ONE

"I baptize with water, but there stands
One among you whom you do not know."

—John 1:26

John came in the spirit and power of Elijah, to do such a work as Elijah did. If the Jews had received him, it would have been accomplished for them. But they did not receive his message. To them he was not Elijah. He could not fulfill for them the mission he came to accomplish.

Many of those gathered at the Jordan had been present at the baptism of Jesus; but the sign then given had been manifest to but few among them. During the preceding months of the Baptist's ministry, many had refused to heed the call to repentance. Thus they had hardened their hearts and darkened their understanding. When Heaven bore testimony to Jesus at His baptism, they perceived it not. Eyes that had never been turned in faith to Him that is invisible beheld not the revelation of the glory of God; ears that had never listened to His voice heard not the words of witness. So it is now. Often the presence of Christ and the ministering angels is manifest in the assemblies of the people, and yet there are many who know it not. They discern nothing unusual. But to some the Saviour's presence is revealed. Peace and joy animate their hearts. They are comforted, encouraged, and blessed.

The deputies from Jerusalem had demanded of John, "Why baptizest thou?" and they were awaiting his answer. Suddenly, as his glance swept over the throng, his eye kindled, his face was lighted up, his whole being was stirred with deep emotion. With outstretched hands he cried, "I baptize in water: in the midst of you standeth One whom ye know not, even He that cometh after me, the latchet of whose shoe I am not worthy to unloose." (John 1:26, 27, R. V.)

The message was distinct and unequivocal, to be carried back to the Sanhedrin. The words of John could apply to no other than the **long-promised One**. The Messiah was among them! In amazement priests and rulers gazed about them, hoping to discover Him of whom John had spoken. But He was not distinguishable among the throng. When at the baptism of Jesus, John pointed to Him as the Lamb of God, a new light was shed upon the Messiah's work. The prophet's mind was directed to the words of Isaiah, "He is brought as a lamb to the slaughter." (Isaiah 53:7)—*The Desire of Ages*, pp. 135, 136.

Further Reflection: *How would it feel to be in the presence of Jesus, yet completely fail to recognize Him?*

GREAT MEDIATOR

"I counsel you to buy from Me gold refined in the fire."
—Revelation 3:18

Let the solemn question come home to everyone who is a member of our churches, How am I standing before God as a professed follower of Christ? Is my light shining forth to the world in clear, steady rays? Have we as a people who have taken vows of dedication to God, preserved our union with the Source of all light? Are not the symptoms to declension and decay painfully visible among the Christian churches of today? Spiritual death has come upon many who should be examples of zeal, purity, and consecration. Their practices speak more loudly than their professions, and witness to the fact that some power has cut the cable that anchored them to the eternal Rock, and they are drifting without chart or compass.

The True Witness desires to remedy the perilous condition in which His professed people are placed, and He says: "I have somewhat against thee, because thou hast left thy first love. Remember therefore from whence thou art fallen, and repent, and do the first works; or else I will come unto thee quickly, and will remove thy candlestick out of his place, except thou repent." Christ will cease to take the names of those who fail to turn to Him and do their first works, and will no longer make intercession for them before the Father. . . . Yet the case of those who are rebuked is not a hopeless one; it is not beyond the power of the **great Mediator**. He says: "I counsel thee to buy of Me gold tried in the fire, that thou mayest be rich; and white raiment, that thou mayest be clothed, and that the shame of thy nakedness do not appear; and anoint thine eyes with eyesalve, that thou mayest see." Though the professed followers of Christ are in a deplorable condition, they are not yet in so desperate a strait as were the foolish virgins whose lamps were going out, and there was no time in which to replenish their vessels with oil. When the bridegroom came, those that were ready went in with him to the wedding; but when the foolish virgins came, the door was shut, and they were too late to obtain an entrance. But the counsel of the True Witness does not represent those who are lukewarm as in a hopeless case. There is yet a chance to remedy their state, and the Laodicean message is full of encouragement; for the backslidden church may yet buy the gold of faith and love, may yet have the white robe of the righteousness of Christ. —*Review and Herald*, August 28, 1894.

Further Reflection: *Do I know the true spiritual condition of my soul?*

SAVIOUR OF SINNERS

The LORD said to Satan, "The LORD rebuke you, Satan! The LORD who has chosen Jerusalem rebuke you! Is this not a brand plucked from the fire?"

—Zechariah 3:2

In vision the prophet beholds "Joshua the high priest," "clothed with filthy garments" (Zechariah 3:1, 3), standing before the Angel of the Lord, entreating God's mercy in behalf of His afflicted people. As he pleads for the fulfillment of God's promises, Satan stands up boldly to resist him. He points to the transgressions of Israel as a reason why they should not be restored to the favor of God. He claims them as his prey, and demands that they be given into his hands.

The high priest cannot defend himself or his people from Satan's accusations. He does not claim that Israel is free from fault. In filthy garments, symbolizing the sins of the people, which he bears as their representative, he stands before the Angel, confessing their guilt, yet pointing to their repentance and humiliation, and relying upon the mercy of a sin-pardoning Redeemer. In faith he claims the promises of God.

Then the Angel, who is Christ Himself, the **Saviour of sinners**, puts to silence the accuser of His people, declaring, "The Lord rebuke thee, O Satan; even the Lord that hath chosen Jerusalem rebuke thee: is not this a brand plucked out of the fire?" (Verse 2) Long had Israel remained in the furnace of affliction. Because of their sins they had been well-nigh consumed in the flame kindled by Satan and his agents for their destruction, but God had now set His hand to bring them forth.

As the intercession of Joshua is accepted, the command is given, "Take away the filthy garments from him;" and to Joshua the Angel says, "Behold, I have caused thine iniquity to pass from thee, and I will clothe thee with change of raiment." "So they set a fair miter upon his head, and clothed him with garments." (Verses 4, 5) His own sins and those of his people were pardoned. Israel was clothed with "change of raiment"—the righteousness of Christ imputed to them. The miter placed upon Joshua's head was such as was worn by the priests, and bore the inscription, "Holiness to the Lord" (Exodus 28:36), signifying that notwithstanding his former transgressions, he was now qualified to minister before God in His sanctuary.—*Prophets and Kings*, pp. 583, 584.

Further Reflection: *Am I okay with Jesus choosing the time and place of my deliverance?*

FINISHER OF THE WORK

So when Jesus had received the sour wine,
He said, "It is finished!"

—John 19:30

The Lord does not come to this world with gold and silver to advance His work. He supplies men and women with resources, that by their gifts and offerings they may keep His work advancing. The one purpose above all others for which God's gifts should be used is the sustaining of workers in the great harvest field. And if men, and women as well, will become channels of blessing to other souls, the Lord will keep the channels supplied. It is not returning to God His own that makes people poor; it is withholding that tends to poverty.

The work of imparting that which has been received will constitute every member of the church a laborer together with God. Of yourself you can do nothing; but Christ is the great worker. It is the privilege of every human being who receives Christ to be a worker together with Him.

The Saviour said: "I, if I be lifted up from the earth, will draw all men unto Me." (John 12:32) For the joy of seeing souls redeemed, Christ endured the cross. He became the living sacrifice for a fallen world. Into that act of self-sacrifice was put the heart of Christ, the love of God; and through this sacrifice was given to the world the mighty influence of the Holy Spirit. It is through sacrifice that God's work must be carried forward. Of every child of God self-sacrifice is required. Christ said: "If any man will come after Me, let him deny himself; and take up his cross daily, and follow Me." (Luke 9:23) To all who believe, Christ gives a new character. This character, through His infinite sacrifice, is the reproduction of His own.

The Author of our salvation will be the **Finisher of the work**. One truth received into the heart will make room for still another truth. And the truth, wherever received, quickens into activity the powers of the receiver. When our church members are truly lovers of God's Word, they will reveal the best and strongest qualities; and the nobler they are, the more childlike in spirit they will be, believing the Word of God against all selfishness.

A flood of light is shining from the Word of God, and there must be an awakening to neglected opportunities.—*Testimonies for the Church,* vol. 6, pp. 448–450.

Further Reflection: *Do I view the work of God as a privilege, a God-given opportunity to work with the One who is the Finisher of the work?*

JEHOVAH IMMANUEL

And the LORD shall be King over all the earth.
In that day it shall be—
"The LORD is one,"
And His name one.

—Zechariah 14:9

The kingdom of God's grace is now being established, as day by day hearts that have been full of sin and rebellion yield to the sovereignty of His love. But the full establishment of the kingdom of His glory will not take place until the Second Coming of Christ to this world. "The kingdom and dominion, and the greatness of the kingdom under the whole heaven," is to be given to "the people of the saints of the Most High." (Daniel 7:27) They shall inherit the kingdom prepared for them "from the foundation of the world." (Matthew 25:34) And Christ will take to Himself His great power and will reign.

The heavenly gates are again to be lifted up, and with ten thousand times ten thousand and thousands of thousands of holy ones, our Saviour will come forth as King of kings and Lord of lords. **Jehovah Immanuel** "shall be king over all the earth: in that day shall there be one Lord, and His name one." "The tabernacle of God" shall be with men, "and He will dwell with them, and they shall be His people, and God Himself shall be with them, and be their God." (Zechariah 14:9; Revelation 21:3)

But before that coming, Jesus said, "This gospel of the kingdom shall be preached in all the world for a witness unto all nations." (Matthew 24:14) His kingdom will not come until the good tidings of His grace have been carried to all the earth. Hence, as we give ourselves to God, and win other souls to Him, we hasten the coming of His kingdom. Only those who devote themselves to His service, saying, "Here am I; send me" (Isaiah 6:8), to open blind eyes, to turn human beings "from darkness to light and from the power of Satan unto God, that they may receive forgiveness of sins and inheritance among them which are sanctified" (Acts 26:18)—they alone pray in sincerity, "Thy kingdom come."—*Thoughts From the Mount of Blessing,* pp. 108, 109.

Further Reflection: *Am I actively looking and working for the second coming of Jehovah Immanuel? Can anyone tell that I am?*

OCTOBER

WELLSPRING OF LIFE

And do not be drunk with wine, in which is dissipation;
but be filled with the Spirit.

—Ephesians 5:18

Not through the excitement or oblivion produced by unnatural or unhealthful stimulants; not through indulgence of the lower appetites or passions, is to be found true healing or refreshment for the body or the soul. Among the sick are many who are without God and without hope. They suffer from ungratified desires, disordered passions, and the condemnation of their own consciences; they are losing their hold upon this life, and they have no prospect for the life to come. Let not the attendants upon the sick hope to benefit these patients by granting them frivolous, exciting indulgences. These have been the curse of their lives. The hungry, thirsting soul will continue to hunger and thirst so long as it seeks to find satisfaction here. Those who drink at the fountain of selfish pleasure are deceived. They mistake hilarity for strength, and when the excitement ceases, their inspiration ends, and they are left to discontent and despondency.

Abiding peace, true rest of spirit, has but one Source. It was of this that Christ spoke when He said, "Come unto Me, all ye that labor and are heavy-laden, and I will give you rest." (Matthew 11:28.) "Peace I leave with you, My peace I give unto you: not as the world giveth, give I unto you." (John 14:27.) This peace is not something that He gives apart from Himself. It is in Christ, and we can receive it only by receiving Him.

Christ is the **wellspring of life**. That which many need is to have a clearer knowledge of Him; they need to be patiently and kindly, yet earnestly, taught how the whole being may be thrown open to the healing agencies of heaven. When the sunlight of God's love illuminates the darkened chambers of the soul, restless weariness and dissatisfaction will cease, and satisfying joys will give vigor to the mind and health and energy to the body.

We are in a world of suffering. Difficulty, trial, and sorrow await us all along the way to the heavenly home. But there are many who make life's burdens doubly heavy by continually anticipating trouble. . . . Let them look away from the dark picture, which is imaginary, to the benefits which God has strewn in their pathway, and beyond these to the unseen and eternal.—*The Ministry of Healing*, pp. 246, 247.

Further Reflection: *In what area(s) of my life might I be restless or dissatisfied?*

TRUE PASCHAL LAMB

Then He said to them, "With fervent desire I have desired to eat this Passover with you before I suffer."

—Luke 22:15

In the upper chamber of a dwelling at Jerusalem, Christ was sitting at table with His disciples. They had gathered to celebrate the Passover. The Saviour desired to keep this feast alone with the twelve. He knew that His hour was come; He Himself was the **true paschal Lamb**, and on the day the Passover was eaten He was to be sacrificed. He was about to drink the cup of wrath; He must soon receive the final baptism of suffering. But a few quiet hours yet remained to Him, and these were to be spent for the benefit of His beloved disciples.

The whole life of Christ had been a life of unselfish service. "Not to be ministered unto, but to minister," (Matthew 20:28), had been the lesson of His every act. But not yet had the disciples learned the lesson. At this last Passover supper, Jesus repeated His teaching by an illustration that impressed it forever on their minds and hearts.

The interviews between Jesus and His disciples were usually seasons of calm joy, highly prized by them all. The Passover suppers had been scenes of special interest; but upon this occasion Jesus was troubled. His heart was burdened, and a shadow rested upon His countenance. As He met the disciples in the upper chamber, they perceived that something weighed heavily upon His mind, and although they knew not its cause, they sympathized with His grief.

As they were gathered about the table, He said in tones of touching sadness, "With desire I have desired to eat this Passover with you before I suffer: for I say unto you, I will not any more eat thereof, until it be fulfilled in the kingdom of God. And He took the cup, and gave thanks, and said, Take this, and divide it among yourselves: for I say unto you, I will not drink of the fruit of the vine, until the kingdom of God shall come."

Christ knew that the time had come for Him to depart out of the world, and go to His Father. And having loved His own that were in the world, He loved them unto the end.—*The Desire of Ages*, pp. 642, 643.

Further Reflection: *What would it be like to live with the knowledge that your entire life was angling toward a singular moment of suffering, pain, and death?*

CHILD OF NAZARETH

"For there is born to you this day in the city of David a Savior, who is Christ the Lord."

—Luke 2:11

Every child may gain knowledge as Jesus did. As we try to become acquainted with our heavenly Father through His word, angels will draw near, our minds will be strengthened, our characters will be elevated and refined. We shall become more like our Saviour. And as we behold the beautiful and grand in nature, our affections go out after God. While the spirit is awed, the soul is invigorated by coming in contact with the Infinite through His works. Communion with God through prayer develops the mental and moral faculties, and the spiritual powers strengthen as we cultivate thoughts upon spiritual things.

The life of Jesus was a life in harmony with God. While He was a child, He thought and spoke as a child; but no trace of sin marred the image of God within Him. Yet He was not exempt from temptation. The inhabitants of Nazareth were proverbial for their wickedness. The low estimate in which they were generally held is shown by Nathanael's question, "Can there any good thing come out of Nazareth?" (John 1:46) Jesus was placed where His character would be tested. It was necessary for Him to be constantly on guard in order to preserve His purity. He was subject to all the conflicts which we have to meet, that He might be an example to us in childhood, youth, and manhood.

Satan was unwearied in his efforts to overcome the **Child of Nazareth**. From His earliest years Jesus was guarded by heavenly angels, yet His life was one long struggle against the powers of darkness. That there should be upon the earth one life free from the defilement of evil was an offense and a perplexity to the prince of darkness. He left no means untried to ensnare Jesus. No child of humanity will ever be called to live a holy life amid so fierce a conflict with temptation as was our Saviour.

The parents of Jesus were poor, and dependent upon their daily toil. He was familiar with poverty, self-denial, and privation. This experience was a safeguard to Him. In His industrious life there were no idle moments to invite temptation.—*The Desire of Ages*, pp. 70–72.

Further Reflection: *How can I prevent the environment and culture in which I live from shaping my character?*

LORD OF LIFE

God has given us eternal life, and this life is in His Son.
—1 John 5:11

The Divine Husbandman planted a goodly vine upon the hills of Palestine. But the people of Israel despised this root of heavenly origin. In a rage they cast it over their vineyard wall; they bruised it, and trampled it under their indignant feet, and hoped that they had destroyed it forever. The Husbandman removed the broken vine, and concealed it from their sight. Again he planted it, but in such a manner that the stock was no longer visible. The branches hung over the wall, and grafts might be joined to it, but the stem itself was placed beyond the power of human beings to reach or harm.

To this world, dark with the shadows of sin, sorrow, and death, came the Son of God with the light of pardon, peace, and immortal life. "As the Father hath life in Himself, so hath He given to the Son to have life in Himself." But the world hated Christ because His perfect purity was in such contrast to their own vileness. They rejected and crucified the **Lord of life**. God raised Him from the dead, and hid Him from mortal view; but He is still the Saviour of humanity. He is still the vine-stock, the source and sustainer of spiritual life. Still may grace, strength, and salvation be derived from His fullness. Though the Vine itself is unseen, its branches are visible. While Christ is removed from human sight, His life and power are manifested in His followers.

Grafts may still be united with the Vine. As the severed branch, leafless, and apparently lifeless, is engrafted into the living stock, and, fiber by fiber, and vein by vein, drinks in the life and strength of the vine until it buds and blossoms and bears fruit, even so may the sinner, by repentance and faith, connect himself with Christ, become a partaker of the divine nature, and bring forth in words and deeds the fruit of a holy life.

Jesus "has life in Himself," and this life He offers to impart freely to souls that are dead in trespasses and sins. Yea, He shares with them His purity, His honor, and exaltation. "Behold, what manner of love the Father hath bestowed upon us that we should be called the sons of God." The sapless branch, engrafted into the living vine, becomes a part of the vine. It lives while united to the vine. So the Christian lives by virtue of his union with Christ. The sinful and human is linked to the holy and divine.—*Review and Herald*, September 11, 1883.

Further Reflection: *Has anyone ever told me that they saw Jesus in me?*

SOURCE OF ALL TRUE PLEASURE AND SATISFACTION

In Your presence is fullness of joy; at Your right hand are pleasures forevermore.

—Psalm 16:11

Of all the features of an education to be given in our school homes, the religious exercises are the most important. They should be treated with the greatest solemnity and reverence, yet all the pleasantness possible should be brought into them. They should not be prolonged till they become wearisome, for the impression thus made upon the minds of the youth will cause them to associate religion with all that is dry and uninteresting; and many will be led to cast their influence on the side of the enemy, who, if properly taught, would become a blessing to the world and to the church. The Sabbath meetings, the morning and evening service in the home and in the chapel, unless wisely planned and vitalized by the Spirit of God, may become the most formal, unpleasant, unattractive, and to the youth the most burdensome, of all the school exercises. The social meetings and all other religious exercises should be so planned and managed that they will be not only profitable, but so pleasant as to be positively attractive. Praying together will bind hearts to God in bonds that will endure; confessing Christ openly and bravely, exhibiting in our characters His meekness, humility, and love, will charm others with the beauty of holiness.

On all these occasions Christ should be set forth as "the chiefest among ten thousand," the One "altogether lovely." (Song of Solomon 5:10, 16) He should be presented as the **Source of all true pleasure and satisfaction**, the Giver of every good and perfect gift, the Author of every blessing, the One in whom all our hopes of eternal life are centered. In every religious exercise let the love of God and the joy of the Christian experience appear in their true beauty. Present the Saviour as the restorer from every effect of sin.

To accomplish this result all narrowness must be avoided. Sincere, earnest, heartfelt devotion will be needed. Ardent, active piety in the teachers will be essential. But there is power for us if we will have it. There is grace for us if we will appreciate it. The Holy Spirit is waiting our demand if we will only demand it with that intensity of purpose which is proportionate to the value of the object we seek.—*Testimonies for the Church,* vol. 6, pp. 174, 175.

Further Reflection: *What do I find most meaningful in my private devotional time with God? What do I enjoy most about worshiping God at church?*

ONLY SAFE GUIDE

Who is the man that fears the LORD?
Him shall He teach in the way He chooses.

—Psalm 25:12

The apostle exalted Christ before his friends as the One by whom God had created all things and by whom He had wrought out their redemption. He declared that the hand that sustains the worlds in space, and holds in their orderly arrangements and tireless activity all things throughout the universe of God, is the hand that was nailed to the cross for them. "By Him were all things created," Paul wrote, "that are in heaven, and that are in earth, visible and invisible, whether they be thrones, or dominions, or principalities, or powers: all things were created by Him, and for Him: and He is before all things, and by Him all things consist." . . .

The Son of God stooped to uplift the fallen. For this He left the sinless worlds on high, the ninety and nine that loved Him, and came to this earth to be "wounded for our transgressions" and "bruised for our iniquities." (Isaiah 53:5) He was in all things made like unto His brethren. He became flesh, even as we are. He knew what it meant to be hungry and thirsty and weary. He was sustained by food and refreshed by sleep. He was a stranger and a sojourner on the earth—in the world, but not of the world; tempted and tried as men and women of today are tempted and tried, yet living a life free from sin. Tender, compassionate, sympathetic, ever considerate of others, He represented the character of God. "The Word was made flesh, and dwelt among us, . . . full of grace and truth." (John 1:14)

Surrounded by the practices and influences of heathenism, the Colossian believers were in danger of being drawn away from the simplicity of the gospel, and Paul, in warning them against this, pointed them to Christ as the **only safe guide**. "I would that ye knew," he wrote, "what great conflict I have for you, and for them at Laodicea, and for as many as have not seen my face in the flesh; that their hearts might be comforted, being knit together in love, and unto all riches of the full assurance of understanding, to the acknowledgment of the mystery of God, and of the Father, and of Christ; in whom are hid all the treasures of wisdom and knowledge."—*The Acts of the Apostles*, pp. 471, 472.

Further Reflection: *Why was Paul so bold in his witness about Jesus? Does my fear prevent me from talking to others about Jesus?*

DEFENDER

The LORD is my rock and my fortress and my deliverer.
—Psalm 18:2

I am thankful that the Lord has not left us in ignorance of how to gain His blessing. Read the eighth and ninth chapters of Second Corinthians, and you will find the whole matter outlined in a few words. Read how the believers came to the apostles and laid their offerings at their feet, praying with much entreaty that they would receive the gift. When God by His Spirit stirs the hearts of His people, leading them to see the necessities of this work, there will be a denying of self, and gifts will flow into the treasury for the proclamation of the message for this time.

If there are those who think they are making large sacrifices for the work, let them consider the sacrifice that Christ made in their behalf. The human race was under sentence of death, but the Son of God clothed His divinity with humanity and came to this world to live and die in our behalf. He came to stand against the host of fallen angels. We must have a **Defender**, and when our Defender came, He was clothed with humanity; for He must be subject to the temptations wherewith humanity is beset, that He might understand how to deliver the godly out of temptation. He took His stand at the head of the fallen race, that men and women might be enabled to stand on vantage ground.

Christ did not come to this world with a legion of angels. Laying aside His royal robes and kingly crown, He stepped down from His high command, and for our sake became poor, that we through His poverty might be made rich. This was the plan laid in the heavenly courts. The Redeemer of humanity was to be born in poverty, and He was to be a worker with His hands. He labored with His father at the carpenter's trade, and into all that He did He brought perfection. His companions sometimes found fault with Him because He was so thorough. What is the use of being so particular? they said. But He would work till He had brought what He was doing as near perfection as He could, and then He would look up with the light of heaven shining from His face, and those who had criticized Him would turn away ashamed of themselves. Instead of retaliating when found fault with, He would begin to sing one of the psalms, and before those who had found fault with Him realized it, they, too, were singing.—Manuscript 58, 1905.

Further Reflection: *Jesus willingly became humanity's Defender, choosing even to share our weaknesses. For what other reasons did He volunteer to come to our sin-cursed planet?*

PROPHET OF GALILEE

"This is truly the Prophet who is to come into the world."
—John 6:14

Many educated and influential people had come to hear the **Prophet of Galilee**. Some of these looked with curious interest upon the multitude that had gathered about Christ as He taught by the sea. In this great throng all classes of society were represented. There were the poor, the illiterate, the ragged beggar, the robber with the seal of guilt upon his face, the maimed, the dissipated, the merchant and the person of leisure, high and low, rich and poor, all crowding upon one another for a place to stand and hear the words of Christ. As these cultured people gazed upon the strange assembly, they asked themselves, Is the kingdom of God composed of such material as this? Again the Saviour replied by a parable: "The kingdom of heaven is like unto leaven, which a woman took, and hid in three measures of meal, till the whole was leavened."

Among the Jews leaven was sometimes used as an emblem of sin. At the time of the Passover the people were directed to remove all the leaven from their houses as they were to put away sin from their hearts. Christ warned His disciples, "Beware ye of the leaven of the Pharisees, which is hypocrisy." (Luke 12:1) And the apostle Paul speaks of the "leaven of malice and wickedness." (1 Corinthians 5:8) But in the Saviour's parable, leaven is used to represent the kingdom of heaven. It illustrates the quickening, assimilating power of the grace of God.

None are so vile, none have fallen so low, as to be beyond the working of this power. In all who will submit themselves to the Holy Spirit a new principle of life is to be implanted; the lost image of God is to be restored in humanity.

But persons cannot transform themselves by the exercise of the will. He or she possesses no power by which this change can be effected. The leaven—something wholly from without—must be put into the meal before the desired change can be wrought in it. So the grace of God must be received by the sinner before he can be fitted for the kingdom of glory. All the culture and education which the world can give will fail of making a degraded child of sin a child of heaven. The renewing energy must come from God. The change can be made only by the Holy Spirit.—*Christ's Object Lessons*, pp. 95–97.

Further Reflection: *How has the leaven of God's grace changed my attitude and behavior?*

JUST ONE

And you know that He was manifested to take away our sins,
and in Him there is no sin.

—1 John 3:5

When Stephen was questioned as to the truth of the charges against him, he began his defense in a clear, thrilling voice, which rang through the council hall. In words that held the assembly spellbound, he proceeded to rehearse the history of the chosen people of God. He showed a thorough knowledge of the Jewish economy and the spiritual interpretation of it now made manifest through Christ. He repeated the words of Moses that foretold of the Messiah: "A Prophet shall the Lord your God raise up unto you of your brethren, like unto me; Him shall ye hear." He made plain his own loyalty to God and to the Jewish faith, while he showed that the law in which the Jews trusted for salvation had not been able to save Israel from idolatry. He connected Jesus Christ with all the Jewish history. He referred to the building of the temple by Solomon, and to the words of both Solomon and Isaiah: "Howbeit the Most High dwelleth not in temples made with hands; as saith the prophet, Heaven is My throne, and earth is My footstool: what house will ye build Me? saith the Lord: or what is the place of My rest? . . ."

When Stephen reached this point, there was a tumult among the people. When he connected Christ with the prophecies and spoke as he did of the temple, the priest, pretending to be horror-stricken, rent his robe. To Stephen this act was a signal that his voice would soon be silenced forever. He saw the resistance that met his words and knew that he was giving his last testimony. Although in the midst of his sermon, he abruptly concluded it.

Suddenly breaking away from the train of history that he was following, and turning upon his infuriated judges, he cried: "Ye stiff-necked and uncircumcised in heart and ears, ye do always resist the Holy Ghost: as your fathers did, so do ye. Which of the prophets have not your fathers persecuted? and they have slain them which showed before of the coming of the **Just One**; of whom ye have been now the betrayers and murderers: who have received the law by the disposition of angels, and have not kept it."

At this, priests and rulers were beside themselves with anger. . . . In the cruel faces about him the prisoner read his fate; but he did not waver.—*The Acts of the Apostles*, pp. 99, 100.

Further Reflection: *Why don't I face more opposition for my faith in Jesus Christ?*

LOVING SAVIOUR

"Blessing and honor and glory and power be to Him who sits on the throne, and to the Lamb, forever and ever!"
—Revelation 5:13

Christ yielded not in the least degree to the torturing foe, even in His bitterest anguish. Legions of evil angels were all about the Son of God, yet the holy angels were bidden not to break their ranks and engage in conflict with the taunting, reviling foe. Heavenly angels were not permitted to minister unto the anguished spirit of the Son of God. It was in this terrible hour of darkness, the face of His Father hidden, legions of evil angels enshrouding Him, the sins of the world upon Him, that the words were wrenched from His lips: "My God, My God, why hast Thou forsaken Me?" (Matthew 27:46)

The death of the martyrs can bear no comparison with the agony endured by the Son of God. We should take broader and deeper views of the life, sufferings, and death of God's dear Son. When the atonement is viewed correctly, the salvation of souls will be felt to be of infinite value. In comparison with the enterprise of everlasting life, every other sinks into insignificance. But how have the counsels of this **loving Saviour** been despised! The heart has been devoted to the world, and selfish interests have closed the door against the Son of God. Hollow hypocrisy and pride, selfishness and gain, envy, malice, and passion, have so filled the hearts of many that Christ can have no room.

He was eternally rich, yet for our sakes He became poor, that we through His poverty might be made rich. He was clothed with light and glory, and was surrounded with hosts of heavenly angels waiting to execute His commands. Yet He put on our nature and came to sojourn among sinful mortals. Here is love that no language can express. It passes knowledge. Great is the mystery of godliness. Our souls should be enlivened, elevated, and enraptured with the theme of the love of the Father and the Son to humanity. The followers of Christ should here learn to reflect in some degree that mysterious love preparatory to joining all the redeemed in ascribing "blessing, and honor, and glory, and power . . . unto Him that sitteth upon the throne, and unto the Lamb for ever and ever." (Revelation 5:13)—*Testimonies for the Church*, vol. 2, pp. 214, 215.

Further Reflection: *When will I set aside time to contemplate the life and death of Jesus?*

REDEEMER AND DELIVERER OF HIS PEOPLE

For by grace you have been saved through faith, and that not of yourselves; it is the gift of God.
—Ephesians 2:8

Meekness and lowliness of heart are the conditions for strength and victory. The crown of glory awaits those who bow at the foot of the cross. Blessed are these mourners, for they shall be comforted. . . .

As the people of God afflict their souls before Him, pleading for purity of heart, the command is given, "Take away the filthy garments" from them, and the encouraging words are spoken, "Behold, I have caused thine iniquity to pass from thee, and I will clothe thee with change of raiment." The spotless robe of Christ's righteousness is placed upon the tried, tempted, yet faithful children of God. The despised remnant are clothed in glorious apparel, nevermore to be defiled by the corruptions of the world. Their names are retained in the Lamb's book of life, enrolled among the faithful of all ages. They have resisted the wiles of the deceiver; they have not been turned from their loyalty by the dragon's roar. Now they are eternally secure from the tempter's devices. Their sins are transferred to the originator of sin.

And the remnant are not only pardoned and accepted, but honored. "A fair miter" is set upon their heads. They are to be as kings and priests unto God. While Satan was urging his accusations and seeking to destroy this company, holy angels, unseen, were passing to and fro, placing upon them the seal of the living God. These are they that stand upon Mount Zion with the Lamb, having the Father's name written in their foreheads. They sing the new song before the throne, that song which no person can learn save the hundred and forty and four thousand, which were redeemed from the earth. . . .

Now is reached the complete fulfillment of those words of the Angel: "Hear now, O Joshua the high priest, thou, and thy fellows that sit before thee: for they are men wondered at: for, behold, I will bring forth My servant the Branch." Christ is revealed as the **Redeemer and Deliverer of His people**. Now indeed are the remnant "men wondered at," as the tears and humiliation of their pilgrimage give place to joy and honor in the presence of God and the Lamb.—*Testimonies for the Church*, vol. 5, pp. 475, 476.

Further Reflection: *How does it feel to know that while Satan is accusing, God is sealing?*

ETERNAL ROCK OF SALVATION

"No one is holy like the LORD, for there is none besides You, nor is there any rock like our God."

—1 Samuel 2:2

The Lord frequently places us in difficult positions to stimulate us to greater exertion. In His providence special annoyances sometimes occur to test our patience and faith. God gives us lessons of trust. He would teach us where to look for help and strength in time of need. Thus we obtain practical knowledge of His divine will, which we so much need in our life experience. Faith grows strong in earnest conflict with doubt and fear. Brother, you may be a conqueror if you take careful heed to your ways. You should devote your young life to the cause of God and pray for success. You should not close your eyes to your danger, but should resolutely prepare for every difficulty in your Christian advancement. Take time for reflection and for humble, earnest prayer. Your talents are marked, and you are hopeful in regard to your future success; but unless you comprehend the weakness of your natural heart you will be disappointed.

You are just starting out in life; you have arrived at an age to bear responsibilities for yourself. This is a critical period in your life. Now, in your youth, you are sowing in the field of life. That which you sow you will also reap; as was the seed, so will be the harvest. If you are neglectful and indifferent concerning eternal things you will sustain a great loss yourself and, through your influence, will prevent others from fulfilling their obligations to God.

Both worlds are before you. Which will you choose? Be wise and lay hold of eternal life. Swerve not from your integrity, however unpleasant your duties may appear in the present emergency. It may seem that you are about to make great sacrifices to preserve your purity of soul, but do not hesitate; press forward in the fear of God, and He will bless your efforts and recompense you a thousand-fold. Do not yield your religious claims and privileges in order to gratify the wishes of your unconsecrated friends and relatives. You are called to take your position for the truth, even if it should be in direct opposition to those who are closely connected with you. . . .

Lay the foundation of your Christian character upon the **eternal Rock of salvation** and let the structure be firm and sound.—*Testimonies for the Church*, vol. 4, pp. 116, 117.

Further Reflection: *How will I prepare for today's difficulties in my spiritual journey?*

ONE WISER THAN SOLOMON

But to those who are called, both Jews and Greeks, Christ the power of God and the wisdom of God.

—1 Corinthians 1:24

The wonderful personage whom John had announced had been among them for more than thirty years, and they had not really known Him as the One sent from God. Remorse took hold of the disciples because they had allowed the prevailing unbelief to leaven their opinions and becloud their understanding. The Light of this dark world had been shining amid its gloom, and they had failed to comprehend whence were its beams. They asked themselves why they had pursued a course that made it necessary for Christ to reprove them. They often repeated His conversations, and said, "Why did we allow earthly considerations and the opposition of priests and rabbis to confuse our senses, so that we did not comprehend that a greater than Moses was among us, that **One wiser than Solomon** was instructing us? How dull were our ears! how feeble was our understanding!"

Thomas would not believe until he had thrust his finger into the wound made by the Roman soldiers. Peter had denied Him in His humiliation and rejection. These painful remembrances came before them in distinct lines. They had been with Him, but they had not known or appreciated Him. But how these things now stirred their hearts as they recognized their unbelief!

As priests and rulers combined against them, and they were brought before councils and thrust into prison, the followers of Christ rejoiced "that they were counted worthy to suffer shame for His name." (Acts 5:41) They rejoiced to prove, before human beings and angels, that they recognized the glory of Christ, and chose to follow Him at the loss of all things.

It is as true now as in apostolic days, that without the illumination of the divine Spirit, humanity cannot discern the glory of Christ. The truth and the work of God are unappreciated by a world-loving and compromising Christianity. Not in the ways of ease, of earthly honor or worldly conformity, are the followers of the Master found. They are far in advance, in the paths of toil, and humiliation, and reproach, in the front of the battle "against the principalities, against the powers, against the world rulers of this darkness, against the spiritual hosts of wickedness in the heavenly places." (Ephesians 6:12, R. V.)—*The Desire of Ages*, p. 508.

Further Reflection: *How can I make the wisdom of Jesus my own, and let it guide my life?*

NEWBORN KING

And when they had come into the house, they saw the young Child with Mary His mother, and fell down and worshiped Him.
—Matthew 2:11

The wise men departed alone from Jerusalem. The shadows of night were falling as they left the gates, but to their great joy they again saw the star, and were directed to Bethlehem. They had received no such intimation of the lowly estate of Jesus as was given to the shepherds. After the long journey they had been disappointed by the indifference of the Jewish leaders, and had left Jerusalem less confident than when they entered the city. At Bethlehem they found no royal guard stationed to protect the **newborn King.** None of the world's honored men and women were in attendance. Jesus was cradled in a manger. His parents, uneducated peasants, were His only guardians. Could this be He of whom it was written, that He should "raise up the tribes of Jacob," and "restore the preserved of Israel;" that He should be "a light to the Gentiles," and for "salvation unto the end of the earth"? (Isaiah 49:6)

"When they were come into the house, they saw the young child with Mary His mother, and fell down, and worshiped Him." Beneath the lowly guise of Jesus, they recognized the presence of Divinity. They gave their hearts to Him as their Saviour, and then poured out their gifts—"gold, and frankincense, and myrrh." What a faith was theirs! It might have been said of the wise men from the East, as afterward of the Roman centurion, "I have not found so great faith, no, not in Israel." (Matthew 8:10)

The wise men had not penetrated Herod's design toward Jesus. When the object of their journey was accomplished, they prepared to return to Jerusalem, intending to acquaint him with their success. But in a dream they received a divine message to hold no further communication with him. Avoiding Jerusalem, they set out for their own country by another route.

In like manner Joseph received warning to flee into Egypt with Mary and the child. And the angel said, "Be thou there until I bring thee word: for Herod will seek the young child to destroy Him." Joseph obeyed without delay, setting out on the journey by night for greater security.

Through the wise men, God had called the attention of the Jewish nation to the birth of His Son.—*The Desire of Ages*, pp. 63, 64.

Further Reflection: *Might God ever use a non-Christian to do what He desires me to do?*

REJECTED STONE

"This is the 'stone which was rejected by you builders, which has become the chief cornerstone.' "

—Acts 4:11

With holy boldness and in the power of the Spirit, Peter fearlessly declared: "Be it known unto you all, and to all the people of Israel, that by the name of Jesus Christ of Nazareth, whom ye crucified, whom God raised from the dead, even by Him doth this man stand here before you whole. This is the stone which was set at naught of you builders, which is become the head of the corner. Neither is there salvation in any other: for there is none other name under heaven given among men, whereby we must be saved."

This courageous defense, in which Peter boldly avowed whence his strength was obtained, appalled the Jewish leaders. They had supposed that the disciples, being only ignorant fishermen, would be overcome with fear and confusion when brought before the Sanhedrin. But instead, the disciples spoke as Christ had spoken, with a convincing power that silenced their adversaries. There was no trace of fear in Peter's voice as he declared of Christ, "This is the stone which was set at naught of you builders, which is become the head of the corner."

Peter here used a figure of speech familiar to the priests. The prophets had spoken of the **rejected stone**, and Christ Himself, speaking on one occasion to the priests and elders, said, "Did ye never read in the Scriptures, The stone which the builders rejected, the same is become the head of the corner: this is the Lord's doing, and it is marvelous in our eyes? Therefore I say unto you, The kingdom of God shall be taken from you, and given to a nation bringing forth the fruits thereof. And whosoever shall fall on this stone shall be broken: but on whomsoever it shall fall, it will grind him to powder."

As the priests listened to Peter's fearless words, "they took knowledge of them, that they had been with Jesus." Of the disciples after the transfiguration of Christ, it is written that at the close of this wonderful scene, they "saw no man, save Jesus only." (Matthew 17:8) "Jesus only"—in these words is contained the secret of the life and power that marked the history of the early church. When the disciples first heard the words of Christ, they felt their need of Him.—*The Acts of the Apostles*, pp. 63, 64.

Further Reflection: *How can I make "Jesus only" the guiding principle of my life?*

PRINCE OF LIFE

And Jesus went about all Galilee, teaching in their synagogues, preaching the gospel of the kingdom, and healing all kinds of sickness and all kinds of disease among the people.

—Matthew 4:23

Upon all who are engaged in the Lord's work rests the responsibility of fulfilling the commission: "Go ye therefore, and teach all nations, baptizing them in the name of the Father, and of the Son, and of the Holy Ghost: teaching them to observe all things whatsoever I have commanded you." (Matthew 28:19, 20)

Christ Himself has given us an example of how we are to work. Read the fourth chapter of Matthew, and learn what methods Christ, the **Prince of life**, followed in His teaching. "Leaving Nazareth, He came and dwelt in Capernaum, which is upon the seacoast, in the borders of Zabulon and Nephthalim: that it might be fulfilled which was spoken by Esaias the prophet, saying, The land of Zabulon, and the land of Nephthalim, by the way of the sea, beyond Jordan, Galilee of the Gentiles; the people which sat in darkness saw great light; and to them which sat in the region and shadow of death light is sprung up." (Matthew 4:13–16)

"And Jesus, walking by the sea of Galilee, saw two brethren, Simon called Peter, and Andrew his brother, casting a net into the sea: for they were fishers. And He saith unto them, Follow Me, and I will make you fishers of men. And they straightway left their nets, and followed Him. And going on from thence, He saw other two brethren, James the son of Zebedee, and John his brother, in a ship with Zebedee their father, mending their nets; and He called them. And they immediately left the ship and their father, and followed Him." (Matthew 4:18–22)

These humble fishermen were Christ's first disciples. He did not say that they were to receive a certain sum for their services. They were to share with Him His self-denial and sacrifices. . . .

In every sense of the word Christ was a medical missionary. He came to this world to preach the gospel and to heal the sick. He came as a healer of the bodies as well as the souls of human beings. His message was that obedience to the laws of the kingdom of God would bring men and women health and prosperity.—*Counsels on Health*, pp. 316, 317.

Further Reflection: *Have I ever studied the methods Jesus used to minister to the physical and spiritual needs of the lost? What can I learn from how Jesus worked?*

ONLY SOURCE OF HELP

"But you are not willing to come to Me that you may have life."
—John 5:40

It is not merely servants, delegates, and prophets, whom thou hast refused and rejected, but the Holy One of Israel, thy Redeemer. If thou art destroyed, thou alone art responsible. . . .

Christ saw in Jerusalem a symbol of the world hardened in unbelief and rebellion, and hastening on to meet the retributive judgments of God. The woes of a fallen race, pressing upon His soul, forced from His lips that exceeding bitter cry. He saw the record of sin traced in human misery, tears, and blood; His heart was moved with infinite pity for the afflicted and suffering ones of earth; He yearned to relieve them all. But even His hand might not turn back the tide of human woe; few would seek their **only Source of help**. He was willing to pour out His soul unto death, to bring salvation within their reach; but few would come to Him that they might have life.

The Majesty of heaven in tears! The Son of the infinite God troubled in spirit, bowed down with anguish! The scene filled all heaven with wonder. That scene reveals to us the exceeding sinfulness of sin; it shows how hard a task it is, even for Infinite Power, to save the guilty from the consequences of transgressing the law of God. Jesus, looking down to the last generation, saw the world involved in a deception similar to that which caused the destruction of Jerusalem. The great sin of the Jews was their rejection of Christ; the great sin of the Christian world would be their rejection of the law of God, the foundation of His government in heaven and earth. The precepts of Jehovah would be despised and set at naught. Millions in bondage to sin, slaves of Satan, doomed to suffer the second death, would refuse to listen to the words of truth in their day of visitation. Terrible blindness! Strange infatuation!

Two days before the Passover, when Christ had for the last time departed from the temple, after denouncing the hypocrisy of the Jewish rulers, He again went out with His disciples to the Mount of Olives and seated Himself with them upon the grassy slope overlooking the city. Once more He gazed upon its walls, its towers, and its palaces. Once more He beheld the temple in its dazzling splendor, a diadem of beauty crowning the sacred mount.—*The Great Controversy*, pp. 22, 23.

Further Reflection: *In what area of my life might I be refusing the appeal of Jesus?*

SUSTAINER OF THE HUMAN RACE

"Come to Me, all you who labor and are heavy laden,
and I will give you rest."

—Matthew 11:28

Make Christ's work your example. Constantly He went about doing good—feeding the hungry and healing the sick. No one who came to Him for sympathy was disappointed. The commander of the heavenly courts, He was made flesh and dwelt among us, and His lifework is an example of the work we are to do. His tender, pitying love rebukes our selfishness and heartlessness.

Christ stood at the head of humanity in the garb of humanity. So full of sympathy and love was His attitude that the poorest was not afraid to come to Him. He was kind to all, easily approached by the most lowly. He went from house to house, healing the sick, feeding the hungry, comforting the mourners, soothing the afflicted, speaking peace to the distressed. . . . He was willing to humble Himself, to deny Himself. He did not seek to distinguish Himself. He was the servant of all. It was His meat and drink to be a comfort and a consolation to others, to gladden the sad and heavy-laden one with whom He daily came in contact.

Christ stands before us as a pattern Man, the great Medical Missionary—an example for all who should come after. His love, pure and holy, blessed all who came within the sphere of its influence. His character was absolutely perfect, free from the slightest stain of sin. He came as an expression of the perfect love of God, not to crush, not to judge and condemn, but to heal every weak, defective character, to save men and women from Satan's power. He is the Creator, Redeemer, and **Sustainer of the human race**. He gives to all the invitation, "Come unto Me, all ye that labour and are heavy laden, and I will give you rest. Take My yoke upon you, and learn of Me; for I am meek and lowly in heart: and ye shall find rest unto your souls. For My yoke is easy, and My burden is light."

What, then, is the example that we are to set to the world? We are to do the same work that the great Medical Missionary undertook in our behalf. We are to follow the path of self-sacrifice trodden by Christ. —*Welfare Ministry*, pp. 53, 54.

Further Reflection: *What is preventing me from taking the yoke of Jesus and learning of Him?*

WONDERFUL COUNSELOR

You will guide me with Your counsel,
and afterward receive me to glory.

—Psalm 73:24

God calls upon human beings to oppose the powers of evil. He says: "Let not sin therefore reign in your mortal bodies, that ye should obey it in the lusts thereof. Neither yield ye your members as instruments of unrighteousness unto sin; but yield yourselves unto God, as those that are alive from the dead, and your members as instruments of righteousness unto God."

The Christian life is a warfare. But "we wrestle not against flesh and blood, but against principalities, against powers, against the rulers of the darkness of this world, against spiritual wickedness in high places." In this conflict of righteousness against unrighteousness, we can be successful only by divine aid. Our finite will must be brought into submission to the will of the Infinite; the human will must be blended with the divine. This will bring the Holy Spirit to our aid; and every conquest will tend to the recovery of God's purchased possession, to the restoration of His image in the soul.

The Lord Jesus acts through the Holy Spirit; for It is His representative. Through It He infuses spiritual life into the soul, quickening its energies for good, cleansing from moral defilement, and giving it a fitness for His kingdom. Jesus has large blessings to bestow, rich gifts to distribute among humanity. He is the **wonderful Counselor**, infinite in wisdom and strength; and if we will acknowledge the power of His Spirit, and submit to be molded by It, we shall stand complete in Him. What a thought is this! In Christ "dwelleth all the fulness of the Godhead bodily. And ye are complete in Him." Never will the human heart know happiness until it is submitted to be molded by the Spirit of God. The Spirit conforms the renewed soul to the model, Jesus Christ. Through Its influence, enmity against God is changed into faith and love, and pride into humility. The soul perceives the beauty of truth, and Christ is honored in excellence and perfection of character. As these changes are effected, angels break out in rapturous song, and God and Christ rejoice over souls fashioned after the divine similitude.—*Review and Herald*, August 25, 1896.

Further Reflection: *When was the last time that angels rejoiced over a positive change in my life brought about by the Holy Spirit?*

UNSEEN

For he who does not love his brother whom he has seen, how can he love God whom he has not seen?
—1 John 4:20

After the ascension of Christ, John stands forth as a faithful, earnest laborer for the Master. With the other disciples he enjoyed the outpouring of the Spirit on the Day of Pentecost, and with fresh zeal and power he continued to speak to the people the words of life, seeking to lead their thoughts to the **Unseen**. He was a powerful preacher, fervent, and deeply in earnest. In beautiful language and with a musical voice he told of the words and works of Christ, speaking in a way that impressed the hearts of those who heard him. The simplicity of his words, the sublime power of the truths he uttered, and the fervor that characterized his teachings, gave him access to all classes.

The apostle's life was in harmony with his teachings. The love for Christ which glowed in his heart led him to put forth earnest, untiring labor for his fellow men and women, especially for his brethren in the Christian church.

Christ had bidden the first disciples love one another as He had loved them. Thus they were to bear testimony to the world that Christ was formed within, the hope of glory. "A new commandment I give unto you," He had said, "That ye love one another; as I have loved you, that ye also love one another." (John 13:34) At the time when these words were spoken, the disciples could not understand them; but after they had witnessed the sufferings of Christ, after His crucifixion and resurrection, and ascension to heaven, and after the Holy Spirit had rested on them at Pentecost, they had a clearer conception of the love of God and of the nature of that love which they must have for one another. Then John could say to his fellow disciples: "Hereby perceive we the love of God, because He laid down His life for us: and we ought to lay down our lives for the brethren."

After the descent of the Holy Spirit, when the disciples went forth to proclaim a living Saviour, their one desire was the salvation of souls. They rejoiced in the sweetness of communion with saints. They were tender, thoughtful, self-denying, willing to make any sacrifice for the truth's sake.—*The Acts of the Apostles*, pp. 546, 547.

Further Reflection: *How can I witness to all classes of people as the apostle John did?*

FIRST-BORN OF HEAVEN

Knowing that you were not redeemed with corruptible things, like silver or gold, from your aimless conduct received by tradition from your fathers, but with the precious blood of Christ, as of a lamb without blemish and without spot.
—1 Peter 1:18, 19

About forty days after the birth of Christ, Joseph and Mary took Him to Jerusalem, to present Him to the Lord, and to offer sacrifice. This was according to the Jewish law, and as man's substitute Christ must conform to the law in every particular. He had already been subjected to the rite of circumcision, as a pledge of His obedience to the law.

As an offering for the mother, the law required a lamb of the first year for a burnt offering, and a young pigeon or a turtledove for a sin offering. But the law provided that if the parents were too poor to bring a lamb, a pair of turtledoves or two young pigeons, one for a burnt offering, the other for a sin offering, might be accepted.

The offerings presented to the Lord were to be without blemish. These offerings represented Christ, and from this it is evident that Jesus Himself was free from physical deformity. He was the "lamb without blemish and without spot." (1 Peter 1:19) His physical structure was not marred by any defect; His body was strong and healthy. And throughout His lifetime He lived in conformity to nature's laws. Physically as well as spiritually, He was an example of what God designed all humanity to be through obedience to His laws.

The dedication of the first-born had its origin in the earliest times. God had promised to give the **First-born of heaven** to save the sinner. This gift was to be acknowledged in every household by the consecration of the first-born son. He was to be devoted to the priesthood, as a representative of Christ among human beings.

In the deliverance of Israel from Egypt, the dedication of the first-born was again commanded. While the children of Israel were in bondage to the Egyptians, the Lord directed Moses to go to Pharaoh, king of Egypt, and say, "Thus saith the Lord, Israel is My son, even My first-born: and I say unto thee, Let My son go, that he may serve Me: and if thou refuse to let him go, behold, I will slay thy son, even thy first-born." (Exodus 4:22, 23)—*The Desire of Ages*, pp. 50, 51.

Further Reflection: *If Jesus was my perfect "example," how can I pattern my life after Him?*

TRUE WARDEN OF THE TEMPLE COURTS

"These things says He who holds the seven stars in His right hand, who walks in the midst of the seven golden lampstands."
—Revelation 2:1

The names of the seven churches are symbolic of the church in different periods of the Christian Era. The number 7 indicates completeness, and is symbolic of the fact that the messages extend to the end of time, while the symbols used reveal the condition of the church at different periods in the history of the world.

Christ is spoken of as walking in the midst of the golden candlesticks. Thus is symbolized His relation to the churches. He is in constant communication with His people. He knows their true state. He observes their order, their piety, their devotion. Although He is high priest and mediator in the sanctuary above, yet He is represented as walking up and down in the midst of His churches on the earth. With untiring wakefulness and unremitting vigilance, He watches to see whether the light of any of His sentinels is burning dim or going out. If the candlesticks were left to mere human care, the flickering flame would languish and die; but He is the true watchman in the Lord's house, the **true Warden of the temple courts**. His continued care and sustaining grace are the source of life and light.

Christ is represented as holding the seven stars in His right hand. This assures us that no church faithful to its trust need fear coming to nought, for not a star that has the protection of Omnipotence can be plucked out of the hand of Christ. . . .

. . . These words are spoken to the teachers in the church—those entrusted by God with weighty responsibilities. The sweet influences that are to be abundant in the church are bound up with God's ministers, who are to reveal the love of Christ. The stars of heaven are under His control. He fills them with light. He guides and directs their movements. If He did not do this, they would become fallen stars. So with His ministers. They are but instruments in His hands, and all the good they accomplish is done through His power. . . . If they will look to Him as He looked to the Father they will be enabled to do His work. As they make God their dependence, He will give them His brightness to reflect to the world.—*The Acts of the Apostles*, pp. 585–587.

Further Reflection: *How comforting is it to know that Jesus is in the very midst of His church, no matter its challenges?*

RIGHTFUL RULER

"Get behind Me, Satan! For it is written, 'You shall worship the LORD your God, and Him only you shall serve.' "

—Luke 4:8

Satan brought all his strength to bear upon this last temptation; for this last effort was to decide his destiny as to who should be victor. He claimed the world as his dominion, and that he was the prince of the power of the air.

He bore Jesus to the top of an exceeding high mountain, and then in a panoramic view presented before Him all the kingdoms of the world that had been so long under his dominion, and offered them to Him in one great gift. He told Christ that He could come into possession of all these kingdoms without suffering or peril. Satan promises to yield his scepter and dominion, and to make Christ the **rightful Ruler**, for one favor from Him. All he requires in return for making over to Him the kingdoms of the world that day presented before Him, is that Christ shall do him homage as to a superior.

The eye of Jesus for a moment rested upon the glory presented before Him; but He turned away and refused to look upon the entrancing spectacle. He would not endanger His steadfast integrity by dallying with the tempter. When Satan solicited homage Christ's divine indignation was aroused, and He could no longer tolerate his blasphemous assumption or even permit him to remain in His presence. Here Christ exercised His divine authority and commanded Satan to desist. "Get thee hence, Satan: for it is written, Thou shalt worship the Lord thy God, and Him only shalt thou serve."

Satan, in his pride and arrogance, had declared himself to be the rightful and permanent ruler of the world, the possessor of all its riches and glory, claiming homage of all who lived in it, as if he had created the world and all things that were therein. Said he to Christ, "All this power will I give Thee, and the glory of them: for that is delivered unto me; and to whomsoever I will I give it." He endeavored to make a special contract with Christ, to make over to Him at once the whole of his claim, if He would worship him.

This insult to the Creator moved the indignation of the Son of God to rebuke and dismiss him.—*Confrontation*, pp. 52, 53.

Further Reflection: *What will it be like when Jesus takes ownership of the earth made new, a perfect place where sin will never rise again?*

WONDERFUL TEACHER

Now early in the morning He came again into the temple, and all the people came to Him; and He sat down and taught them.
—John 8:2

The priests and rulers of the Jews hated Jesus, but multitudes thronged to listen to His words of wisdom and to witness His mighty works. The people were stirred with the deepest interest and anxiously followed Jesus to hear the instructions of this **wonderful Teacher**. Many of the rulers believed on Him, but dared not confess their faith lest they should be put out of the synagogue. The priests and elders decided that something must be done to draw the attention of the people from Jesus. They feared that all people would believe on Him. They could see no safety for themselves. They must lose their position or put Jesus to death. And after they should put Him to death, there would still be those who were living monuments of His power.

Jesus had raised Lazarus from the dead, and they feared that if they should kill Jesus, Lazarus would testify of His mighty power. The people were flocking to see him who was raised from the dead, and the rulers determined to slay Lazarus also, and put down the excitement. Then they would turn the people to the traditions and doctrines of men, to tithe mint and rue, and again have influence over them. They agreed to take Jesus when He was alone, for if they should attempt to take Him in a crowd, when the minds of the people were all interested in Him, they would be stoned.

Judas knew how anxious they were to obtain Jesus and offered to betray Him to the chief priests and elders for a few pieces of silver. His love of money led him to agree to betray his Lord into the hands of His bitterest enemies. Satan was working directly through Judas, and in the midst of the impressive scene of the last supper the traitor was devising plans to betray his Master. Jesus sorrowfully told His disciples that all of them would be offended because of Him that night. But Peter ardently affirmed that although all others should be offended because of Him, he would not be offended. Jesus said to Peter, "Satan hath desired to have you, that he may sift you as wheat: but I have prayed for thee, that thy faith fail not: and when thou art converted, strengthen thy brethren." (Luke 22:31, 32)—*The Story of Redemption*, pp. 209, 210.

Further Reflection: *Do I ever get jealous about how the Holy Spirit is using someone else to do great things for God?*

INEXHAUSTIBLE SOURCE

"And this is eternal life, that they may know You, the only true God, and Jesus Christ whom You have sent."

—John 17:3

I Nebuchadnezzar lifted up mine eyes unto heaven, and mine understanding returned unto me, and I blessed the Most High, and I praised and honoured Him that liveth for ever, whose dominion is an everlasting dominion, and His kingdom is from generation to generation. . . . At the same time my reason returned unto me; and for the glory of my kingdom mine honour and brightness returned unto me; and my counsellors and my lords sought unto me; and I was established in my kingdom, and excellent majesty was added unto me. Now I Nebuchadnezzar praise and extol and honour the King of heaven, all whose works are truth, and His ways judgment; and those that walk in pride He is able to abase."

Those who act a part in the work of God do good only because God is behind them, doing the work. Shall we then praise people, and give thanks to them, neglecting to recognize God? If we do, God will not co-operate with us. When men and women put themselves first and God second, they show that they are losing their wisdom and righteousness. All that is ever done towards restoring the moral image of God in humanity is done because God is the efficiency of the worker. Christ in His prayer to His Father, declared, "This is life eternal, that they might know Thee, the only true God, and Jesus Christ, whom Thou hast sent."

Said the great Apostle Paul, "Let a man so account of us, as ministers of Christ, and stewards of the mysteries of God. Moreover it is required in stewards, that a man be found faithful." Let every steward understand that as he strives to advance the glory of God in our world, whether he stands before Christians or infidels, peasants or princes, he is to make God first, and last, and best in everything. Humans cannot show greater weakness than by thinking they will find greater acceptance in the sight of fellow mortal if they leave God out of their assemblies. God must stand the highest. The wisdom of the greatest person is foolishness with Him. The true Christian will realize that he has a right to his name only as he uplifts Christ with a steady, persevering, and ever increasing force. No ambitious motive will chill his energy; for it comes from an **inexhaustible Source**—"the Light of life."—*The Present Truth* (UK), September 7, 1899.

Further Reflection: *How do I humble myself while uplifting Christ?*

LORD OF GLORY

"If we let Him alone like this, everyone will believe in Him, and the Romans will come and take away both our place and nation."

—John 11:48

The Jewish leaders had supposed that the work of Christ would end with His death; but, instead of this, they witnessed the marvelous scenes of the Day of Pentecost. They heard the disciples, endowed with a power and energy hitherto unknown, preaching Christ, their words confirmed by signs and wonders. In Jerusalem, the stronghold of Judaism, thousands openly declared their faith in Jesus of Nazareth as the Messiah.

The disciples were astonished and overjoyed at the greatness of the harvest of souls. They did not regard this wonderful ingathering as the result of their own efforts; they realized that they were entering into other people's labors. Ever since the fall of Adam, Christ had been committing to chosen servants the seed of His word, to be sown in human hearts. During His life on this earth He had sown the seed of truth and had watered it with His blood. The conversions that took place on the Day of Pentecost were the result of this sowing, the harvest of Christ's work, revealing the power of His teaching.

The arguments of the apostles alone, though clear and convincing, would not have removed the prejudice that had withstood so much evidence. But the Holy Spirit sent the arguments home to hearts with divine power. The words of the apostles were as sharp arrows of the Almighty, convicting men and women of their terrible guilt in rejecting and crucifying the **Lord of glory**.

Under the training of Christ the disciples had been led to feel their need of the Spirit. Under the Spirit's teaching they received the final qualification, and went forth to their lifework. No longer were they ignorant and uncultured. No longer were they a collection of independent units or discordant, conflicting elements. No longer were their hopes set on worldly greatness. They were of "one accord," "of one heart and of one soul." (Acts 2:46; 4:32) Christ filled their thoughts; the advancement of His kingdom was their aim. In mind and character they had become like their Master, and people "took knowledge of them, that they had been with Jesus." (Acts 4:13)—*The Acts of the Apostles*, pp. 44, 45.

Further Reflection: *The disciples received "the final qualification" before beginning their life's work. What qualification do I need before I go about my life's work?*

OCTOBER 27

ORIGINATOR OF EVERY GOOD THING

Every good gift and every perfect gift is from above.
—James 1:17

The sin of Adam and Eve caused a fearful separation between God and human beings. And Christ steps in between fallen humanity and God, and says to men and women: "You may yet come to the Father; there is a plan devised through which God can be reconciled to humanity, and humanity to God; through a mediator you can approach God." . . .

I thank God that we have a Saviour. And there is no way whereby we can be exalted, except through Christ. Then let no one think that it is a great humiliation on his part to accept of Christ; for when we take that step we take hold of the golden cord that links finite human beings with the infinite God; we take the first step toward true exaltation, that we may be fitted for the society of pure and heavenly angels in the kingdom of glory.

Be not discouraged; be not fainthearted. Although you may have temptations, although you may be beset by the wily foe, yet if you have the fear of God before you, angels that excel in strength will be sent to your help, and you can be more than a match for the powers of darkness. Jesus lives. He died to make a way of escape for the fallen race, and He lives today to make intercession for us, that we may be exalted to His own right hand. Hope in God. The world is traveling the broad way; and as you travel in the narrow way, and have to contend with principalities and powers, and to meet the opposition of foes, remember that provision has been made for you. Help has been laid upon One that is mighty, and through Him you can conquer.

Come out from among them, and be separate, saith the Lord, and I will receive you, and ye shall be sons and daughters of the Lord Almighty. What a promise is this! It is a pledge to you that you shall become members of the royal family, heirs of the heavenly kingdom. If a person is honored by, or becomes connected with, any of the monarchs of earth, how it goes the rounds of the periodicals of the day and excites the envy of those who think themselves less fortunate. But here is One who is King over all, the monarch of the universe, the **originator of every good thing**; and He says to us: "I will make you My sons and daughters; I will unite you to Myself; you shall become members of the royal family and children of the heavenly King."—*Testimonies for the Church*, vol. 2, pp. 591, 592.

Further Reflection: *How can I be fitted today for the society of the angels in heaven?*

REVEALER OF THE INFINITE MIND

The only begotten Son, who is in the bosom of the Father, He has declared Him.

—John 1:18

Through varied channels the heavenly messengers are in active communication with every part of the world; and when men and women call upon the Lord with a true and earnest heart, God is represented as bending from His throne above. He listens to every yearning cry, and answers, "Here am I." . . .

In every precept that Christ taught, He was expounding His own life. God's holy law was magnified in this living representative. He was the **revealer of the Infinite mind**. He uttered no uncertain sentiments or opinions, but pure and holy truth. "Every one that is of the truth," He said, "heareth my voice." He has built no walls so high that the nations of the earth cannot be benefited by His light-bearers, His representatives. He invites men and women to take a close view of God in Himself, in the infinite love therein expressed. "For God so loved the world, that He gave His only begotten Son, that whosoever believeth in Him should not perish, but have everlasting life." He so loved the world that He could give nothing less. Having undertaken the work of humanity's redemption, the Father would spare nothing, however dear, which was essential for the completion of His work. He would make opportunities for humanity; He would pour upon them His blessings; He would heap favor upon favor, gift upon gift, until the whole treasury of heaven was open to those whom He came to save. Having collected all the riches of the universe, and laid open all the resources of His divine nature, God gave them all for the use of human beings. They were His free gift. What an ocean of love is circulating, like a divine atmosphere, around the world! What manner of love is this, that the eternal God should adopt human nature in the person of His Son, and carry the same into the highest heaven!

All the heavenly intelligences were watching with intense interest the warfare that was going on upon the earth—the earth that Satan claimed as his dominion. . . . But lo, mercy prevailed. When the Son of God might have come to the world to condemn, He came as righteousness and peace, to save not merely the descendants of Abraham, Isaac, and Jacob, but all the world.—*The Youth's Instructor*, July 29, 1897.

Further Reflection: *How can I take advantage of the blessing of knowing that my world, and the entire planet, is enveloped in an ocean of God's love?*

SEAL OF THE PROMISES MADE

"My soul is exceedingly sorrowful, even to death. Stay here and watch with Me."

—Matthew 26:38

As Christ felt His unity with the Father broken up, He feared that in His human nature He would be unable to endure the coming conflict with the powers of darkness. In the wilderness of temptation the destiny of the human race had been at stake. Christ was then conqueror. Now the tempter had come for the last fearful struggle. For this he had been preparing during the three years of Christ's ministry. Everything was at stake with him. If he failed here, his hope of mastery was lost; the kingdoms of the world would finally become Christ's; he himself would be overthrown and cast out. But if Christ could be overcome, the earth would become Satan's kingdom, and the human race would be forever in his power. With the issues of the conflict before Him, Christ's soul was filled with dread of separation from God. Satan told Him that if He became the surety for a sinful world, the separation would be eternal. He would be identified with Satan's kingdom, and would nevermore be one with God.

And what was to be gained by this sacrifice? How hopeless appeared the guilt and ingratitude of human beings! In its hardest features Satan pressed the situation upon the Redeemer: The people who claim to be above all others in temporal and spiritual advantages have rejected You. They are seeking to destroy You, the foundation, the center and **seal of the promises made** to them as a peculiar people. One of Your own disciples, who has listened to Your instruction, and has been among the foremost in church activities, will betray You. One of Your most zealous followers will deny You. All will forsake You. Christ's whole being abhorred the thought. That those whom He had undertaken to save, those whom He loved so much, should unite in the plots of Satan, this pierced His soul. The conflict was terrible. Its measure was the guilt of His nation, of His accusers and betrayer, the guilt of a world lying in wickedness. The sins of humans weighed heavily upon Christ, and the sense of God's wrath against sin was crushing out His life.

Behold Him contemplating the price to be paid for the human soul. In His agony He clings to the cold ground, as if to prevent Himself from being drawn farther from God.—*The Desire of Ages*, pp. 686, 687.

Further Reflection: *Have do I handle the weight that results from the guilt of my sins?*

SIN-PARDONING SAVIOUR

If we confess our sins, He is faithful and just to forgive us our sins and to cleanse us from all unrighteousness.

—1 John 1:9

God does not give us up because of our sins. We may make mistakes and grieve His Spirit, but when we repent and come to Him with contrite hearts, He will not turn us away. There are hindrances to be removed. Wrong feelings have been cherished, and there have been pride, self-sufficiency, impatience, and murmurings. All these separate us from God. Sins must be confessed; there must be a deeper work of grace in the heart. Those who feel weak and discouraged may become strong men and women of God and do noble work for the Master. But they must work from a high standpoint; they must be influenced by no selfish motives.

We must learn in the school of Christ. Nothing but His righteousness can entitle us to one of the blessings of the covenant of grace. We have long desired and tried to obtain these blessings but have not received them because we have cherished the idea that we could do something to make ourselves worthy of them. We have not looked away from ourselves, believing that Jesus is a living Saviour. We must not think that our own grace and merits will save us; the grace of Christ is our only hope of salvation. Through His prophet the Lord promises, "Let the wicked forsake his way, and the unrighteous man his thoughts: and let him return unto the Lord, and He will have mercy upon him; and to our God, for He will abundantly pardon." (Isaiah 55:7) We must believe the naked promise, and not accept feeling for faith. When we trust God fully, when we rely upon the merits of Jesus as a **sin-pardoning Saviour** we shall receive all the help that we can desire.

We look to self, as though we had power to save ourselves; but Jesus died for us because we are helpless to do this. In Him is our hope, our justification, our righteousness. We should not despond and fear that we have no Saviour or that He has no thoughts of mercy toward us. At this very time He is carrying on His work in our behalf, inviting us to come to Him in our helplessness and be saved. We dishonor Him by our unbelief.—*Selected Messages*, book 1, pp. 350, 351.

Further Reflection: *What is the role of feelings in my spiritual experience? How do I make faith rather than feelings the source of my actions?*

VINDICATOR OF TRUTH

For the law was given through Moses,
but grace and truth came through Jesus Christ.

—John 1:17

Christ here gives all His people an example of the manner of His working for the salvation of men and women. The Son of God identified Himself with the office and authority of His organized church. His blessings were to come through the agencies He has ordained, thus connecting humanity with the channel through which His blessings come.

Paul's being strictly conscientious in his work of persecuting the saints does not make him guiltless when the knowledge of his cruel work is impressed upon him by the Spirit of God. He is to become a learner of the disciples. He learns that Jesus, whom in his blindness he considered an imposter, is indeed the Author and foundation of all the religion of God's chosen people from Adam's day, and the Finisher of the faith now so clear to his enlightened vision.

He saw Christ as the **Vindicator of the truth**, the fulfiller of all prophecies. Christ had been regarded as making of none effect the law of God, but when his spiritual vision was touched by the finger of God, he learned of the disciples that Christ was the originator and foundation of the entire Jewish system of sacrifices, that in the death of type met antitype, [and] that Christ came into the world for the express purpose of vindicating His Father's law. In the light of the law, he saw himself a sinner. That very law which he thought he had been keeping so zealously, he finds he has transgressed. In the light of the law he finds himself a sinner, and he dies to sin and becomes obedient to the claims of God's law. He repents of his sins and has faith in Jesus Christ as his Saviour, is baptized, and preaches Jesus as earnestly and as zealously as he once condemned Him.

In the conversion of Paul are given us important principles which we should ever bear in mind. The Redeemer of the world does not sanction the experience and exercise in religious matters independent of His organized and acknowledged church, where He has a church.—Letter 54, 1874.

Further Reflection: *Have I ever caught a vision of Jesus, and if so, what difference has it made in the way I practice my faith?*

NOVEMBER

PRINCE OF TEACHERS

And He taught in their synagogues, being glorified by all.
—Luke 4:15

Never man spake like this man." (John 7:46) This would have been true of Christ had He taught only in the realm of the physical and the intellectual, or in matters of theory and speculation solely. He might have unlocked mysteries that have required centuries of toil and study to penetrate. He might have made suggestions in scientific lines that, till the close of time, would have afforded food for thought and stimulus for invention. But He did not do this. He said nothing to gratify curiosity or to stimulate selfish ambition. He did not deal in abstract theories, but in that which is essential to the development of character; that which will enlarge humanity's capacity for knowing God, and increase their power to do good. He spoke of those truths that relate to the conduct of life and that unite humanity with eternity.

Instead of directing the people to study human theories about God, His Word, or His works, He taught them to behold Him, as manifested in His works, in His Word, and by His providences. He brought their minds in contact with the mind of the Infinite. . . .

. . . Never before spoke one who had such power to awaken thought, to kindle aspiration, to arouse every capability of body, mind, and soul.

Christ's teaching, like His sympathies, embraced the world. Never can there be a circumstance of life, a crisis in human experience, which has not been anticipated in His teaching, and for which its principles have not a lesson. The **Prince of teachers**, His words will be found a guide to His co-workers till the end of time.

To Him the present and the future, the near and the far, were one. He had in view the needs of all humanity. Before His mind's eye was outspread every scene of human effort and achievement, of temptation and conflict, of perplexity and peril. All hearts, all homes, all pleasures and joys and aspirations, were known to Him.

He spoke not only for, but to, all humanity. To the little child, in the gladness of life's morning; to the eager, restless heart of youth; to men and women in the strength of their years . . . ; to the aged in their weakness and weariness.—*Education*, pp. 81, 82.

Further Reflection: *Jesus is an amazing Teacher. What kind of student would He say I am?*

ROCK OF ISRAEL'S SALVATION

"And I also say to you that you are Peter, and on this rock I will build My church."

—Matthew 16:18

The word Peter signifies a stone—a rolling stone. Peter was not the rock upon which the church was founded. The gates of hell did prevail against him when he denied his Lord with cursing and swearing. The church was built upon One against whom the gates of hell could not prevail.

Centuries before the Saviour's advent Moses had pointed to the **Rock of Israel's salvation**. The psalmist had sung of "the Rock of my strength." Isaiah had written, "Thus saith the Lord God, Behold, I lay in Zion for a foundation a stone, a tried stone, a precious cornerstone, a sure foundation." (Deuteronomy 32:4; Psalm 62:7; Isaiah 28:16) Peter himself, writing by inspiration, applies this prophecy to Jesus. He says, "If ye have tasted that the Lord is gracious: unto whom coming, a living stone, rejected indeed of men, but with God elect, precious, ye also, as living stones, are built up a spiritual house." (1 Peter 2:3–5, R. V.)

"Other foundation can no man lay than that is laid, which is Jesus Christ." (1 Corinthians 3:11) "Upon this rock," said Jesus, "I will build My church." In the presence of God, and all the heavenly intelligences, in the presence of the unseen army of hell, Christ founded His church upon the living Rock. That Rock is Himself—His own body, for us broken and bruised. Against the church built upon this foundation, the gates of hell shall not prevail.

How feeble the church appeared when Christ spoke these words! There was only a handful of believers, against whom all the power of demons and evil human beings would be directed; yet the followers of Christ were not to fear. Built upon the Rock of their strength, they could not be overthrown.

For six thousand years, faith has builded upon Christ. For six thousand years the floods and tempests of satanic wrath have beaten upon the Rock of our salvation; but it stands unmoved.

Peter had expressed the truth which is the foundation of the church's faith, and Jesus now honored him as the representative of the whole body of believers.—*The Desire of Ages*, p. 413.

Further Reflection: *What part do I play in helping Christ to sustain and protect His Church?*

SOURCE OF ALL SPIRITUAL GROWTH

Ask the Lord for rain
In the time of the latter rain.
The Lord will make flashing clouds;
He will give them showers of rain,
Grass in the field for everyone.

—Zechariah 10:1

The Spirit of the Almighty is moving upon men's hearts, and those who respond to Its influence become witnesses for God and His truth. In many places consecrated men and women may be seen communicating to others the light that has made plain to them the way of salvation through Christ. And as they continue to let their light shine, as did those who were baptized with the Spirit on the Day of Pentecost, they receive more and still more of the Spirit's power. Thus the earth is to be lightened with the glory of God. . . .

It is true that in the time of the end, when God's work in the earth is closing, the earnest efforts put forth by consecrated believers under the guidance of the Holy Spirit are to be accompanied by special tokens of divine favor. Under the figure of the early and the latter rain, that falls in Eastern lands at seedtime and harvest, the Hebrew prophets foretold the bestowal of spiritual grace in extraordinary measure upon God's church. The outpouring of the Spirit in the days of the apostles was the beginning of the early, or former, rain, and glorious was the result. To the end of time the presence of the Spirit is to abide with the true church.

But near the close of earth's harvest, a special bestowal of spiritual grace is promised to prepare the church for the coming of the Son of man. This outpouring of the Spirit is likened to the falling of the latter rain; and it is for this added power that Christians are to send their petitions to the Lord of the harvest "in the time of the latter rain." In response, "the Lord shall make bright clouds, and give them showers of rain." "He will cause to come down . . . the rain, the former rain, and the latter rain." (Zechariah 10:1; Joel 2:23)

But unless the members of God's church today have a living connection with the **Source of all spiritual growth**, they will not be ready for the time of reaping. Unless they keep their lamps trimmed and burning, they will fail of receiving added grace in times of special need.—*The Acts of the Apostles*, pp. 54, 55.

Further Reflection: *Could the latter rain be falling on others around me and I be left untouched? When was the last time that I prayed for this rain to fall on me?*

LOOKED-FOR DELIVERER

"The Spirit of the LORD is upon Me,
Because He has anointed Me
To preach the gospel to the poor;
He has sent Me to heal the brokenhearted."

—Luke 4:18

The Galileans who returned from the Passover brought back the report of the wonderful works of Jesus. The judgment passed upon His acts by the dignitaries at Jerusalem opened His way in Galilee. Many of the people lamented the abuse of the temple and the greed and arrogance of the priests. They hoped that this Man, who had put the rulers to flight, might be the **Looked-for Deliverer**. Now tidings had come that seemed to confirm their brightest anticipations. It was reported that the prophet had declared Himself to be the Messiah.

But the people of Nazareth did not believe on Him. For this reason, Jesus did not visit Nazareth on His way to Cana. The Saviour declared to His disciples that a prophet has no honor in his own country. Men and women estimate character by that which they themselves are capable of appreciating. The narrow and worldly-minded judged of Christ by His humble birth, His lowly garb, and daily toil. They could not appreciate the purity of that spirit upon which was no stain of sin.

The news of Christ's return to Cana soon spread throughout Galilee, bringing hope to the suffering and distressed. In Capernaum the tidings attracted the attention of a Jewish nobleman who was an officer in the king's service. A son of the officer was suffering from what seemed to be an incurable disease. Physicians had given him up to die; but when the father heard of Jesus, he determined to seek help from Him. The child was very low, and, it was feared, might not live till his return; yet the nobleman felt that he must present the case in person. He hoped that a father's prayers might awaken the sympathy of the Great Physician. . . .

Like Jacob he prevailed. The Saviour cannot withdraw from the soul that clings to Him, pleading its great need. "Go thy way," He said; "thy son liveth." The nobleman left the Saviour's presence with a peace and joy he had never known before. Not only did he believe that his son would be restored, but with strong confidence he trusted in Christ as the Redeemer.—*The Desire of Ages*, pp. 196–199.

Further Reflection: *Why does Jesus sometimes leave me in the furnace of affliction?*

INNOCENT REDEEMER

"Which of you convicts Me of sin?
And if I tell the truth, why do you not believe Me?"

—John 8:46

From the fall of Jerusalem the thoughts of Jesus passed to a wider judgment. In the destruction of the impenitent city He saw a symbol of the final destruction to come upon the world. He said, "Then shall they begin to say to the mountains, Fall on us; and to the hills, Cover us. For if they do these things in a green tree, what shall be done in the dry?" By the green tree, Jesus represented Himself, the **innocent Redeemer**. God suffered His wrath against transgression to fall on His beloved Son. Jesus was to be crucified for the sins of humanity. What suffering, then, would the sinner bear who continued in sin? All the impenitent and unbelieving would know a sorrow and misery that language would fail to express.

Of the multitude that followed the Saviour to Calvary, many had attended Him with joyful hosannas and the waving of palm branches as He rode triumphantly into Jerusalem. But not a few who had then shouted His praise, because it was popular to do so, now swelled the cry of "Crucify Him, crucify Him." When Christ rode into Jerusalem, the hopes of the disciples had been raised to the highest pitch. They had pressed close about their Master, feeling that it was a high honor to be connected with Him. Now in His humiliation they followed Him at a distance. They were filled with grief, and bowed down with disappointed hopes. How were the words of Jesus verified: "All ye shall be offended because of Me this night: for it is written, I will smite the shepherd, and the sheep of the flock shall be scattered abroad." (Matthew 26:31)

Arriving at the place of execution, the prisoners were bound to the instruments of torture. The two thieves wrestled in the hands of those who placed them on the cross; but Jesus made no resistance. The mother of Jesus, supported by John the beloved disciple, had followed the steps of her Son to Calvary. She had seen Him fainting under the burden of the cross, and had longed to place a supporting hand beneath His wounded head, and to bathe that brow which had once been pillowed upon her bosom. But she was not permitted this mournful privilege. With the disciples she still cherished the hope that Jesus would manifest His power, and deliver Himself from His enemies. Again her heart would sink as she recalled the words in which He had foretold the very scenes that were then taking place.—*The Desire of Ages*, pp. 743, 744.

Further Reflection: *How do I treat those I love when they hurt me?*

MAN OF SORROWS

He is despised and rejected by men,
A Man of sorrows and acquainted with grief.
And we hid, as it were, our faces from Him;
He was despised, and we did not esteem Him.

—Isaiah 53:3

In the providence of God, John was placed where Christ could give him a wonderful revelation of Himself and of divine truth for the enlightenment of the churches.

In exiling John, the enemies of truth had hoped to silence forever the voice of God's faithful witness; but on Patmos the disciple received a message, the influence of which was to continue to strengthen the church till the end of time. Though not released from the responsibility of their wrong act, those who banished John became instruments in the hands of God to carry out Heaven's purpose; and the very effort to extinguish the light placed the truth in bold relief.

It was on the Sabbath that the Lord of glory appeared to the exiled apostle. The Sabbath was as sacredly observed by John on Patmos as when he was preaching to the people in the towns and cities of Judea. He claimed as his own the precious promises that had been given regarding that day. "I was in the Spirit on the Lord's day," John writes, "and heard behind me a great voice, as of a trumpet, saying, I am Alpha and Omega, the first and the last. . . . And I turned to see the voice that spake with me. And being turned, I saw seven golden candlesticks; and in the midst of the seven candlesticks One like unto the Son of man." (Revelation 1:10–13)

Richly favored was this beloved disciple. He had seen his Master in Gethsemane, His face marked with the blood drops of agony, His "visage . . . marred more than any man, and His form more than the sons of men." (Isaiah 52:14) He had seen Him in the hands of the Roman soldiers, clothed with an old purple robe and crowned with thorns. He had seen Him hanging on the cross of Calvary, the object of cruel mockery and abuse. Now John is once more permitted to behold his Lord. But how changed is His appearance! He is no longer a **Man of Sorrows**, despised and humiliated by humanity. He is clothed in a garment of heavenly brightness. . . . His voice is like the music of many waters. His countenance shines as the sun. In His hand are seven stars, and out of His mouth issues a sharp two-edged sword, an emblem of the power of His word. Patmos is made resplendent with the glory of the risen Lord.—*The Acts of the Apostles*, pp. 581, 582.

Further Reflection: *How has God revealed Himself to me during trying circumstances?*

PRINCE IMMANUEL

"He will not fail nor be discouraged, till He has established justice in the earth; and the coastlands shall wait for His law."

—Isaiah 42:4

The church that would prove successful in the Master's service must be an aggressive one. Its members must not allow their interest in the work to lag. Heavenly intelligences are ready to co-operate with the human agent to press forward the work. At whatever cost press the battle to the gates of the enemy; yea, storm the very citadel. Do not allow yourselves to fail nor be discouraged. Christ's authority is supreme. His power is invincible. Through the Holy Spirit the Lord works with the human agent. "He hath appointed us to preach good tidings unto the meek; He hath sent us to bind up the broken-hearted; to proclaim liberty to the captives; and the opening of the prison to them that are bound; to proclaim the acceptable year of the Lord, and the day of vengeance of our God: to comfort all that mourn, to appoint unto them that mourn in Zion; to give unto them beauty for ashes, the oil of joy for mourning, and the garment of praise for the spirit of heaviness; that they might be called trees of righteousness, the planting of the Lord, that He might be glorified." The Sun of Righteousness has arisen. Christ is waiting to clothe His people with the garments of salvation. And "He shall not fail nor be discouraged, till He have set judgment in the earth; and the isles shall wait for His law." His glory shall be seen upon thee. And the Gentiles shall come to thy light, the kings to the brightness of thy rising.

The Lord does not wish to have one true soldier of the cross remain in ignorance or darkness. He calls us up, high above the earth, that He may show us the vast confederacy of evil that is arrayed against us. He would remind us that "we wrestle not against flesh and blood, but against principalities, against powers, against the rulers of the darkness of this world, against spiritual wickedness in high places." But He assures us all who are engaged in this warfare that they are fighting under the "Captain of the Lord's hosts," and that the angels of heaven are assisting them in their struggle for the "crown that fadeth not away." Let us rally under the banner of **Prince Immanuel**, and in the name and strength of Jesus Christ press the battle home.—*Bible Training School*, June 1, 1911.

Further Reflection: *How does it make me feel to know that as God's people work for the lost, all of heaven will be right there with us as we press the battle home?*

EXAMPLE

"And shall God not avenge His own elect who cry out day and night to Him."

—Luke 18:7

"Judgment is turned away backward, and justice standeth afar off; for truth is fallen in the street, and equity cannot enter. Yea, truth faileth; and he that departeth from evil maketh himself a prey." (Isaiah 59:14, 15) This was fulfilled in the life of Christ on earth. He was loyal to God's commandments, setting aside the human traditions and requirements which had been exalted in their place. Because of this He was hated and persecuted. This history is repeated. The laws and traditions of men are exalted above the law of God, and those who are true to God's commandments suffer reproach and persecution. Christ, because of His faithfulness to God, was accused as a Sabbath-breaker and blasphemer. He was declared to be possessed of a devil, and was denounced as Beelzebub. In like manner His followers are accused and misrepresented. Thus Satan hopes to lead them to sin, and cast dishonor upon God.

The character of the judge in the parable, who feared not God nor regarded human beings, was presented by Christ to show the kind of judgment that was then being executed, and that would soon be witnessed at His trial. He desires His people in all time to realize how little dependence can be placed on earthly rulers or judges in the day of adversity. Often the elect people of God have to stand before people in official positions who do not make the word of God their guide and counselor, but who follow their own unconsecrated, undisciplined impulses.

In the parable of the unjust judge, Christ has shown what we should do. "Shall not God avenge His own elect, which cry day and night unto Him?" Christ, our **example**, did nothing to vindicate or deliver Himself. He committed His case to God. So His followers are not to accuse or condemn, or to resort to force in order to deliver themselves.

When trials arise that seem unexplainable, we should not allow our peace to be spoiled. However unjustly we may be treated, let not passion arise. By indulging a spirit of retaliation we injure ourselves. We destroy our own confidence in God, and grieve the Holy Spirit. There is by our side a witness, a heavenly messenger, who will lift up for us a standard against the enemy. He will shut us in with the bright beams of the Sun of Righteousness. Beyond this Satan cannot penetrate. He cannot pass this shield of holy light.—*Christ's Object Lessons*, pp. 170–172.

Further Reflection: *If I do not retaliate when wronged, how will God vindicate me?*

GREAT CENTER

And He is before all things, and in Him all things consist.
—Colossians 1:17

All the disciples had serious faults when Jesus called them to His service. Even John, who came into closest association with the meek and lowly One, was not himself naturally meek and yielding. He and his brother were called "the sons of thunder." While they were with Jesus, any slight shown to Him aroused their indignation and combativeness. Evil temper, revenge, the spirit of criticism, were all in the beloved disciple. He was proud, and ambitious to be first in the kingdom of God. But day by day, in contrast with his own violent spirit, he beheld the tenderness and forbearance of Jesus, and heard His lessons of humility and patience. He opened his heart to the divine influence, and became not only a hearer but a doer of the Saviour's words. Self was hid in Christ. He learned to wear the yoke of Christ and to bear His burden.

Jesus reproved His disciples, He warned and cautioned them; but John and his brethren did not leave Him; they chose Jesus, notwithstanding the reproofs. The Saviour did not withdraw from them because of their weakness and errors. They continued to the end to share His trials and to learn the lessons of His life. By beholding Christ, they became transformed in character.

The apostles differed widely in habits and disposition. There were the publican, Levi-Matthew, and the fiery zealot Simon, the uncompromising hater of the authority of Rome; the generous, impulsive Peter, and the mean-spirited Judas; Thomas, truehearted, yet timid and fearful, Philip, slow of heart, and inclined to doubt, and the ambitious, outspoken sons of Zebedee, with their brethren. These were brought together, with their different faults, all with inherited and cultivated tendencies to evil; but in and through Christ they were to dwell in the family of God, learning to become one in faith, in doctrine, in spirit. They would have their tests, their grievances, their differences of opinion; but while Christ was abiding in the heart, there could be no dissension. His love would lead to love for one another; the lessons of the Master would lead to the harmonizing of all differences, bringing the disciples into unity, till they would be of one mind and one judgment. Christ is the **great center**, and they would approach one another just in proportion as they approached the center.—*The Desire of Ages*, pp. 295, 296.

Further Reflection: *What has changed about me since I began walking with Jesus? Has my family noticed a difference?*

REST-GIVER

"Come aside by yourselves to a deserted place and rest a while."
—Mark 6:31

Christ spoke no words revealing His importance, or showing His superiority; He did not ignore His fellow beings. He made no assumptions of authority because of His relation to God, but His words and actions showed Him to be possessed of a knowledge of His mission and character. He spoke of heavenly things as one to whom everything heavenly was familiar. He spoke of His intimacy and oneness with the Father as a child would speak of its connection with its parents. He spoke as one who had come to enlighten the world with His glory. He never patronized the schools of the rabbis, for He was the Teacher sent by God to instruct humanity. As one in whom all restorative power is found, Christ spoke of drawing all humanity unto Him, and of giving them life everlasting. In Him there is power to heal every physical and spiritual disease.

Christ came to our world with a consciousness of more than human greatness, to accomplish a work that was to be infinite in its results. Where do you find Him when doing this work? In the house of Peter the fisherman; resting by Jacob's well, telling the Samaritan woman of the living water. He generally taught in the open air; but sometimes in the temple, for He attended the gatherings of the Jewish people. But oftenest He taught when sitting on a mountainside, or in a fisherman's boat. He entered into the lives of these humble fishermen. His sympathy was enlisted in behalf of the needy, the suffering, the despised; and many were attracted to Him.

When the plan of redemption was laid, it was decided that Christ should not appear in accordance with His divine character, for then He could not associate with the distressed and the suffering. He must come as a poor man. He could have appeared in accordance with His exalted station in the heavenly courts; but no; He must reach to the very lowest depths of human suffering and poverty, that His voice might be heard by the burdened and disappointed, that to the weary, sin-sick soul He might reveal Himself as the Restorer, the desire of all nations the **Rest-giver**. And to those who are longing for rest and peace today, just as truly as those who listened to His words in Judea, He is saying, "Come unto me, all ye that labor and are heavy laden, and I will give you rest." (Matthew 11:28)—Manuscript 14, 1897.

Further Reflection: *How willing am I to give up the privileges of status to serve those in need?*

UNSEEN ONE

By faith he forsook Egypt, not fearing the wrath of the king; for he endured as seeing Him who is invisible.

—Hebrews 11:27

The education that Moses had received in Egypt was a help to him in many respects; but the most valuable preparation for his lifework was that which he received while employed as a shepherd. Moses was naturally of an impetuous spirit. In Egypt a successful military leader and a favorite with the king and the nation, he had been accustomed to receiving praise and flattery. He had attracted the people to himself. He hoped to accomplish by his own powers the work of delivering Israel. Far different were the lessons he had to learn as God's representative. As he led his flocks through the wilds of the mountains and into the green pastures of the valleys, he learned faith and meekness, patience, humility, and self-forgetfulness. He learned to care for the weak, to nurse the sick, to seek after the straying, to bear with the unruly, to tend the lambs, and to nurture the old and the feeble.

In this work Moses was drawn nearer to the Chief Shepherd. He became closely united to the Holy One of Israel. No longer did he plan to do a great work. He sought to do faithfully as unto God the work committed to his charge. He recognized the presence of God in his surroundings. All nature spoke to him of the **Unseen One**. He knew God as a personal God, and, in meditating upon His character he grasped more and more fully the sense of His presence. . . .

After this experience, Moses heard the call from heaven to exchange his shepherd's crook for the rod of authority; to leave his flock of sheep and take the leadership of Israel. The divine command found him self-distrustful, slow of speech, and timid. He was overwhelmed with a sense of his incapacity to be a mouthpiece for God. But he accepted the work, putting his whole trust in the Lord. The greatness of his mission called into exercise the best powers of his mind. God blessed his ready obedience, and he became eloquent, hopeful, self-possessed, fitted for the greatest work ever given to human beings. Of him it is written: "There hath not arisen a prophet since in Israel like unto Moses, whom Jehovah knew face to face." (Deuteronomy 34:10, A.R.V.)—*The Ministry of Healing*, pp. 474, 475.

Further Reflection: *What have I learned that I must I unlearn in order to do greater service for God?*

KING OF KINGS AND LORD OF LORDS

"Behold, the bridegroom is coming; go out to meet him!"
—Matthew 25:6

The coming of Christ as our high priest to the most holy place, for the cleansing of the sanctuary, brought to view in Daniel 8:14; the coming of the Son of man to the Ancient of Days, as presented in Daniel 7:13; and the coming of the Lord to His temple, foretold by Malachi, are descriptions of the same event; and this is also represented by the coming of the bridegroom to the marriage, described by Christ in the parable of the ten virgins, of Matthew 25.

In the summer and autumn of 1844 the proclamation, "Behold, the Bridegroom cometh," was given. The two classes represented by the wise and foolish virgins were then developed—one class who looked with joy to the Lord's appearing, and who had been diligently preparing to meet Him; another class that, influenced by fear and acting from impulse, had been satisfied with a theory of the truth, but were destitute of the grace of God. In the parable, when the bridegroom came, "they that were ready went in with him to the marriage." The coming of the bridegroom, here brought to view, takes place before the marriage. The marriage represents the reception by Christ of His kingdom. The Holy City, the New Jerusalem, which is the capital and representative of the kingdom, is called "the bride, the Lamb's wife." Said the angel to John: "Come hither, I will show thee the bride, the Lamb's wife." "He carried me away in the spirit," says the prophet, "and showed me that great city, the holy Jerusalem, descending out of heaven from God." (Revelation 21:9, 10) Clearly, then, the bride represents the Holy City, and the virgins that go out to meet the bridegroom are a symbol of the church. In the Revelation the people of God are said to be the guests at the marriage supper. (Revelation 19:9) If *guests*, they cannot be represented also as the *bride*. Christ, as stated by the prophet Daniel, will receive from the Ancient of Days in heaven, "dominion, and glory, and a kingdom;" He will receive the New Jerusalem, the capital of His kingdom, "prepared as a bride adorned for her husband." (Daniel 7:14; Revelation 21:2) Having received the kingdom, He will come in His glory, as **King of kings and Lord of lords**, for the redemption of His people who are to . . . partake of the marriage supper of the Lamb.—*The Great Controversy*, pp. 426, 427.

Further Reflection: *What would it be like to share a meal with Jesus alone?*

SUN OF RIGHTEOUSNESS

"The people who sat in darkness have seen a great light."
—Matthew 4:16

We must pray more, and walk more humbly and more by faith. Christ was perfect in His humanity, and the more faith we have in Him as our sufficiency, the more humbly we walk with God, and the more entire our consecration, the less intrusion of self will there be between God and humanity. The grace of Christ must be an abiding presence in the soul day by day. Only thus can we endure the seeing of Him who is invisible.

Christ came to our world to manifest God to men and women, to lead them to God. "I am the light of the world," He declared. (John 8:12) What was it that consecrated Him the Light of the world? It was this. He came down from heaven. He is the true Teacher sent from God. He was the One chosen to reveal God's character to the world. He is the bright and morning Star. He is the **Sun of Righteousness**, a Light to Lighten the Gentiles, and the glory of His people Israel. John declared of Him, "That was the true Light, which lighteth every man that cometh into the world." (John 1:9)

We may ask of our Lord, knowing that we shall receive. We need more of Christ's humility and meekness, that we may have fervent charity among ourselves; then we may pray, then we may intercede with God. Thus we shall prove the truth of the word, "The effectual fervent prayer of a righteous man availeth much." (James 5:16) "The secret of the Lord is with them that fear Him." (Psalm 25:14) But those whom the Lord would use are in great danger of getting on human stilts. There is earnest work to be done. There is need of walking with God. Then tracts right to the point will be issued.

Prayer and faith will do what no power upon earth can accomplish. We need not be so anxious and troubled. The human agent cannot go everywhere and do everything that needs to be done. Often imperfections manifest themselves in the work, but if we show unwavering trust in God, not depending upon the ability or talent of human beings, the truth will advance. Let us place all things in God's hands, leaving Him to do the work in His own way according to His own will, through whomsoever He may choose. Those who seem to be weak God will use if they are humble.—Manuscript 120, 1898.

Further Reflection: *How have prayer and faith affected the way in which I witness for Christ? How have these spiritual blessings changed my walk with God?*

GREAT MASTER BUILDER

For every house is built by someone,
but He who built all things is God.

—Hebrews 3:4

The Jewish temple was built of hewn stones quarried out of the mountains; and every stone was fitted for its place in the temple, hewed, polished, and tested before it was brought to Jerusalem. And when all were brought to the ground, the building went together without the sound of ax or hammer. This building represents God's spiritual temple, which is composed of material gathered out of every nation, and tongue, and people, of all grades, high and low, rich and poor, learned and unlearned. These are not dead substances to be fitted by hammer and chisel. They are living stones, quarried out from the world by the truth; and the **great Master Builder**, the Lord of the temple, is now hewing and polishing them, and fitting them for their respective places in the spiritual temple. When completed, this temple will be perfect in all its parts, the admiration of angels and of human beings; for its Builder and Maker is God. . . .

. . . There is no person, no nation, that is perfect in every habit and thought. One must learn of another. Therefore God wants the different nationalities to mingle together, to be one in judgment, one in purpose. Then the union that there is in Christ will be exemplified.

I was almost afraid to come to this country because I heard so many say that the different nationalities of Europe were peculiar and had to be reached in a certain way. But the wisdom of God is promised to those who feel their need and who ask for it. God can bring the people where they will receive the truth. Let the Lord take possession of the mind and mold it as the clay is molded in the hands of the potter, and these differences will not exist. Look to Jesus, brethren; copy His manners and spirit, and you will have no trouble in reaching these different classes.

We have not six patterns to follow . . . only one, and that is Christ Jesus. If the Italian brethren, the French brethren, and the German brethren try to be like Him, they will plant their feet upon the same foundation of truth; the same spirit that dwells in one will dwell in the other—Christ in them, the hope of glory. I warn you, brethren and sisters, not to build up a wall of partition between different nationalities. On the contrary, seek to break it down wherever it exists. We should endeavor to bring all into the harmony that there is in Jesus, laboring for the one object, the salvation of our fellow human beings.—*Testimonies for the Church*, vol. 9, pp. 180, 181.

Further Reflection: *What ethnic or cultural differences continue to separate the church?*

GUILTLESS ONE

"For the Father judges no one, but has committed all judgment to the Son."

—John 5:22

Between the first and the second advent of Christ a wonderful contrast will be seen. No human language can portray the scenes of the second coming of the Son of Man in the clouds of heaven. He is to come with His own glory, and with the glory of the Father and of the holy angels. He will come clad in the robe of light, which He has worn from the days of eternity. Angels will accompany Him. Ten thousand times ten thousand will escort Him on His way. . . . The voice of Christ will penetrate the tomb, and pierce the ears of the dead, "and all that are in the graves . . . shall come forth."

"And before Him shall be gathered all nations." The very One who died for humanity is to judge them in the last day; for the Father "hath committed all judgment unto the Son: . . . and hath given Him authority to execute judgment also, because He is the Son of man." What a day that will be, when those who rejected Christ will look upon Him whom their sins have pierced. They will then know that He proffered them all heaven if they would but stand by His side as obedient children; that He paid an infinite price for their redemption; but that they would not accept freedom from the galling slavery of sin. . . .

As they gaze upon His glory, there flashes before their minds the memory of the Son of Man clad in the garb of humanity. They remember how they treated Him, how they refused Him, and pressed close to the side of the great apostate. The scenes of Christ's life appear before them in all their clearness. All He did, all He said, the humiliation to which He descended to save them from the taint of sin, rises before them in condemnation. . . .

Again they hear the voice of Pilate, saying, "I find in Him no fault at all." They see the shameful scene in the judgment-hall, when Barabbas stood by the side of Christ, and they had the privilege of choosing the **Guiltless One**. They hear again the words of Pilate, "Whom will ye that I release unto you? Barabbas, or Jesus, which is called Christ?" They hear the response, "Away with this man, and release unto us Barabbas." To the question of Pilate, "What shall I do then with Jesus?" the answer comes, "Let Him be crucified."—*Review and Herald*, September 5, 1899.

Further Reflection: *What strikes me most about this judgment scene?*

ONE GREATER THAN MOSES

"The case that is too hard for you, bring to me, and I will hear it."
—Deuteronomy 1:17

Let us believe the Lord will hear our united petitions. With Him nothing is impossible. The words spoken by Moses, the Mighty Counselor speaks to us, "And the cause that is too hard for you, bring it unto Me, and I will hear it." (Deuteronomy 1:17) What a cheering, hopeful message is this. Shall not we comply with this gracious invitation? **One greater than Moses** speaks these words, and it comes down along the line of ages to the Israel of God in these days. The case that is baffling to human wisdom, too difficult for the acutest skill of human beings, take it then to Jesus, and He who has spoken so encouragingly "bring it unto Me" will not disappoint our expectations.

That which He requires of us is simply to exercise faith in His word that He will remove all our difficulties and perplexities and make all that is complex clear, and all that is dark light. With Him nothing is impossible. One thing I know, we must rest upon the promise of God without one doubt. Look and live. "Looking unto Jesus, who is the Author and Finisher of our faith." (Hebrews 12:2) Here, as on a stable foundation, we rest. Faith can there act its way—often sunless and starless, while everything in appearance is an intricate wilderness. "Now faith is the substance of things hoped for, the evidence of things not seen." (Hebrews 11:1)

Faith can travel through trials, endure temptations, bear and live under disappointments. Bear up under apparent forbidding providences, saying, "Thou are my refuge, in Thee I trust implicitly believing His word because the eye of faith sees in Jesus the substitute and surety for humanity, and Jesus is the ever-living witness that God is true." The promise is then to us, yea and amen in Christ Jesus.

The waves of trial and temptation may be rolling at our feet, and to all appearances we are sinking beneath the white-capped billows that seem to be talking with death, and our souls exclaim in anguish. Will He be favorable no more? Will the Lord cease to be gracious? Hath He in anger shut up His tender mercies? Look up upon the face of His anointed. Behold the glory of God's verity and His truth and loving kindness and tender compassion beaming in the face of Jesus Christ, and doubt no more.—Letter 80, 1893.

Further Reflection: *What case is too hard for me to bear today? Why do I not bring it to Jesus?*

PRINCE OF HEAVEN

For we do not have a High Priest who cannot sympathize with our weaknesses, but was in all points tempted as we are, yet without sin.

—Hebrews 4:15

It was incomprehensible to the selfish soul of Satan that there could exist benevolence and love for the deceived race so great as to induce the **Prince of Heaven** to leave His home and come to a world marred with sin and seared with the curse. He had knowledge of the inestimable value of eternal riches that humans had not. He had experienced the pure contentment, the peace, exalted holiness, and unalloyed joys of the heavenly abode. He had realized, before his rebellion, the satisfaction of the full approval of God. He . . . knew that there was no limit to His power.

Satan knew what he had lost. He now feared that his empire over the world was to be contested, his right disputed, and his power broken. He knew, through prophecy, that a Saviour was predicted and that His kingdom would not be established in earthly triumph and with worldly honor and display. He knew that ancient prophecies foretold a kingdom to be established by the Prince of Heaven upon the earth, which he claimed as his dominion. This kingdom would embrace all the kingdoms of the world, and then his power and his glory would cease and he would receive his retribution for the sins he had introduced into the world, and for the misery he had brought upon man. He knew that everything which concerned his prosperity was pending upon his success or failure in overcoming Christ with his temptations in the wilderness. He brought to bear upon Christ every artifice and force of his powerful temptations to allure Him from His allegiance.

It is impossible for human beings to know the strength of Satan's temptations to the Son of God. Every temptation that seems so afflicting to man in his daily life, so difficult to resist and overcome, was brought to bear upon the Son of God in as much greater degree as His excellence of character was superior to that of fallen man.

Christ was tempted in all points . . . As man's representative He stood the closest test and proving of God. He met the strongest force of Satan. His most wily temptations Christ has tested and conquered in behalf of humanity. It is impossible for humans to be tempted above what they are able to bear while relying upon Jesus, the infinite Conqueror.—*Confrontation*, pp. 30, 31.

Further Reflection: *What cherished sin makes me most vulnerable temptation?*

REFINER

The refining pot is for silver and the furnace for gold,
but the Lord *tests the hearts.*

—Proverbs 17:3

We believe without a doubt that Christ is soon coming. This is not a fable to us; it is a reality. . . . When He comes He is not to cleanse us of our sins, to remove from us the defects in our characters, or to cure us of the infirmities of our tempers and dispositions. If wrought for us at all, this work will all be accomplished before that time.

When the Lord comes, those who are holy will be holy still. Those who have preserved their bodies and spirits in holiness, in sanctification and honor, will then receive the finishing touch of immortality. But those who are unjust, unsanctified, and filthy will remain so forever. No work will then be done for them to remove their defects and give them holy characters. The **Refiner** does not then sit to pursue His refining process and remove their sins and their corruption. This is all to be done in these hours of probation. It is now that this work is to be accomplished for us. . . .

We are in a world that is opposed to righteousness and purity of character, and to a growth in grace. Wherever we look we see corruption and defilement, deformity and sin. And what is the work that we are to undertake here just previous to receiving immortality? It is to preserve our bodies holy, our spirits pure, that we may stand forth unstained amid the corruptions teeming around us in these last days. . . .

"Know ye not that your body is the temple of the Holy Ghost which is in you, which ye have of God, and ye are not your own? For ye are bought with a price: therefore glorify God in your body, and in your spirit, which are God's." (1 Corinthians 6:19, 20)

We are not our own. We have been purchased with a dear price, even the sufferings and death of the Son of God. If we could understand this, and fully realize it, we would feel a great responsibility resting upon us to keep ourselves in the very best condition of health, that we might render to God perfect service. But when we take any course which expends our vitality, decreases our strength, or beclouds the intellect we sin against God.—*Testimonies for the Church*, vol. 2, pp. 354–356.

Further Reflection: *How does the purity of my life affect the power of my witness?*

SENT OF GOD

"They shall be Mine," says the LORD of hosts,
"on the day that I make them My jewels."

—Malachi 3:17

Christ, the heavenly merchantman seeking goodly pearls, saw in lost humanity the pearl of price. In humanity, defiled and ruined by sin, He saw the possibilities of redemption. Hearts that have been the battleground of the conflict with Satan, and that have been rescued by the power of love, are more precious to the Redeemer than are those who have never fallen. God looked upon humanity, not as vile and worthless; He looked upon it in Christ, saw it as it might become through redeeming love. He collected all the riches of the universe, and laid them down in order to buy the pearl. And Jesus, having found it, resets it in His own diadem. . . . "They shall be Mine, saith the Lord of hosts, in that day when I make up My jewels." (Malachi 3:17)

But Christ as the precious pearl, and our privilege of possessing this heavenly treasure, is the theme on which we most need to dwell. It is the Holy Spirit that reveals to humanity the preciousness of the goodly pearl. The time of the Holy Spirit's power is the time when in a special sense the heavenly gift is sought and found. In Christ's day many heard the gospel, but their minds were darkened by false teaching, and they did not recognize in the humble Teacher of Galilee the **Sent of God**. But after Christ's ascension His enthronement in His mediatorial kingdom was signalized by the outpouring of the Holy Spirit. On the day of Pentecost the Spirit was given. Christ's witnesses proclaimed the power of the risen Saviour. The light of heaven penetrated the darkened minds of those who had been deceived by the enemies of Christ. They now saw Him exalted to be "a Prince and a Saviour, for to give repentance to Israel, and forgiveness of sins." (Acts 5:31) They saw Him encircled with the glory of heaven, with infinite treasures in His hands to bestow upon all who would turn from their rebellion. As the apostles set forth the glory of the Only-Begotten of the Father, three thousand souls were convicted. They were made to see themselves as they were, sinful and polluted, and Christ as their friend and Redeemer. Christ was lifted up, Christ was glorified, through the power of the Holy Spirit resting upon men and women.—*Christ's Object Lessons*, pp. 118–120.

Further Reflection: *Has the Holy Spirit brought to my view just how precious Jesus is? What in my spiritual life demonstrates that Jesus is precious to me?*

SERVANT OF ALL

"If I then, your Lord and Teacher, have washed your feet, you also ought to wash one another's feet."

—John 13:14

For I have given you an example, that ye should do as I have done to you. Verily, verily, I say unto you, The servant is not greater than his lord; neither he that is sent greater than he that sent him. If ye know these things, happy are ye if ye do them." (John 13:12–17)

There is in human beings a disposition to esteem themselves more highly than others, to work for self, to seek the highest place; and often this results in evil surmisings and bitterness of spirit. The ordinance preceding the Lord's Supper is to clear away these misunderstandings, to bring men and women out of their selfishness, down from their stilts of self-exaltation, to the humility of heart that will lead them to serve each other.

The holy Watcher from heaven is present at this season to make it one of soul searching, of conviction of sin, and of the blessed assurance of sins forgiven. Christ in the fullness of His grace is there to change the current of the thoughts that have been running in selfish channels. The Holy Spirit quickens the sensibilities of those who follow the example of their Lord. As the Saviour's humiliation for us is remembered, thought links with thought; a chain of memories is called up, memories of God's great goodness and of the favor and tenderness of earthly friends. . . .

. . . Whenever this ordinance is rightly celebrated, the children of God are brought into a holy relationship, to help and bless each other. They covenant that the life shall be given to unselfish ministry. And this, not only for one another. Their field of labor is as wide as their Master's was. The world is full of those who need our ministry. The poor, the helpless, the ignorant, are on every hand. Those who have communed with Christ in the upper chamber will go forth to minister as He did.

Jesus, the served of all, came to be the **servant of all**. And because He ministered to all, He will again be served and honored by all. And those who would partake of His divine attributes, and share with Him the joy of seeing souls redeemed, must follow His example of unselfish ministry.—*The Desire of Ages*, pp. 650, 651.

Further Reflection: *Jesus who came to save fallen humanity often served the lost, expecting nothing in return. Do I practice this spirit of service when I minister to those in need?*

TRUE EDUCATOR

For the LORD gives wisdom; from His mouth come knowledge and understanding.

—Proverbs 2:6

And they shall build the old wastes, they shall raise up the former desolations, and they shall repair the waste cities, the desolations of many generations." "And thou shalt be called, The repairer of the breach, The restorer of paths to dwell in." (Isaiah 61:4; 58:12) These words of Inspiration present before believers in present truth the work that should now be done in the education of our children and youth. When the truth for these last days came to the world in the proclamation of the first, second, and third angel's messages, we were shown that in the education of our children a different order of things must be brought in; but it has taken much time to understand what changes should be made.

Our work is reformatory; and it is the purpose of God that through the excellence of the work done in our educational institutions the attention of the people shall be called to the last great effort to save the perishing. In our schools the standard of education must not be lowered. It must be lifted higher and still higher, far above where it now stands; but the education given must not be confined to a knowledge of textbooks merely. The study of textbooks alone cannot afford students the discipline they need, nor can it impart true wisdom. The object of our schools is to provide places where the younger members of the Lord's family may be trained according to His plan of growth and development.

Satan has used the most ingenious methods to weave his plans and principles into the systems of education, and thus gain a strong hold on the minds of the children and youth. It is the work of the **true educator** to thwart his devices. We are under solemn, sacred covenant to God to bring up our children for Him and not for the world; to teach them not to put their hands into the hand of the world, but to love and fear God, and to keep His commandments. They should be impressed with the thought that they are formed in the image of their Creator and that Christ is the pattern after which they are to be fashioned. Most earnest attention must be given to the education which will impart a knowledge of salvation, and will conform the life and character to the divine similitude. It is the love of God, the purity of soul woven into the life like threads of gold, that is of true worth.—*Testimonies for the Church,* vol. 6, pp. 126, 127.

Further Reflection: *Was I educated according to God's plan of growth and development?*

COMPASSIONATE INTERCESSOR

As a father pities his children, so the LORD pities those who fear Him.
—Psalm 103:13

Shall any man or woman be indifferent to the very souls for whom Christ is pleading in the courts of heaven? Shall you in your course of action, imitate the Pharisees, who would be merciless, and Satan, who will accuse and destroy? O will you individually humble your own souls before God, and [let] that stern nerve and iron will be subdued and broken?

Step away from the sound of Satan's voice and acting his will, and stand by the side of Jesus, possessing His attributes, the possessor of keen and tender sensibilities, who can make the cause of the afflicted, suffering ones His own. The person who has had much forgiven will love much. Jesus is a **compassionate Intercessor**, a merciful and faithful high priest. He, the Majesty of heaven—the King of glory—can look upon finite men and women, subject to the temptations of Satan, knowing [that] He has felt the power of Satan's Wiles. "Wherefore in all things it behooved Him to be made like unto His brethren, (clothing His divinity with humanity) that He might be a merciful and faithful high priest in things pertaining to God, to make reconciliation for the sins of the people. For in that He himself hath suffered being tempted, He is able to succor them that are tempted." (Hebrews 2:17, 18)

Then I call upon you, my brethren, to practice working in the lines that Christ worked. You must never put on the cloak of severity and condemn and denounce and drive away from the fold poor, tempted mortals; but as laborers together with God, heal the spiritually diseased. This you will do if you have the mind of Christ. (Hebrews 4:15; also Isaiah 40:28) He "fainteth not neither is weary."—Manuscript 34, 1893.

Further Reflection: *If there is a spirit of condemnation in me, how can I overcome it? If there is a tendency in my church to denounce those who err, what can I do to change it?*

SURETY FOR A SINFUL WORLD

"O My Father, if it is possible, let this cup pass from Me; nevertheless, not as I will, but as You will."

—Matthew 26:39

As one surprised, Christ addressed them, saying, "What, could ye not watch with Me one hour?" They roused themselves, and looked sorrowfully at their Lord. "Watch and pray," He said, "that ye enter not into temptation." Then the divine Sufferer excused the disciples, saying, "The spirit indeed is willing, but the flesh is weak."

Christ went away the second time, and prayed earnestly, "O My Father, if this cup may not pass away from Me, except I drink it, Thy will be done." Again darkness pressed upon His soul with almost unbearable agony, and again He felt a longing for companionship, for some words which would bring relief, and break the spell of darkness that well-nigh overpowered Him. "And He came and found them asleep again; for their eyes were heavy;" "neither wist they what to answer him." They saw His face marked with the bloody sweat of agony, and they were filled with sorrow; for "His visage was so marred, more than any man."

Again Christ went away, and prayed that if it were possible this cup might pass from Him. His soul was filled with an overpowering fear of separation from God in consequence of sin. Satan told Him that if He became the substitute and **surety for a sinful world**, He would nevermore be one with God, but would be under his control.

Three times the prayer ascended to God, "O my Father, if it be possible, let this cup pass from Me," always followed by the words, "Not My will, but Thine, be done." Shall the cup pass from the Suffering One? Shall the sacrifice of Christ, ordained before the foundation of the world, and symbolized in every sacrifice offered since Adam's transgression, be given up? . . . Shall that which angels eagerly desired to look into and understand, that which had been the burden of prophecy, that which lay at the foundation of types and shadows, fail after all, leaving Satan and his apostate forces and confederacy of evil to come off triumphant?

O, how much Christ had already suffered as the Son of man, in order to redeem and save men and women!—*The Signs of the Times,* June 3, 1897.

Further Reflection: *In every consequential moment when humanity's fate hung in the balance, Jesus made the right decision. How can I remain faithful in my hour of trial?*

COMPASSIONATE SAVIOUR

"And often he has thrown him both into the fire and into the water to destroy him. But if You can do anything, have compassion on us and help us."

—Mark 9:22

How many a sin-burdened soul has echoed that prayer. And to all, the pitying Saviour's answer is, "If thou canst believe, all things are possible to him that believeth." It is faith that connects us with heaven, and brings us strength for coping with the powers of darkness. In Christ, God has provided means for subduing every sinful trait, and resisting every temptation, however strong. But many feel that they lack faith, and therefore they remain away from Christ. Let these souls, in their helpless unworthiness, cast themselves upon the mercy of their **compassionate Saviour**. Look not to self, but to Christ. He who healed the sick and cast out demons when He walked among human beings is the same mighty Redeemer today. Faith comes by the word of God. Then grasp His promise, "Him that cometh to Me I will in no wise cast out." (John 6:37) Cast yourself at His feet with the cry, "Lord, I believe; help Thou mine unbelief." You can never perish while you do this—never.

In a brief space of time the favored disciples have beheld the extreme of glory and of humiliation. They have seen humanity as transfigured into the image of God, and as debased into the likeness of Satan. From the mountain where He has talked with the heavenly messengers, and has been proclaimed the Son of God by the voice from the radiant glory, they have seen Jesus descend to meet that most distressing and revolting spectacle, the maniac boy, with distorted countenance, gnashing his teeth in spasms of agony that no human power could relieve. And this mighty Redeemer, who but a few hours before stood glorified before His wondering disciples, stoops to lift the victim of Satan from the earth where he is wallowing, and in health of mind and body restores him to his father and his home.

It was an object lesson of redemption—the Divine One from the Father's glory stooping to save the lost. It represented also the disciples' mission. Not alone upon the mountaintop with Jesus, in hours of spiritual illumination, is the life of Christ's servants to be spent. There is work for them down in the plain. Souls whom Satan has enslaved are waiting for the word of faith and prayer to set them free.—*The Desire of Ages*, p. 429.

Further Reflection: *How "low" am I willing to go to save the lost people around me?*

DEAREST BELOVED

"He who touches you touches the apple of His eye."
—Zechariah 2:8

Only the sense of God's presence can banish the fear that, for the timid child, would make life a burden. Let him fix in his memory the promise, "The angel of the Lord encampeth round about them that fear Him, and delivereth them." (Psalm 34:7) Let him read that wonderful story of Elisha in the mountain city, and, between him and the hosts of armed foemen, a mighty encircling band of heavenly angels. Let him read how to Peter, in prison and condemned to death, God's angel appeared; how, past the armed guards, the massive doors and great iron gateway with their bolts and bars, the angel led God's servant forth in safety. Let him read of that scene on the sea, when the tempest-tossed soldiers and seamen, worn with labor and watching and long fasting, Paul the prisoner, on his way to trial and execution, spoke those grand words of courage and hope: "Be of good cheer: for there shall be no loss of any man's life among you. . . . For there stood by me this night the angel of God, whose I am, and whom I serve, saying, Fear not, Paul; thou must be brought before Caesar: and, lo, God hath given thee all them that sail with thee." . . .

These things were not written merely that we might read and wonder, but that the same faith which wrought in God's servants of old might work in us. In no less marked a manner than He wrought then will He work now wherever there are hearts of faith to be channels of His power.

Let the self-distrustful, whose lack of self-reliance leads them to shrink from care and responsibility, be taught reliance upon God. Thus many a one who otherwise would be but a cipher in the world, perhaps only a helpless burden, will be able to say with the apostle Paul, "I can do all things through Christ which strengtheneth me." (Philippians 4:13)

For the child also who is quick to resent injuries, faith has precious lessons. The disposition to resist evil or to avenge wrong is often prompted by a keen sense of justice and an active, energetic spirit. Let such a child be taught that God is the eternal guardian of right. He has a tender care for the beings whom He has so loved as to give His **dearest Beloved** to save. He will deal with every wrongdoer.—*Education*, pp. 255–257.

Further Reflection: *In a world where justice often seems elusive, how can I help those who are wronged find hope in the Dearest Beloved of heaven?*

LORD OF THE SABBATH

For the Son of Man is Lord even of the Sabbath.
—Matthew 12:8

Bidding His hearers marvel not, Christ opened before them, in still wider view, the mystery of the future. "The hour cometh," He said, "in which all that are in the tombs shall hear His voice, and shall come forth; they that have done good, unto the resurrection of life; and they that have done ill, unto the resurrection of judgment." (John 5:28, 29, R. V.)

This assurance of the future life was that for which Israel had so long waited, and which they had hoped to receive at the Messiah's advent. The only light that can lighten the gloom of the grave was shining upon them. But self-will is blind. Jesus had violated the traditions of the rabbis, and disregarded their authority, and they would not believe.

The time, the place, the occasion, the intensity of feeling that pervaded the assembly, all combined to make the words of Jesus before the Sanhedrin the more impressive. The highest religious authorities of the nation were seeking the life of Him who declared Himself the restorer of Israel. The **Lord of the Sabbath** was arraigned before an earthly tribunal to answer the charge of breaking the Sabbath law. When He so fearlessly declared His mission, His judges looked upon Him with astonishment and rage; but His words were unanswerable. They could not condemn Him. He denied the right of the priests and rabbis to question Him, or to interfere with His work. They were invested with no such authority. Their claims were based upon their own pride and arrogance. He refused to plead guilty of their charges, or to be catechized by them.

Instead of apologizing for the act of which they complained, or explaining His purpose in doing it, Jesus turned upon the rulers, and the accused became the accuser. He rebuked them for the hardness of their hearts, and their ignorance of the Scriptures. He declared that they had rejected the word of God, inasmuch as they had rejected Him whom God had sent. "Ye search the Scriptures, because ye think that in them ye have eternal life; and these are they which bear witness of Me." (John 5:39), R. V.

In every page, whether history, or precept, or prophecy, the Old Testament Scriptures are irradiated with the glory of the Son of God. So far as it was of divine institution, the entire system of Judaism was a compacted prophecy of the gospel.—*The Desire of Ages*, p. 211

Further Reflection: *What can I learn from the way in which Jesus handled the Sanhedrin?*

INFINITE HELPER

Great is our Lord, and mighty in power; His understanding is infinite.
—Psalm 147:5

Many suppose that the Catholic religion is unattractive, and that its worship is a dull, stupid round of ceremony. Here they mistake. While Romanism is based upon deception, it is not a coarse and clumsy imposture. The religious service of the Romish Church is a most impressive ceremonial. Its gorgeous display and solemn rites fascinate the senses of the people, and silence the voice of reason and of conscience. The eye is charmed. Magnificent churches, imposing processions, golden altars, jeweled shrines, choice paintings, and exquisite sculpture appeal to the love of beauty. The ear also is captivated. There is nothing to excel the music. The rich notes of the deep-toned organ, blending with the melody of many voices as it swells through the lofty domes and pillared aisles of her grand cathedrals, cannot fail to impress the mind with awe and reverence.

This outward splendor, pomp, and ceremony, that only mocks the longings of the sin-sick soul, is an evidence of inward corruption. The religion of Christ needs not such attractions to recommend it. In the light shining from the cross, true Christianity appears so pure and lovely that external decorations only hide its true worth. It is the beauty of holiness, a meek and quiet spirit, which is of value with God.

Brilliancy of style is not an index of pure, elevated thought. The highest conceptions of art, the most delicate refinement of taste, often spring from minds wholly earthly and sensual. They are often employed by Satan to lead people to forget the necessities of the soul, to lose sight of the future, immortal life, to turn away from their **infinite Helper**, and to live for this world alone.

A religion of externals is attractive to the unrenewed heart. The pomp and ceremony of the Catholic worship have a seductive, bewitching power by which many are deceived; and they come to look upon the Roman Church as the very gate of heaven. None are proof against her influence but those who have planted their feet firmly upon the foundation of truth, and whose hearts are renewed by the Spirit of God.—*The Signs of the Times*, June 30, 1898.

Further Reflection: *Do the beautiful things in life obscure or illumine my view of God?*

KING OF ISRAEL

"How lovely are your tents, O Jacob!
Your dwellings, O Israel!
Like valleys that stretch out,
Like gardens by the riverside,
Like aloes planted by the LORD,
Like cedars beside the waters."

—Numbers 24:5, 6

The prosperity of God's people is here represented by some of the most beautiful figures to be found in nature. The prophet likens Israel to fertile valleys covered with abundant harvests; to flourishing gardens watered by never-failing springs; to the fragrant sandal tree and the stately cedar. The figure last mentioned is one of the most strikingly beautiful and appropriate to be found in the inspired word.

The cedar of Lebanon was honored by all the people of the East. The class of trees to which it belongs is found wherever human beings have gone throughout the earth. From the arctic regions to the tropic zone they flourish, rejoicing in the heat, yet braving the cold; springing in rich luxuriance by the riverside, yet towering aloft upon the parched and thirsty waste. They plant their roots deep among the rocks of the mountains and boldly stand in defiance of the tempest. Their leaves are fresh and green when all else has perished at the breath of winter. Above all other trees the cedar of Lebanon is distinguished for its strength, its firmness, its undecaying vigor; and this is used as a symbol of those whose life is "hid with Christ in God." (Colossians 3:3) Says the Scripture, "The righteous . . . shall grow like a cedar." (Psalm 92:12) The divine hand has exalted the cedar as king over the forest. "The fir trees were not like his boughs, and the chestnut trees were not like his branches" (Ezekiel 31:8); nor any tree in the garden of God. The cedar is repeatedly employed as an emblem of royalty, and its use in Scripture to represent the righteous shows how heaven regards those who do the will of God.

Balaam prophesied that Israel's king would be greater and more powerful than Agag. This was the name given to the kings of the Amalekites, who were at this time a very powerful nation; but Israel, if true to God, would subdue all her enemies. The **King of Israel** was the Son of God; and His throne was one day to be established in the earth, and His power to be exalted above all earthly kingdoms.—*Patriarchs and Prophets*, p. 450.

Further Reflection: *Have you ever thought of how sin prevented Jesus from establishing His throne as earth's rightful ruler? When will Christ's rulership be reestablished?*

LIGHT OF SUN, MOON, AND STAR

This is the message which we have heard from Him and declare to you, that God is light and in Him is no darkness at all.

—1 John 1:5

In the manifestation of God to His people, light had ever been a symbol of His presence. At the creative word in the beginning, light had shone out of darkness. Light had been enshrouded in the pillar of cloud by day and the pillar of fire by night, leading the vast armies of Israel. Light blazed with awful grandeur about the Lord on Mount Sinai. Light rested over the mercy seat in the tabernacle. Light filled the temple of Solomon at its dedication. Light shone on the hills of Bethlehem when the angels brought the message of redemption to the watching shepherds.

God is light; in the words, "I am the light of the world," Christ declared His oneness with God, and His relation to the whole human family. It was He who at the beginning had caused "the light to shine out of darkness." (2 Corinthians 4:6) He is the **light of sun and moon and star**. He was the spiritual light that in symbol and type and prophecy had shone upon Israel. But not to the Jewish nation alone was the light given. As the sunbeams penetrate to the remotest corners of the earth, so does the light of the Sun of Righteousness shine upon every soul.

"That was the true light, which lighteth every man that cometh into the world." The world has had its great teachers, men and women of giant intellect and wonderful research, persons whose utterances have stimulated thought, and opened to view vast fields of knowledge; and these persons have been honored as guides and benefactors of their race. But there is One who stands higher than they.

"As many as received Him, to them gave He power to become the sons of God." "No man hath seen God at any time; the only-begotten Son, which is in the bosom of the Father, He hath declared Him." (John 1:12, 18) We can trace the line of the world's great teachers as far back as human records extend; but the Light was before them. As the moon and the stars of the solar system shine by the reflected light of the sun, so, as far as their teaching is true, do the world's great thinkers reflect the rays of the Sun of Righteousness. Every gem of thought, every flash of the intellect, is from the Light of the world.—*The Desire of Ages*, pp. 464, 465.

Further Reflection: *How has the Holy Spirit helped me in areas of personal weakness?*

KING OF SAINTS

"Great and marvelous are Your works,
Lord God Almighty!
Just and true are Your ways,
O King of the saints!"

—Revelation 15:3

God designed that the Prince of sufferers in humanity should be judge of the whole world. He who came from the heavenly courts to save humanity from eternal death; He who men and women despised, rejected, and upon whom they heaped all the contempt of which human beings, inspired by Satan, are capable; He who submitted to be arraigned before an earthly tribunal, and who suffered the ignominious death of the cross—He alone is to pronounce the sentence of reward or of punishment. He who submitted to the suffering and humiliation of the cross here, in the counsel of God is to have the fullest compensation, and ascend the throne acknowledged by all the heavenly universe as the **King of saints**. He has undertaken the work of salvation, and shown before unfallen worlds and the heavenly family that the work He has begun He is able to complete. It is Christ who gives human beings the grace of repentance; His merits are accepted by the Father in behalf of every soul that will help to compose the family of God.

In that day of final punishment and reward, both saints and sinners will recognize in Him who was crucified the Judge of all living. Every crown that is given to the saints of the Most High will be bestowed by the hands of Christ—those hands that cruel priests and rulers condemned to be nailed to the cross. He alone can give to men and women the consolation of eternal life.

A sign in the heavens was given to the wise men of the East who were searching for Christ. To shepherds who were keeping their flocks on the hills of Bethlehem, the angel host appeared. All heaven recognized the advent of Christ. Unseen angels were present in the judgment-hall. When Christ was scourged with the cruel thongs, they could scarcely endure the sight. Angels of heaven were present at His death. The darkness that covered the earth at His crucifixion concealed the company of heaven's powerful agencies; but the earth quaked beneath the tread of the heavenly throng. The rocks were rent. For three hours the earth was shrouded in impenetrable darkness; nature with her dark robes hid the sufferings of the Son of God.—*Review and Herald*, November 22, 1898.

Further Reflection: *What will I say to Jesus when He gives me my crown?*

DECEMBER

INFINITE PURITY

And everyone who has this hope in Him purifies himself,
just as He is pure.

—1 John 3:3

The discourse ended, Jesus turned to Peter, and bade him launch out into the sea, and let down his net for a draught. But Peter was disheartened. All night he had taken nothing. During the lonely hours he had thought of the fate of John the Baptist, who was languishing alone in his dungeon. He had thought of the prospect before Jesus and His followers, of the ill success of the mission to Judea, and the malice of the priests and rabbis. Even his own occupation had failed him; and as he watched by the empty nets, the future had seemed dark with discouragement. "Master," he said, "we have toiled all the night, and have taken nothing: nevertheless at Thy word I will let down the net."

Night was the only favorable time for fishing with nets in the clear waters of the lake. After toiling all night without success, it seemed hopeless to cast the net by day; but Jesus had given the command, and love for their Master moved the disciples to obey. Simon and his brother together let down the net. As they attempted to draw it in, so great was the quantity of fish enclosed that it began to break. They were obliged to summon James and John to their aid. When the catch was secured, both the boats were so heavily laden that they were in danger of sinking.

But Peter was unmindful now of boats or lading. This miracle, above any other he had ever witnessed, was to him a manifestation of divine power. In Jesus he saw One who held all nature under His control. The presence of divinity revealed his own unholiness. Love for his Master, shame for his own unbelief, gratitude for the condescension of Christ, above all, the sense of his uncleanness in the presence of **infinite purity**, overwhelmed him. While his companions were securing the contents of the net, Peter fell at the Saviour's feet, exclaiming, "Depart from me; for I am a sinful man, O Lord."

It was the same presence of divine holiness that had caused the prophet Daniel to fall as one dead before the angel of God.—*The Desire of Ages*, pp. 245, 246.

Further Reflection: *When was my Peter moment—the moment when I felt how sinful I was in comparison to the purity of Jesus?*

WITNESS

Then she called the name of the LORD who spoke to her, You-Are-the-God-Who-Sees; for she said, "Have I also here seen Him who sees me?"
—Genesis 16:13

We should not be discouraged if things of a trying nature arise. Do not let your passion rise. Control yourself. When things occur which seem unexplainable, which do not appear to be in harmony with the great Counsel Book, do not allow your own peace to be spoiled. Remember that there is a **Witness**, a heavenly Messenger by your side, who is your shield, your fortress. Into it you can run, and be safe. But a word of retaliation will destroy your peace, and your confidence in God. Who then is injured?—Yourself. Who is grieved and wounded?—The Holy Spirit of God.

On every occasion be armed and equipped with "It is Written." God is your armor, on the right hand, and on the left. A flood of hasty words may seek for expression, but say, No; no. I will not place my feet on Satan's ground. I will not sacrifice my peace and honor as a child of God. I will keep in the only safe path, close beside Jesus, who has done so much for me. . . .

Do not be surprised if great changes are made. Do not wonder if the persons who felt themselves capable of handling the consciences of their fellow human beings, and of controlling the minds and talents God has given them should go back, and walk no more with these who believe the truth. The truth makes too great a demand upon them. When they see that they must die to self, and practice the principles of self-denial, they are displeased because they cannot gratify their ambitious desire to rule other people. Their true characters will appear. Some will make total shipwreck of the faith. "They went out from us, but they were not of us," said John, and so it will be again.

Hold fast to the truth, the precious, sanctifying truth. You are then in the best of company, and the very highest intelligences are beholding your course of action. You are a spectacle to the world, to angels, and to humanity. Under provocation, your work is to hold the faith and a good conscience, "Which some having put away concerning faith have made shipwreck."—*Christian Leadership*, p. 64.

Further Reflection: *Does God expect me to be a witness even when falsely attacked or ridiculed?*

HEAVENLY VISITANT

He was in the world, and the world was made through Him, and the world did not know Him.

—John 1:10

Have you not been afraid of the Holy Spirit? At times It has come with all-pervading influence into the school at Battle Creek and into the schools in other localities. Did you recognize It? Did you accord It the honor due to a heavenly Messenger? When the Spirit seemed to be striving with the youth, did you say, "Let us put aside all study; for it is evident that we have among us a heavenly Guest. Let us give praise and honor to God?" Did you, with contrite hearts, bow in prayer with your students, pleading that you might receive the blessing that the Lord was offering you?

The Great Teacher Himself was among you. How did you honor Him? Was He a stranger to some of the educators? Was there need to send for someone of supposed authority to welcome or repel this Messenger from heaven? Though unseen, His presence was among you. But was not the thought expressed that in school the time ought to be given to study, and that there was a time for everything?—as if the hours devoted to common study were too precious to be given up to the working of the heavenly Messenger.

If you have in this way restricted and repulsed the Holy Spirit of God, I entreat you to repent of it as quickly as possible. If any have closed and padlocked the door of your heart to the Spirit of God, I urge you to unlock the door and to pray with earnestness, "Abide with me." . . .

Let me tell you what I know of this heavenly Guest. The Holy Spirit was brooding over the youth during the school hours; but some hearts were so cold and dark that they had no desire for the Spirit's presence, and the light of God was withdrawn. The **heavenly Visitant** would have opened the understanding, would have given wisdom and knowledge in all lines of study that could be employed to the glory of God. He came to convince of sin and to soften the hearts hardened by long estrangement from God. He came to reveal the great love wherewith God has loved these youth.—*Counsels to Parents, Teachers, and Students*, pp. 363, 364.

Further Reflection: *Can I recognize the presence of Jesus when He visits me through the indwelling power of the Holy Spirit?*

GREAT SIN OFFERING

So Moses made a bronze serpent, and put it on a pole; and so it was, if a serpent had bitten anyone, when he looked at the bronze serpent, he lived.

—Numbers 21:9

Moses was divinely commanded to make a serpent of brass resembling the living ones, and to elevate it among the people. To this, all who had been bitten were to look, and they would find relief. He did so, and the joyful news was sounded throughout the encampment that all who had been bitten might look upon the brazen serpent and live. Many had already died, and when Moses raised the serpent upon the pole, some would not believe that merely gazing upon that metallic image would heal them; these perished in their unbelief. Yet there were many who had faith in the provision which God had made. Fathers, mothers, brothers, and sisters were anxiously engaged in helping their suffering, dying friends to fix their languid eyes upon the serpent. If these, though faint and dying, could only once look, they were perfectly restored.

The people well knew that there was no power in the serpent of brass to cause such a change in those who looked upon it. The healing virtue was from God alone. In His wisdom He chose this way of displaying His power. By this simple means the people were made to realize that this affliction had been brought upon them by their sins. They were also assured that while obeying God they had no reason to fear, for He would preserve them.

The lifting up of the brazen serpent was to teach Israel an important lesson. They could not save themselves from the fatal effect of the poison in their wounds. God alone was able to heal them. Yet they were required to show their faith in the provision which He had made. They must look in order to live. It was their faith that was acceptable with God, and by looking upon the serpent their faith was shown. They knew that there was no virtue in the serpent itself, but it was a symbol of Christ; and the necessity of faith in His merits was thus presented to their minds. Heretofore many had brought their offerings to God, and had felt that in so doing they made ample atonement for their sins. They did not rely upon the Redeemer to come, of whom these offerings were only a type. The Lord would now teach them that their sacrifices, in themselves, had no more power or virtue than the serpent of brass, but were, like that, to lead their minds to Christ, the **great sin offering**.—*Patriarchs and Prophets*, p. 430.

Further Reflection: *Has God ever hidden a blessing for me in a seemingly odd command?*

ONE LIKE THE SONS OF MEN

For you know the grace of our Lord Jesus Christ, that though He was rich, yet for your sakes He became poor, that you through His poverty might become rich.

—2 Corinthians 8:9

Jesus, the brightness of the Father's glory, thought "it not a thing to be grasped to be on an equality with God, but emptied Himself, taking the form of a servant." (Philippians 2:6, 7, R.V., margin.) Through all the lowly experiences of life He consented to pass, walking among the children of men and women, not as a king, to demand homage, but as one whose mission it was to serve others. There was in His manner no taint of bigotry, no cold austerity. The world's Redeemer had a greater than angelic nature, yet united with His divine majesty were meekness and humility that attracted all to Himself.

Jesus emptied Himself, and in all that He did, self did not appear. He subordinated all things to the will of His Father. When His mission on earth was about to close, He could say, "I have glorified Thee on the earth: I have finished the work which Thou gavest Me to do." (John 17:4) And He bids us, "Learn of Me; for I am meek and lowly in heart." "If any man will come after Me, let him deny himself" (Matthew 11:29; 16:24); let self be dethroned and no longer hold the supremacy of the soul.

He who beholds Christ in His self-denial, His lowliness of heart, will be constrained to say, as did Daniel, when he beheld **One Like the Sons of Men**, "My comeliness was turned in me into corruption." (Daniel 10:8) The independence and self-supremacy in which we glory are seen in their true vileness as tokens of servitude to Satan. Human nature is ever struggling for expression, ready for contest; but he who learns of Christ is emptied of self, of pride, of love of supremacy, and there is silence in the soul. Self is yielded to the disposal of the Holy Spirit. Then we are not anxious to have of highest place. We have no ambition to crowd and elbow ourselves into notice; but we feel that our highest place is at the feet of our Saviour. We look to Jesus, waiting for His hand to lead, listening for His voice to guide.—*Thoughts From the Mount of Blessing*, pp. 14, 15.

Further Reflection: *Jesus never allowed self to appear in any of His actions. How can I practice such a high standard of selflessness in my life?*

SOVEREIGN OF HEAVEN

"I and My Father are one."

—John 10:30

All heaven had rejoiced to reflect the Creator's glory and to show forth His praise. And while God was thus honored, all had been peace and gladness. But a note of discord now marred the celestial harmonies. The service and exaltation of self, contrary to the Creator's plan, awakened forebodings of evil in minds to whom God's glory was supreme. The heavenly councils pleaded with Lucifer. The Son of God presented before him the greatness, the goodness, and the justice of the Creator, and the sacred, unchanging nature of His law. God Himself had established the order of heaven; and in departing from it, Lucifer would dishonor his Maker, and bring ruin upon himself. But the warning, given in infinite love and mercy, only aroused a spirit of resistance. Lucifer allowed jealousy of Christ to prevail, and he became the more determined.

Pride in his own glory nourished the desire for supremacy. The high honors conferred upon Lucifer were not appreciated as the gift of God and called forth no gratitude to the Creator. He gloried in his brightness and exaltation, and aspired to be equal with God. He was beloved and reverenced by the heavenly host. Angels delighted to execute his commands, and he was clothed with wisdom and glory above them all. Yet the Son of God was the acknowledged **Sovereign of heaven**, one in power and authority with the Father. In all the councils of God, Christ was a participant, while Lucifer was not permitted thus to enter into the divine purposes. "Why," questioned this mighty angel, "should Christ have the supremacy? Why is He thus honored above Lucifer?"

Leaving his place in the immediate presence of God, Lucifer went forth to diffuse the spirit of discontent among the angels. Working with mysterious secrecy, and for a time concealing his real purpose under an appearance of reverence for God, he endeavored to excite dissatisfaction concerning the laws that governed heavenly beings, intimating that they imposed an unnecessary restraint. Since their natures were holy, he urged that the angels should obey the dictates of their own will. . . .

God in His great mercy bore long with Lucifer.—*The Great Controversy*, pp. 494, 495.

Further Reflection: *Have I ever been used by Satan to spread dissension among my family, friends, or coworkers? How do I avoid allowing Satan to use me in this way?*

TRUE FOUNDATION

Having been built on the foundation of the apostles and prophets, Jesus Christ Himself being the chief cornerstone, in whom the whole building, being fitted together, grows into a holy temple in the Lord.
—Ephesians 2:20, 21

In the Galatian churches, open, unmasked error was supplanting the gospel message. Christ, the **true foundation** of the faith, was virtually renounced for the obsolete ceremonies of Judaism. The apostle saw that if the believers in Galatia were saved from the dangerous influences which threatened them, the most decisive measures must be taken, the sharpest warnings given.

An important lesson for every minister of Christ to learn is that of adapting his labors to the condition of those whom he seeks to benefit. Tenderness, patience, decision, and firmness are alike needful; but these are to be exercised with proper discrimination. To deal wisely with different classes of minds, under varied circumstances and conditions, is a work requiring wisdom and judgment enlightened and sanctified by the Spirit of God.

In his letter to the Galatian believers Paul briefly reviewed the leading incidents connected with his own conversion and early Christian experience. By this means he sought to show that it was through a special manifestation of divine power that he had been led to see and grasp the great truths of the gospel. It was through instruction received from God Himself that Paul was led to warn and admonish the Galatians in so solemn and positive a manner. . . .

The apostle urged the Galatians to leave the false guides by whom they had been misled, and to return to the faith that had been accompanied by unmistakable evidences of divine approval. The people who had attempted to lead them from their belief in the gospel were hypocrites, unholy in heart and corrupt in life. Their religion was made up of a round of ceremonies, through the performance of which they expected to gain the favor of God. They had no desire for a gospel that called for obedience to the word. . . .

. . . It is Satan's studied effort to divert minds from the hope of salvation through faith in Christ and obedience to the law of God.—*The Acts of the Apostles*, pp. 385–387.

Further Reflection: *How do I use God's divine manifestations in my life to give others a view of my True Foundation?*

DECEMBER 8

SON OF GOD

But may the God of all grace, who called us to His eternal glory by Christ Jesus, after you have suffered a while, perfect, establish, strengthen, and settle you.
—1 Peter 5:10

After his expulsion from Eden Adam's life on earth was filled with sorrow. Every dying leaf, every victim of sacrifice, every blight upon the fair face of nature, every stain upon humanity's purity, were fresh reminders of their sin. Terrible was the agony of remorse as he beheld iniquity abounding and, in answer to his warnings, met the reproaches cast upon himself as the cause of sin. With patient humility he bore for nearly a thousand years the penalty of transgression. Faithfully did he repent of his sin and trust in the merits of the promised Saviour, and he died in the hope of a resurrection. The **Son of God** redeemed humanity's failure and fall; and now, through the work of the atonement, Adam is reinstated in his first dominion.

Transported with joy, he beholds the trees that were once his delight—the very trees whose fruit he himself had gathered in the days of his innocence and joy. He sees the vines that his own hands have trained, the very flowers that he once loved to care for. His mind grasps the reality of the scene; he comprehends that this is indeed Eden restored, more lovely now than when he was banished from it. The Saviour leads him to the tree of life and plucks the glorious fruit and bids him eat. He looks about him and beholds a multitude of his family redeemed, standing in the Paradise of God. Then he casts his glittering crown at the feet of Jesus and, falling upon His breast, embraces the Redeemer. He touches the golden harp, and the vaults of heaven echo the triumphant song, "Worthy, worthy, worthy is the Lamb that was slain, and lives again!" The family of Adam take up the strain and cast their crowns at the Saviour's feet as they bow before Him in adoration.

This reunion is witnessed by the angels who wept at the fall of Adam and rejoiced when Jesus, after His resurrection, ascended to heaven, having opened the grave for all who should believe on His name. Now they behold the work of redemption accomplished, and they unite their voices in the song of praise.—*The Adventist Home*, pp. 540, 541.

Further Reflection: *What would you to say to Adam after witnessing his wonderful reunion with God in heaven?*

REPRESENTATIVE IN HEAVEN

"Father, I desire that they also whom You gave Me may be with Me where I am."

—John 17:24

God has a church, a chosen people; and could all see as I have seen how closely Christ identifies Himself with His people, no such message would be heard as the one that denounces the church as Babylon. God has a people who are laborers together with Him, and they have gone straight forward, having His glory in view. Listen to the prayer of our **Representative in heaven**: "Father, I will that they also, whom Thou hast given Me, be with Me where I am; that they may behold My glory." Oh, how the divine Head longed to have His church with Him! They had fellowship with Him in His suffering and humiliation, and it is His highest joy to have them with Him to be partakers of His glory. Christ claims the privilege of having His church with Him. "I will that they also, whom Thou hast given Me, be with Me where I am." To have them with Him is according to covenant promise and agreement with His Father. He reverently presents at the mercy seat His finished redemption for His people. The bow of promise encircles our Substitute and Surety as He pours out His petition of love, "Father, I will that they also, whom Thou hast given Me, be with Me where I am; that they may behold My glory." We shall behold the King in His beauty, and the church will be glorified.

Like David, we may now pray, "It is time for Thee, Lord, to work: for they have made void Thy law." Human beings have gone on in disobedience to God's law until they have reached a point of insolence that is unparalleled. Men and women are training in disobedience, and are fast approaching the limit of God's forbearance and love, and God will surely interfere. He will surely vindicate His honor, and repress the prevailing iniquity. Will God's commandment-keeping people be carried away with the prevailing iniquity? Will they be tempted, because universal scorn is placed upon the law of God, to think less of that law which is the foundation of His government both in heaven and in earth? No. To His church His law becomes more precious, holy, honorable, as people cast upon it scorn and contempt.—*Testimonies to Ministers and Gospel Workers*, pp. 20, 21.

Further Reflection: *If Jesus longs to have His church with Him in glory, what can I do today to add more members to God's remnant church?*

STEPPINGSTONE

Behold, I lay in Zion a chief cornerstone, elect, precious.
—1 Peter 2:6

That nation which God had declared was a royal nation, a peculiar people, a holy priesthood, Moses heard crying for the blood of Christ. He saw them crucify his Saviour. To him was revealed Christ's agony as He hung upon the cross. . . .

When he beheld the Saviour's ascension and saw that he himself would be one of those who should attend the Saviour and open to Him the everlasting gates, what a change took place in the expression on his face! The joy, the glory, the light that shone from his countenance no language can describe, no pen can picture. Moses was one of those who comforted Christ on the mount of transfiguration.

Then was presented to him a view of the multitude of captives who rose at the time Jesus was raised from the dead and who went into the city and revealed themselves unto many. Notwithstanding the fact that a lie had been put into the mouths of the Roman guard that watched the sepulcher lest the disciples should come at night and steal away the body of Christ, the raising of these captives to life established the certainty of Christ Himself having risen from the dead. . . .

But when multitudes began to believe on the Son and to receive divine truth from the lips of the disciples of Jesus, Satan saw that he must do something else to counter the work that the disciples were doing. So he determined to lead men and women to reject the Father and His law, as the Jews had rejected Christ. . . . Because of his deceptions humanity would fail of glorifying God by obeying His law, the foundation of His government in heaven and on earth.

The Old Testament, containing the prophecies of the coming of Christ, is now made of small account. The cry now is, "The Christ, the Christ! The gospel, the gospel!" But the gospel is taught all the way through the Bible, from Genesis to Revelation. The gospel is revealed in all the prophecies of the first advent of Christ as the Saviour of humanity. Every act of the old dispensation to turn men and women away from sin or to bring them forgiveness was done with reference to the Saviour who was to come. He was the **Steppingstone** by which humanity was to be exalted.—*Manuscript Releases*, vol. 10, pp. 155, 156.

Further Reflection: *How do I completely depend on the Steppingstone instead of myself?*

GREAT HEALER OF HUMAN WOE

And the Spirit and the bride say, "Come!" And let him who hears say, "Come!" And let him who thirsts come. Whoever desires, let him take the water of life freely.
—Revelation 22:17

I Jesus have sent Mine angel to testify unto you these things in the churches. I am the root and the offspring of David, and the bright and morning star. And the Spirit and the bride say, Come. And let him that heareth say, Come. And let him that is athirst come. And whosoever will, let him take the water of life freely." (Revelation 22:16, 17)

Here is your work—leading souls to the fountain of the water of life. All who have the truth in their own hearts as a living principle, an all-pervading influence, will have a living testimony to bear to those who are in the darkness of error. There is, thank God, an ever-living Spirit to guide us into all truth. But it is to be communicated, not shut up to our own individual selves. This Spirit, who will guide us into all truth, must be made known to others, and will guide them. The Word, the precious Word, is to be eaten as the flesh of the Son of God. Let there be no listless, sleepy testimonies.

Instead of stimulating doubt, strengthen faith by every word, attitude, and practice. Make known that we have a living Saviour, a real, spiritual life, to receive and to impart. Guide others who are now on sliding sand to plant their feet on solid rock. There are souls to be revived, many to receive the joy of salvation into their own souls. They have erred, they have not been building a right character; but God has joy to restore to them, even the joy of His anointed. This will give efficiency and happiness and sanctified assurance, a living testimony. Tell the poor desponding ones who have gone astray from straight paths, tell them that they need not despair. There is healing, cleansing, for every soul who will come to Christ. . . .

In hours when clouds encompass the soul, Christ is not far from every one of us. To whom shall we go if not to the Sinbearer, the **great Healer of human woe**? "Thou hast the words of eternal life." (John 6:68) There is joy for all who put their trust in Him, and exercise the faith that works by love and purifies the soul. Jesus says, My joy shall be in you, and your joy shall be full. (John 15:11) "Without faith it is impossible to please Him." (Hebrews 11:6) A paralysis has stolen upon the spiritual nerve and muscle of the children of God. Arouse now, just now, without delay.—Letter 93, September 30, 1896.

Further Reflection: *Does my every word, attitude, and practice strengthen faith?*

DECEMBER 12

SOURCE OF UNERRING WISDOM

"The words that I speak to you are spirit, and they are life."
—John 6:63

Christ's words contain nothing that is nonessential. The Sermon on the Mount is a wonderful production, yet so simple that a child can study it without misunderstanding. The mount of beatitudes is a symbol of the spiritual elevation on which Christ ever stood. Every word He uttered came from God, and He spoke with the authority of heaven. "The words that I speak unto you," He said, "they are spirit, and they are life." (John 6:63) His teaching is full of ennobling, saving truth, to which humanity's highest ambitions and most profound investigations can bear no comparison. He was alive to the terrible ruin hanging over the race, and He came to save souls by His own righteousness, bringing to the world definite assurance of hope and complete relief.

It is because Christ's words are disregarded, because the Word of God is given a second place in education, that infidelity is riot and iniquity is rife. Things of minor consequence occupy the minds of many of the teachers of today. A mass of tradition, containing merely a semblance of truth, is brought into the courses of study given in the schools of the world. The force of much human teaching is found in assertion, not in truth. The teachers of the present day can use only the ability of previous teachers; and yet with all the weighty importance that may be attached to the words of the greatest human authors there is a conscious inability to trace back to the first great principle, the **Source of Unerring Wisdom**. There is a painful uncertainty, a constant searching, a reaching for assurance, that can be found only in God. The trumpet of human greatness may be sounded, but it is with an uncertain sound; it is not reliable, and the salvation of souls cannot be assured by it.

In acquiring earthly knowledge, men and women have thought to gain a treasure; and they have laid the Bible aside, ignorant that it contains a treasure worth everything else. A failure to study and obey God's word has brought confusion into the world. Human beings have left the guardianship of Christ for the guardianship of the great rebel, the prince of darkness. Strange fire has been mingled with the sacred.—*Counsels to Parents, Teachers, and Students*, pp. 439, 440.

Further Reflection: *If Jesus is not my ultimate Source of unerring wisdom, whom do I consult to help me make right decisions in life?*

WATCHER

The eyes of the Lord *are in every place,*
keeping watch on the evil and the good.
—Proverbs 15:3

Every nation that has come upon the stage of action has been permitted to occupy its place on the earth, that the fact might be determined whether it would fulfill the purposes of the **Watcher** and the Holy One. Prophecy has traced the rise and progress of the world's great empires—Babylon, Medo-Persia, Greece, and Rome. With each of these, as with the nations of less power, history has repeated itself. Each has had its period of test; each has failed, its glory faded, its power departed.

While nations have rejected God's principles, and in this rejection have wrought their own ruin, yet a divine, overruling purpose has manifestly been at work throughout the ages. It was this that the prophet Ezekiel saw in the wonderful representation given him during his exile in the land of the Chaldeans, when before his astonished gaze were portrayed the symbols that revealed an overruling Power that has to do with the affairs of earthly rulers.

Upon the banks of the river Chebar, Ezekiel beheld a whirlwind seeming to come from the north, "a great cloud, and a fire infolding itself, and a brightness was about it, and out of the midst thereof as the color of amber." A number of wheels intersecting one another were moved by four living beings. High above all these "was the likeness of a throne, as the appearance of a sapphire stone: and upon the likeness of the throne was the likeness as the appearance of a man above upon it." "And there appeared in the cherubims the form of a man's hand under their wings." (Ezekiel 1:4, 26; 10:8) The wheels were so complicated in arrangement that at first sight they appeared to be in confusion; yet they moved in perfect harmony. Heavenly beings, sustained and guided by the hand beneath the wings of the cherubim, were impelling those wheels; above them, upon the sapphire throne, was the Eternal One; and round about the throne was a rainbow, the emblem of divine mercy.

As the wheellike complications were under the guidance of the hand beneath the wings of the cherubim, so the complicated play of human events is under divine control. Amidst the strife and tumult of nations He that sitteth above the cherubim still guides the affairs of this earth. —*Prophets and Kings*, pp. 535, 536.

Further Reflection: *Do I have the peace that comes from God controlling all things?*

PRINCE OF SUFFERERS

And He Himself is the propitiation for our sins,
and not for ours only but also for the whole world.

—1 John 2:2

The perfect example of Christ's filial love shines forth with undimmed luster from the mist of ages. For nearly thirty years Jesus by His daily toil had helped bear the burdens of the home. And now, even in His last agony, He remembers to provide for His sorrowing, widowed mother. The same spirit will be seen in every disciple of our Lord. Those who follow Christ will feel that it is a part of their religion to respect and provide for their parents. From the heart where His love is cherished, father and mother will never fail of receiving thoughtful care and tender sympathy.

And now the Lord of glory was dying, a ransom for the race. In yielding up His precious life, Christ was not upheld by triumphant joy. All was oppressive gloom. It was not the dread of death that weighed upon Him. It was not the pain and ignominy of the cross that caused His inexpressible agony. Christ was the **prince of sufferers**; but His suffering was from a sense of the malignity of sin, a knowledge that through familiarity with evil, humanity had become blinded to its enormity. Christ saw how deep is the hold of sin upon the human heart, how few would be willing to break from its power. He knew that without help from God, humanity must perish, and He saw multitudes perishing within reach of abundant help.

Upon Christ as our substitute and surety was laid the iniquity of us all. He was counted a transgressor, that He might redeem us from the condemnation of the law. The guilt of every descendant of Adam was pressing upon His heart. The wrath of God against sin, the terrible manifestation of His displeasure because of iniquity, filled the soul of His Son with consternation. All His life Christ had been publishing to a fallen world the good news of the Father's mercy and pardoning love. Salvation for the chief of sinners was His theme. But now with the terrible weight of guilt He bears, He cannot see the Father's reconciling face. The withdrawal of the divine countenance from the Saviour in this hour of supreme anguish pierced His heart with a sorrow that can never be fully understood by human beings. So great was this agony that His physical pain was hardly felt.—*The Desire of Ages*, pp. 752, 753.

Further Reflection: *How amazing is it to know that He who was cut off from His Father in the hour of His deepest anguish refuses to let anything separate me from His love?*

GUEST

"Behold, I stand at the door and knock.
If anyone hears My voice and opens the door,
I will come in to him and dine with him, and he with Me."
—Revelation 3:20

Our Saviour appreciated a quiet home and interested listeners. He longed for human tenderness, courtesy, and affection. Those who received the heavenly instruction He was always ready to impart were greatly blessed. As the multitudes followed Christ through the open fields, He unfolded to them the beauties of the natural world. He sought to open the eyes of their understanding, that they might see how the hand of God upholds the world. In order to call out an appreciation of God's goodness and benevolence, He called the attention of His hearers to the gently falling dew, to the soft showers of rain and the bright sunshine, given alike to good and evil. He desired men and women to realize more fully the regard that God bestows on the human instrumentalities He has created. But the multitudes were slow of hearing, and in the home at Bethany Christ found rest from the weary conflict of public life. Here He opened to an appreciative audience the volume of Providence. In these private interviews He unfolded to His hearers that which He did not attempt to tell to the mixed multitude. . . .

As Christ gave His wonderful lessons, Mary sat at His feet, a reverent and devoted listener. On one occasion, Martha, perplexed with the care of preparing the meal, went to Christ, saying, "Lord, dost Thou not care that my sister hath left me to serve alone? bid her therefore that she help me." This was the time of Christ's first visit to Bethany. The Saviour and His disciples had just made the toilsome journey on foot from Jericho. Martha was anxious to provide for their comfort, and in her anxiety she forgot the courtesy due to her **Guest**. Jesus answered her with mild and patient words, "Martha, Martha, thou art careful and troubled about many things: but one thing is needful: and Mary hath chosen that good part, which shall not be taken away from her." Mary was storing her mind with the precious words falling from the Saviour's lips. . . .

The "one thing" that Martha needed was a calm, devotional spirit, a deeper anxiety for knowledge concerning the future, immortal life, and the graces necessary for spiritual advancement. She needed less anxiety for the things which pass away, and more for those things which endure forever.—*The Desire of Ages*, pp. 524, 525.

Further Reflection: *What can I do to welcome Jesus into my home and heart today?*

PROMISED ONE

"This is He of whom I said, 'After me comes a Man who is preferred before me, for He was before me.' "

—John 1:30

Jesus and John the Baptist were cousins, and closely related by the circumstances of their birth; yet they had had no direct acquaintance with each other. The life of Jesus had been spent at Nazareth in Galilee; that of John, in the wilderness of Judea. Amid widely different surroundings they had lived in seclusion, and had had no communication with each other. Providence had ordered this. No occasion was to be given for the charge that they had conspired together to support each other's claims.

John was acquainted with the events that had marked the birth of Jesus. He had heard of the visit to Jerusalem in His boyhood, and of what had passed in the school of the rabbis. He knew of His sinless life, and believed Him to be the Messiah; but of this he had no positive assurance. The fact that Jesus had for so many years remained in obscurity, giving no special evidence of His mission, gave occasion for doubt as to whether He could be the **Promised One**. The Baptist, however, waited in faith, believing that in God's own time all would be made plain. It had been revealed to him that the Messiah would seek baptism at his hands, and that a sign of His divine character should then be given. Thus he would be enabled to present Him to the people.

When Jesus came to be baptized, John recognized in Him a purity of character that he had never before perceived in any person. The very atmosphere of His presence was holy and awe-inspiring. Among the multitudes that had gathered about him at the Jordan, John had heard dark tales of crime, and had met souls bowed down with the burden of myriad sins; but never had he come in contact with a human being from whom there breathed an influence so divine. All this was in harmony with what had been revealed to John regarding the Messiah. Yet he shrank from granting the request of Jesus. How could he, a sinner, baptize the Sinless One? And why should He who needed no repentance submit to a rite that was a confession of guilt to be washed away?—*The Desire of Ages,* pp. 109, 110.

Further Reflection: *When Jesus came to John the Baptist, John recognized in Him a purity of character he had never seen before. Is it possible for me to possess even a fraction of the purity of character that Jesus had? How?*

ORIGINATOR OF ALL TRUTH

And the Word became flesh and dwelt among us, and we beheld His glory, the glory as of the only begotten of the Father, full of grace and truth.

—John 1:14

In Christ, divinity and humanity were combined. Divinity was not degraded to humanity; divinity held its place, but humanity by being united to divinity withstood the fiercest test of temptation in the wilderness. The prince of this world came to Christ after His long fast, when He was an hungered, and suggested to Him to command the stones to become bread. But the plan of God, devised for the salvation of men and women, provided that Christ should know hunger, and poverty, and every phase of humanity's experience. He withstood the temptation, through the power that humanity may command. He laid hold on the throne of God, and there is not a man or woman who may not have access to the same help through faith in God. Men and women may become partakers of the divine nature; not a soul lives who may not summon the aid of Heaven in temptation and trial. Christ came to reveal the source of His power, that human beings might never rely on their unaided human capabilities.

Those who would overcome must put to the tax every power of their being. They must agonize on their knees before God for divine power. Christ came to be our example, and to make known to us that we may be partakers of the divine nature. How?—By having escaped the corruptions that are in the world through lust. Satan did not gain the victory over Christ. He did not put his foot upon the soul of the Redeemer. He did not touch the head though he bruised the heel. Christ, by His own example, made it evident that men and women may stand in integrity. Human beings may have a power to resist evil—a power that neither earth, nor death, nor hell can master; a power that will place them where they may overcome as Christ overcame.

It was the work of Christ to present the truth in the framework of the gospel, and to reveal the precepts and principles that He had given to fallen humanity. Every idea He presented was His own. He needed not to borrow thoughts from any, for He was the **originator of all truth**. He could present the ideas of prophets and philosophers, and preserve His originality; for all wisdom was His; He was the source, the fountain, of all truth. He was in advance of all, and by His teaching He became the spiritual leader for all ages.—*Selected Messages*, book 1, pp. 408, 409.

Further Reflection: *If Jesus is the Originator of all truth, who is the source of all lies?*

REDEEMER

That I may know Him and the power of His resurrection, and the fellowship of His sufferings, being conformed to His death.

—Philippians 3:10

Paul's labors in Ephesus were concluded. His ministry there had been a season of incessant labor, of many trials, and of deep anguish. He had taught the people in public and from house to house, with many tears instructing and warning them. Continually he had been opposed by the Jews, who lost no opportunity to stir up the popular feeling against him.

And while thus battling against opposition, pushing forward with untiring zeal the gospel work, and guarding the interests of a church yet young in the faith, Paul was bearing upon his soul a heavy burden for all the churches.

News of apostasy in some of the churches of his planting caused him deep sorrow. He feared that his efforts in their behalf might prove to be in vain. Many a sleepless night was spent in prayer and earnest thought as he learned of the methods employed to counteract his work. As he had opportunity and as their condition demanded, he wrote to the churches, giving reproof, counsel, admonition, and encouragement. In these letters the apostle does not dwell on his own trials, yet there are occasional glimpses of his labors and sufferings in the cause of Christ. Stripes and imprisonment, cold and hunger and thirst, perils by land and by sea, in the city and in the wilderness, from his own countrymen, from the heathen, and from false brethren—all this he endured for the sake of the gospel. He was "defamed," "reviled," made "the offscouring of all things," "perplexed," "persecuted," "troubled on every side," "in jeopardy every hour," "alway delivered unto death for Jesus' sake."

Amidst the constant storm of opposition, the clamor of enemies, and the desertion of friends the intrepid apostle almost lost heart. But he looked back to Calvary and with new ardor pressed on to spread the knowledge of the Crucified. He was but treading the blood-stained path that Christ had trodden before him. He sought no discharge from the warfare till he should lay off his armor at the feet of his **Redeemer.**—*The Acts of the Apostles*, pp. 296, 297.

Further Reflection: *How do I build a legacy of faithfulness in trial as Paul did during his long sojourn in ministry? Who is gaining faith by watching how I handle times of suffering?*

NEVER-FAILING HELPER

"Fear not, for I am with you."

—Isaiah 41:10

As the shepherd goes before his sheep, himself first encountering the perils of the way, so does Jesus with His people. "When He putteth forth His own sheep, He goeth before them." The way to heaven is consecrated by the Saviour's footprints. The path may be steep and rugged, but Jesus has traveled that way; His feet have pressed down the cruel thorns, to make the pathway easier for us. Every burden that we are called to bear He Himself has borne.

Though now He has ascended to the presence of God, and shares the throne of the universe, Jesus has lost none of His compassionate nature. Today the same tender, sympathizing heart is open to all the woes of humanity. Today the hand that was pierced is reached forth to bless more abundantly His people that are in the world. "And they shall never perish, neither shall any man pluck them out of My hand." The soul that has given himself to Christ is more precious in His sight than the whole world. The Saviour would have passed through the agony of Calvary that one might be saved in His kingdom. He will never abandon one for whom He has died. Unless His followers choose to leave Him, He will hold them fast.

Through all our trials we have a **never-failing Helper**. He does not leave us alone to struggle with temptation, to battle with evil, and be finally crushed with burdens and sorrow. Though now He is hidden from mortal sight, the ear of faith can hear His voice saying, Fear not; I am with you. "I am He that liveth, and was dead; and, behold, I am alive forevermore." (Revelation 1:18) I have endured your sorrows, experienced your struggles, encountered your temptations. I know your tears; I also have wept. The griefs that lie too deep to be breathed into any human ear, I know. Think not that you are desolate and forsaken. Though your pain touch no responsive chord in any heart on earth, look unto Me, and live. "The mountains shall depart, and the hills be removed; but My kindness shall not depart from thee, neither shall the covenant of My peace be removed, saith the Lord that hath mercy on thee." (Isaiah 54:10)

However much a shepherd may love his sheep, he loves his sons and daughters more. Jesus is not only our shepherd; He is our "everlasting Father."—*The Desire of Ages*, pp. 480–483.

Further Reflection: *If I have given my life to Christ, I am worth more to God than the whole world. What is my total value in God's eyes?*

TRUE INTERPRETER

Every word of God is pure.

—Proverbs 30:5

Outside of the Jewish nation there were people who foretold the appearance of a divine instructor. These persons were seeking for truth, and to them the Spirit of Inspiration was imparted. One after another, like stars in the darkened heavens, such teachers had arisen. Their words of prophecy had kindled hope in the hearts of thousands of the Gentile world.

For hundreds of years the Scriptures had been translated into the Greek language, then widely spoken throughout the Roman Empire. The Jews were scattered everywhere, and their expectation of the Messiah's coming was to some extent shared by the Gentiles. Among those whom the Jews styled heathen were people who had a better understanding of the Scripture prophecies concerning the Messiah than had the teachers in Israel. There were some who hoped for His coming as a deliverer from sin. Philosophers endeavored to study into the mystery of the Hebrew economy. But the bigotry of the Jews hindered the spread of the light. Intent on maintaining the separation between themselves and other nations, they were unwilling to impart the knowledge they still possessed concerning the symbolic service. The **true Interpreter** must come. The One whom all these types prefigured must explain their significance.

Through nature, through types and symbols, through patriarchs and prophets, God had spoken to the world. Lessons must be given to humanity in the language of humanity. The Messenger of the covenant must speak. His voice must be heard in His own temple. Christ must come to utter words which should be clearly and definitely understood. He, the Author of truth, must separate truth from the chaff of human utterance, which had made it of no effect. The principles of God's government and the plan of redemption must be clearly defined. The lessons of the Old Testament must be fully set before men and women.—*The Desire of Ages*, pp. 33, 34.

Further Reflection: *Christ came to earth that humanity might hear the words of life directly from His lips. How often do I ask Jesus to speak directly to me? What do I do when divine silence becomes deafening?*

UNSPEAKABLE GIFT

"For the Son of Man did not come to destroy men's lives but to save them."

—Luke 9:56

We are nearing the close of another year. Christmas and New Year's will soon be here. Let us candidly and carefully review our life during the year that is about to pass, with its burden of history, into eternity, and consider the many tokens we have had of the favor of God in the blessings He has bestowed upon us. The most **unspeakable gift** which God could bestow upon the world was the Gift of His beloved Son.

We do not half appreciate the grandeur of the plan of salvation. He who was one with the Father stepped down from the glorious throne in heaven, laid aside His royal robe and crown, and clothed His divinity with humanity, thus bringing Himself to the level of man's feeble faculties. "For your sakes He became poor, that ye through His poverty might be rich." Infinite was the sacrifice on the part of the Father; infinite the sacrifice of the Son! The highest gift that Heaven could bestow was given to ransom fallen humanity. O, what divine benevolence! It would have been far easier to crush the world out of existence than to reform it. But Christ declares, "The Son of man is not come to destroy men's lives, but to save them." The Son of God understood the desperate situation, and Himself came to our world, that humanity through Him might have eternal life. Son of the Most High though He was, He submitted Himself to insult, mockery, and a cruel death because He loved human beings, and would save them from ruin. But, as if determined to cut themselves off from all communication with Heaven, as if scorning God's mercy and defying Omnipotence, the world whom He came to save, crucified the Lord of glory. Can we, my dear brethren and sisters, behold such love, such infinite sacrifice, unmoved? O, what abundant resources divine power has provided for the fallen race!

Let us look to Jesus, and see the amazing love for fallen humanity of which the cross of Calvary gives evidence. The great sacrifice has been made, and Christ has purchased men and women at an infinite cost. "Ye are bought with a price," even the precious blood of the Son of God. And now Jesus says, "I have claims upon the human heart . . ." Thus He asserts His ownership of the consciences of human beings.—*Review and Herald*, December 11, 1888.

Further Reflection: *How is my value to God positively or negatively affected by sin?*

PERSONAL SAVIOUR

For as many of you as were baptized into Christ have put on Christ.
—Galatians 3:27

In ancient times, Abraham, Isaac, Jacob, Moses with his meekness and wisdom, and Joshua with his varied capabilities, were all enlisted in God's service. The music of Miriam, the courage and piety of Deborah, the filial affection of Ruth, the obedience and faithfulness of Samuel, the stern fidelity of Elijah, the softening, subduing influence of Elisha—all were needed. So now all upon whom God's blessing has been bestowed are to respond by actual service; every gift is to be employed for the advancement of His kingdom and the glory of His name.

All who receive Christ as a **personal Saviour** are to demonstrate the truth of the gospel and its saving power upon the life. God makes no requirement without making provision for its fulfillment. Through the grace of Christ we may accomplish everything that God requires. All the riches of heaven are to be revealed through God's people. "Herein is My Father glorified," Christ says, "that ye bear much fruit; so shall ye be My disciples." (John 15:8)

God claims the whole earth as His vineyard. Though now in the hands of the usurper, it belongs to God. By redemption no less than by creation it is His. For the world Christ's sacrifice was made. "God so loved the world, that He gave His only begotten Son." (John 3:16) It is through that one gift that every other is imparted to men. Daily the whole world receives blessing from God. Every drop of rain, every ray of light shed on our unthankful race, every leaf and flower and fruit, testifies to God's long forbearance and His great love.

And what returns are made to the great Giver? How are human beings treating the claims of God? To whom are the masses of humanity giving the service of their lives? They are serving mammon. Wealth, position, pleasure in the world, is their aim. Wealth is gained by robbery, not of people only, but of God. Men and women are using His gifts to gratify their selfishness. Everything they can grasp is made to minister to their greed and their love of selfish pleasure.—*Christ's Object Lessons*, pp. 301, 302.

Further Reflection: *How do I avoid worshiping at the twin altars of consumerism and materialism?*

SINLESS ONE

*"Woman, where are those accusers of yours?
Has no one condemned you?"*

—John 8:10

Jesus arose, and looking at the woman said, "Woman, where are those thine accusers? hath no man condemned thee? She said, No man, Lord. And Jesus said unto her, Neither do I condemn thee: go, and sin no more."

The woman had stood before Jesus, cowering with fear. His words, "He that is without sin among you, let him first cast a stone," had come to her as a death sentence. She dared not lift her eyes to the Saviour's face, but silently awaited her doom. In astonishment she saw her accusers depart speechless and confounded; then those words of hope fell upon her ear, "Neither do I condemn thee: go, and sin no more." Her heart was melted, and she cast herself at the feet of Jesus, sobbing out her grateful love, and with bitter tears confessing her sins.

This was to her the beginning of a new life, a life of purity and peace, devoted to the service of God. In the uplifting of this fallen soul, Jesus performed a greater miracle than in healing the most grievous physical disease; He cured the spiritual malady which is unto death everlasting. This penitent woman became one of His most steadfast followers. With self-sacrificing love and devotion she repaid His forgiving mercy.

In His act of pardoning this woman and encouraging her to live a better life, the character of Jesus shines forth in the beauty of perfect righteousness. While He does not palliate sin, nor lessen the sense of guilt, He seeks not to condemn, but to save. The world had for this erring woman only contempt and scorn; but Jesus speaks words of comfort and hope. The **Sinless One** pities the weakness of the sinner, and reaches to her a helping hand. While the hypocritical Pharisees denounce, Jesus bids her, "Go, and sin no more."

It is not Christ's follower that, with averted eyes, turns from the erring, leaving them unhindered to pursue their downward course. Those who are forward in accusing others, and zealous in bringing them to justice, are often in their own lives more guilty than they. People hate the sinner, while they love the sin. Christ hates the sin, but loves the sinner. This will be the spirit of all who follow Him.—*The Desire of Ages*, pp. 461, 462.

Further Reflection: *When has God forgiven my sin and protected me from public shame and ridicule?*

WISEST TEACHER

For the word of God is living and powerful,
and sharper than any two-edged sword.

—Hebrews 4:12

It is God's purpose that the poor and uneducated shall have, in His Word, a sure guide in the path of righteousness. If they are sincere, and desire earnestly to know the will of God, they will not be left in darkness. It is the privilege of everyone to understand the Word of God for himself. The great truths necessary for salvation are made as clear as noonday; and none need mistake and lose their way except those who follow their own judgment instead of the plainly revealed will of God. A single text has proved in the past, and will prove in the future, to be a savor of life unto life to many a soul. As men and women diligently search, the Bible opens new treasures of truth, which are as bright jewels to the mind.

If the unlearned are not capable of understanding the Bible, then the mission of Christ to our world was useless. . . .

The command to search the Scriptures, Christ addressed not only to the scribes and Pharisees, but to the great multitude of the common people, who crowded about Him. If the Bible is not to be understood by every class of people, whether they be rich or poor, what would be the need of the Saviour's charge to search the Scriptures? What profit would there be in searching that which could never be understood? What would be the consistency of this command, if the searching of the Scriptures would not dispel the clouds of error, or lead to an understanding of the revealed will of God?

Let everyone who has been blessed with reasoning faculties take up the Bible and search its pages, that they may understand the will of God concerning themselves. In this Book divine instruction is given to all. The Bible is addressed to everyone—to every class of society, to those of every clime and age. Everyone should read the Bible for himself. Do not depend on the minister to read it for you. The Bible is God's Word to you. And Christ has made this Word so plain that in reading it, no one need misunderstand. Let the humble cottager read and understand the Word given by the **wisest Teacher** the world has ever known, and among kings, governors, statesmen, there is none greater than He.—*The Signs of the Times,* July 11, 1906.

Further Reflection: *How has studying the Bible changed my mind?*

PROMISED SEED

For it is evident that our Lord arose from Judah,
of which tribe Moses spoke nothing concerning priesthood.
—Hebrews 7:14

Skepticism could not deny the existence of Eden while it stood just in sight, its entrance barred by watching angels. The order of creation, the object of the garden, the history of its two trees so closely connected with humanity's destiny, were undisputed facts. And the existence and supreme authority of God, the obligation of His law, were truths which people were slow to question while Adam was among them.

Notwithstanding the prevailing iniquity, there was a line of holy men and women who, elevated and ennobled by communion with God, lived as in the companionship of heaven. They were men of massive intellect, of wonderful attainments. They had a great and holy mission—to develop a character of righteousness, to teach a lesson of godliness, not only to the people of their time, but for future generations. Only a few of the most prominent are mentioned in the Scriptures; but all through the ages God had faithful witnesses, truehearted worshipers.

Of Enoch it is written that he lived sixty-five years, and begat a son. After that he walked with God three hundred years. During these earlier years Enoch had loved and feared God and had kept His commandments. He was one of the holy line, the preservers of the true faith, the progenitors of the **promised seed**. From the lips of Adam he had learned the dark story of the Fall, and the cheering one of God's grace as seen in the promise; and he relied upon the Redeemer to come. But after the birth of his first son, Enoch reached a higher experience; he was drawn into a closer relationship with God. He realized more fully his own obligations and responsibility as a son of God. And as he saw the child's love for its father . . . he learned a precious lesson of the wonderful love of God to humanity in the gift of His Son, and the confidence which the children of God may repose in their heavenly Father. The infinite, unfathomable love of God through Christ became the subject of his meditations day and night; and with all the fervor of his soul he sought to reveal that love to the people among whom he dwelt.—*Patriarchs and Prophets*, p. 84.

Further Reflection: *What would happen in my spiritual experience if I meditated daily on the gift of Jesus to fallen humanity?*

RIGHTFUL KING

That the Most High rules in the kingdom of men,
gives it to whomever He will.

—Daniel 4:17

When Satan declared to Christ, The kingdom and glory of the world are delivered unto me, and to whomsoever I will I give it, he stated what was true only in part, and he declared it to serve his own purpose of deception. Satan's dominion was that wrested from Adam, but Adam was the vicegerent of the Creator. His was not an independent rule. The earth is God's, and He has committed all things to His Son. Adam was to reign subject to Christ. When Adam betrayed his sovereignty into Satan's hands, Christ still remained the **rightful king**. . . . Satan can exercise his usurped authority only as God permits.

When the tempter offered to Christ the kingdom and glory of the world, he was proposing that Christ should yield up the real kingship of the world, and hold dominion subject to Satan. This was the same dominion upon which the hopes of the Jews were set. They desired the kingdom of this world. If Christ had consented to offer them such a kingdom, they would gladly have received Him. But the curse of sin, with all its woe, rested upon it. Christ declared to the tempter, "Get thee behind Me, Satan: for it is written, Thou shalt worship the Lord thy God, and Him only shalt thou serve."

By the one who had revolted in heaven the kingdoms of this world were offered Christ, to buy His homage to the principles of evil; but He would not be bought; He had come to establish a kingdom of righteousness, and He would not abandon His purpose. With the same temptation Satan approaches men and women, and here he has better success than with Christ. To human beings he offers the kingdom of this world on condition that they will acknowledge his supremacy. He requires that they sacrifice integrity, disregard conscience, indulge selfishness. Christ bids them seek first the kingdom of God, and His righteousness; but Satan walks by their side and says: Whatever may be true in regard to life eternal, in order to make a success in this world you must serve me. . . . While he allures them with the hope of worldly dominion, he gains dominion over the soul. But he offers that which is not his to bestow, and which is soon to be wrested from him.—*The Desire of Ages*, pp. 129, 130.

Further Reflection: *What do I say to people who see the wicked prospering while the righteous suffer?*

SPOTLESS LAMB OF GOD

All who dwell on the earth will worship him,
whose names have not been written in the
Book of Life of the Lamb slain from the foundation of the world.
—Revelation 13:8

As we read of Luther, Knox, and other noted Reformers, we admire the strength, fortitude, and courage possessed by these faithful servants of God, and we would catch the spirit that animated them. We desire to know from what source they were out of weakness made strong. Although these great men and women were used as instruments for God, they were not faultless. They were erring people, and made great mistakes. We should seek to imitate their virtues, but we should not make them our criterion. These persons possessed rare talents to carry forward the work of the Reformation. They were moved upon by a power above themselves; but it was not them, the instruments that God used, that should be exalted and honored, but the Lord Jesus who let His light and power come upon them. Let those who love truth and righteousness, who gather up the hereditary trusts given to these standard-bearers, praise God, the Source of all light.

If it should be announced that angel messengers were to open before humanity the treasures of the knowledge which relate to heavenly things, what a stir would it create in the Christian world! The atmosphere of heaven would be about the messengers, and how eagerly would many listen to the words that should fall from their lips! Men and women would write books calling attention to the angels' words, but a greater Being than angels has been in our world; the Lord Himself has come to reflect upon human beings the light of heaven. He has announced Himself as one with the Father, full of grace and truth, God manifest in the flesh.

The Lord Jesus, who is the image of the invisible God, gave His own life to save perishing humanity, and, oh, what light, what power, He brings with Him! In Him dwells all the fullness of the Godhead, bodily. What a mystery of mysteries! It is difficult for the reason to grasp the majesty of Christ, the mystery of redemption. The shameful cross has been upraised, the nails have been driven through His hands and feet, the cruel spear has pierced to His heart, and the redemption price has been paid for the human race. The **spotless Lamb of God** bore our sins in His own body upon the tree; He carried our sorrows.—*Selected Messages*, book 1, pp. 402, 403.

Further Reflection: *What would it feel like to become sin when I have never sinned? How did Jesus feel as my sins slowly invaded His perfect purity?*

SOURCE OF LIGHT

"A little while longer the light is with you. Walk while you have the light."

—John 12:35

The gospel of Christ is aggressive and diffusive. In the day of God not one will be excused for being shut up to his own selfish interests. There is work for every mind, and for every hand, work adapted to different minds and varied capabilities. Everyone who is connected with God will impart light to others. If there are any who have no light to give, it is because they have no connection with the **Source of light**. Is it any marvel that God does not visit the churches with greater manifestations of His power, when so large a number are shut up in themselves, engrossed in their own interests? It is thus that their piety becomes weakened, and they grow bigoted and self-caring; but by working for others they would keep their souls alive. If they would become co-laborers with Jesus, we should see the light in our churches steadily burning brighter and brighter, sending forth its rays to penetrate the darkness beyond our own border.

Oh, if the church would arise, and put on her beautiful garments, the righteousness of Christ, what a change would be realized in her influence, and in her spiritual condition! The jealousies and fault-finding, the heart-burnings, the envy and dissensions, the strife for supremacy, would cease. A close sympathy with Christ and His mission of love and mercy, would bring the workers into sympathy with one another, and there would be no disposition to cherish these evils, which, if indulged, are the curse of the church. In giving attention to the work of saving souls, they would be stimulated themselves to greater piety and purity; there would be a unity of purpose, and the salvation of precious souls would be felt to be of such great importance that all little differences would be completely swallowed up.

The Lord holds the church responsible for the souls whom they might save. If His people were to see themselves as God sees them, they could not endure to look their responsibilities and delinquencies in the face. Self-reproach would overwhelm them. . . . If you claim to be the children of God, you are your brother's keeper. God has entrusted to you sacred truths. Christ abiding in the individual members of the church is a well of water, springing up into everlasting life. You are guilty before God if you do not make every effort possible to dispense this living water to others.—*Review and Herald*, October 12, 1886.

Further Reflection: *What blessing from God does my church desperately need?*

NEVER-FAILING SOURCE OF STRENGTH

The name of the Lord is a strong tower;
The righteous run to it and are safe.
—Proverbs 18:10

I have been praying most earnestly for wisdom to place in print the very things that, should I not live, will be a help and strength to those who will be pleased to use them. My heart is filled with thanksgiving and praise. Heaven is full of richest blessings to bestow upon all who need these precious blessings, if they ask the Lord with heart and soul and have a strong desire to receive to impart. The Lord Jesus has passed through every temptation that human beings have had. We read that He "knoweth how to deliver the godly out of temptations," for He hath been "in all points tempted like as we are"—tempted in His human nature that He might know how to succor those who shall be tempted. (2 Peter 2:9; Hebrews 4:15; 2:17, 18)

I am so thankful that this long siege of temptation, sadness, and grief is past. I can see my Redeemer, in whom I have fresh encouragement to trust as a **never-failing Source of strength**. I take up my service with renewed courage, yet not knowing which shall prosper, this or that. Every soul must walk by faith. Our service is a continual warfare against the satanic science coming in through deceptive guise to take us unawares. Therefore angels are on guard to protect all who are watching and believing and walking and working.

There are continuous battles to fight, and we are not safe a moment unless we place ourselves under the guardianship of One who gave His own precious life to make it possible for everyone who will believe in Him as the Son of God, while meeting the strain of Satan's varied science, to escape the corruptions that are in the world through lust. He is fully able, in response to our faith, to unite our human with His divine nature. We are, while trusting in the partaking of the divine nature and strengthening our own efforts, proclaiming Christ's mission on earth to be peace on earth and good will towards human beings. We are bound to speak of the dangers of the warfare with invisible foes and to keep the armor on, for we war not merely against flesh and blood, but against principalities and powers and spiritual wickedness in high places. This means that people of influence will depart from the faith, giving heed to seducing spirits. Therefore we need to keep under the constant guardianship of holy angels.—Manuscript 156, 1907.

Further Reflection: *Am I dressed for today's battles? Have I put on the whole armor of God that I might be able to stand?*

SECOND ADAM

The first man was of the earth, made of dust;
the second Man is the Lord from heaven.
—1 Corinthians 15:47

When the Saviour imparts His peace to the soul, the heart will be in perfect harmony with the Word of God, for the Spirit and the Word agree. The Lord honors His Word in all His dealings with human beings. It is His own will, His own voice, that is revealed to men and women, and He has no new will, no new truth, aside from His Word, to unfold to His children. If you have a wonderful experience that is not in harmony with expressed directions of God's Word, you may well doubt it, for its origin is not from above. The peace of Christ comes through the knowledge of Jesus whom the Bible reveals.

If happiness is drawn from outside sources and not from the Divine Fount, it will be as changeable as varying circumstances can make it; but the peace of Christ is a constant and abiding peace. It does not depend on any circumstance in life, on the amount of worldly goods, or the number of earthly friends. Christ is the fountain of living waters, and happiness and peace drawn from Him will never fail, for He is a well-spring of life. Those who trust in Him can say: "God is our refuge and strength, a very present help in trouble. Therefore will not we fear, though the earth be removed, and though the mountains be carried into the midst of the sea." (Psalm 46:1–4) . . .

We have reason for ceaseless gratitude to God that Christ, by His perfect obedience, has won back the heaven that Adam lost through disobedience. Adam sinned, and the children of Adam share his guilt and its consequences; but Jesus bore the guilt of Adam, and all the children of Adam that will flee to Christ, the **Second Adam**, may escape the penalty of transgression. Jesus regained heaven for human beings by bearing the test that Adam failed to endure; for He obeyed the law perfectly, and all who have a right conception of the plan of redemption will see that they cannot be saved while in transgression of God's holy precepts. They must cease to transgress the law and lay hold on the promises of God that are available for us through the merits of Christ.—*Faith and Works*, pp. 88, 89.

Further Reflection: *Another year has come and gone. Am I any more ready to meet Jesus than I was at the end of last year?*

SURETY FOR THE HUMAN RACE

For the wages of sin is death,
but the gift of God is eternal life in Christ Jesus our Lord.
—Romans 6:23

Then the portals of the city of God are opened wide, and the angelic throng sweep through the gates amid a burst of rapturous music.

There is the throne, and around it the rainbow of promise. There are cherubim and seraphim. The commanders of the angel hosts, the sons of God, the representatives of the unfallen worlds, are assembled. The heavenly council before which Lucifer had accused God and His Son, the representatives of those sinless realms over which Satan had thought to establish his dominion,—all are there to welcome the Redeemer. They are eager to celebrate His triumph and to glorify their King.

But He waves them back. Not yet; He cannot now receive the coronet of glory and the royal robe. He enters into the presence of His Father. He points to His wounded head, the pierced side, the marred feet; He lifts His hands, bearing the print of nails. He points to the tokens of His triumph; He presents to God the wave sheaf, those raised with Him as representatives of that great multitude who shall come forth from the grave at His second coming. He approaches the Father, with whom there is joy over one sinner that repents; who rejoices over one with singing. Before the foundations of the earth were laid, the Father and the Son had united in a covenant to redeem men and women if they should be overcome by Satan. They had clasped Their hands in a solemn pledge that Christ should become the **Surety for the Human Race**. This pledge Christ has fulfilled. When upon the cross He cried out, "It is finished," He addressed the Father. The compact had been fully carried out. Now He declares: Father, it is finished. I have done Thy will, O My God. I have completed the work of redemption. If Thy justice is satisfied, "I will that they also, whom Thou hast given Me, be with Me where I am." (John 19:30; 17:24)

The voice of God is heard proclaiming that justice is satisfied. Satan is vanquished. Christ's toiling, struggling ones on earth are "accepted in the Beloved." (Ephesians 1:6)—*The Desire of Ages*, pp. 833, 834.

Further Reflection: *How does the acceptance of Jesus' sacrifice by God and the vanquishing of Satan empower me to walk in victory every day until Jesus comes?*